2nd

E D I T I O N

Management Policy and Strategy

George A. Steiner
University of California, Los Angeles

John B. Miner
Georgia State University

Macmillan Publishing Co., Inc.
NEW YORK

Collier Macmillan Publishers
LONDON

Earlier edition copyright © 1977 by Macmillan
Publishing Co., Inc.

This is the text portion of *Management Policy and
Strategy: Text, Readings, and Cases,* with minor
alterations, copyright © 1977 and 1982 by Macmillan
Publishing Co., Inc.

Macmillan Publishing Co., Inc.
866 Third Avenue, New York, New York 10022

Collier Macmillan Canada, Inc.

Library of Congress Cataloging in Publication Data

Steiner, George Albert (date)
   Management policy and strategy.

   Bibliography: p.
   Includes indexes.
   1. Management.   2. Corporate planning.   1. Miner,
John B.   II. Title.
HD31.S6887   1982   658.4   81–6061
ISBN 0–02–416790–8   AACR2

Printing: 2 3 4 5 6 7 8   Year: 3 4 5 6 7 8 9

ISBN   0-02-416790-8

*To
scholars who have
been engaged in research in
organizational strategy*

Preface

A sufficient body of knowledge has now been developed directly in the field of organizational policy and strategy to justify its compilation and its use by students as background for their study of actual business situations. In years past the tendency in business policy courses has been to review either the management process literature or the functional areas of business, such as marketing and finance, as a preliminary to the analysis of cases, business games, experiences in real organizations, and the like. We believe it is much more important to focus directly on policy and strategy formation and implementation. Furthermore, we believe enough is now known from theory, research, and practical experience to justify such a focus. This is not to say that a knowledge of management process and business functions is unimportant; however, these topics are covered elsewhere in the business curriculum. The subject matter of this book typically is not covered; in any case it is not covered in the depth provided here.

Discussions with many instructors of policy courses, together with an examination of the books used, reveals the development of some significant new trends and needs in policy courses: a focus on top management and the total organization rather than on functional areas; stress on strategic management in contrast with operational management; the use of top management strategy as a new integrating concept of analysis; the introduction into classroom discussion of basic research on the identification, evaluation, and implementation of strategy; expansion of analysis beyond the business sector to include the not-for-profit sector; the addition of materials concerning business ethics and morality; and the use of descriptive materials to complement cases. This book supports these basic trends and needs that we detect in the teaching of policy courses.

There are, of course, two types of management in organizations (except in the very smallest)—strategic management, which is conducted at the top of the pyramid, and operational management, which is performed in other areas of the organization. These two types differ significantly. Most books that deal with the management process focus almost entirely on operational management. Our hope is that our book will be useful in general management courses where students wish more exposure to strategic management.

In Chapter 1 we set forth in more detail the ways in which we hope this book will support the trends and fill the needs mentioned above. The remainder of the book is divided into five parts.

Part I briefly defines what is meant by policy and strategy and describes the critical roles they play in organizations.

Part II is concerned with overall forces that have important effects on the formulation and implementation of strategy. Here, for instance, we discuss the impact of changing environment on policy and strategy, the changing social role of business in society, and the impact of various managerial styles and organizational life cycles on policy and strategy. Our intent is to provide an overview of important considerations needed as a background for understanding material in later chapters.

In Part III we examine in depth the approaches to formulating business policy and strategy. Heavy stress is placed on systematic strategic planning and the roles of people in this process.

Part IV deals with the implementation of policy and strategy. Here the preferred methods for implementation are examined.

Part V deals with policy and strategy in different contexts. One chapter is concerned with entrepreneurship. Another deals with the special aspects of formulating and implementing policy and strategy in nonprofit organizations. Finally, we discuss contingency theories of policy and strategy formulation and implementation generally.

Although this comparatively short book, short at least for the policy field, is designed primarily to support trends in teaching in the policy area, as noted above, we do not recommend that it be used alone. We believe that learning about policy and strategy in operational settings must also include real or vicarious experience in actual situations. This can often be accomplished by the use of cases. Conversely, it is our view that cases alone are not enough. If cases alone are used, there is a real danger that each will be considered separately, and students will fail to comprehend those generalizations that will enrich their understanding of the policy/strategy formulation and implementation process. Furthermore, case evaluations and student understanding of managerial policy/strategy problems and processes should be enriched by an examination of the research in the field, which has now grown to sizable proportions. Students can, of course, dig out the research literature for themselves. Realistically, however, they are better served if the available relevant research and/or references can be organized for them in one place. Thus, we believe that the best approach is to combine research findings and references with cases. Although the book is for both graduate and undergraduate courses in business policy and general management, there are, of course, many different ways in which it can be mixed with cases and other readings.

While coming to operationally successful policy and strategy conclusions is more a matter of art and wisdom than of skill in using tools and specific pieces of knowledge, we believe that research findings in this field have powerful pragmatic applications. It is our hope, therefore, that line managers and staff specialists in all organizations will find valuable uses for the volume.

We are deeply indebted to the many scholars and practitioners who have written about policy and strategy. Many of them and their written works are recognized in this book.

We wish to thank the following for their helpful comments based on experience with the First Edition:

Thomas V. Atwater, Eastern Washington University
J. M. Bertotti, University of South Florida
B. G. Bizzell, Stephen F. Austin State University

Richard J. Butler, Rochester Institute of Technology
Curtis W. Cook, Southern Illinois University/Edwardsville
Robert I. Corless, Plymouth State College
D. James Day, University of Pittsburgh
Robert J. Ellis, Boston College
John B. Gayle, Florida Institute of Technology
Peter M. Ginter, University of Arkansas
Paul J. Gordon, Indiana University
Peter Goulet, University of Northern Iowa
Paul V. Grambsch, University of Minnesota
Robert H. Harrison, Northeast Louisiana University
O. J. Krasner, Pepperdine University
Martin K. Marsh, Humboldt State University
Edward V. Sedgwick, University of California, Los Angeles
Albert K. Steigerwalt, Central Michigan University
Abraham Stein, Hofstra University

We also wish to thank Laura Anderson, Mary Blanton, and Barbara Miner for their help with all phases of manuscript preparation.

G. A. S.
J. B. M.

Contents

PART I

The Nature and Importance of Business Policy/Strategy

Chapter 1
INTRODUCTION   3
Chapter 2
THE NATURE OF POLICY/STRATEGY   15
Chapter 3
THE CENTRAL ROLE OF POLICY/STRATEGY IN
ORGANIZATIONS   27

PART II

Key Overall Forces in Policy/Strategy Formulation and Implementation

Chapter 4
THE CHANGING ORGANIZATIONAL ENVIRONMENT   43
Chapter 5
CORPORATE SOCIAL RESPONSIBILITIES AND RESPONSES
TO THEM   57
Chapter 6
MANAGERIAL AND ORGANIZATIONAL STYLES   71

PART III

Formulating Business Policy/Strategy

Chapter 7
SYSTEMATIC PLANNING IN STRATEGIC MANAGEMENT   93
Chapter 8
IDENTIFYING POLICIES AND STRATEGIES TO EVALUATE   119

Chapter 9
EVALUATING AND CHOOSING AMONG POLICY/STRATEGY
ALTERNATIVES   149
Chapter 10
INDIVIDUALS IN POLICY/STRATEGY FORMATION   169
Chapter 11
GROUP ASPECTS OF POLICY/STRATEGY FORMATION   185
Chapter 12
ALTERNATIVE APPROACHES TO DECISION MAKING   205

PART IV

Implementing Policy/Strategy

Chapter 13
ORGANIZATIONAL STRUCTURES AND PROCESSES FOR
IMPLEMENTING POLICIES AND STRATEGIES   223
Chapter 14
FORMAL SYSTEMS FOR IMPLEMENTING POLICIES
AND STRATEGIES   239
Chapter 15
THE ROLE OF PEOPLE IN IMPLEMENTATION   255

PART V

Policy/Strategy in Varied Contexts

Chapter 16
ENTREPRENEURSHIP   271
Chapter 17
SPECIAL ASPECTS OF POLICY/STRATEGY IN NOT-FOR-PROFIT
ORGANIZATIONS   289
Chapter 18
CONTINGENCY THEORY OF POLICY/STRATEGY   303

References   317

Author Index   343

Subject Index   351

The Nature
and Importance
of Business
Policy/Strategy

C H A P T E R

1

Introduction

Most schools of business in the United States, as well as those in other countries of the world, have a capstone course in their curriculum that is concerned with "business policy." This book is designed for such a course. The nature of the business policy course, the changes taking place in the concept of such courses, and the objectives of the policy course, as well as the structure of the book are discussed in this introductory chapter.

THE BUSINESS POLICY COURSE

The impetus to the widespread introduction of business policy courses into school of business curriculums came in 1959 with reports sponsored by the Ford Foundation and the Carnegie Corporation of New York. Both reports were evaluations of course content in schools of business and both made recommendations about curriculum revisions that were designed to strengthen programs of study. The Gordon and Howell report [1959:206–207]* sponsored by the Ford Foundation, made the following recommendation:

The capstone of the core curriculum should be a course in "business policy" which will give students an opportunity to pull together what they have learned in the separate business fields and utilize this knowledge in the analysis of complex business problems. The business policy course can offer the student something he (or she†) will find nowhere else in the curriculum: consideration of business problems which are not prejudged as being marketing problems, finance problems, etc.; emphasis on the development of skill in identifying, analyzing, and solving problems in a situation which is as close as the classroom can ever be to the real business world; opportunity to consider problems which draw on a wide range of substantive areas in business; opportunity to consider the external, nonmarket implications of problems at the same time that internal decisions must be made; situations which enable the student to exercise qualities of judgment and of mind which were not explicitly called for in any prior course. Questions of social responsibility and

---

* References, shown in square brackets, will be found in the bibliography at the end of the book.

† Whenever *he* or *she* is used to refer to a person we mean either *he* or *she*. This is done without prejudice and only to avoid the awkwardness of saying each time he or she, his or her, or he/she.

of personal attitudes can be brought in as a regular aspect of this kind of problem-solving practice. Without the responsibility of having to transmit some specific body of knowledge, the business policy course can concentrate on integrating what already has been acquired and on developing further the student's skill in using that knowledge. The course can range over the entire curriculum and beyond [Gordon and Howell, 1959, pp. 206–207].

This point of view was also taken by the Pierson report [1959] sponsored by the Carnegie Corporation of New York. In 1969 the American Assembly of Collegiate Schools of Business included in its revised statement of curriculum standards for accreditation the provision that "study of administrative processes under conditions of uncertainty including integrating analyses and policy determination at the overall management level," be required of all students in business and administration programs.

Business policy courses have evolved in different directions but, generally, they can be characterized as capstone integrative courses much as Gordon and Howell recommended in their report. When details of course content and teaching methods are examined, however, there is a great diversity.

One common characteristic of many policy courses is a heavy reliance on business cases as subjects of study. Through the use of cases covering all aspects of management, students apply the skills they have learned, come to understand better the attitudes of managers, and pick up knowledge about management that derives from the case. The use of this method has a long tradition extending back to 1908 when the Harvard Business School first announced its intention of using cases in its classroom discussions [Copeland, in McNair, 1954].

NEW TRENDS IN POLICY COURSES

In recent years several trends in business policy courses are noticeable. First, the focus is on top management and the total organization, rather than on functional areas. Second, the core synthesizing concept of study is strategic management. Third, research findings about these two aspects of the area are introduced into policy course work. Fourth, policy issues and cases have been added for organizations in the nonbusiness sector. Fifth, although separate case books have long been available concerning business social responsibilities and business ethics, the traditional policy course did not cover such subjects. The trend now is to introduce such cases in the policy course. Each of these trends will be examined now in greater detail.

The View from the Top

The central view of this book is the role of the chief executive officer (CEO) of an organization as he looks at his total organization. The CEO is not necessarily singular but can be plural in the case of joint top executive authority in "offices of the president." The CEO can be plural, also, in the sense that different top executives may have types of plenary power over an organization under certain circumstances. So, in the present frame of reference, a CEO can be a top manager of an organization and not necessarily the *one* person who has that title. However, for ease of presentation the discussion here does adopt the singular mode.

The view of the top manager is unique. No one else in an organization has the same perspective. He alone is responsible for relating his organization to a changing environment. He alone is responsible for assuring the proper balance among various competing subsystems in his organization. He alone is responsible for determining the total thrust of the organization and for assuring that performance matches his design. Additional unique responsibilities of the CEO will be set forth in later chapters.

It is significant to note here that just as the role of the CEO is unique so is his way of thinking. Not all CEOs, of course, think alike, but there is a special way of thinking associated with the functioning of the top executive. It concentrates on the total enterprise rather than parts of it. Forrester [1964:60] has correctly pointed out that an understanding of the functioning of a total business system does not merely extend the phenomena of simpler situations. "Entirely new phenomena take place." CEOs think in these terms. There are two types of management in an organization—strategic management that exists at the very top and all other management, which might be called operational management. The thought processes, the attitudes, the perspective, the frames of reference, the methods of analysis, and the skills differ between the two.

To illustrate differences in perspective, consider the specialist versus the general top level manager. The specialist is an expert on a particular subject because his life has been devoted to mastering that subject. On other subjects he generally is no more informed than the average person. Specialists' thought patterns differ depending upon their specialties, but each specialist establishes standards for rationality drawn from his discipline and each seeks to decide matters in those terms. The standards may be equity, justice, and legal precedence *(stare decisis)* for the lawyer; cost reduction with acceptable quality for the engineer; quantitative solutions that optimize output for the operations research specialist; or profit maximization for the economist. The general top manager thinks in different terms. He must consider all relevant specialist criteria and then decide, based on what is in the best interests of his organization as he sees those interests. What that means depends upon the organization, the problem, the philosophies of the manager, and pressures placed upon him.

In looking at the entirety of an organization, the top manager also approaches decision making differently than major division line managers. A major division line manager considers himself to be a part of a larger organization. But within the larger organization he thinks differently than the CEO at central headquarters. Indeed, the two may be and often are in conflict. For example, the divisional manager may desire a capital allocation to meet needs that the CEO may not grant because of other higher level priorities of the total organization. Such conflicts are natural and understandable.

CEO's also think differently than functional departmental managers. Again, managers of such departments certainly consider themselves "team members" of a larger organization. But, again, their thought patterns are much different than those of top executives responsible for a total enterprise. For instance, sales managers tend to place greatest emphasis on increasing sales, market share, and reputation with customers. This emphasis, if unchecked, may be at the expense of profits. Financial executives, on the other hand tend to think in terms of profit, liquidity, low risk, and high return on investment. This viewpoint, if not balanced, may stifle growth and reduce risk taking and initiative. Research and development scientists may concentrate on new technical breakthroughs, top quality products, and research that interests them. This attitude, too, may result in costly research with limited applicability to the organization. Other functional departments have different driving motivations. All must be related to and integrated in the larger organization of which they are a part, and that is done by the CEO and his closely associated line managers and staff.

The student might ask at this point: "Why should I study the work and thinking of the top level managers of organizations? I will never get there." There are a number of answers to this legitimate question. To begin with, most business students will find their careers in organizations, especially large business organizations. Whether they become staff experts or general functional managers, the more they know about the top management of organizations the better they will be able to contribute. Also, the more they know about the top, the less frustrated they are likely to be in dealing with it. Although the focus is on top management, the analysis of cases, which will be discussed later, requires a perspective and methodological approach that students will find helpful in entering the world of organizations no matter at what level and job. For the student as well as the layman interested in policy, the study of top management can be stimulating in itself. We are dealing here with an extremely important talent in organizations, which in one way or another has a very significant impact on our lives, individually and as a society. Finally, who knows which student will eventually wind up at the top of an organization? The policy course may help many to get there and to do a better job when they arrive.

Strategic Management, Strategy, and Strategic Planning

Strategic management is the phrase currently in use to identify top corporate policy/strategy formulation and its implementation in private and public organizations. In a real sense this is what this book is all about. Policy/strategy formulation is a responsibility that top management has always had. Why then the new words to describe it?

The emphasis on strategic management distinguishes it from operational management. This reflects the growing significance of environmental impacts on organizations and the need for top managers to react appropriately to them. As Organ [1971:74] has observed, ". . . there is a growing suspicion that the more relevant criterion of organizational effectiveness is not, as it used to be, that of efficiency, but rather that of adaptability to changes in the environment." Although strategic management emphasizes adaptation to the environment, external and internal, it does not neglect tactical management of internal affairs. Both are important; however, the emphasis has shifted significantly from older concepts of the managerial job.

Strategy is the central and unique core of strategic management. Strategy refers to the fomulation of basic organizational missions, purposes, and objectives; policies and program strategies to achieve them; and the methods needed to assure that strategies are implemented to achieve organizational ends. A more detailed examination of the meaning of strategy and policy will be given in Chapter 2, but the reader is asked to accept this definition in this introductory chapter. Again, because of its importance, the emphasis is on strategy (and policy) rather than on tactics. "Leaders will be judged," says Boettinger [1973:3] ". . . not by tactical nimbleness but by the robustness of their strategic decisions for the organizations they head."

In a growing number of corporations, particularly the larger companies, one framework by means of which strategy is devised is the formal strategy planning process. This is a process that varies from firm to firm but, increasingly, has become inextricably interwoven with the entire strategic management process. In effect, strategic planning is a new way to manage.

The dominant themes of this book, the unifying threads are, therefore, strategic management, strategy (and policy), and strategic planning. The organizing framework of the book's contents is, centrally, the formulation and implementation of strategy (and policy). It can also be called strategic thinking.

Research on Organizational Policy and Strategy

One reason frequently used to justify exclusive use of cases in the policy course, although by no means the only reason, is that no underlying systematic body of theory exists upon which to build a different basis for teaching. It certainly has been true that research in the policy area has lagged. In light of the great significance of policy, one may ask why there has been so little research until recently. The principal answer is that the policy/strategy process is extremely complicated. It involves many variables that are difficult to measure. It involves many disciplines. It favors intensive field research, and it is not easily structured. Indeed, conceptual models to guide research and practice have been slow in developing [Mintzberg, 1977].

The pure case method certainly can be justified for policy courses when there is insufficient research and theory to teach, but that is no longer the case. Today cases alone cannot give students the understanding they should have about the strategy-policy-making processes of top managers. There is a growing body of research that can and should be used to strengthen and supplement cases.

Business and Nonbusiness Organizations

The primary focus of this book is on business organizations but not to the complete neglect of policy and strategy in nonbusiness organizations. Many of the accepted fundamentals about business strategic management and strategy are applicable to nonbusiness organizations. On the other hand, there are some significant differences between policy and strategy formulation and implementation in business and nonbusiness organizations. These are noted throughout the book but particularly in Chapter 17. If possible even more discussion of nonbusiness organizations would have been included, but limitations and higher priorities for space prevented it.

Social Responsibilities and Ethical Standards

Social responsibilities traditionally have been defined in terms of both economic and social goals of organizations. Until recent years, however, the greatest emphasis has been placed on the economic objective, namely, to be efficient in the production of goods and services that society wanted and at prices people were willing to pay. If this was done well, it was reasoned, profits would be maximized. Profit maximization, therefore, became the dominant goal of a business. Today, for many reasons, which will be explained in some detail in Chapters 4 and 5, much greater emphasis is being placed on the social aspects of organizational obligations to society and to those working in the organizations.

This new emphasis is creating major policy and strategy problems for organizations. To begin with, there is no clear theory or set of practices that managers can consult to tell them precisely what are the social responsibilities and ethical standards that they should incorporate in their policy/strategy decisions. Also, different constituents of and managers in an organization will have different views about what social and ethical standards should be established for decision making. The net result is, of course, considerable uncertainty about what policy and strategy should be in many situations. Although the profit objective is still dominant, it is becoming more intertwined with social and ethical objectives, particularly in the large publicly exposed corporation.

OBJECTIVES OF THE ORGANIZATIONAL POLICY AND STRATEGY COURSE

The policy course has a focus and thrust that seeks to achieve a set of objectives different from any other course. Several writers have classified the objectives of the policy course into three categories: knowledge, skills, and attitudes [Christensen, Andrews and Bower, 1978; Glueck, 1980, Broom, 1969, to mention a few]. To these may be added a few special instructor-student objectives. These general classes of aims are not, of course, unique to the policy and strategy course, nor are all the detailed objectives that may be listed under each. Together, however, they provide a set of objectives for a unique course of study. Some of the detailed objectives are as follows:

Knowledge
1. To understand the central significance of policy and strategy to top managers and their organizations. This means among other things, an understanding of how environments, external and internal, affect the functioning of an organization. It means an ability to evaluate environment so as to detect opportunities and threats in it to which alert managers must respond. It means an understanding of the processes through which managers can best determine those missions and objectives their organizations should seek; it means the ability to formulate and evaluate the best policies and strategies to achieve these ends, and the methods to assure that policies and strategies are implemented. An important aim of the course should be to underscore for the student the importance of implementation. The best of policies and strategies are ineffective if they are not implemented, and problems of implementation are far too frequently underestimated, both in teaching management subjects and in actual practice.

2. To learn about and understand the interrelationships among subsystems in organizations and the problems top managers have in avoiding suboptimization of parts.
3. To learn the limits of specialized knowledge for strategic problems.
4. To understand better the uniqueness in settings and operations of different industries and individual companies.
5. Top managers of organizations have attitudes, values, and ways of thinking that are unique to them and which also have a distinctive impact on all processes and decision making. The requirements for effective management in general and high quality policy/strategy formulation and implementation in particular will vary among top managers in different organizations and at different times. It is important that students understand and have an appreciation of these phenomena.
6. To learn about, understand, and appreciate the best research that has been done on the preceding subjects.

Attitudes

A central purpose of the policy and strategy course is to put the students "in the shoes of the top manager." This means a number of things.

1. Look at the subject matter from the point of view of generalists, which top managers are rather than specialists, which they are not. This attitude results in decision making on the basis of all relevant disciplines rather than on the basis of one alone. It means not hesitating to use judgment when facts are unknown or uncertain. Specialists tend to withhold decision pending the acquisition of more and more facts. The generalist knows there must be an end to the search for facts and does not hesitate to determine when fact gathering shall cease and decisions should be made.
2. Make decisions as a practitioner in contrast to a research specialist. General managers are pragmatic, results oriented, and realistic. The practitioner, perhaps more so than the specialist, is interested in identifying the right problem to solve rather than in finding a problem to solve. The practitioner is less interested (compared with the specialist) in an optimum solution than in an acceptable solution. The practitioner is constantly concerned with cost tradeoffs in terms of the timing of decisions, the nature of the solution, problems of implementation, and so on.
3. Make decisions from the perspective of the total organization in contrast to the point of view of subparts. The differences have been noted previously.
4. View the subject matter as a professional manager, who accepts new research and specialists' dogma about decision making but refuses to be a captive of it. As Summer and O'Connell [1964:3] point out, scientific research findings and theories have great potential power in decision making but they also ". . . have serious, sometimes even dangerous, limitations for managers who must make decisions in large complex policy systems of today." The professional managerial mind understands both the power and the limitations of technology pertinent to his decision making and is able to bridge the gap between the two.

This attitude does not, of course, reject the scientific method *per se.* Indeed as Patz [1975] observes, a well-developed policy and strategy formulation and implementation process *is* the employment of the scientific method and is perfected by the more successful managers.

Professional managers keep open minds, mindful of the limitations of past knowledge and of the need to search for new knowledge that will aid them. They are alert to unexpected situations requiring new thinking. They accept Hutchins' comment [1975:23] "If I had a single message for the younger generation I would say, 'Get ready for anything,' because *anything* is what's going to happen. We don't know what it is, and it's very likely that whatever it is it won't be what we now think it is."

Skills

Students in the policy and strategy course should be expected to demonstrate such skills as the following in dealing with specific cases and in using the research findings presented:

1. Size up quickly and accurately the situation presented in terms of identifying the core problems and/or issues; and in evaluating management's policy and strategy in relation to the environment, top management values, societal expectations, the financial position of the organization, and so on.
2. Analyze facts to identify opportunities and threats in the environment and the strengths and weaknesses of the organization so as to get in a position to appraise managerial behavior and/or prepare a situation audit useful in formulating, evaluating, and implementing policies and strategies.
3. Identify policies and strategies that are appropriate to each situation and evaluate alternatives in terms of all relevant criteria, top management values, societal expectations, internal financial, production, technical, and facility situation, and so on.
4. Recommend specific courses of action in terms of (when appropriate) detailed strategies and plans, organizational changes, financial requirements and implications, timing, personnel relations, etc.
5. To sharpen analytical skills acquired in functional areas—production, finance, marketing, operations research, personnel, etc.—in dealing with problems of the total organization. This is the skill of integrating the knowledge a student has so as to deal with a total enterprise.
6. Link theory and practice. Develop an understanding of when and how to use what tools, and their limitations, in particular problem-solving situations. As demonstrated in this book there is a rich pallette of tools (quantitative and qualitative) that decision makers can use. The student who can choose the most appropriate tools for analysis and know correctly how far to employ them in a particular situation has a highly valuable and marketable skill.
7. In most policy/strategy courses students must prepare written analyses of cases and their recommendations for action. This presents an opportunity for both the instructor and the student to improve writing capability, a skill that has high market value.
8. Policy/strategy courses provide an excellent opportunity for students to improve their oral skills in making presentations. In mind here is not only the art of expressive speech but of developing visual presentations. There is a definite art to doing both

well, and the most effective abilities for each differ in the business and government world from those needed in the academic world.

Instructor-Student Objectives

There are several additional overarching objectives of the policy and strategy course that should be mentioned. One is to stimulate students to think for themselves in dealing with specific business problems without depending upon the instructor for "the answer." Another is to help students make a transition from the academic world to the world of operations by providing them with the opportunity to deal with problems, patterns of thinking, and so on, that are encountered in the organizational world. Finally, the policy course should seek to give students a rich learning experience which is achieved with pleasure and high interest.

A NOTE ON CASE ANALYSIS AND CLASSROOM DISCUSSION

The following discussion assumes that students in business policy courses will be required to engage in case analysis to some extent or at the very least that they should be knowledgeable about the use of the case method.

There is no correct way to analyze or discuss cases. For most problems a manager faces there are a number of possible and equally acceptable courses of action. Often, too, the decision as to what is the best course of action rests on one's values.

Instead of looking for the "right" answer or one about which there is a concensus in the class, students should be more concerned about identifying the critical problem; finding feasible alternative courses of action; evaluating alternatives in terms of available knowledge, concepts, tested practices, lessons of experience, and relevant scientific techniques; testing alternatives against evaluations of company strengths and weaknesses; developing detailed plans to determine the credibility of chosen policies and strategies; matching potential gains against calculated risks; thinking through carefully the timing of action and how to make sure action is in conformance with plans; and so on.

More important than finding a "solution" is the analysis and interchange of ideas that takes place in the class discussion. There should be a maximum of discussion among students so that various views about the cases can be aired. Students need the opportunity to present their analyses and conclusions and to engage in debate with their peers in advancing their positions. The opportunity for students to think for themselves without domination from their peers and the instructor is important.

Students often find it interesting to "update" cases in the sense of finding out what really happened after the end of the case. This is, of course, interesting but not vital. What one person did in the past is not germane to the analysis of the case itself. It may be interesting for students to compare their recommendations with those decisions actually made, however. Yet if there is a difference between the two, not too much can be concluded from the variation because circumstances change very quickly, managers on the spot have more information at the time of a decision than students with only case materials, and, in any event, no one really knows what would have happened had a different decision been made by either the students or the practicing managers.

More important than finding the solution which the managers actually adopted is the creativity, insight, and appropriateness of student recommendations made in light of the materials in the case and any other information that can be marshalled for dealing with the issue at hand.

Not all cases involve making recommendations. A number of them are concerned with problem identification. Some involve analysis of courses of action managers did take. Others are directed more at generating understanding of managerial problems than in reaching conclusions about what should be done. In a number of instances, cases have been disguised and it is not, therefore, possible to "update."

The role of the instructor will vary depending upon pedagogical preferences, the composition and size of the class, and the particular subject under discussion [Dooley and Skinner, 1977; Charan, 1976]. Usually, instruction is a combination of student-centered learning and instructor lecturing with the greatest emphasis on the former. Certainly, the instructor may expand upon and expound on the significance of research, such as that contained in this volume, as it relates to different incidents and cases. However, whatever lecturing is done at this point typically is intended to broaden and deepen the understanding of the students about issues related to and/or suggested by the cases. In addition, of course, time may be set aside in class for discussion of research and knowledge about policy and strategy without reference to any particular case.

In most instances the posture for the instructor with respect to cases is to stimulate a free and creative discussion by students without the instructor standing between them and their peers. Only rarely will the instructor accept the role of the "authority" in answering student questions about a case. This does not mean the instructor does nothing. He can and will stop a fruitless discussion and/or subtly redirect the discussion if the situation seems to warrant it. He may find it desirable to summarize a discussion up to a point in time. He may correct a misstatement of fact if no one else does. He may draw attention to areas of knowledge that are applicable to the discussion if it does not inhibit student discussion. Before cases are discussed he may emphasize that the student discussion must be as informed, creative, and rational as possible as opposed to being uninformed, off-the-cuff, and vague in analysis and recommendations.

There is no one correct way to discuss cases in the classroom. A few alternatives are as follows. An instructor may "lead" the discussion, perhaps for the first case, to emphasize different approaches to case discussion. If he "leads" a case he will seek to draw out the views of students about their perceptions of issues, their analyses of different aspects of the case, their opinions about what should be done, and so on. There is such a tendency, built into existing educational traditions, for students to look to the instructor for guidance, approval, and answers, that careful efforts may be required to avoid inhibiting the free thinking of students.

THE STRUCTURE OF THE BOOK

In 1973 Anshen and Guth pointed out that the "policy area" lagged others in the management field in research and that the area was ripe for a major burst of research effort. They were right. Since that time there has been a significant increase in research in the field. But there still is vast opportunity for additional research [Saunders and Thompson, 1980; Bower, 1980].

This book covers an enormous territory. It is relatively brief rather than definitive for many reasons. Although the literature and research findings are not discussed in detail, all major relevant literature is included. This literature is placed in a conceptual framework, and every effort is made to indicate its significance for policy and strategy.

The formulation and implementation of policy and strategy in organizations is the basic framework of the book. Before dealing with these subjects, however, the authors define what is meant by policy and strategy and the central role they play in organizations. The reader must be made aware at the very beginning that there is no consensus about nomenclature in this field. No effort is made to try to settle the semantic problem, but those definitions used throughout the book are presented. A number of overall considerations of importance in policy and strategy, such as, the way in which environment affects organizations, the changing social role of business in society, and how managerial and organizational styles affect policy and strategy also are considered. Following detailed examination of the formulation and implementation of policy and strategy the book concludes with chapters on entrepreneurship, the special aspects of policy and strategy in not-for-profit organizations, and a discussion of the current status of a contingency theory in policy and strategy formulation and implementation.

Throughout this book, research in all areas relevant to policy and strategy is drawn upon; the major emphasis, however, is on what might be called operational theory and organizational theory. To oversimplify, the former is more concerned with what managers do (their functions and activities) and the second emphasizes the elements and processes that interrelate what they do. An attempt is made to marry these two approaches and also to blend into this body of thought relevant materials from other disciplines.

WHAT THIS BOOK IS NOT

First of all, this is not a book on general management. It does not take the place of books dealing with the management of organizations and the way they function.

Second, it is not definitive in the areas it presumes to cover. Space limitations obviously restrict coverage of research, theory, and practice.

Third, this book is by no means an effort to substitute lecture and text for cases and discussions.

Finally, this book is not an attempt to train students to be chief executive officers. The intent is to permit them to simulate the position of top managers so as to gain a better appreciation of their views, role, and functioning.

Before discussing research and knowledge about the formulation and implementation of policy and strategy, it is essential that the definitions of the key words policy and strategy used in this book be set forth in some detail. This is done in Chapter 2. The present chapter touches on the significant role played by policy and strategy, but this point deserves considerably more emphasis and elaboration. That is done in Chapter 3.

QUESTIONS

Discussion Guides on Chapter Content
1. Briefly trace the evolution of the business policy course.
2. What new trends are noticeable today in the content of business policy courses?
3. Define strategic management and explain how strategy and strategic planning are related to it.
4. What objectives do the authors establish for the business policy course? If achieved, how important may that be to you?
5. What guides and recommendations do the authors suggest for classroom discussion of policy cases?

Mind Stretching Question
1. A number of scholars and teachers today think that the study of business policy should not be confined to a single capstone course but should expand into a field of study. If you were developing a curriculum in a business school with this in mind, what would you include?

2

The Nature
of Policy/Strategy

INTRODUCTION

In the last chapter we noted a lack of concensus about the meaning of the words policy and strategy. In this chapter we present in detail what we mean by these as well as other closely related words.

In this general area there are serious semantic problems because words are sometimes used as nouns and sometimes as verbs. They are often used to signify concepts and at other times to denote specific actions. They are used interchangeably. Long usage has encrusted words in this area with implications and characteristics no longer applicable.

Policy and strategy are important words and change meaning with new developments. In this light we do not seek to forge definitions with which every one will agree. That is impossible. Our purpose is to develop a general understanding of meaning upon which basis the remainder of the book can proceed.

STRATEGIC PLANNING, STRATEGIC PLANS, STRATEGY, AND POLICY

A useful starting point to clarify terms is our model of a company-wide planning process, shown in Figure 2-1. This is a conceptual as contrasted with an operational model and will be examined in detail in Chapter 7. This model displays a process that can be completed solely in the mind of one individual, and never written down on paper, or it can be pursued by many managers and staff on the basis of precise procedures that eventually produce detailed written plans. In other words, the model may be followed (conceptually or operationally) to design a very simple strategic planning system or a very complex comprehensive formal strategic planning system. This point deserves under-scoring. However, we are not so much interested in such designs at this point as in concepts.

The chart divides the entire planning process into four major parts: strategic planning, medium-range programming and programs, short-range planning, implementation and

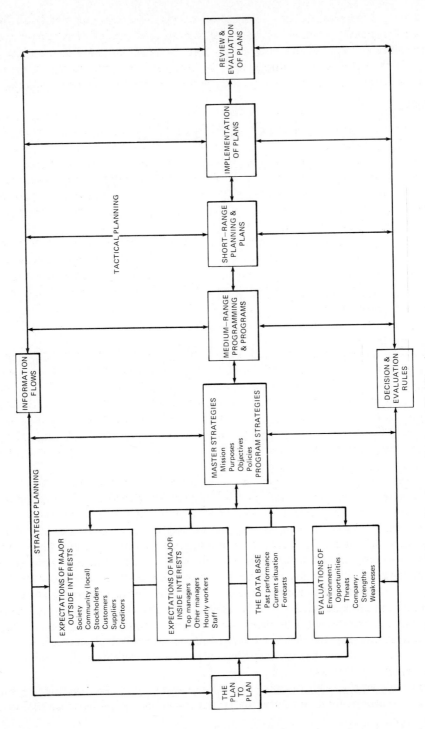

Figure 2-1 Structure and process of business company-wide planning.

review. Strategic planning, as noted in the chart, covers the entire process of determining major outside interests focused on the organization; expectations of dominant inside interests; information about past, current, and projected performance; and evaluations of company strengths and weaknesses. With these data in hand, managers are in a position to determine company missions, basic purposes, objectives, policies, and program strategies.

Medium-range programming and programs refer to specific functional plans that are required to implement strategies, which in turn will achieve fundamental corporate aims.

Short-range planning and plans refers to actions that must be taken today or in the near-term future to implement medium-range programs and company strategies.

Implementation refers to all those activities required to activate people and use resources to achieve plans that have been devised in the planning process. Review and evaluation of plans refers, of course, to the analysis of actions taken to determine whether they are in conformance with plans.

A number of persons have commented about different possible meanings of the arrows in the chart. The arrows are intended only to indicate that the planning process does flow from left to right but that it is a highly iterative process when done properly.

The nature of the planning process shown in Figure 2-1 will be examined in detail in later chapters, particularly Chapters 7, 8, and 9.

Semantic Confusion

Semantic difficulties exist in the field because there are many different definitions of terms used by various writers. This is due in no small measure to the fact that words like strategy, policy, objectives are "accordianlike" as Andrews puts it [1971:27]. Each embraces a range of statements from broad and important to narrow and comparatively unimportant. For example, policies shade into procedures and procedures into rules. Strategies shade into tactics. Overall corporate objectives shade into minute budget ceilings. At the extremes it is easy to distinguish among these words, but as they shade into one another it is not.

In this field we also are confronted with an ends-means continuum in which words alter meaning as the decision making process proceeds. For example, suppose a company has an objective of sales growth of 25 per cent a year. Suppose also it decides to try to achieve this objective by acquiring other companies rather than through in-house research and development. It would be correct to say that acquisition was the strategy chosen by the company. Once that has been decided, however, seeking a company to acquire becomes an objective. The strategy choice then may be between acquiring a large rather than a small company. Suppose the decision is to acquire a large company. Search for a large company to acquire then becomes an objective, and so on. Depending upon inclination, the word policy can be substituted in this illustration for strategy. (For an extended discussion of this subject see Gross [1964:Ch. 19].)

Strategy and Policy Defined

Unfortunately, there is no consensus about the meaning of the words strategy or policy either in management literature or practice. As a result one must be careful to understand what writers and practitioners have in mind when using them. As noted in Figure 2–1 we refer to missions, purposes, objectives, and policies as *master strategies. Program strategies,* in contrast, refer to the choice of specific methods to achieve an already established mission or objective. For instance, a master strategy might be to diversify away from one product line, as did Coca Cola a few years ago. A program strategy would be the decision to acquire a specific company in a different industry.

As Hofer and Schendel [1978] demonstrate at length, scholars in the field are divided on the definition of strategy. Many accept the definition of master strategy previously given, and more seem to be moving in this direction. However, in industry the word strategy is not typically used so broadly. The word in industry usually refers only to what is identified previously as program strategies. Mission statements are labeled as such and so are company purposes, long-range planning objectives, and policies.

The word strategy entered the literature and practice of management only in recent years. At first the word was used in its military sense to mean that which a manager does to offset actual or potential actions of competitors. The word is still used in this sense, but by fewer people.

Our concept of strategy is more in line with its original meaning. Strategy derives from the Greek *strategos,* which meant general. The word strategy, therefore, literally meant "the art of the general." It refers to that which is of major concern to top managements of organizations. Specifically, strategy is the forging of company missions, setting objectives for the organization in light of external and internal forces, formulating specific policies and strategies to achieve objectives, and assuring their proper implementation so that the basic purposes and objectives of the organization will be achieved.

Strategy is now the more common term for what used to be called policy, but there is no concensus about that. Some writers today refer to what we have called master strategy as policy. For us these words are used interchangeably for major decisions and/or at high levels of abstraction. But for detailed decisions there are differences in meaning that must be defined. These differences are set forth in the following detailed examination of strategies and policies.

Types of Strategies

There is no classification of strategies that is generally accepted. The following groupings are given to clarify some dimensions of strategies.

First, is classification based on scope. As noted previously, strategy may be defined broadly as we have done in defining master strategies. Some writers refer to these as grand strategies or root strategies. Or, as also noted before, strategies may be defined more narrowly, such as program strategies. Detailed strategies may be devised to implement program strategies, and these might be designed as substrategies.

Second, strategies may be classified in terms of organizational level. In a divisionalized company one would find at least two levels, corporate headquarter strategies and divisional strategies. If the latter are developed in pursuit of the former, they might be called substrategies.

Third, strategies may be classified as to whether they are concerned with material or nonmaterial resources. Most strategies deal with physical resources. But strategy can deal with the use of managers, scientific personnel, and other employees. Strategy can be concerned with styles of management, patterns of thinking, or philosophy about such matters as a company's attitudes towards social responsibilities.

Fourth, strategies may be classified as to purpose and/or function. For instance, growth is a major objective of most companies and there are many and preferred strategies to secure growth [Guth, 1980; Clifford, 1973b; and Gutman, 1964].

Product-market strategies is another important classification. Included would be strategies designed to develop and exploit new products, strategies designed to expand sales and markets served, diversification strategies, and strategies related to product life cycle. For a good classification of such strategies see Luck and Prell [1968:177–188].

Financial strategies are vitally important to the survival and growth of a company. Indeed, all strategies are successful or unsuccessful depending upon the extent to which they affect the financial position of the company. This is an ultimate test of strategy. Here again, the area covered can be very broad. Financial strategies can include such areas as divestment of unwanted assets, customer credit, sources of funds, dividend policy, capital allocation, and transfer of balances among companies scattered around the world.

Fifth, are personal strategies of managers. The higher the level of the manager the more significant these strategies are to the life of an organization. Personal strategies are rules of thumb that capture a manager's values, motivations, protections from a hostile environment; methods to change their environment; techniques for dealing with people and getting things done; and ways to maximize their self-satisfactions and basic needs. These personal strategies constitute a fundamental, and generally unwritten, framework within which business strategy is developed. Classification of such strategies is a matter of personal choice. They may be aggressive, such as, strike when the iron is hot, divide and conquer, or in union there is strength. They may be mild, or passive, such as, time is a great healer, avoid action until success is certain, start small, or avoid decisive engagements when in a weak position [McFarland, 1967:159]. Other strategies may relate to timing, personal power, dealing with others, career paths, and so on.

An illustration of how personal values may affect a firm's strategy is that of a large research and development company, which had most of its work in government contracts and was considering three strategies, as follows: (1) Try to triple sales over the next three to five years by expanding the research base and getting a larger share of growing government contracts; (2) achieve the same sales goal but through production of hardware, on the commercial market, which grows out of the research activity; and (3) aim for a slower growth rate and keep within the same type business.

Three vice presidents of the company had different values that had a bearing on the acceptability of these strategies. One was business-science oriented and wanted to make as much money as possible while still being part of an intellectually stimulating firm. He wanted profits but from an exclusively research company. Another had the value orientations of a materialist who wanted growth and profitability from widening markets and internal efficiency. He saw that the best path to this goal lay in the commercialization of hardware production. The third was more scientifically oriented. He wanted to continue present research activities and viewed with alarm getting into commercial production.

Taking these motivations and values into consideration, the president felt the best strategy would be to double sales over the next five years by continuing the business along the lines that had brought it to its present position. In this way he was best accommodating the values of his top executives [Guth and Tagiuri, 1965].

The Web of Successful Strategies

A successful strategy is usually not a single decision but a web of interrelated strategies, substrategies, sub-substrategies, policies, and tactics. For instance, in the mid-1950s when Timex rapidly increased its sales and profits, the company followed three interrelated strategies all of which were essential for success. They were (1) produce an inexpensive disposable product that looked like an expensive watch; (2) undertake an effective national advertising campaign to promote the sale of the product; and (3) pursue a radical new approach to distribution (instead of depending upon jewelry stores for sales, place watches in drug stores, grocery stores, department stores, garages, and so on). Each of these strategies, of course, had to be supported by interrelated substrategies, policies, and tactics.

Strategy versus Tactics

Organizational decisions range across a spectrum, having a broad master strategy at one end and minute tactics at the other. It is useful to distinguish between these two types of decisions because the way they are formulated and implemented are very different. The following distinctions are in no particular order of importance.

1. *Level of conduct.* Strategy is developed at the highest levels of management (at headquarters and in major divisions) and relates exclusively to decisions in the province of these levels. Tactics are employed at and relate to lower levels of management.
2. *Regularity.* The formulation of strategy is both continuous and irregular. The process is continuous but the timing of decision is irregular for it depends upon and is triggered by the appearance of opportunities, new ideas, management initiative, crises, and other nonroutine stimuli. Tactics are determined, for many companies, on a periodic cycle with a fixed time schedule, such as the annual budget process.
3. *Subjective values.* Strategic decision making is more heavily weighted with subjective values of managers than is tactical decision making.
4. *Range of alternatives.* The total possible range of alternatives from which a management must choose is far greater in strategic than in tactical decision making.
5. *Uncertainty.* Uncertainty is usually much greater in both the formulation and implementation of strategy than in deciding upon and knowing the results of tactical decisions. Not only is the time dimension much shorter in tactical decisions but risks are more easily assessed than with respect to strategies.
6. *Nature of problems.* Strategic problems are generally unstructured and tend to be one of a kind. Tactical problems are more structured and often repetitive in nature.
7. *Information needs.* Formulating strategy requires large amounts of information de-

rived from, and relating to, areas of knowledge outside the corporation. Most of the more relevant data needed relate to the future, are difficult to get with accuracy, and are tailored to each problem. In mind, for example, is information about competitors, future technology, social and political changes affecting corporate decisions, and economic developments altering markets. Tactical informational needs, in contrast rely more heavily on internally generated data, particularly from accounting systems, and involve a higher proportionate use of historical information. For example, tactical plans to control production rest heavily upon internal records of past experience.

8. *Time horizons.* Strategies, especially when successful, are intended to, and do, last for long periods of time. However, sometimes the time dimension is very short. Tactics cover a shorter duration and are more uniform for all parts of an operating program, such as the contents of an annual budget.

9. *Reference.* Strategy is original in the sense that it is the source or origin for the development of tactics. Tactics are formulated within and in pursuit of strategies.

10. *Detail.* Strategies are usually broad and have many fewer details than tactics.

11. *Type of personnel involved in formulation.* Strategies for the most part are formulated by top management and its staff. The numbers of people involved are comparatively few as contrasted with the formulation of tactics where large numbers of managers and employees usually participate in the process.

12. *Ease of evaluation.* It is usually considerably easier to measure the effectiveness and efficiency of tactics than of strategies. Results of strategies may become evident only after a number of years. Very frequently it is difficult to disentangle the forces that led to the results. In sharp contrast, tactical results are quickly evident and much more easily identified with specific actions.

13. *Point of view.* Strategies are formulated from a corporate point of view, whereas tactics are developed principally from a functional point of view.

14. *Importance.* Strategies, by definition, are of the highest importance to an organization. Tactics are of considerably less significance.

Blurring Differences

Both conceptually and operationally, the lines of demarcation between strategy and tactics are blurred. At the extremes their differences are crystal clear, as in the preceding comparisons. But these distinctions do not always hold. For instance, both in theory and practice, strategy gives rise to tactics, and tactics may be considered a substrategy which, in turn, employs tactics for execution. What is one manager's strategy is another's tactics; what is one manager's tactics is another's strategy. For example, strategies are developed in the strategic planning process at company headquarters. Substrategies within this strategic plan may then be pursued in the major divisions of the company. Concretely, a corporation may decide that its strategy is to penetrate the European market by divisional acquisitions of foreign companies. Part of the headquarters' tactical plan might be for the Electronics Division to buy a majority interest in a plant in Germany that produces a product similar to one of its own. But this may be considered a strategy by the Division. The Division may devise a tactical plan to acquire an interest in a specific plant through an exchange of stock rather than cash. From this illustration, it is clear that in an operational setting what is strategy and what is tactics may depend upon who is looking.

THE NATURE OF POLICIES

There is no concensus about the meaning of policy. Policies have characteristics that distinguish them from strategies, but there are times when it is difficult if not impossible to separate the two, as noted.

Policies are generally considered to be guides to action or channels to thinking. More specifically, policies are guides to carrying out an action. They establish the universe in which action is to be taken. This universe can be very broad if a policy deals, for example, with a general statement of managerial intent, such as, "it is our policy to be a good corporate citizen." The universe can be a much more restricted area for action in such a directive as, "It is our policy to retain 50 per cent of net earnings and to distribute the other half to stockholders in the form of dividends." Policies may be thought of as codes that state the directions in which action may take place. They set boundaries. Policies stand as ready guides to answering thousands of questions that may arise in the operation of a business.

Policies usually enjoy a long life. As a matter of fact there is too much of a tendency in business for them to live too long without review and revision. At any rate, policies are generally formulated with the long view in mind.

Policies direct action to the achievement of an objective or goal. They explain how aims are to be reached by prescribing guideposts to be followed. They are designed to secure a consistency of purpose and to avoid decisions that are short-sighted and based on expediency.

A business policy can be defined as management's expressed or implied intent to govern action in the achievement of a company's aims. This definition is at a high level of abstraction. It is necessary to dig deeper into the anatomy of a policy to understand its operational character.

Policy Verbs

Policies are generally expressed in a qualitative, conditional, and general way. The verbs most often used in stating policies are: to maintain, to continue, to follow, to adhere, to provide, to assist, to assure, to employ, to make, to produce, and to be. For example, "It is the policy of the Ajax Corporation to control the release to the public, employees, stockholders, and others all information that may disclose company plans, policies, and activities in such a way as to assure a favorable reaction toward the company, its interests, and its products." Or, "It is company policy to protect the assets of the corporation by having an adequate corporate insurance program."

Policy and Role Theory

From what has been said, it is clear that policy is quite important in role theory. For example, policies are means to ends and, as such, explain what people should do as contrasted with what they are doing. Policies, when enforced, permit prediction of roles with certainty [Miner, 1978].

Procedures, Standard Operating Plans, and Rules

Procedures, standard operating plans, and rules, differ from policies only in degree. All provide guidance about how a particular problem should be solved.

A procedure is usually considered to be a series of related steps or tasks expressed in chronological order and sequence to achieve a specific purpose. When a sequence of actions becomes well established and is, in a sense, a basic rule of conduct, it is called a standard operating procedure. For instance, a series of steps in filling a customer order, in making a purchase of an office machine, in hiring an employee, or in handling crank letters, becomes a standard operating procedure when it is formalized. Procedures are methods, techniques, and detailed ways by and through which policies are achieved.

Most companies have literally hundreds of standard operating procedures. Depending upon subject matter, of course, there are degrees of leeway in compliance. But most procedures specify patterns and/or steps of action that must be followed with minimum deviation.

Rules are prescribed courses of action that usually are stated in such a way as to leave no doubt about what is to be done. They are specific and permit a minimum of flexibility and freedom of interpretation. "Each operating division will be responsible for the direct export sales of its own products," is a rule. "All quantity discounts must be approved by the Vice-President, Sales," is a rule. Rules limit flexibility of managers. Rules cannot substitute for procedures and policies, nor vice versa. All companies, therefore, have the problem of developing a proper blend of policies, procedures, and rules.

Like strategies and tactics, rules and procedures and policies may be clearly demarcated by definition but in practice it may be difficult if not impossible to distinguish among them. A change in verb can blur the line of demarcation among these words. Or, the ends-means continuum noted earlier can create semantic problems. Also, as with strategies and tactics, much depends upon who is defining terms.

The Business Pyramid of Policies

It is clear from the preceding discussion that in every business there is a pyramid of policies. At the top of the pyramid are very broad fundamental policies concerned with company purpose, company thrust, and ways of doing business. At this point policies and strategies are indistinguishable. Falling below this level are policies of lesser scope and importance that shade into procedures and rules.

At lower managerial levels more attention is directed to implementation of higher level policies and controlling operations than to making subpolicies. When subpolicies are formulated the time horizon tends to be shorter and the policy statement tends to get more specific.

Although no company can or should have a policy to cover every action and contingency, there is a tendency, particularly in the larger companies, to have an organized written register of policies. Problems that are unusual in a small company may come frequently enough to be covered by a policy in a larger company. In larger companies a structure tends to be developed, a comprehensive body, a more or less integrated set of policies and their derivatives, which becomes something like a legal system for management and other employees. These policies stretch from the highest level of generality in a company to low operating details. They may be broad in specification or specific, concrete or vague, quantitative or qualitative, flexible or inflexible, narrow or long in time, written or unwritten.

Types and Classifications of Business Policies

Business policies may be classified in the same groupings as previously presented for strategies. Here again, however, there is no consensus.

First, policies may be classified in terms of scope and importance. One may speak of *master policy* or grand policy which covers the same area as *master strategy*. The two concepts are the same. At a lower level *program policies* can be identified. These are comparable to program strategies previously defined but are much more numerous in a company and cover many more activities. Program strategies are more selective. Then, of course, at lower levels of importance and scope are found procedures and rules.

Second, policies, like strategies, may be classified in terms of organizational levels. As Paul Appleby [1949] put it, everything decided at a particular managerial level, and above, is policy. Everything below is administration.

Third, policies, like strategies, may be classified in terms of material or nonmaterial subjects.

Fourth, policies may be classified according to purpose or function. In each of the following functional areas, for example, a large company will have policies: marketing, production, procurement, research, finance, facilities, personnel, public relations, law, dealings with foreign governments, and general management. Some corporate policy manuals literally contain hundreds of policies covering activities in these areas.

Fifth, are personal policies of managers. A surprising number of companies have written creeds, philosophies, and standards of conduct that are policies. These creeds usually express the basic purposes of the companies and the beliefs of top managers about the ways in which the company will operate. They set forth moral codes of top management concerning such matters as honesty, integrity, fairness in dealings, efficiency, devotion to the public interest, devotion to profits, quality of work, and consumer service. Most creeds tend to be short rather than long. Some are for public relations purposes; others are taken very seriously as company policy [Chatov, 1980; Steiner, 1969b:144–150, 158; Gross 1964:488; Thompson, 1958].

Public Policy

In the public sector the word policy attaches today to decisions and actions of the highest significance, widest ramifications, and longest time perspective. To be sure, they could be called strategy, but the fact of the matter is they are not. When the President speaks of his major actions to deal with the energy problem or the economic problems of the United States he does not speak of "strategy" but of "policy." Most pieces of major legislation begin with a statement that explains the "policies" set forth in the legislation.

CONCLUDING COMMENT

In one sense the word policy is the older word for today's concept of strategy. But this is not quite so, for the words strategy and policy, as discussed in this chapter, do have some characteristics that differ. In this chapter we have pointed out the similarities and dissimilarities between the two words. We think the words are interchangeable when concerned with the major decisions of top managers but have different meanings at lower levels of organizational operations. Since the primary focus of this book is on the top levels of managers, the reader can decide whether he likes the sound of policy or strategy. For the purposes of this book we speak of policy/strategy. Behind that phrase, however, there are distinctions that have been set forth in this chapter.

QUESTIONS

Discussion Guides on Chapter Content
1. Distinguish among strategic planning, strategic plans, strategy, and policy.
2. What are some of the reasons for the semantic confusion concerning these words?
3. What classifications of strategies and policies do you see?
4. Explain the differences between strategies and tactics.
5. "Policy is quite important in role theory." Explain this quotation.

Mind Stretching Questions
1. If you were to try to straighten out the semantic problems discussed in this chapter, what different words would you suggest for the major concepts?
2. Upon the basis of a little library research, trace the evolution of the definition of the word strategy.

3

The Central Role
of Policy/Strategy
in Organizations

INTRODUCTION

The conceptual understanding of policy/strategy presented in the last chapter will be expanded in the present chapter to examine why it is so important to organizations. It is our thesis that the policy/strategy responsibilities of top managers of an organization are of equal if not superior importance to all other responsibilities. In explaining why this is so, it is convenient to look at policy/strategy as a product of top management's strategic planning process. (We recognize, of course, that policy/strategy is a wider concept than strategic planning.) The chapter also will describe some successful and unsuccessful strategies.

TASKS OF TOP MANAGERS

Peter Drucker [1974:611] points out that there is no prescribed set of top management functions performed uniformly throughout industry. There are prescribed top management tasks, but these vary from one organization to another. Furthermore, says Drucker, these tasks are unique to top managements of organizations. This is true for public institutions as well as for business firms.

The tasks that Drucker identifies as belonging to top managers are as follows:

First, what we have designated as master policy/strategy.

Second, setting standards, as for example the "conscience" guides.

Third, is the "responsibility to build and maintain the human organization."

Fourth, assuring the proper relationships between the top managers and others, such as government, major suppliers, banks, other businesses, and so on.

Fifth, performing the countless "ceremonial" functions required of top managers.

Sixth, standing ready to lead when things go wrong. Drucker [1974:612] calls this a "stand-by organ for major crises."

There are other tasks, says Drucker, but this list serves to show that the tasks of top management are unique to it. Top management is a distinct type of work. "The ideal top management," he goes on to observe, "is the one that does the things that are right and proper for its enterprise here and now" [Drucker, 1974:613].

PRIMACY OF POLICY/STRATEGY

It is not our purpose to elaborate here on the functions of top management. More will be said about that in Chapter 6. Our intent is to note first of all the priority that Drucker gives to the policy/strategy function and to observe that the policy/strategy task influences and is influenced by the other functions. The significance of master policy/strategy is framed in a comment made by Robert E. Wood when Chairman of the Board of Sears, Roebuck and Company. He said, "Business is like war in one respect, if its grand strategy is correct, any number of tactical errors can be made and yet the enterprise proves successful [Chandler, 1962:235]. He is saying that a company can be rather inefficient in its uses of resources but can be successful if its grand strategy is right. On the other hand, a company may be very efficient in organizing its production but will fail if its grand strategy is inadequate. Both, of course, are important but a company that has the "right" master policy/strategy can be inefficient and yet financially successful.

Business success generally is not the happy result of one accidental brilliant strategy. Rather, success is the product of continuous attention to the changing environment and the insightful adaptations to it. A classic illustration is Sears, Roebuck and Company, which will be discussed later in this chapter.

The Policy/Strategy Process

In explaining further why master policy/strategy is so important, it is in order to comment on the strategic planning process where master policy/strategy is formulated. Details of this process will be given in Chapter 7 and following chapters. At this point it is only necessary to note that all companies have grand policies/strategies. In this regard, companies can be divided into two categories. First, there are those that live from day to day and whose policies/strategies are reactive to current events. The second group consists of those who seek to anticipate the future and to prepare suitable guidelines for making better current decisions. The second group can be divided again into two different types: those companies whose managers engage in what we call intuitive anticipatory planning, and those that do systematic formal planning. In Chapter 7 we shall say more about these two types, but at this point we wish to observe that the outcome of both types of planning are similar in that they produce grand policy/strategy, which involves an understanding of the organization's environment and the formulation of basic missions, purposes, objectives, and the policies and strategies to achieve the objectives. In the case of intuitive anticipatory planning, the results tend not to be written or are only sketchily written. The formal systems result in written sets of plans. It is rare to find a large company today, especially in the United States, Western Europe, and Japan, that does not have some sort of formal strategic planning system.

It is our thesis that to a large extent the success of a company will depend upon how well it formulates its policy/strategy in light of its evolving environment, how well it defines and articulates its policy/strategy, and how well it assures its implementation. Why is this so?

The Importance of Policy/Strategy

Simply stated, the elements of the strategic planning process, as shown in Figure 2-1, concern an understanding of the changing environment in which a company finds itself, the basic missions of the organization, basic company purposes, long range planning objectives, and program/policies and strategies. We shall comment on each of these elements.

The strategic planning process would be invaluable to a company if it did nothing more than force top management to be aware of its changing environment. As shall be shown in the next chapter, the environment of business is changing rapidly and it is opening up surprising new opportunities as well as spawning frightening new threats. Failure to adjust to either can bring disaster. The strategic planning process focuses attention on opportunities and threats, but it also asks fundamental questions the answers to which are indispensable to good management. In mind are questions such as: What are the basic strengths and weaknesses of our company? What are our competitors doing and likely to do? When will our present products require modification? What is our cash flow? What are our capital needs? Is our share of the market acceptable? Are we headed in the direction we wish?

The strategic planning process also addresses itself to defining the mission of the company. This includes the basic products and/or businesses of the company and the markets in which they are distributed. An understanding of mission permits management to deal explicitly with a number of fundamental strategic issues such as the following: What is the competitive area in which we find ourselves? What are the requirements for success in this competitive environment? Are we the proper size for success? What are our relative strengths and weaknesses in our basic businesses? Is our basic mission appropriate in light of our desires, capabilities, and opportunities?

The basic purposes refer to fundamental aims the company seeks for such factors as product quality, customer service, response to community interests, and ethical conduct. These ends are usually broadly stated, for example: "We seek to set the technical standard that other companies in the industry will strive to meet." Formulating purposes obviously forces top managers to come to grips with major questions, such as: What emphasis will be placed on customer service? In what ways will we try to capture consumer confidence? What will be our ethical posture with respect to customers, suppliers, employees, government and creditors? The answers to these questions will have profound impacts on operations.

A third major element of strategic planning is the formulation of specific long range objectives. Platitudes such as: "Our objective is to make a profit," do not provide proper direction for a company's activities. In the strategic planning process, specific objectives are set for sales, profits, share of market, return on investment, and other factors that top management thinks are important and for which it seeks measurement of progress.

A fourth component of strategic planning is the specification of program policies and strategies. These are the decisions concerning deployment of resources and guidelines developed to direct more detailed decisions in their implementation. They provide a framework within which managerial decisions throughout an enterprise can be made consistent with the basic missions, purposes, and objectives of the firm, as established by top management.

Overall, the singular significance of master policy/strategy is that it addresses itself to the core responsibility of top management, that is, to assure the success of the business today and tomorrow. To do this top management must be continuously involved in the process of surveying the environment, determining the nature of the business, setting goals for it, devising program policies and strategies to achieve objectives, and assuring that actions take place in such a fashion that the policies and strategies chosen really do result in the achievement of objectives and basic company purposes.

The strategic planning process provides a unified framework within which managers can deal with the major issues managers should face, for dealing with major problems that are unique to the company, for identifying more easily new opportunities, and for assessing strengths that can be capitalized upon and weaknesses that must be corrected. It can enable managers "without benefit of inspiration, to make solid contributions that would otherwise be lost" [Bower, 1966:50]. It is a training ground for managers to be better managers because it forces thought processes that are essential to better management and raises and answers questions that good managers must address.

STRATEGIC MANAGEMENT

The concept of strategic management was presented in Chapter 1. So important is it, however, that a few additional comments are useful here. There is no concensus about the precise meaning of strategic management, but most writers on the subject would agree, we think, with the general thrust of the following definitions.

Strategic management is concerned primarily with relating the organization to its environment, formulating strategies to adapt to that environment, and assuring that implementation of strategies takes place. This is a process that, among other things, involves (1) surveillance of the changing environment (externally and internally in all major aspects so far as the company is concerned), (2) identification in that environment of opportunities to exploit and dangers to avoid, (3) evaluation of company strengths and weaknesses of importance in formulating and evaluating strategies, (4) formulating missions and objectives, (5) identifying strategies to achieve company aims, (6) evaluating the strategies and choosing those which will be implemented, and (7) establishing and monitoring processes to make sure that strategies are properly implemented. Each of these processes, as will be explained in detail in later chapters, contains many subprocesses.

Thus, strategic management involves, of course, establishing a framework to perform these various processes. In addition, the concept of strategic management must embody all general management principles and practices devoted to strategy formulation and its implementation in the organization [Glueck, Kaufman, and Walleck, 1980; Hofer and Schendel, 1978].

A significant feature of the concept of strategic management is its focus on top management strategic activities in contrast to more routine operational management. This is a new perspective that highlights the importance, in both theory and practice, to a company of this process as well as its uniqueness compared with other managerial functions.

Central to strategic management is the process of defining the strategic thrusts and directions of the business in light of the changing environment and devising strategies to achieve them. This reflects the fact that in recent years the business environment has become increasingly turbulent, complex, and threatening. The result is that top managements find it necessary to spend more and more time on environmental forces and company relationships to them. At the same time more and more companies have grown significantly in size and complexity. Managerial strategies to deal with such organizations are considerably different from operational strategies needed to administer smaller, less complex organizations.

In most companies in the not too distant past, success was achieved when virtually the entire focus of the manager's job was on running the day-to-day affairs of the company as efficiently as possible. This is still true of many small companies today. Among most companies today, especially the larger ones, it is not enough to be efficient in operating the business. That is still important, but, in addition, a strategy to adapt a company properly to its changing environment is essential for success.

The increasing time demands of strategic management have forced top managements among the larger companies to delegate more and more of the operating authority for running the business to lower-level managers. Some companies today have chief executive officers (CEOs) who are concerned essentially with outside environmental forces, and chief operating officers (COOs) who are concerned primarily with running the day-to-day affairs of the business. In these cases, as well as in others where there is no COO or its equivalent, more authority is usually being delegated to middle managers [Steiner, 1981 a and b].

This does not mean that top managers delegate responsibility over routine business operations and are unconcerned about them. Not at all. Delegation does not mean abdication. Top managements are still much concerned about the way in which their business operates. But their managerial job is considerably different from that of the past. They are forced to spend much less time on such matters and to delegate an increasing amount of authority in managing them.

Notice should be given to the fact that strategic planning is not the same thing as strategic management. Strategic planning as conceived in this book is a major aspect of strategic management. Indeed, it may be considered a central pillar of strategic management. The two are inextricably interrelated. But, as noted previously, strategic management involves more than planning per se.

Ansoff [1979b, 1980], Bracker [1980], Channon [1977], and Ansoff, Declerck, and

Hayes [1976] have described the development of the concept of strategic management for those interested in it. The concept is still evolving and will continue to undergo change. Nothing that has been said here, however, implies any rejection of tested theories of effective management. They can be embraced as appropriate within the concept of strategic management. The concept of strategic management is simply a way to give needed emphasis to a major function of top managements of organizations. As the publisher of *Business Week* observed, "Strategic management has become the major thrust and emphasis in the management of U.S. corporations . . ." [*Business Week,* 1978]. Upon this premise, he introduced a new feature in his magazine concerned with corporate strategies. From its inception, this section has been one of the longest, if not the longest, in each issue. In recent years other business publications have carried more stories about explicit company strategies. To underscore further this new managerial thrust, it is noteworthy that new scholarly books which focus on strategy have used the words strategic management in their titles [Glueck, 1980; Schendel and Hofer, 1979; Ansoff, 1979b). Two new scholarly journals dealing with this subject were launched in 1980, namely, *Strategic Management Journal,* and *The Journal of Business Strategy.*

In essence, strategic management is a new perspective that highlights the significance, in both theory and practice, to a company of the need to pay more attention to environment and the formulation of strategies to relate to it.

To underscore the central role of policy/strategy in the ebb and flow of organizational fortunes a few illustrations of experience are presented. It will be readily observed that some strategies have resulted in remarkable successes for some companies, whereas other companies met with disaster in choosing the wrong strategy. It should be observed, also, that the following sketches are oversimplifications. Success and/or failure in industry can come from a great many causes, ranging from luck to the timing of the introduction of a strategy. This point, however, does not diminish the fact that strategy and its implementation are of central importance to the success or failure of a company.

CROWN CORK AND SEAL COMPANY, INC.

About 25 years ago this company found itself in a financial crisis where it could not cover its preferred dividends. At that time, John F. Connelly a substantial stockholder assumed the presidency of the company. He is now Chairman of the Board and Chief Executive Officer. Under his management the company has been very successful. Sales rose from $115 million in 1956 to $1.40 billion in 1979. Profits were nonexistant in 1956 but rose steadily to $70 million in 1979. Earnings per share have risen steadily from nothing in 1956 to $4.65 in 1979. The following policies/strategies were responsible for this performance, as revealed in case analysis of the company [Christensen, Andrews, and Bower, 1978].

• Maintain a strong position in the production and distribution of cans, closures, and bottling machinery.

- Concentrate on producing cans for "hard-to-hold" products, such as beer and soft drinks, that require high strength in their containers and/or use conveniences in packaging such as aerosol dispensers and "tear-top" lids.
- Seek steadily rising sales and profit levels.
- Concentrate on reducing and holding down costs.
- Centralize the control function but make plant managers responsible for plant profitability.
- Maintain a geographic distribution of plants close to high-density population centers.
- Build plants abroad in areas where growth potential seems to be high.
- Develop wholly owned subsidiaries but have them operated by nationals in each country.
- Maintain technically advanced equipment in producing plants.
- Finance capital requirements through retained earnings and use of long-term debt.
- Maintain a high level of customer service.
- Be skilled at solving customer problems quickly.
- Invest in more equipment than is needed for standard production in order to assure quick service.
- Maintain sufficient research capability to solve customer problems and avoid unpleasant technical surprises but do not go overboard in supporting basic research.

SEARS, ROEBUCK AND COMPANY AND MARCOR

Sears' success over a long period of time supports the hypothesis that a corporation that can make the right strategic decisions at the right time can build a foundation of strength which can last for years. This company has faced stiff competition from its inception. It has competed against discounters and their price cutting, department stores, and foreign-favored nationals. Yet it has been highly successful.

In 1886 Richard Warren Sears saw an opportunity to sell a shipment of watches, which had been rejected by a Chicago wholesale jeweler, by mail-order to customers. This had not been done before. He was successful and expanded his success by adopting a strategy of selling at low prices, accepting a low margin of profit per item, and turning over merchandise fast through heavy advertising [Hidy and Cawein, 1967:72–73].

Beginning with the modern era of Sears, around 1925, there were a number of major strategic moves that maintained the momentum of the company, such as:

- The fateful decision in the mid-1920s to add retail stores to the original catalog business as the farm population came to town in automobiles.
- The decision to centralize merchandising (all buying, promotional, and advertising operations) in Chicago, and to control store operations from territorial headquarters— a unique management structure that forms the warp and woof of Sears today.
- The decision to control the cost, quality, and quantity of Sears' merchandise by having deliveries made to its own specifications. Sears today is responsible for the design details of 95 per cent of the goods it sells.

· The sweeping decision after World War II to expand aggressively, to relocate old stores, and to put new stores in new locations. Thus Sears very early preempted the prize locations as the population went from East to West and from the city to the suburbs.
· The decision in the mid-1950s to expand its sale of soft goods in retail stores, that is, to go to full-line department stores in place of the old hardware sort of stores featuring tools and fishing tackle.

In the late 1960s and early 1970s Sears embarked on a strategy to upgrade its product line and to add merchandise at the higher price end. This was a decision to play up style and fashion along with economy, a decision that was to modernize Sears' image. It led, for example, to Sears becoming one of the largest mink and diamond merchants in the United States. The strategy did attract more affluent customers to the stores and, with the increase in sales of merchandize with higher margins, Sears' profits rose. However, while sales continued to rise, after 1973 profits began to fall. Sears's image as a seller of low-priced merchandize gradually eroded. During most of the 1970s Sears' share of the market remained stable, but market share of companies like K Mart and J. C. Penney increased.

As Sears enters the 1980s it is reverting to its strategy of 15 years ago. The marks of Sears past success are being revived and strengthened—sell to the middle-class, home-owning families and put renewed emphasis on product service and value. As Joseph T. Moran, Vice President for Merchandising, put it:

"We are not a Bloomingdale's or Marshall Field. It (Sears) has connotations of a barn or farm to some people. But Sears is a store that was built for, and helped create, an American middle class, a homeowning, car-owning Middle America with all the things that are bad or good—or that more sophisticated folks might look down their noses at. But that's what we are—an organization designed to serve and capitalize on these people [*Business Week,* January 8, 1979:80].

This overarching theme is being translated into a web of other strategies to support it—advertising, store layout, parking lots, organizational design, qualities sought in managers, pay scales, product lines, and so on.

GENERAL MOTORS' PRICING POLICY

A classic example of a strategy that was the foundation of a highly successful business experience concerns GM's decision to avoid competing with Ford head-on and to produce different automobiles at varying prices. The decision was made prior to World War I at which time Ford had about 50 per cent of the automobile market divided between two cars, the high-volume, low-priced Model T and the low-volume, high-priced Lincoln. GM had approximately 12 per cent of the market. At the time the company had a line of ten cars, some of which were in the same price range, but none were at the low end of a price range. GM decided to compete over a wide range of prices (from

$450 to $3500 in six price classifications). The strategy was explained by Alfred Sloan, one of its architects, as follows:

We proposed in general that General Motors should place its cars at the top of each price range and make them of such a quality that they would attract sales from below that price, selling to those customers who might be willing to pay a little more for the additional quality, and attract sales also from above that price, selling to those customers who would see the price advantage in a car of close to the quality of higher priced competition. This amounted to quality competition against cars below a given price tag, and price competition against cars above that price tag. Of course, a competitor could respond in kind, but where we had little volume we could thereby chip away an increase from above and below, and where we had volume it was up to us to maintain it. Unless the number of models was limited, we said, and unless it was planned that each model should cover its own grade and also overlap into the grades above and below its price, a large volume could not be secured for each car. This large volume, we observed, was necessary to gain the advantages of quantity production, counted on as a most important factor in earning a position of preeminence in all the grades [Sloan, 1964:67–68].

In commenting on this strategy, one of the authors said elsewhere: "Ford monopolized the low-price field, but General Motors' strategy was not to meet Ford head-on with the same type and price automobile; rather, the strategy was to produce a better car than Ford and price it at the top end of the low-price field. The price was near that of Ford's, but with the superior car the idea was that demand would be drawn from the Ford grade of car to the slightly higher price in preference to Ford's utility design. This strategy worked and was the basis for the rise of a major corporation. This was a strategy that Ford used after World War II" (Steiner, 1969b:246).

IBM VERSUS RCA

In matters of master policy/strategy what is one company's formula for great success may be another's booby trap. This was the case with respect to RCA's entrance into the computer market with a policy/strategy to copy IBM's policy/strategy.

RCA decided to enter the computer business in 1957. It was a logical move since RCA had a strong electronics capability and the market for computers at the time promised to grow rapidly. IBM at the time held some 70 per cent of the market and its strategies reinforced one another. Its products were high quality and kept pace with technology. It emphasized solving both software and hardware problems of customers. IBM built a powerful and effective sales organization. It also decided to lease its equipment rather than sell it. One advantage of this strategy was that the machines could be depreciated more rapidly than they disappeared from the market. The result was a valuable asset that did not appear as an investment on the books of the company but produced substantial revenues.

RCA's strategy appeared to be that of competing "head-on" with IBM. RCA, for instance, introduced a series of computers aimed at capturing IBM's Series/360 users. RCA's machines had more capacity and were lower priced than IBM's series. This strategy failed, however, because RCA did not have as well-trained a sales force and stable of engineers as did IBM to deal with software and hardware problems of customers. In addition, IBM's customers were "locked in" because of past satisfaction with IBM's performance. Underneath it all, RCA committed itself to making its computer business a main thrust, but it appears the commitment was never really fulfilled. The result was that in 1971 RCA wrote off its computer business and took a loss between $400 and $500 million [Ross and Kami, 1973:70–76].

CHRYSLER CORPORATION

Early in August 1979 Chrysler Corporation petitioned the United States Government for $1 billion immediate cash aid. Top management of Chrysler said that it had a cash flow crisis and that if it was not corrected the company would be forced into bankruptcy. Following a national debate on the subject, President Carter on January 7, 1980, signed legislation to bail out Chrysler with $1.5 billion in federal loan guarantees. Our interest in this case is not at this point whether the loan guarantee was or was not a proper decision by the Federal government but rather some of the strategy failures of Chrysler that led to this crisis.

Chrysler's profits have been up and down in recent years. In 1973 they were $255 million. Then in 1974 there was a loss of $52 million, followed by a loss of $260 million in 1975. The years 1976 and 1977 were profitable, $423 million and $163 million respectively. In the 18 months ending in mid-August 1980, Chrysler lost more money ($2 billion) than any other company in the history of American business in the same period of time. This situation is not unique with Chrysler, since both Ford Motors and General Motors currently (Fall 1980) show losses, a point which will be noted later.

There are many people who believe that Chrysler's basic current troubles are rooted in poor strategies stretching back many years. In the 1960s Chrysler's top management adopted a strategy of investing heavily in European companies to make cars for that market to soften the profit impact of downturns in the domestic United States auto market. As it turned out Chrysler began this investment program too late and found itself buying failing companies like Simca, in France, and Rootes Motors Ltd., in Great Britain, which required huge cash infusions. Unfortunately, this was cash that was to be needed in renovating Chrysler plants in the United States.

A second strategic error was cutting too deeply into engineering and design staffs in order to ride out the recession of 1974–75. The result of this move was to deprive the company of needed talent to compete in the small car era to come. Chrysler was much too slow in moving to small cars. It depended on large, heavy gas-consuming cars too long for its profits. When it did turn to the small car market its funds were too limited to build a plant to produce the four-cylinder engines needed for its forthcoming Omni and Horizon cars. As a result it contracted with Volkswagen, a large German automobile company, to buy 300,000 engines a year. This ceiling, and the lack of its own engine plant, hurt Chrysler badly because, in the summer of 1979, it appeared clear that the

Omni was popular and might well have sold 600,000 if its engines had been available [Eaton, 1979].

A third managerial shortcoming has been apparent poor quality control. In the mid-1970s Chrysler's Volare and Aspen displayed problems with stalling engines, fading brakes, and hoods flying open. In 1977 Chrysler recalled 4,608,074 cars, or triple its output of that year [Eaton, 1979].

Another strategic error of Chrysler has been its policy of building cars on speculation rather than on firm orders from dealers. This is in contrast to the policy of Ford and General Motors to build cars only on the basis of orders from dealers. Chrysler's policy resulted in excessive inventories in periods of recession. In 1979 rebates up to $1000 to clear the show rooms contributed significantly to Chrysler's deficit.

As a result of such strategies Chrysler has been in difficulty for years. It has long been known as "the sick man of Detroit." However, as noted above, all of the automobile producers in the United States are in deep trouble. As of this writing (Fall 1980) automobile sales are one third below a year ago. In mid-August 1980 sales were less than in any year since 1967. As a result of poor sales Ford Motor is expected to lose more than $2 billion from its North American car operations in 1980, but a good bit of this will be offset by profits from overseas operations. Even mighty General Motors is expected to lose money in 1980 for the first time since 1921 [Taylor, 1980].

The underlying cause of these difficulties, of course, is a sharp drop in consumer demand for American automobiles. But American automobile producers are much to blame for their current difficulties. They did not devise strategies to produce automobiles that the American public now wants. They emphasized for too long large automobiles, which were not gasoline efficient. When consumers demanded quality small, gasoline-efficient automobiles, they simply were not in a position to satisfy the demand.

OTHER BRIEF ILLUSTRATIONS OF MAJOR POLICY/STRATEGY

Simple one-line statements of company strategy miss the rich detail that inevitably is required really to describe the strategy. Nevertheless, a few comparatively simple additional illustrations of strategies that either payed off or resulted in failure are useful in underscoring the significance of strategy in corporate health.

- W. T. Grant was founded in 1906 and by 1975 had approximately 1200 stores in 43 states with sales of $2 billion. In 1976 the company went bankrupt. A major cause was a disasterous strategy in the period 1968–74 of expanding too rapidly. Grant sought a strategic goal of growth without much reference to profit. Also, many of the stores were in poor locations. In addition, however, the company offered a too-liberal credit policy, established policies and strategies that resulted in poor inventory management, and failed to establish a distinct image for its customers [Clark, 1979].
- McDonald's Corporation was founded in 1955 and rapidly grew to become the largest food-service organization in the world. The core strategies for its success have been:

a limited menu with top quality food, low price, heavy advertising, carefully chosen locations for each restaurant, fast service, cleanliness of surroundings, community service of each licensee, and rigorous training of managers [Clark, 1979].

• In mid-1975 Xerox Corporation announced that its $910 million acquisition of Scientific Data Systems Inc., in 1969, to compete head on with IBM, was a mistake and it decided to withdraw from the basic computer business.

• Harry Gray assumed the presidency of stodgy United Aircraft in 1971. United Aircraft had sales of around $2 billion but its primary product, aircraft engines, registered plummeting sales. Today, through an aggressive acquisition program, the company has transformed itself as United Technologies into a giant corporation with sales of $10.6 billion and profits of $326 million [Ehrbar, 1980].

• The Lockheed Aircraft Corporation was a successful, highly profitable aerospace company until 1968 when it changed its basic mission from no commercial aircraft to that of becoming a producer of commercial aircraft. The decision to produce the L-1011, a highly technically successful aircraft, created such a huge demand for development capital that the company was on the verge of bankruptcy for several years.

• Rolls-Royce, Ltd., rushed a new technology (the RB 211 engine destined for the Lockheed L-1011) to the market and was forced into bankruptcy when the engine did not perform as required and was disastrously underpriced.

• Rohr Industries Inc., a successful manufacturer of jet engine pod assemblies decided to enter the presumably growing and lucrative urban mass transit market. It won contracts to build cars for the San Francisco and Washington, D.C., new subway systems and achieved a new record—a $52 million loss in 1976 which was the largest for any *Fortune* 500 company that year. With a new CEO in 1977, Rohr returned to its basic business and is once again a successful aerospace subcontractor.

• Baldwin Locomotive was the most efficient producer of steam locomotives in the 1930s but did not appreciate the competition of the diesel locomotives and was forced out of the locomotive business.

Not so dramatic are the scores of strategic decisions made concerning operating matters, such as redesigning a product to cut costs, increasing advertising to improve sales, reducing price to increase share of market, and so on. Depending upon circumstances and who is making a decision, many of these actions may be considered tactics or strategies. Hall examined 64 of the largest companies in eight major domestic manufacturing industries that are generally conceded to be mature and in trouble. He found that a number of companies achieved enviable financial results even when contrasted with the high performers in industry generally. Two basic strategies were found by Hall to be the source of this success: "Achieve the lowest delivered cost position relative to competition, coupled with both an acceptable delivered quality and a pricing policy to gain profitable volume and market share growth. Achieve the highest product/service/ quality differentiated position relative to competition, coupled with both an acceptable delivered cost structure and a pricing policy to gain margins sufficient to fund reinvestment in product/service differentiation" [1980:78–79].

CONCLUDING COMMENT

Throughout the remainder of this book illustrations of the importance of the policy/ strategy function of top management will be found. The next chapter will describe the rapidly changing environment of business, which not only complicates the problems encountered in formulating policy/strategy but underscores its significance to organizational fortunes.

QUESTIONS

Discussion Guides on Chapter Content

1. What are the functions of top managers according to Drucker?
2. Why is policy/strategy of such great importance to an organization?
3. What is strategic management, and how does it differ from operations management?
4. Discuss some of the policy/strategy illustrations in the chapter and comment on why you believe they were successes or failures?

Mind Stretching Question

1. Choose one of the following organizations and, with a little library research, explain some of the recent strategies employed by the organization that brought either success or deep trouble:

A & P	New York City
AMTRAK	Pan Am
General Motors Corp.	Penn Central Railroad
IBM	RCA
Mattel	Xerox

Key Overall Forces in Policy/Strategy Formulation and Implementation

4

The Changing Organizational Environment

INTRODUCTION

The most important single influence on organizational policy and strategy is the environment outside and inside the organization. The more complex, turbulent, and changing is the environment, the greater is its impact on human attitudes, organizational structures, and processes. Since today's environment has rarely been exceeded in complexity, turbulence, rapidity of change, and significance of change, all organizations, large and small, for their survival must pay more attention than ever before to their environments when formulating and implementing policies and strategies.

The purpose of this chapter is to develop a perspective about environment as a backdrop for the remainder of the book. The chapter will seek to do this first of all by presenting an overview of the interconnections between environment and organizational changes. Second, a brief factual review will be given of how major environments are changing. Third, we shall present a thumbnail sketch of the ways in which environment influences policy and strategy with respect to managerial tasks and organizational processes.

ENVIRONMENT AND ORGANIZATIONAL CHANGE

Scope of Environmental Impacts

Figure 4-1 is designed to reveal a number of relationships between an organization's environment and policies and strategies concerned with the functioning of the enterprise. First of all it is clear that an organization does not operate in one but in many environments. In the past, managers concentrated attention on their economic and technical environments. In recent years, however, changes in human attitudes, social values, political forces, and legal liabilities have forced managers to broaden the scope of the environmental forces they consider.

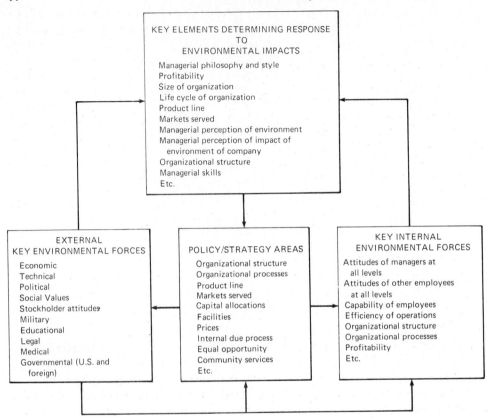

Figure 4-1 Environmental impacts on business policy and strategy.

Second, the forces in environments can affect many different parts of an enterprise. The influence is extremely complex. Some influences may be direct and dramatic, such as a sudden and unexpected change in a vital raw material availability and/or price in a foreign country. Other impacts are indirect, subtle, yet significant, such as changes in worker attitudes toward authority.

Third, the responses of an organization to environmental changes are not always obvious. Much will depend upon managerial philosophy, profitability, the life cycle of the organization, what managers see happening in the environment, how they perceive environmental forces affecting their organization, and so on. The profitability of an enterprise will also affect the way managers respond to outside pressures. For instance, two managers may recognize the importance of responding to society's demands for improving the quality of life in the community. One firm may be operating at a deficit and the other may be making handsome profits. This fact will influence their reactions.

Fourth, the influence process is extremely complex because most things influence all other things. To illustrate, managerial philosophy about the treatment of employees may be influenced by employee atitudes. Managerial philosophy may also influence employee attitudes. Factors in the external environment may influence managerial philosophies as well as employee attitudes. In addition, the interplay between policy/strategy decisions and the internal environment is constant. Changes in organizational structures and processes, for instance, will influence employee attitudes and vice versa.

Fifth, rates of change among different environments will vary. This is an obvious point but deserves mention. A company may find itself, for example, with a congenial economic environment but a hostile social environment. Such was the case of Eastman Kodak when in 1966 it became embroiled in a bitter fight with the black community [Sethi, 1974]. A number of classifications of environments based on rates of change have been suggested by scholars [Rhenman, 1973; Newman, 1971; Emery and Trist, 1965].

Finally, the influence of environment on business is not a unilateral force. Business firms individually and collectively have an important impact on environment. We shall return to this point later.

We turn now to demonstrating, by a few examples, major environmental forces that managers must take into account in formulating and implementing strategy for their enterprises.*

THE ECONOMIC ENVIRONMENT

The economic environment covers a vast territory and is, of course, of arresting significance to business. It is a source of great opportunity as well as a serious threat. The managerial task today is far more complex than in the past, in large part because of the rapid changes taking place in the economic environment to which a firm must adapt for its survival and profitable growth.

Inflation is a serious economic problem plaguing both government and business. Business profits are rising in current dollars but falling in constant dollars, a fact not generally recognized by the public, which continues to consider business profits excessive. The failure of corporations to account fully for the inflation factor has resulted in understatements in their accounting records of capital and inventory replacement and has also caused many corporations to pay more in dividends than their total inflation-adjusted profits [Neal, 1978]. Aside from the depletion of capital resulting from accounting practices not in tune with inflation, inflation blurs a manager's ability to foresee future costs, prices, markets, and long-term growth prospects. Corporations, like the rest of us, also pay taxes on inflationary reevaluations of their earnings and assets.

At a different level, to illustrate the complexities of the economic environment, risks of production are rising. The life cycle of a typical product is becoming shorter. Simultaneously, the research and development time and costs to produce a typical product are increasing. Uncertainties about the availability and price of energy are today and for the foreseeable future a major concern of business managers.

---

* The following environmental analysis draws heavily on Steiner [1980]. See also Steiner and Steiner [1980] for an extended discussion of this subject.

In a different direction, society is demanding that more ethical consideration be injected into technical business decision making. For instance, it is becoming more unethical to produce goods and services that pollute the atmosphere, waste energy, or have built-in obsolescence features. Although such considerations may advance the public welfare, they do complicate the managerial decision-making processes.

In the international economic area, exporters of products and services and multinational corporations are encountering new and perplexing economic problems. To mention just a few, they face a declining but fluctuating value of the dollar in foreign exchange, competition from powerful companies partly subsidized by governments, increasing competition from highly efficient foreign producers, and demands from host governments to assume increased social responsibilities (as are defined by the host governments). Generally, their operations are being more and more restricted by both the government of the United States and the countries in which they do business.

On the other hand, there are elements in the economic environment that provide great profit opportunities. The size of the American market is itself a source of opportunity. Despite undulations above and below GNP trend lines, business activity in the past three decades has shown remarkably stable growth when compared with the past. This, of course, reduces substantially the previous uncertainties facing business with respect to general economic conditions. The fact that the world is not witnessing any wars of great violence is a stabilizing force for world business. There are also opportunities for new technologies and for government partnership with business in such areas as communication and energy.

GOVERNMENT

For most businesses government is a partner—sometimes silent and sometimes highly vocal. Never before in our history, except in wartime, has government been so deeply involved in business as it now is.

The range of government relationships to business spreads from Christmaslike generosity to virtually complete regulation of all industry in time of national emergency. For most businesses the government, particularly the federal government, is one of the most significant influences on operations—growth, pricing, production, product quality, competition, wages, profits, investments, markets, and interest rates paid on capital. The impacts of government on business in recent years have increased in response to tough socioeconomic problems and rising demands and expectations of people for a better life.

Government supports business. To illustrate, it directly benefits business in making research grants, providing financial aids, negotiating tariff arrangements with foreign countries, purchasing the output of business, and commiting itself to a policy of producing economic growth and full employment of resources.

On the other hand, government restricts business. To illustrate, it directly regulates business in many ways—competition, prices, product quality, advertising, sale of securities, labor relations, and air pollution. There is a tendency in many areas, automobile safety for example, for government to get more deeply involved in business' operating details.

Business and government in the past have tended to be antagonistic towards one another. This condition still exists, but there seems to be a change taking place that is bringing about more cooperation between the two. This is illustrated by the government-business complexes developed by the National Aeronautics and Space Administration in its Apollo Program, the forming of COMSAT, and the production of military hardware in the aerospace industry.

This is not meant to imply that the governmental environment for business will necessarily become more friendly and stable. On the contrary, there is evidence that in its dealing with business the government is quite capable of lodging unexpected burdens on particular industries and companies.

THE SOCIOPOLITICAL ENVIRONMENT

Changes in the sociopolitical environment have, within the past several decades, introduced new major forces into the formulation and implementation of policy/strategy for all organizations, especially the large business firm. This has come as a direct reflection of social change and through the indirect impact of social change on economic, technical, and political forces of importance to business. So significant is this change and its impact on business that one observer speaks of the second American Revolution in a book with that title [Rockefeller, 1973]. There are many facets to this phenomenon so the following sections are only illustrative.

Changing Values

Highly important in the turbulence of the business environment are changes in the values that people hold. In recent years changes in these values have stimulated massive regulations, deep criticisms, new demands, and challenges of the very fundamental values on which the business institution rests. For example, more and more people are less and less willing to accept the impartial operation of the market mechanism as the best way to allocate resources. As a result they are relying increasingly on government to intervene in their behalf.

New concepts of egalitarianism are challenging older distributive principles. Traditionally, equality meant that conditions should permit individuals, whatever their origins, to make a life on the basis of ability and character. It was believed that everyone should have an equal place at "the starting line." In recent years the concept of equality has broadened to include rights to receive a wide range of political, social, and economic demands. One authority has called this the "Revolution of Rising Entitlements" [Bell, 1975a]. More recently this concept has turned into one of equality of results, or an equal outcome for all. This value, according to *Business Week,* is "the greatest single force changing and expanding the role of the federal government in the U.S. today [Cobbs, 1975].

There are many other value changes that directly or indirectly influence business.

For example, people today seek self-gratification now rather than later. They want the good things of life immediately. They want to lead lives that are continuously improving in quality. There is a growing challenge of cynicism toward authority. There seems to be an erosion of that part of the Protestant ethic that motivates people to high standards of work performance. People seem to want a more comfortable and less risky life. People are no longer willing to accept traditional rights of property ownership, but want to influence how property is used. Profit is no longer universally accepted as the end purpose of business. Society is coming more and more to expect that societal interests be considered, as well as business self-interest, in pursuing profit objectives. Some observers see in such trends a serious erosion of the fundamental institutional values of the classical free enterprise system [Lodge, 1974, 1975].

Criticism of Business

Opinion polls show that Americans are highly critical of all their institutions, but the business institution has elicited special criticisms, especially the larger corporations. Public respect for business has declined drastically during the past decade and is now at a very low level [Lipset and Schneider, 1978]. The average person, according to polls, has a deep mistrust of the motives of business people. There is a strong belief that those in business serve their own self-interests rather than those of their customers and that they act immorally much too often.

Attitudes such as these accentuate and accelerate government regulation of business. They lead to punitive forms of regulation that are costly and disruptive, and they adversely affect economic/political balances. Criticism, when justified, can be effective in improving business performance. When it is distorted, ill-founded, and exorbitant, however, it can easily lead to excessive government regulation.

Pluralism

We are a pluralistic society. This means our society is composed of semiautonomous and autonomous groups through which power is diffused. One feature of our pluralism is that these groups are growing in total numbers and more of them have deep antipathy toward business or espouse a point of view that is in sharp contrast to traditional business practices. Also, more and more groups are armed with talented, dedicated members who understand how to use their power and existing laws to meet their objectives.

A fact of political life, of course, is the right of these groups to exert their influence in the seat of government. Government decisions are made in response to these pressures. Their influence on business is felt, therefore, through the legislative process. In addition, however, these groups are exercising more and more influence directly on business. In the distant past a business manager could be successful if, working within the rules of the game laid down by government, he or she tried to satisfy only customers and stockholders. Today the managers of a large corporation must pay attention to a growing number of diverse constituent groups (Vogel, 1978). Dealing with the often conflicting, and sometimes disruptive, pressures of such groups is consuming an increasing share of managerial time.

To make matters worse we are moving inexorably "toward becoming a special interest society. . . . Too many lobbyists and interest groups today either care absolutely nothing about the national interest as long as they get theirs or blithely assume that getting theirs is in the national interest. . . . The result has been an increasing polarization pitting those identified as supporters of the 'public interest' against backers of 'private interest,' as if the two were neatly and simply defined and opposed" (Williams, 1975:9). One writer looks at the same phenomenon and says, "The result is an increase in community conflict and in the politics of 'stymie' " (Bell, 1975b:21).

It cannot be denied, of course, that business exerts power in the legislative and executive branches of government. But empirical observation makes quite clear the fact that business has lost relative power in the political arena. Aside from the power issue, however, the current trends in pluralism clearly complicate the managerial task in operating a business.

The Internal Environment

Individuals within organizations are demanding that their interests be considered in the managerial decision-making process. In the past business could legally make decisions wholly on the basis of economic factors. This is no longer possible. Individuals want more creative jobs, they want to participate in the decision-making process, they want to avoid routine mind-numbing jobs, they want more pleasant surroundings, they want higher wages and more generous pensions, and they want shorter hours and more vacations. Meeting such demands, within the competitive conditions facing most companies, is a difficult managerial task. But it is a challenge that managers of more and more companies accept. As Irving Shapiro, Chairman of the Board of Du Pont puts it:

The whole thrust of our society is toward greater individuality and better utilization of human potential. Our people are going to need a great deal of personal breadth and versatility. Our institutions are going to have to be flexible and offer a diversity of incentives and rewards.

Our employee relations programs will have to take into account not just the job requirements as management sees them, but the plans and ambitions and preferences of individual employees as well. Finding the right fit between the goals of organizations and the goals of people working in them will be one of management's main tasks in the future [Williams, 1975].

THE LEGAL ENVIRONMENT

An executive of a large company remarked recently that 10 years ago his principal legal worries centered on antitrust matters and that everything else was lumped together as a poor second. Not today, he commented. Now, there are many areas of great urgency the priorities of which change from month to month, and the number of problems, as well as attorney and other legal costs, has exploded. Indeed, he said that he has set a goal of having annual earnings five times the legal fees of his company!

Thomas Ehrlich, Dean of the Law School at Stanford University, has used the phrase "legal pollution" to describe what he calls the growing feeling that it is virtually impossible to move "without running into a law or a regulation or a legal problem" [*U.S. News*

& World Report, 1978:44]. The complex legal environment of business is due not only to increased government regulations but also to a new propensity in society to litigate. Such litigation is encouraged by the massive details of current laws, opportunities for different interpretations, and incentives to resist obeying the rules.

Not only are corporations subject to vastly expanded legal liabilities, but so are directors, officers, and other managers of businesses. Public demands are mounting for managers of corporations to be held personally liable for illegal acts. The demands are not only for higher monetary levies for infractions of the law but for jail sentences [Sethi, 1978]. This trend is of concern to executives because new laws are often vague, and the body of legal opinion to establish standards has not yet been built. Furthermore, well-financed "public interest" groups are an established part of the business environment these days and are ready to bring suit on slight provocation. In addition, discovery of noncompliance with laws and regulations is much more likely today with the wide-ranging inspection right of agencies like the Occupational Safety and Health Administration, the Internal Revenue Service, and the Securities and Exchange Commission. As a result of Watergate and the foreign-payoff scandals of recent years, corporate ethical performance, too, is high on the list of public concerns.

Finally, there are laws and statutes today that implicate managers in criminal actions even though they have not participated in that action. For instance, John R. Park, president of the multibillion-dollar food chain Acme Markets Inc., was personally held liable by the Supreme Court because he failed to ensure that the company kept rats out of a Baltimore warehouse, as required by law (*U.S. v. Park,* 1974).

THE TECHNOLOGICAL ENVIRONMENT

Those in business, no less than the ordinary citizen, are subject to "future shock," a term Toffler [1970:4] coined "to describe the shattering stress and disorientation that we induce in individuals by subjecting them to too much change in too short a time." The pace of technological change has increased rapidly during the past several decades and, although there are those who urge that it be slowed [Ehrlich and Ehrlich, 1974; Schumacher, 1973; Meadows, 1972; and Mishan, 1971], it is likely to continue.

During the past few years we have had one spectacular technological development after another, for example, the computer, laser beams, xerography, miniature integrated circuits, color television, synthetic leather, birth-control pills, the discovery of DNA, nuclear power plants, human body organ transplants, artificial hearts, synthetic foods, new high-productive food grains, and two-way television. Within these developments are others as spectacular as the original invention. Today, for example, we have computers the size of typewriters with the capability of equipment that could only be housed in a two-story building 20 years ago. We are able to send men to the moon and return them safely to earth. We can send men to ocean depths unheard of only a few years ago. With new medicines we save millions of lives of people who would have died in the past.

This environment offers great opportunities as well as serious threats to the businessman. He has opportunities, of course, in finding new technical solutions to meet new demands and in identifying existing technologies that can be exploited. He faces threats in two ways. First, a technology may suddenly appear that makes his product obsolete. Second, new technology sets in motion forces that in turn result in changes in the values people hold. These value changes can be beneficial or threatening to business [Steiner and Steiner, 1980:77–90].

WORLDWIDE FORCES

To this description of environment there should be added worldwide forces. Possibilities for war exist, particularly limited war, and this casts a cloud of uncertainty on the total world environment. World population growth is projected to rise from 4.4 billion today to about 6 billion in the year 2000. The rate of growth is slowing down in the industrial nations of the world but is still rapid in the less developed countries. Unchecked population growth can bring instability in political systems and tensions throughout the world as the rich nations get richer and the poor get poorer, and as underdeveloped nations face mounting food shortages.

There are offsetting counterforces. One is increasing efforts around the world to check population growth. New technology is creating new foods and higher yield grains. Industrial technology is spreading to underdeveloped countries and developed countries are still concerned about and are helping underdeveloped countries to achieve a better life.

Whatever one's perception of the state of the world environment, there is one thing certain about it; it adds to rather than reduces the risks and uncertainty in our domestic environment.

THE IMPACT OF BUSINESS POLICY/STRATEGY ON ENVIRONMENT

As noted earlier, the policies and strategies of business have a significant impact on environment. The majority of new technologies are introduced into the social system by business. The policy/strategy choices of business obviously have an influence on what is introduced, when, and how much. Business decisions concerning negotiations with labor unions, capital expenditures, transfers of foreign trade balances, foreign investments, and pricing certainly influence environment. Finally, it may be noted that business has lost power relative to other groups in influencing the various governments, but it still has significant power in legislative halls.

THE FUTURE ENVIRONMENT

Most of the preceding discussion concerned current environments, but enough was said to indicate that the future environments of organizations are not likely to be calm.

A few comments, added to what has already been said, will reinforce this conclusion.

Pluralism in this society is likely to expand rather than recede, which means further challenge to business power. An educated population will likely be more rather than less critical and demanding of all organizations, including business. Growing affluence will lead to less attention to material necessities and more to a richer life, self-satisfactions, and self-fulfillment. All organizations, including businesses, will be held accountable for their performance. For business this means accountability for social as well as economic performance. The economic environment will be supportive for business with a steady expansion of general economic activity. However, it will also be threatening because of serious problems associated with price inflation, growing scarcity of selected raw materials, problems in financing capital requirements, and so on.

We do not know precisely what the future holds for business as an institution and for individual business organizations, but certainly there will be continuing challenges to managers to adapt properly to rapidly changing environmental forces. The pressures on managers to formulate and execute appropriate policies/strategies for their enterprises will increase rather than decline.

IMPACT OF ENVIRONMENT ON BUSINESS ORGANIZATION

Environmental forces affect management and organizations in very specific ways. Beginning with Chandler's classic book on *Strategy and Structure* [1962] scholars have been increasingly interested in the interrelationships among environment, company strategic reaction, and organizational arrangements. Throughout this book references will be made to the results of research in this area.

Comparatively little attention has been paid in academic circles to the ways in which environmental forces are changing the managerial job, especially among top managers in our largest corporations, and how that in turn is changing the internal infrastructure and decision-making processes. In 1969 the Conference Board surveyed CEOs and found only one among 127 who rated contact with the community and especially government as being of most importance in the CEOs task [Stieglitz, 1969]. Chase surveyed CEOs of the *Fortune* 1000 companies and found that they said they spent in 1976 an average of 20 per cent of their time on public issues that affect the company and that had increased to 40 per cent in 1978 [Fegley, 1979]. More recently Buchholz [1979] surveyed CEOs and found that time spent on external matters ranged from 20 to 75 per cent with a mode of 50 per cent. Steiner interviewed CEOs of large corporations and confirmed these findings [Steiner, 1981a and b].

Not only do managers of large corporations spend much more time than in the past on environmental forces but they have also changed the ways in which they manage and their philosophy of management. For instance, they are much more involved in political activities today than ever before. They spend far more time than ever before involved not only in the political processes in Washington, D.C., but among the governmental regulatory agencies. They are much more involved in public debate about public issues affecting their companies and business in general. The requirements for effective management of our largest companies, in brief, are very different from those of only a comparatively few years ago. For a full analysis of these changes see *The New Class of Chief Executive Officer* [Steiner, 1981a and b].

Because of these changes in the activities of CEOs of large companies there have been significant changes in the internal organization and decision-making processes. As noted in the last chapter, CEOs are delegating more of the day-to-day management to lower-level managers. But much more is going on than that. Relationships with boards of directors are changing, the public affairs function has expanded significantly, new staff groups have been formed, new programs have been launched to sensitize managers to environmental forces, and new programs have been developed to get company constituents involved in the political processes (Steiner, 1981a and b]. These changes will be further elaborated in later chapters.

Many other aspects of management practice, organizational structure, and organizational processes are influenced by environmental changes. The many environmental changes taking place today have profoundly affected the ways in which managers manage and organizations operate. There are deep and fundamental changes taking place in the business organization as a result of environmental forces and, as a result, future business organizations, especially of the larger companies, will operate much differently than their current-day counterparts. Table 4-1 summarizes some of the major changes likely to continue and is presented without further comment at this point.

CONCLUDING COMMENT

This short overview permits a few outstanding conclusions. First, the top management task in organizations, especially that related to the policy/strategy formulation and implementation task, is unbelievably complex and is destined to become more so because of rapidly changing, enigmatic, and uncertain environments. The environment will pose many more questions for managers than can be answered by the old quantitative economic calculus. Nonquantifiable parameters concerning political, social, ethical and human factors will be injected more and more into decision making. This all is further complicated by many changing attitudes of people in organizations.

Second, the environment is constantly changing. Suitable managerial solutions today to adapt to a changing environment may be completely inadequate tomorrow. This, of course, significantly complicates the policy/strategy formulation and implementation process.

Third, it must be quite obvious by now that the decisions made by top managers in the policy/strategy process, especially as they relate to environment, are the most critical decisions they are called upon to make. The only possible exception is the choice of other top managers to follow in their footsteps. Generally, however, that choice is the person whose capabilities best fit him or her to meet the challenges of the organization's environment.

TABLE 4-1
Recent Past Versus Current and Future Managerial Practices

RECENT PAST	TOWARD	CURRENT AND FUTURE
1. Assumption that a business manager's sole responsibility is to optimize stockholder wealth; operational management dominant		Profit still dominant but modified by the assumption that a business manager has other social responsibilities; strategic management dominant
2. Business performances measured only by economic standards		Application of both an economic and social measure of performance
3. Emphasis on quantity of production		Emphasis on quantity and quality
4. Authoritarian management		Permissive/democratic management
5. Short-term intuitive planning		Long-range comprehensive structured planning
6. Entrepreneural managers who prosper by concentrating on exploiting opportunities they perceive in the environments		Renaissance managers who have the capability of entrepreneurs but who also understand political, technical, social, human, and other forces influencing their organizations
7. People subordinate		People dominant
8. Financial accounting		Financial, human resources, and social accounting
9. Caveat emptor		Ombudsman
10. Centralized decision making		Decentralized and small group decision making
11. Dominance of solely economic forecasts in decision making		Major use of social, technical, and political forecasts as well as economic forecasts
12. Business ideology calls for aloofness from government		Business-government cooperation and convergence of planning
13. Business has little concern for social costs of production		Increasing concern for internalizing social costs of production
14. Managerial emphasis on internal efficiency		Emphasis on devising strategy to adapt to turbulent environment *plus* internal efficiency
15. Decisions based on assumption of price stability		Assumption of continuing inflation
16. Decisions based on assumption of cheap and abundant energy		Expensive and uncertain energy supplies
17. Most companies not involved in foreign trade and international competition		Many multinational corporations facing stiff foreign competition

SOURCE: Adapted from Steiner [1972a].

QUESTIONS

Discussion Guides on Chapter Content

1. Discuss the conceptual interrelationships between a business' environment and its policy and strategy.
2. Explain briefly how the following domestic environments are changing for business: economic, government, legal, technological, social, worldwide forces. For each, appraise briefly whether the change is beneficial or threatening to business.
3. In what ways does business have an impact on its environment?
4. Explain in what ways environment has affected the way in which businesses are organized.
5. Explain briefly what is meant by each of the comparisons shown in Table 4-1 of the differences in management practices (past and future) brought about by changing environments. Can you add others to this table?

Mind Stretching Questions

1. You are now in the year 2000. Assuming that the practices of management of organizations change as asserted by the authors in Table 4-1, do you think the structures, operation, and role of the business institution will be radically different from today, only a little different from today, or about the same as today? Explain.
2. If you accept the changes in the way businesses will be managed in the future, as discussed in this chapter, how would you revise today's curriculum in schools of business to prepare students better to meet the needs and challenges of future business life?

5

Corporate Social Responsibilities and Responses to Them

Environmental changes discussed in the last chapter have added significant new dimensions to managerial decision making. One very important new force concerns the social responsibilities that corporations are presumed to have, especially the larger companies, and how policies/strategies are changing to respond to them. This is the subject of this chapter.

THE SOCIAL RESPONSIBILITIES OF BUSINESS

Managers of all organizations, including business institutions, have always had social responsibilities, but the meaning of this phrase and its importance in decision making is significantly different today than in the past. The following discussion applies to all organizations, but the focus will be on business.

Shifting Managerial Philosophies

Traditionally, managers of business enterprises have been asked by society to concentrate on using efficiently the resources at their disposal to produce goods and services that consumers wanted at prices they were willing to pay. If this was done well, said classical economists, stockholder wealth would be maximized. This view came to mean that the managerial task was to maximize profits within, of course, the "rules of the game" laid down by law and custom. The decision-making calculus focused on the short time span, and was predominantly economic with very little if any concern for social matters. This is the classical philosophy.

The first major break in this philosophy came in the 1930s when managers of large corporations asserted that they were obliged to make decisions in such a way as to balance equitably the claims on the enterprise of stockholders, employees, customers, suppliers, and the general public. Managers were considered to be trustees for these interests. If the balancing was done well, it was reasoned, the long-run profits of the corporation would be maximized. There were some who felt that actions not directly related to profits might be taken, but their acceptable range was negligible. This is the balanced-interest managerial philosophy.

Another major break from the older concept is now taking place. It is the socioeconomic managerial philosophy. In this view the business enterprise reacts to the total societal environment and not merely to markets [Jacoby, 1973:194]. There is no concensus about what this means. This view is rooted in the idea that there is a social contract upon which basis corporations function [Anshen, 1974]. Society grants corporations various rights and in turn expects them to operate in certain ways. In the past a corporation was only expected to use resources efficiently; now it is expected to assume social responsibilities that go well beyond mere efficiency. There is a growing recognition among corporate leaders, especially in the larger firms, that they do indeed have social responsibilities to try to meet some of society's new expectations, but there is no concensus about what to do. Although the policy/strategy implications are not clear in specific cases, there is no doubt that the underlying philosophy of managerial social responsibility identified here is distinctly different from the past views of balancing interests and of profit maximization [Adizes and Weston, 1973]. Today sociopolitical forces are as important to managerial decision making in the larger corporation as economic and technical forces.

These three views—the classical, the balanced-interest, and the socioeconomic—are not, of course, sequential. Among business managers and the general public each idea has some degree of acceptance as an operational philosophy [Richman, 1973]. Generally speaking the classical philosophy is more readily accepted for and among small enterprises and the social philosophy is more demanded of and accepted by managers of larger companies.

What Is Meant by the Social Responsibility of Business?

In the classical view, a business was acting in a socially responsible manner when it used efficiently the resources at its disposal. The current concept of social responsibility includes this action but much more. We define the new social responsibility from two points of view—the conceptual and in terms of specific programs.

CONCEPTUAL. At a high level of abstraction, business social responsibilities refer to "the businessman's decisions and actions taken for reasons at least partially beyond the firm's direct economic or technical interest" [Davis, 1960:70]. A broader view is that there are obligations to "pursue those policies, to make those decisions, or to follow those lines of action that are desirable in terms of the objectives and values of our society" [Bowen, 1953:6]. An even broader view is the following: "By 'social responsibility' we mean the intelligent and objective concern for the welfare of society that restrains individual and corporate behavior from ultimately destructive activities, no matter how immediately profitable, and leads to the direction of positive contributions to human betterment, variously as the latter may be defined" [Andrews, 1971:120]. Basically, these definitions say that business men in their decision making should consider the social interests of people in society.

SPECIFIC CORPORATE SOCIAL PROGRAMS. At an operational level, social responsibilities can be defined in terms of specific action programs that a corporation may take. Several lists of such programs have been compiled, the first by the Committee for Economic Development (CED) [1971:31–40]. There were ten categories and 57 separate programs in the CED list. Included were the classical responsibilities of business relating to economic efficiency and growth. Other categories were education, employment and training, civil rights and equal opportunity, urban renewal and development, pollution abatement, conservation and recreation, culture and the arts, medical care, and government. In a survey based upon this list respondents were asked what other programs might be included, and from this response these categories were added: product safety, advertising, consumer services, general community services, and improving employee self-satisfactions. McAdam [1973] compiled a more recent and longer list.

OTHER DEFINITIONS. There is no concensus about the definition of business social responsibilities. Different writers approach the subject from different points of view. For instance, social responsibilities have been defined in terms of ethics [Baumhart, 1968]; sociology [Bell, 1971]; aesthetics [Eells, 1968]; internalizing costs [Barkley and Seckler, 1972]; and how future society judges today's performance [Farmer and Hogue, 1973].

Most businessmen prefer words other than social responsibilities to describe the phenomenon. Some synonyms are: public policy, social action, social concern, social challenges, community activities, and public affairs.

SOCIAL RESPONSIBILITIES AND PROFITS. When speaking of social responsibilities many people, including managers, conclude that the pursuit of social responsibilities will *ipso facto* result in a reduction of short-range and perhaps also of long-range profits. This is not so. If one accepts our definitions, a corporation is acting socially responsibly when it improves its productivity and, other things being equal, that will raise both short- and long-range profits. But a corporation may undertake other programs that will raise profits rather than reduce them. For instance, assuring more due process, justice, equity, and morality in employee selection, training, promotion, and firing may well improve morale and productivity and, in turn, profits. Replacing a dangerous machine with a new one may not only eliminate an accident hazard but also raise productivity per man hour. Some social programs can, of course, reduce profits. If a firm installs expensive antipollution devices and the costs cannot be passed on to consumers, the company's profits will certainly be less than before.

The Case Against Business' Assumption of Social Responsibilities

Not everyone agrees that businessmen have social responsibilities beyond their classical function. Milton Friedman, a widely-respected economist, is an outstanding protagonist of this view. He says:

. . . there is one and only one social responsibility of business—to use its resources and engage in activities designed to increase its profits so long as it stays within the rules of the game, which is to say, engages in open and free competition, without deception or fraud. . . . Few trends could so thoroughly undermine the very foundations of our free society as the acceptance by corporate officials of a social responsibility other than to make as much money for their stockholders as possible. This is a fundamentally subversive doctrine [Friedman, 1962:133].

Friedman bases his position on a number of arguments. For example, he says that managers are employees of the owners of an enterprise and are directly responsible to the owners—the shareholders. Since shareholders want to maximize their wealth the managers should pursue that objective without deviation. He also says that if managers spend stockholder money without their consent that amounts to taxation without representation. More cogently, Friedman argues that if corporations pursue social responsibilities, which are really governmental responsibilities, their performance will tend to be measured by criteria used to judge performance of public officials. If so, the economic measure of performance will decline in importance and eventually economic efficiency will erode and society will lose. Friedman is joined by many others in such beliefs [Manne, 1972; Heyne, 1971, 1968; Levitt, 1968; Hayek, 1944].

The Case for Business' Assumption of Social Responsibilities

The number of people opposing such views is growing both in and out of the business world. Generally speaking, the case for the assumption of business social responsibilities is based on three interrelated core ideas. The first, simply put, is that society expects business to assume social responsibilities. Now, since the corporation is a creature sanctioned by society to achieve objectives set for it by society, the corporation must respond when society's will becomes manifest. Gerhard Bleichen [1972], Chairman of the Board of John Hancock Mutual Life Insurance Company succinctly put the position of business this way: ". . . it never occurred to me that there was a time when American business was at liberty to operate in conflict with the interests of society." Many businessmen accept the notion that the corporation operates under a franchise from society, and society can take that franchise away if business does not respond to its desires.

Second, it is in the long-run self-interest of business to assume social responsibilities. This is inherent in the preceding position but can be expressed in different words. In a milestone policy statement of the CED, a group of prominent businessmen concluded: ". . . it is in the enlightened self-interest of corporations to promote the public welfare in a positive way" [Committee for Economic Development, 1971:25]. The statement continued: "Indeed, the corporate interest broadly defined by management can support involvement in helping to solve virtually any social problem, because people who have a good environment, education, and opportunity make better employees, customers, and neighbors for business than those who are poor, ignorant, and oppressed" [1971:26].

The same point holds with respect to other types of social responsibilities. For instance, corporations are understanding better that their best interests are served when corporate goals and personnel goals are in harmony. Arjay Miller [1966] says that a corporation cannot preserve stockholder equity in the long run without behaving with social responsibility.

Third, when business assumes social responsibilities it reduces the pressure for and incidence of federal regulations. In turn, the businessman will reduce his costs because regulation is generally expensive; he will retain some flexibility and freedom in making decisions; and he will restrain further concentration of power in government. Furthermore, says Anshen [1970], the businessman will retain a needed credibility with the public and will be invited to, not restrained from, participating in the political decision-making process when new legislation pertaining to business is being drafted.

Many other arguments are made to support business' assumption of social responsibility but only a few can be added here. Some say that businessmen are concerned citizens, as well as managers, and can be expected to use their corporate powers to help develop a better world. Some managers and scholars say that businessmen take social responsibility seriously in order to assure a legitimacy which today is tenuous and fuzzy. When managers find themselves in control of a giant company in which they possess small stock ownership, and no one else owns anything beyond a fraction of outstanding shares, to whom are they responsible? Finally, as Andrews [1971:133] points out: ". . . corporate executives of the caliber, integrity, intelligence, and humanity required to run substantial companies cannot be expected to confine themselves to their narrow economic activity and to ignore its social consequences."

An Assessment of the Argument

It is our judgment that arguments opposing the assumption of social responsibilities are weak on two grounds. First, they overstate the trend and ultimate magnitude of social responsibilities which businessmen voluntarily take on now and will undertake in the future. Second, they want corporations to do something they cannot do, and that is to ignore societal demands on them. This does not mean the arguments against social responsibilities are without any substance. They do contain warning signals that caution us against any excessive movement away from traditional economic motivations and measures of performance.

Opponents of the social responsibility doctrine like to point to the fact that stockholders are the legal owners of a corporation and that managers, by law and in conformance with the theory of the private enterprise system, must consider the interests of the stockholders as being preeminent. There are many who disagree. Wallich and McGown, for example, point out that this view rests on a simplistic notion of stockholder ownership. They say: "Once it is recognized that corporations are not usually owned by a group of investors who own shares in only one corporation, but by individuals who as a group typically own shares in a very large number of corporations, the whole concept of stockholder interest becomes extremely fuzzy" [in Baumol *et al.,* 1970:55]. If stockholders feel their interests are not being served, they sell their stock.

Opponents of business social responsibilities point to a conflict between socially responsible actions and profits. Earlier we noted that there need not be a conflict. A corporation can improve its profit position and at the same time be socially responsible.

The argument about whether businessmen have or do not have social obligations is by no means settled and will continue. For practical purposes, however, the issue is settled. Businessmen do have social responsibilities! There are questions of more immediate concern. Precisely what are the social responsibilities of a particular business? How can top managers institutionalize the social point of view in the decision-making process of a company? How can and should a corporation account for its social performance? We shall address each of these questions but, before doing so, it is useful to distinguish among major types of business social responsibilities.

The Concept of Voluntarism

In the typical large corporation, the totality of decision making that falls within the realm of social responsibility, as defined previously, may be classified into five categories, as follows: (1) decisions concerned with traditional economic and technical matters; (2) actions generated by irresistible internal human and organizational pressures; (3) responses to government laws, regulations, and other mandates; (4) responses to demands from powerful pressure groups, such as unions, which cannot be denied; and (5) voluntary socially oriented actions.

In the fifth class are new social programs introduced in the corporation and/or the addition of social dimensions to traditional types of decisions made in the other categories. Programs in this area can be divided into the following groups: those actions taken by managers to do more than the law requires, actions that recognize current public expectations and social demands, actions that anticipate new social demands and prepare in advance to meet them, and actions that serve to show that corporate managers are leaders in setting new standards of business social performance [Chamber of Commerce of the United States, 1970; Rockefeller, 1973].

No one knows precisely what volume of decisions, irrespective of how volume is defined, falls into the preceding categories. There seems little question about the fact, however, that the fifth area is growing in volume and significance in most larger and many smaller corporations. For the average corporation, however, it is relatively small compared to the other categories.

CORPORATE RESPONSE TO SOCIAL DEMANDS

The great bulk of socially responsible actions taken by corporations is mandated by market conditions and government edict. But corporations, especially the larger ones, have sought to respond appropriately on a voluntary basis to the legitimate demands of various constituents. This fact has, of course, raised important new dimensions to policy/strategy formulation and implementation. It is not possible in the limited space that can be devoted to this subject here to do more than sketch some of the major dimensions.

What Are an Individual Corporation's Social Responsibilities?

As noted earlier there is an answer to this question at a high level of abstraction. There is no clear answer, however, at the operational or decision-making level. Each company is able to determine for itself how to respond to the many interests and pressures for social action that are focused on it.

Although there are no rules that apply to individual companies in specifying what, when, where, and how much social responsibility should be introduced into the decision-making processes, there are a few generalizations that can give some guidance.

First, the larger a company becomes the more actual and potential influence it has over people and society. Society tends to take a greater interest in what the company does, and the company tends to think more carefully about its social responsibilities. In the words of jurists it tends to be "affected with a public interest." Society does not, on the other hand, expect many social responsibilities from very small corporations other than to produce goods and services efficiently within the law and codes of honesty and integrity.

Second, without regard to size, companies may have different degrees of power over individuals and communities. For example, company A may be smaller than company B, but company A may employ 90 per cent of the workers of town Y whereas company B employs only 1 per cent of the workers of the town. Both companies are planning to move. It would appear that, other things being equal, company A should give much more thought to its social responsibilities in moving than company B. This is what Davis [1960] calls a "socioeconomic responsibility" problem.

Again, although all this may be useful in helping a management that is trying to formulate social policies and strategies, it does not tell a company precisely what it ought to be doing. There is no easy answer to that question, and what may be a suitable answer today may well be insufficient tomorrow as the social environment changes.

The Range of Corporate Social Programs

A comprehensive survey of almost 300 larger corporations showed a widespread commitment to social programs. Using the CED listing referred to earlier, respondents were asked to identify those individual programs to which they were making substantial commitments in time and money. A large number of companies were acting in every one of the CED programs. Table 5-1 shows the programs where most corporations are making heavy commitments [Corson and Steiner, 1974].

TABLE 5-1
Rank Order Listing of Activities that Were Noted Most Frequently by Companies
(N = 284) to Involve Significant Commitments of Money and/or Personnel Time

RANK*	NUMBER OF RESPONSES
1. Ensuring employment and advancement opportunities for minorities	244
2. Direct financial aid to schools, including scholarships, grants, and tuition refunds	238
3. Active recruitment of the disadvantaged	199
4. Improvement of work/career opportunities	191
5. Installation of modern pollution abatement equipment	189
6. Increasing productivity in the private sector of the economy	180
7. Direct financial support to art institutions and the performing arts	177
8. Facilitating equality of results by continued training and other special programs (civil rights and equal opportunity)	176
9. Improving the innovative and performance of business management	174
10. Engineering new facilities for minimum environmental effects	169

* Rank: (1) indicates highest commitment.

Models of Business Social Responsibilities

Managers may choose one or more fundamental models, or basic policy/strategy postures, in assuming social responsibilities. Walton [1967:127–41] suggests six basic models, or ways of looking at a business firm's social responsibilities, to which we will add a seventh. These are rather oversimplified concepts that a manager may have about the principal emphasis he or she takes toward decision making in a company. To the extent that a manager holds views corresponding to these models, the task of determining what his or her social responsibilities are will be simplifed.

1. The austere model. This is the classical model. Here the manager seeks only to maximize stockowner wealth.
2. The household model. Managers in this model believe that their employees (managers and other workers) are their most precious assets and that they have a claim equal, if not superior, to that of the common stockholders. In this view the company is a team, a family, a social organization; the model stresses the importance of the dignity, growth, fulfillment, and abilities of employees. It recognizes a management responsibility to employees going considerably beyond legal obligations to meet their interests and demands.
3. The vendor model. This model focuses attention on the consumer. Over a period of years a substantial body of laws has been enacted to protect the consumer, but this model goes further in seeking to determine consumer wants and to meet the best interests of consumers. A company following this model will not overprice, will not withhold new technologies from the consumer to favor its own financial position, and will incur costs to protect the consumer from defective products.
4. The investment model. This model embodies the concept of long-run enlightened self-interest. Its focus is on long-term profits and the survival of the firm. It recognizes the need to expand its donative powers and to assume social programs that will foster an environment in which business can thrive. This is, according to those who hold this view, a more farsighted view of return on investment.
5. The civic model. In this model, managers recognize a responsibility to the industrial and political system that not only gives them their franchise but provides the means for their growth and prosperity. The managers in this model recognize responsibilities to the community and seek to help the community to fulfill its objectives.
6. The artistic model. This is an emerging model and not a widely accepted one. It focuses on creativity, imagination, and innovation. It manifests concern for and support of the creative arts because it recognizes a close connection between a more humane society and the creative needs of corporate life.
7. The eclectic model. This incorporates two or more of the preceding models. For many companies, the eclectic model is probably a more realistic one than the single-purpose models.

Policies for Social Response

Those corporations choosing to respond to social demands in a manner appropriate for the company will, of course, establish policy/strategy for implementation. A model of a comprehensive set of policies/strategies governing social actions is as follows [Steiner and Steiner, 1980:223–24]:

Each item is prefaced by, "It is the policy/strategy of this company . . ."

1. To think carefully about its social responsibilities. This policy does not commit a company to any particular social program, but it does say that the company feels its first social responsibility is to think carefully about its social responsibilities.
2. To make full use of tax deductibility laws through contributions, when profit margins permit. This policy simply takes advantage of the tax laws but does not commit the company beyond its current minimum philanthropy unless it feels that profit margins are high enough to warrant further giving.
3. To bear the social costs attendant upon its operations when it is possible to do so without jeopardizing its competitive or financial position. This policy says the company wishes to avoid the adverse side effects on society of its operations to the extent that it can do so.
4. To concentrate action programs on limited objectives. No company can take significant action in every area of social responsibility. It can achieve more if it selects areas in which to concentrate its efforts. This policy, therefore, sets limits on social programs.
5. To concentrate action programs on areas strategically related to the present and prospective functions of the business, to begin action programs close to home before acting in far distant regions, and to deal first with what appears to be the most urgent areas of concern to the company. This policy has many facets to it. For example, it does not say that a company should take only that action which is closest to its self-interest. It does say that it should concentrate its efforts in areas that will be importantly related to its survival and healthy growth. To implement this policy it will be necessary for a company to assess carefully the various expectations of its many constituencies, especially those close to it, lay out priorities for action, and then see to implementation. It says, for example, that it is much more important for a public utility to pay attention to what people in and out of the company expect by way of social action than to make contributions to charities far removed geographically from the company.
6. To facilitate employee actions that can be taken as individuals rather than as representatives of the company. This is an encouragement to try to free people who want to to be released. A company should not force employees to go out in the community to do good deeds, but there is a great opportunity for companies to encourage and provide means for their employees to pursue their community interests.
7. To search for product and service opportunities to permit our company and others to make profits while advancing the social interests; but not all social actions should be taken solely for profit. This policy recognizes that there are many things a company can do that are socially responsible and profitable. The combination should be encouraged.
8. To take actions in the name of social responsibilities but not at the expense of that required level of rising profits needed to maintain the economic strength and

dynamism desired by top management. Actions taken in the name of social responsibility should enhance the economic strength of the company and/or the business community. The over-all mission of the company is two-pronged, as follows:

> To set forth and achieve corporate objectives that meet specified social challenges ranging from product quality to the "quality of life" requirements, both internally and externally.

> To increase the company's earnings per share at a rate required to meet shareowner/profit expectations and these new requirements.

This policy does not replace traditional profit policy but expands it.

9. To take socially responsive actions on a continuous basis rather than *ad hoc,* one at a time, or for a short duration. This policy is based upon the conviction that a company will be able to make a much greater impact, at less cost, with continuous as compared with on-again off-again actions.

10. To examine carefully before proceeding the socially responsive needs the company wishes to address, the contributions the company can make, the risks involved for the company, and the potential benefits to both the company and society. This is a warning to "look before you leap." In the past many companies got into trouble because they acted more on impulse than reason. This policy commits the company to take action that is organized, sensible, systematic, and extended over a period of time. It is the opposite of putting out fires or answering alarm bells in response to outside pressures and, after the pressures disappear, going back to practices existing before the stimulus. This policy says, "Let's make a careful cost/benefit analysis before making important commitments."

Institutionalizing Social Policy/Strategy

If the policies/strategies noted in the preceding list are to result in action, they must be defined in more detail and become integrated in day-to-day decision making. Detailed policies, tactics, procedures, control mechanisms, and reward systems must be established to ensure that goals are achieved in conformance with the law, in the case of mandated programs, and top management policies/strategies, for programs that are undertaken voluntarily. Reporting and control mechanisms must, of course, also be prepared, and managers then must exercise the necessary degree of surveillance and control. This is the process of institutionalizing the social point of view in the decision-making process. It is a difficult process and takes much time to implement. Ackerman concluded that this process takes up to eight years [1973, 1975b], a fact confirmed by Murray [1976].

The range of specific policies/strategies, and methods of implementation, that have been developed by corporations is extremely wide [Steiner, 1981a and b; Steiner and Steiner, 1980: Chapter 14]. What follows, therefore, merely illustrates types of social response of corporations.

Most larger corporations and many smaller ones have written statements that reflect their economic and social policies, strategies, and ideologies. ALCOA [1977] for instance, sets forth the following basic policies/strategies, which it calls "Fundamental Objectives":

Aluminum Company of America, as a broadly owned multinational company, is committed to four fundamental, interdependent objectives, all of which are essential to its long-term success. The ideas behind these words have been part of Alcoa's success for many years—as has the company's intention to excel in all these objectives:

- Provide for shareholders a return superior to that available from other investments of equal risk, based on reliable long-term growth in earnings per share
- Provide employees a rewarding and challenging employment environment with opportunity for economic and personal growth
- Provide worldwide customers with products and services of quality
- Direct its skills and resources to help solve the major problems of the societies and communities of which it is a part, while providing these societies with the benefits of its other fundamental objectives [ALCOA, 1977]

Policies and strategies employed by boards of directors increasingly reflect the social point of view. In 1971 Mr. Roche, then chairman of the board of General Motors Corporation named the Reverend Leon H. Sullivan to become the first black member of its board of directors. He also established a Public Policy Committee of outside GM directors. Both actions, according to Roche, were to assure that community action and corporate citizenship would have a permanent place on the highest level of management. Since then a large number of corporations have established public policy committees at the board level. An increasing number of boards of directors have audit committees composed of outside directors. The scope of activities of these committees is widening [Macchiaverna, 1978]. They audit financial, material, and other control systems to make sure that activities are in conformance with law, good management practices, and social expectations. They have become involved in assessing ethical practices to assure not only that they are in conformance with law but also with standards set by top management.

Many corporations have created staff committees with titles such as Social Policy Committee. This committee at the Bank of America [1977] has the following responsibilities.

. . . brings together the expertise of senior managers from many of the bank's operating and administrative departments, including the California and World Banking Divisions, the two largest profit centers, the Personnel, Legal, and Secretary's Departments; the Loan and Controller's Departments; and the Communications and Public Relations Departments . . .

This committee identifies emerging social policy issues and considers the changing needs of groups to which the bank must be responsive—employees, consumers, shareholders, communities, and others. It sets priorities and standards for responsible action and initiates changes in bank policies, positions, and practices. It also plans specific programs to help the bank meet its social responsibilities and monitors the implementation and effectiveness of these undertakings [Bank of America, 1977].

In the past, decision making in the strategic planning process was virtually dominated by economic and technical considerations. Increasingly in the larger corporations social and political considerations stand on equal footing with economic and technical factors. This new dimension has resulted in new programs among corporations to assess the evolving social and political environment. For a brief analysis of how Sears, Roebuck & Co., and General Electric Company do this see, respectively, Barmeier [1980] and Wilson [1980].

Top managers of more and more companies have introduced various programs to help sensitize managers throughout their organizations to social and political considerations that should be understood if not taken into consideration in their decision making. The list of programs is long, but to illustratee the range of programs the following are cited: management memoranda, speeches, and seminars; university faculty invited lectures; attendance at university executive programs; special formal educational programs established for company managers; incentives for employee participation in community affairs; and involving employees and managers in creating social problems or in developing social policy for the company [Buchholz, 1980].

Case narrative and analysis of positive corporate response to social demands is a recently growing literature. A few current samples are Anshen [1980], Frey [1980], McGrath [1980], Brown [1979], Sawyer [1979], Schaeffer and Lynton [1979], and Preston [1978].

THE SOCIAL AUDIT

What Is a Social Audit?

In response to general pressures for corporations to assume social responsibilities and to be held accountable to constituent interests for their performance, companies have made reports of their social activities. These reports have been called social audits.

At a high level of abstraction there probably is agreement that a social audit is a report of social performance in contrast to a financial report, which deals with economic performance. Consensus ends at this point.

There are two fundamentally different types of social audit. One type is required by government agencies to meet reporting requirements for such activities as equal opportunity, pollution abatement, and product performance. Reporting requirements vary widely. The second type covers social audits that concern social programs undertaken voluntarily. These vary from brief comments in annual reports to elaborate research reports [Corson and Steiner, 1974].

What Are Companies Doing?

Corporate social audits are a phenomenon of literally the past decade, although the origins of the approach have been traced back to 1940 [Carroll and Beiler, 1975]. The great majority of social audits that have been made and distributed are inventory-type statements that identify and describe the social programs the company is undertaking and chooses to publicize. They are usually added to the annual financial report. An increasing number of companies, however, prepare separate reports. They range from public-relations statements to thoroughly researched and illuminating reports. A good example of the latter is the annual report of the General Motors Corporation, which carries the title *Report on Progress in Areas of Public Concern.* The great majority of our larger corporations today prepare some form of public statement about their social programs.

Major Policy and Strategy Questions

The idea of a social audit raises a number of important policy/strategy questions for a large company, for instance: Should we undertake a social audit? Why should we do so? To whom should the audit be addressed? If it is addressed to constituents, how shall their interests be identified? What shall we do when constituent interests conflict? How complete shall the audit be? Should we make the audit public? How much should be made public? Who is to measure our social performance?

CONCLUDING COMMENTS

The role of the corporation especially the larger one is undergoing significant change. No longer is society satisfied when it confines its efforts to being efficient. That is still required but, in addition, the corporation is expected to meet new and rising social demands of people. These new demands range from better working conditions in a company to helping society achieve the major objectives it sets for itself.

Not only are corporations expected to undertake social programs that, heretofore, they would not have thought of pursuing but they are also expected to inject into traditional economic and technical decision making a new social point of view. This has clearly added a new dimension to the traditional policy/strategy process. It has immeasurably complicated it because there are no hard and fast guidelines available to a company. Each firm must decide for itself.

An additional complication arises from the fact that corporations, like other institutions, are being held accountable for their social performance. A result of this is the development of the business social audit which is a report on a company's social performance. Here, again, no firm guidelines exist for the business in making a social audit.

QUESTIONS

Discussion Guides on Chapter Content
1. How have the fundamental philsophies of the business managerial role changed over the past 200 years?
2. What is meant by "the social responsibility" of business?
3. Explain the case against businesses' assumption of social responsibilities.
4. What is the case for businesses' assumption of social responsibilities?
5. How do you assess the arguments pro and con of businesses' social responsibilities?
6. In this debate does it make any difference whether one speaks about legally mandated responsibilities versus those voluntarily assumed by business?

7. Do you think the policy recommendations for social responsibilities stated in the chapter should be accepted by every business in the United States? Explain.

8. What are corporations doing to respond to the legitimate demands on them for more and better social performance?

9. Argue the case pro and con that corporations should report publicly on their social activities as they do on their economic activities.

Mind Stretching Questions

1. Mr. Richard Gerstenberg, when Chairman of the Board of General Motors, said, "The most successful business in the years ahead will be the one that not only offers quality products at competitive prices, but also succeeds in matching its resources to society's changing demands, the business that is best able to give creative response to the social aspirations of the people it serves. Conversely, the business that fails in the years ahead will be the one that fails to understand how it is related to the society around it and will, therefore, overlook opportunities for services, for growth, and for profit." (Remarks made at the Institutional Investors Conference, General Motors Technical Center, Warren, Michigan, February 8, 1973.) Is he saying that the business that assumes its proper social responsibilities is likely to be the successful business? Do you agree?

2. John D. Rockefeller, III, examined the role of businessmen in their traditional economic activities and new responsibilities of a social nature and commented as follows: "The challenge is to be successful in business and in serving the needs of society. Is it unreasonable to assume that the same abilities and qualities apply in both cases? I think not." (John D. Rockefeller, III: *The Second American Revolution,* New York, Harper & Row, 1973, p. 95.) Do you agree with Mr. Rockefeller? Explain.

3. What major policy/strategy questions can you enumerate that will face the chief executive officer of a large company who decides that his managers should respond appropriately to the legitimate social demands of constituent groups?

4. Are social responsibilities and moralities the same?

6

Managerial and Organizational Styles

INTRODUCTION

The environments that organizations face vary widely. This is in part a function of the type of organization and the particular industry that a company is in. It is also a function of the stage of development of the company and its current position in its organizational life cycle. These different environments call for different managerial styles, particularly at the top management level, if the company is to cope with its environment effectively. This pressure from the environment is one basis for variations in managerial styles and, thus, in the way companies operate.

Another basis for variation derives directly from within the organization and its members. People differ a great deal in many respects. Many different kinds of people become managers, and for one reason or another rise to top level positions. Thus, two companies in virtually identical environments can be run by chief executive officers who perceive their environments differently, value different things, have different kinds of knowledge and behave quite differently. (A variety of such factors, which may influence managerial decision making, are discussed in Chapter 10.)

These differences among people in their approaches to their jobs constitute differing *managerial* styles. To the extent there are consistencies within companies, so that certain styles tend to be pervasive, one may talk about *organizational* styles. Organizational styles are strongly influenced by top management and by the prevailing organizational climate, particularly by the value and reward structure components of that climate. Managerial and organizational styles in turn exert a great deal of influence on policy and strategy formulation and implementation.

MANAGERIAL JOBS

One approach to dealing with the managerial style question is through the analysis of managerial jobs. Once a knowledge of the range of managerial functions is developed, variations in the extent to which different managers emphasize certain functions and the appropriateness of such an emphasis to the particular situation can be examined.

The Management Process Approach

The approach to the analysis of managerial work with the longest history is the management process approach, which views managing in terms of planning, organizing, and other similar functions. For many years this approach was almost entirely theoretical in nature, and the variety and number of functions considered important in managerial work varied markedly from one theorist to another. More recently a solid underpinning of research has been developing, and certain managerial functions have been identified as playing a central role [Miner, 1971; 1978].

Among the functions proposed by the early theorists, the following have achieved strong research support:

1. Planning
2. Organizing
3. Supervising
4. Coordinating
5. Controlling
6. Communicating

In addition the research indicates that certain other functions, which have appeared in the theoretical literature more recently, are also important:

7. Investigating
8. Evaluating
9. Decision making

Several other functions appear to lack the widespread significance of the preceding nine, but they are important in certain specific kinds of management positions:

10. Staffing
11. Representing
12. Negotiating

If one studies people in upper level management positions, a tendency to concentrate time and effort on certain functions at the expense of others does emerge [Mahoney *et al.,* 1963; 1965]. There are relatively large numbers of top managers who concentrate primarily on planning—approximately 28 per cent in this study. Concentration in this area is much less at lower levels. A second sizable group of top managers (22 per cent) specializes in supervising and directing. These people do relatively little planning; however, this predominance of supervising is even more characteristic of lower management. Another 14 per cent at the top levels concentrate on either the investigative or evaluative aspect of controlling.

Yet top management is also characterized by a disproportionately large number of generalists who spread their time over many functions—20 per cent versus 9 per cent of lower level managers. None of these managers spend as much as 20 per cent of their time in a single function. Yet, only staffing and representing receive very little attention.

Studies of this kind make it clear that managers at the top levels are by no means all generalists in their actual job behavior. This is not to say that a greater shift in the generalist direction might not be desirable. Any conclusion in this regard must await studies relating the use of managerial time to environmental and job requirements. However, the large amount of the top managers' time spent in planning does suggest that policy considerations are often of prime importance.

The Managerial Working Roles Approach

An alternative way of looking at managerial work has recently been developed by Mintzberg [1973; 1975] based primarily on his intensive study of five chief executives. Mintzberg [1979] is very much interested in developing an underlying theory for the field of business policy and in linking this theory into management theory in general. As a starting point he has focused on the working styles of managers. His approach differs from the management process approach because he starts his analysis of the managerial job from different premises and uses a different conceptual framework. That he comes out with a somewhat different result is not so much a repudiation of the process approach as a consequence of cutting up the pie differently in the first place. Yet the ideas that Mintzberg presents regarding the managerial job do provide some valuable insights into managerial styles and differential approaches to policy formation. The essence of his managerial work roles approach is stated in Table 6-1.

Research indicates that as with the management process approach, managerial working roles differ in relation to managerial level [Alexander, 1979]. The entrepreneur and liaison roles are uniquely important in top management, but the figurehead, monitor, disseminator, spokesman, and negotiator roles all are more characteristic at the top than in lower management. The leader, disturbance handler, and resource allocator roles do not differ with level. There are also differences in requirements associated with functional areas, the decisional roles being more characteristic in production, the interpersonal roles in sales, and the informational roles in accounting.

Mintzberg [1973] provides no evidence in support of the particular method of classifying roles set forth in Table 6-1 other than a certain logical coherence. Subsequent studies correlating measures of the roles indicate that only two major categories are needed— informational roles (figurehead, liaison, disseminator, and spokesman) and decisional roles (leader, monitor, entrepreneur, disturbance handler, resource allocator, and negotiator) [Shapira and Dunbar, 1980]. Differentiation along these lines fits well with the decision-making emphasis that characterizes the policy/strategy field.

Roles of the kind Mintzberg [1973] proposed appear to differ in significance, not only from one managerial level or functional area to another but also from organization to organization, depending on the particular problems faced [Morse and Wagner, 1978]. The pattern of role performance that makes for success as a manager in one firm may

TABLE 6-1
Ten Managerial Work Roles

ROLE	DESCRIPTION	TYPICAL ACTIVITIES
Interpersonal Roles		
Figurehead	Symbolic head; performs routine duties of a legal or social nature	Ceremony, status requests
Leader	Responsible for motivation of subordinates and for staffing and training	Almost all managerial activities involving subordinates
Liaison	Maintains network of outside contacts to obtain favors and information	Handling mail, external board work, telephone calls
Informational Roles		
Monitor	Seeks and receives information to obtain thorough understanding of organization and environment	Reading periodicals, observational tours
Disseminator	Transmits information received from outsiders or insiders to other organization members	Forwarding mail, review sessions with subordinates
Spokesman	Transmits information to outsiders on organization plans, policies, actions	Board meetings, handling mail
Decisional Roles		
Entrepreneur	Initiates and supervises design of organizational improvement projects as opportunities arise	Strategy and review sessions regarding change efforts
Disturbance handler	Responsible for corrective action when organization faces unexpected crises	Strategy and review sessions regarding disturbances
Resource allocator	Responsible for allocation of human, monetary, and material resources	Scheduling, requests for authorization, budgeting
Negotiator	Responsible for representing the organization in bargaining and negotiations	Collective bargaining, purchasing

SOURCE: Adapted from Mintzberg [1973:92–93].

differ considerably from the pattern required in another. Clearly different managers may emphasize different combinations of these roles and, accordingly, exhibit widely varying managerial styles.

The number of different managerial styles that may emerge in response to the nature of managerial jobs is sizable. Whether a give style is appropriate can only be determined on the basis of a close analysis of the nature of the specific job and of the demands of that environment. In any event, the existence of different styles can make for extremely varied policies and strategies, as well as considerable variability in the extent to which policies and strategies are formulated at all. Emphasis on one or the other of the decisional roles can produce marked differences in the extent of planning, for instance.

INDIVIDUAL MANAGERIAL STYLES

Another approach to the study and analysis of managerial styles focuses less on the nature of managerial work and more on the nature of managers—their behaviors, predispositions, motives, attitudes, and values. This approach tends to yield somewhat different designations and descriptions of alternative styles than the managerial job approach.

Degree of Subordinate Concern

There has been a long history of research and writing in the leadership area that focuses on style variations associated with such terms as considerate, structuring, autocratic, democratic, laissez-faire, and the like [Miner, 1978]. What these terms have in common is an emphasis on differences in the extent to which managers utilize styles that involve subordinates in the decision-sharing process and exhibit concern for subordinates as individuals. Style variations of this kind continue to provide a major area of study and to yield a wide range of research findings [Miner, 1980a].

Attempts to synthesize this research abound. Thus, Hall, O'Leary, and Williams [1964] utilize concern for subordinate commitment and concern for decision adequacy to identify five prototype styles—eye-to-eye (commitment and adequacy of concern), good neighbor (commitment but not adequacy of concern), self-sufficient (adequacy but not commitment of concern), default (neither commitment nor adequacy of concern), and traditional (both commitment and adequacy of intermediate concern). Bowers and Seashore [1966] expand the number of underlying dimensions from two to four (support, interaction facilitation, goal emphasis, and work facilitation), and accordingly, introduce the possibility of a much more complex array of styles. What characterizes these efforts is a much greater concern with style variations from manager to manager than within the same manager from time to time. Also, there has been relatively little direct application to policy formulation and implementation. In recent years there has been some change in both of these situations, however.

Conditions for Sharing Decisions

It has become increasingly evident that managers do not stick entirely to one style, although because of personal predisposition or environmental pressures a particular style may predominate in their behavior. This viewpoint was expressed some years ago by Tannenbaum and Schmidt [1958], although empirical support has come much more recently. Basically Tannenbaum and Schmidt proposed a continuum of leadership behaviors:

1. Manager makes decision and announces it.
2. Manager sells decision.

3. Manager presents ideas and invites questions.
4. Manager presents tentative decision subject to change.
5. Manager presents problem, gets suggestions, makes decision.
6. Manager defines limits; asks group to make decision.
7. Manager permits subordinates to function within limits defined by superior.

Which of these approaches is taken is said to depend on
1. Forces in the manager including his value system, confidence in his subordinates, leadership inclinations, and feelings of security in an uncertain situation.
2. Forces in the subordinates including their need for independence, readiness to assume responsibility, tolerance for ambiguity, interest in the problem, identification with the goals of the organization, knowledge, and expectation of decision sharing.
3. Forces in the situation, including the type of organization, the effectiveness of the group, the nature of the problem and the pressure of time.

Research conducted since, and elaborated in Chapter 12, indicates that variations in styles of the types indicated do occur within the repertory of a single manager as well as from individual to individual. Furthermore, a number of the forces discussed by Tannenbaum and Schmidt [1958] have been shown to condition the adoption of a particular approach [Heller, 1971; Vroom and Yetton, 1973; Jago and Vroom, 1980].

Leadership Style at the Policy Level
Increasingly, information is being developed on variations in styles of top level executives, especially the chief executive officer. One factor associated with the extent of decision sharing at the top appears to be the degree to which the company is involved in intense competition, and product competition in particular [Khandwalla, 1973]. Where there is a great deal of competition the chief executive tends to delegate and share decisions more in areas such as raising long-term capital, selection of new investments, acquisition of subsidiaries, research and development, new product development, marketing strategy, pricing, top management staffing, and policy change. But it is also true that under highly competitive conditions this decision sharing is much more selective; some types of decisions are delegated and some are not, depending on the circumstances involved.

However, it appears that where a company faces intense competition in its environment, the chief executive not only utilizes a more participative style in decision making but also introduces more controls to be sure the delegated decisions are made and carried out responsibly. Thus, where competition is high, one finds more use of statistical quality control in production, standard costs and cost variance analysis, use of operations research techniques in inventory control and production scheduling, flexible budgeting, investment evaluation by internal rate of return or present value methods, marginal costing for pricing and purchasing decisions, internal auditing, performance (operational) auditing, and systematic evaluation of managerial and senior staff personnel. In fact, the tendency to use these controls when the competition gets heavy is even more pronounced than the tendency to delegate; and once again the use of the approach tends to be highly selective from one control to another, depending on the situation.

Descriptions of individual chief executives make it apparent that sizable differences in style exist. Yet these differences may be entirely appropriate to the external and internal environments with which an executive must cope. Both of the presidents described in Table 6-2 head profitable companies in spite of their very different styles and approaches to policy formation and implementation. Thus, their styles do appear to fit the needs introduced by the nature of company product lines, subordinate competence levels, organizational life cycle position, and the like.

Effective and Ineffective styles

Although those writing about style variations associated with the degree of subordinate concern have generally favored greater participation in decision making, delegation, and consideration for the needs of subordinates, the evidence does not indicate that such managerial styles invariably produce the best results [Miner, 1974; 1978]: that, clearly, is contingent on the situation.

On the other hand, certain categorizations of styles have been developed for the express purpose of contrasting one or more effective styles with certain characteristically ineffective ones. Thus, authoritarian and democratic leadership has been contrasted with a

TABLE 6-2
Descriptions of the Styles of Two Presidents

President Number 1

(45 years old; the company has sales of $225 million, has multiple products, and is divisionally organized)

Sparks subordinates by questioning mind, youthful energy, ideas, and efforts to stretch them.

Pushes executives to set high standards; is a tough evaluator and will replace mediocrity.

Decisions are fact-based and are made after discussions with subordinates.

Use of authority is reasonably permissive within limits of achievement goals; authority is more implied than used.

Seeks change, pushes for it, and is thorough in programming to carry it out.

Is deeply involved in planning, goal setting, and evaluation against targets, with the result that he has a good understanding of each business and has close, frequent contact with each key executive.

President Number 2

(53 years old; the company has sales of $325 million, has a single product, and is functionally organized)

Drives others by the sharpness and toughness of his thinking; he is respected but not held in affection.

Is highly demanding, critical, and imposes his own standards; becomes emotional over difficult people decisions and will by-pass but not fire the mediocre performer.

Makes decisions based heavily on intuition and long experience, which involve relatively little consultation with subordinates and which are held too steadfastly.

Is highly authoritarian, positive in point of view, and imposes decisions with force.

Although intellectually prepared for change, is fearful of it because of anticipation of mistakes and concern over organizational readiness.

In spite of efforts to delegate, maintains over-the-shoulder control; holds onto operations, although much thought is given to strategy.

SOURCE: Adapted from Neuschel [1969:22].

laissez-faire approach, where the manager essentially does nothing unless his subordinates ask him to. Bower [1966] has contrasted his programmed approach, where there is a will to manage an ongoing system, with *ad hoc* management, day-to-day management, piecemeal management, personal management, personal power management, and one-man management. All of the latter are described as "amorphous or mushy. They lack principle. They are indefinite and unclear. They are unfair to able people" [Bower, 1966:12].

Another approach is set forth in Figure 6-1. Here the reconciler is viewed as exhibiting the most effective style, although the other styles may be reasonably appropriate in certain situations.

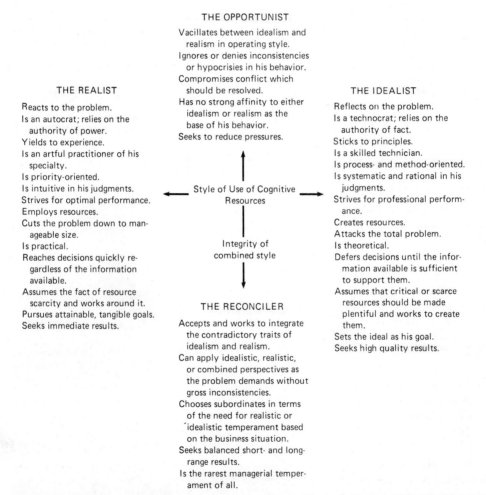

THE OPPORTUNIST

Vacillates between idealism and realism in operating style.
Ignores or denies inconsistencies or hypocrisies in his behavior.
Compromises conflict which should be resolved.
Has no strong affinity to either idealism or realism as the base of his behavior.
Seeks to reduce pressures.

THE REALIST

Reacts to the problem.
Is an autocrat; relies on the authority of power.
Yields to experience.
Is an artful practitioner of his specialty.
Is priority-oriented.
Is intuitive in his judgments.
Strives for optimal performance.
Employs resources.
Cuts the problem down to manageable size.
Is practical.
Reaches decisions quickly regardless of the information available.
Assumes the fact of resource scarcity and works around it.
Pursues attainable, tangible goals.
Seeks immediate results.

Style of Use of Cognitive Resources

Integrity of combined style

THE IDEALIST

Reflects on the problem.
Is a technocrat; relies on the authority of fact.
Sticks to principles.
Is a skilled technician.
Is process- and method-oriented.
Is systematic and rational in his judgments.
Strives for professional performance.
Creates resources.
Attacks the total problem.
Is theoretical.
Defers decisions until the information available is sufficient to support them.
Assumes that critical or scarce resources should be made plentiful and works to create them.
Sets the ideal as his goal.
Seeks high quality results.

THE RECONCILER

Accepts and works to integrate the contradictory traits of idealism and realism.
Can apply idealistic, realistic, or combined perspectives as the problem demands without gross inconsistencies.
Chooses subordinates in terms of the need for realistic or idealistic temperament based on the business situation.
Seeks balanced short- and long-range results.
Is the rarest managerial temperament of all.

Figure 6-1 Polarities of managerial temperament. [From Glenn A. Bassett: "The Qualifications of a Manager," *California Management Review*, Winter 1969, p. 38.]

ORGANIZATIONAL STYLES

When managerial styles coalesce into a meaningful pattern at the upper levels of an organization, it is possible to speak of an organizational style. Not all organizations possess sufficient integration of managerial styles to specify *an* organizational style, although where there has been an extended history of interaction among a reasonably stable group of managers, some semblance of a characteristic style usually does develop. Beyond this, however, the nature, the degree of integration, and the extent of fit with organizational demands can vary tremendously from one company to another.

Variations in Organizational Style

The underpinning of an organizational style is some type of organizational ideology, value structure, or climate. Among the functions thus performed are [Harrison, 1972]

1. Specifying goals and values toward which effort should be directed and by which success and growth should be measured.
2. Prescribing the social contract between individual and organization—what each is and is not supposed to do.
3. Indicating how control should be exercised over behavior—what is and is not legitimate.
4. Establishing which qualities and characteristics of people should be valued or rewarded and which should not.
5. Designating how people in the organization should treat each other—competitively, honestly, distantly, and so on.
6. Providing guides to appropriate methods for dealing with the external environment.

One typology of organizational styles based on variations in these factors is given in Table 6-3. The four alternative styles described are [Harrison, 1972]

1. *Power Orientation.* Such an organization attempts to dominate and control its environment. It makes every effort to avoid control by external law or power, and within the organization those who have power strive to use it.
2. *Role Orientation.* Such an organization attempts to be as rational and orderly as possible. The major concern is with legality, legitimacy, and responsibility.
3. *Task Orientation.* Such an organization devotes its energies to achieving a superordinate goal. The crucial consideration is that structure, functions, and activities are all evaluated in terms of contribution to some such goal—as for instance, profit.
4. *Person Orientation.* Such an organization exists almost entirely to serve the needs of its members. Person-oriented organizations are evaluated as tools by their members. As a result, many have a short life because they outlive their usefulness to members.

It is apparent that different organizational styles among those proposed are differentially effective in alternative internal and external environments.

Another approach to the organizational style issue focuses entirely on alternative

TABLE 6-3
Four Different Organizational Styles

A. INTERESTS OF PEOPLE

	SECURITY AGAINST ECONOMIC, POLITICAL, AND PSYCHOLOGICAL DEPRIVATION	OPPORTUNITIES FOR VOLUNTARY COMMITMENT TO WORTHWHILE GOALS	OPPORTUNITIES TO PURSUE ONE'S OWN GROWTH AND DEVELOPMENT INDEPENDENT OF ORGANIZATION GOALS
Power orientation	Low: At the pleasure of the autocrat	Low: Unless one is in a sufficiently high position to determine organization goals	Low: Unless one is in a sufficiently high position to determine organization goals
Role orientation	High: Secured by law, custom, and procedure	Low: Even if, at times, one is in a high position	Low: Organization goals are relatively rigid and activities are closely prescribed
Task orientation	Moderate: Psychological deprivation can occur when an individual's contributions are redundant	High: A major basis of the individual's relationship to the organization	Low: The individual should not be in the organization if he does not subscribe to some of its goals
Person orientation	High: The individual's welfare is the major concern	High: But only if the individual is capable of generating his own goals	High: Organization goals are determined by individual needs

B. INTERESTS OF THE ORGANIZATION

	EFFECTIVE RESPONSE TO DANGEROUS, THREATENING ENVIRONMENTS	DEALING RAPIDLY AND EFFECTIVELY WITH ENVIRONMENTAL COMPLEXITY AND CHANGE	INTERNAL INTEGRATION AND COORDINATION OF EFFORT—IF NECESSARY, AT THE EXPENSE OF INDIVIDUAL NEEDS
Power orientation	High: The organization tends to be perpetually ready for a fight	Moderate to low: Depends on size, pyramidal communication channels are easily overloaded	High: Effective control emanates from the top
Role orientation	Moderate to low: The organization is slow to mobilize to meet increases in threat	Low: Slow to change programmed procedures, communication channels are easily overloaded	High: Features a carefully planned rational system of work
Task orientation	Moderate to high: The organization may be slow to make decisions but produces highly competent responses	High: Flexible assignment of resources and short communication channels facilitate adaptation	Moderate: Integrated by common goal, but flexible, shifting structure may make coordination difficult
Person orientation	Low: The organization is slow to become aware of threat and slow to mobilize effort against it	High: But response is erratic, assignment of resources to problem depends greatly on individual needs and interests	Low: A common goal is difficult to achieve and activities may shift with individual interests

SOURCE: Harrison [1972:127].

publics [Reimann, 1974]. For certain companies certain publics are more important and/or evaluated more positively than others. Large firms tend to view the national government and the local community relatively negatively as compared with small firms. Creditors are viewed more favorably by independent firms than in branch or subsidiary operations. Labor unions are consistently evaluated negatively. Clearly there is a great variation from firm to firm in the way that the top management group views and values different reference groups in the environment.

Similarly there are differences in those aspects of the firm's managers that are valued and then become part of the organization's style. The following are examples of valued characteristics in different contexts [Miner, 1965; 1967; 1968]:

1. A consulting firm
    Emotional control
    Desire to be with people
    Low interest in implementation
    Desire to be at the center of things
2. A bank devoted to growth
    Youth
    Noncomformity
    Self-confidence
    Dedication to problem solving
3. A department store
    Desire to compete
    Desire to exercise power
    Sense of responsibility
4. A large oil company
    Positive attitudes toward authority
    Desire to compete
    Desire to exercise power
    Assertiveness
    Desire to be at the center of things
5. A large city school district
    Desire to compete
    Assertiveness
    Desire to be at the center of things

Not only do these organizations differ in the style exhibited, but there also appear to be environmentally relevant differences—power motivation is not a consideration in the school district, where external power sources leave the administrators relatively powerless; problem solving is important in the growth-oriented bank; interaction with people is important in the client-oriented consulting firm, and so on. Data such as these suggest that forces in the environment do play an important role in molding organizational style.

The Office of the President

An approach to top level policy formation that relies heavily on an integrated organizational style is the office of the president or office of the chairman. Such an office may be described as follows:

The executives who formerly reported to the chairman or president personally now report to the office of the chairman as an entity. Plans and decisions that formerly were channeled only to the chairman and the president (and their assistants) now can be acted on by one to four more top men, each of whom is formally authorized to act for the office of the chairman. Within individual limits, each member of the office is free to make a decision that binds the entire corporation [Bagley, 1975:104–105].

The objectives are to provide a greater total amount of work time for top level executives, to permit more time to be devoted to external affairs, to facilitate planning and to provide an expanded breadth of expertise. As companies become larger and larger, the difficulty of getting decisions made or approved by one person increases. The office of the president is one way to speed up the decision process and provide organizational flexibility.

The actual forms that top level offices of this kind take vary considerably from company to company. It is not always true that all members are completely coequal or that all can make decisions in all areas. The size typically varies from two to five people, with the most common number being three. Individual company experience with the approach has also varied considerably; a number of firms have abandoned it, whereas others have continued to use it effectively for a number of years. The absolutely crucial ingredient appears to be that an integrated organizational style exist so that members are able to predict each others behavior and can, in fact, stand in for one another.

As Steinmetz and Greenidge [1970:31] have pointed out, the upper levels of management are likely to contain "ascendent-oriented people, who can be trusted to follow their own lead and work toward organizational goals." People of this kind are essential to the effective functioning of a collegial unit, such as the office of the president. Since such people are more likely to be found at or near the top of most companies, the prospects for success when an office of the president is introduced tend to be good. However, the lack of an integrated organizational style can make these favorable prospects worthless. Without the constraints and unifying guidance provided by a consistent organizational style, the probability that internal conflicts will blunt the potential effectiveness of a top level group are very high indeed [McDonald, 1972].

Strategy-Related Styles

Recently there has been a tendency to develop typologies of organizational styles that relate directly to firm strategies and to growth strategies in particular. One such approach, developed by Miles and Snow [1978], is presented in detail in Table 6-4. Of the four styles noted, only the reactors are hypothesized to be consistently poor performers, largely because of a lack of integration in pursuit of goals.

This typology based on strategy has the advantage that it derives from first-hand

TABLE 6-4
A Set of Strategy-Related Organizational Styles

ORGANIZATIONAL STYLES	CHARACTERISTICS
Defenders	1. Narrow and stable product market domain
	2. Success depends on ability to maintain aggressive prominence in chosen market
	3. A tendency to ignore developments outside the domain
	4. Growth by deeper penetration into current markets
	5. Growth is cautious and incremental
	6. Usually only a single core technology
	7. Tendency to integrate vertically
	8. Maintains efficiency by updating current technology
	9. Financial and production experts wield major power
	10. Dominant coalition staffed from functional areas within and has lengthy tenure
	11. Planning is intensive, oriented to problem solving, and precedes action
	12. Structured on a functional basis
	13. Extensive division of labor
	14. High degree of formalization
	15. Control is centralized
	16. Control utilizes long-looped vertical information systems
	17. Coordination is uncomplicated and inexpensive
	18. Conflicts are handled through hierarchical channels
	19. Performance is appraised by comparing present with past indices
Prospectors	1. Domain is broad and continually developing
	2. Capacity to monitor a wide range of environmental variations
	3. Creators of change in their industries
	4. Growth by location of new markets and development of new products
	5. Considerable production of prototype products
	6. Use of multiple technologies
	7. Technologies primarily embedded in people
	8. Dominant coalition is centered around marketing and research
	9. Dominant coalition is large, diverse, and transitory
	10. Executives often hired from the outside
	11. Tenure within the dominant coalition is short
	12. Planning is broad, oriented to problem finding, and contingent on feedback
	13. Structured on a product basis
	14. Division of labor not extensive
	15. Low degree of formalization
	16. Control is results oriented
	17. Control uses short, horizontal feedback loops
	18. Coordination is complex and expensive
	19. Conflict is confronted and resolved by coordinators or integrators
	20. Performance is appraised by comparison with similar organizations
Analyzers	1. Domain is mixed, part stable and part changing
	2. Use of extensive market surveillance mechanisms
	3. An avid follower of change
	4. Growth is through market penetration *and* through product and market development
	5. A dual technological core with the stable and flexible components welded by an applied research unit

TABLE 6-4 *(continued)*
A Set of Strategy-Related Organizational Styles

ORGANIZATIONAL STYLES	CHARACTERISTICS
	6. A moderate degree of technical efficiency
	7. Dominant coalition is centered on marketing, applied research, and production
	8. Planning is intensive and comprehensive
	9. Structured on a matrix basis
	10. Control utilizes several fundamentally different systems
	11. Coordination is both simple and complex
Reactors	1. Management fails to establish any viable organizational strategy, *or*
	2. A strategy is established but without being linked to technologies, structures, and processes appropriately, *or*
	3. Management holds to a strategy/structure long after it has become environmentally irrelevant

SOURCE: Adapted from Miles and Snow [1978:37–82].

study and research in organizations, initially in the college textbook industry but subsequently in several other industries including hospitals. However, much of this early research preceded the theory and thus cannot be considered a test of it. More recently Snow and Hrebiniak [1980] have started to put these ideas to test, with promising results. Of particular significance is the finding that reactors underperformed organizations utilizing other styles with some consistency. However, this does not appear to be true in the highly regulated air transport industry.

Another strategy-related style differentiation has been developed by Leontiades [1980] drawing on the organizational life cycle concept. For Leontiades there are two basic organizational styles—steady-state management and evolutionary management. Under the steady-state style, growth occurs only through expansion of current operations. In contrast, the evolutionary style fosters growth by acquisition, either within the same industry or outside it. These concepts are developed further in relation to various stages of organizational growth. As we will see in the next section, the relationship between managerial and organizational styles and organizational life cycles is indeed a close one.

ORGANIZATIONAL LIFE CYCLES

The idea of an organizational life cycle and the view that there are significant stages of corporate development has been strongly influenced by Alfred Chandler's book *Strategy and Structure* [1962]. It is becoming increasingly clear that the strategies a company uses are influenced by its position in a developmental sequence, and that the appropriate managerial and organizational styles, the styles best suited to the current environment, also vary with the stage of development. In particular, companies at different stages face different competitive conditions in their markets and require different approaches to deal with them.

The Three-Stage Model

One widely utilized view of the developmental sequence represents company evolution as progressing from small to integrated to diversified; there is no implication that companies in the second stage need be any smaller than those in the third [Scott, 1973; Thain, 1969; Tuason, 1973]. The three stages are described in Table 6-5.

The basic theory is that, as companies grow, many tend eventually to resort to a diversified product mix as a protection against the vulnerability inherent in operating within a single industry. The development of the multiproduct strategy foreshadows the move to a diversified, decentralized structure based on product divisions. However, some firms continue to grow while remaining almost entirely within a single industry.

TABLE 6-5
Corporate Life Cycles: Three Stages and Company Characteristics

	STAGES IN CORPORATE LIFE CYCLE		
COMPANY CHARACTERISTICS	STAGE I COMPANY (OR SMALL COMPANY)	STAGE II COMPANY (OR INTEGRATED COMPANY)	STAGE III COMPANY (OR DIVERSIFIED COMPANY)
1. Product line	Single product or single product line	Single product line	Multiple product lines
2. Distribution pipeline	One channel or set of channels	One set of channels	Multiple channels
3. Organization structure	Little formal structure; one-man show	Specialization based on functional areas	Specialization based on market-product relationships
4. Intracompany product/service transactions	No pattern of intracompany transactions	Integrated intracompany transactions	Nonintegrated, pattern of transactions
5. R & D organization process	Not institutionalized; guided by owner-manager	Institutionalized search of product or process improvements	Institutionalized search for new products as well as for improvements
6. Performance measurements	By personal contact and subjective criteria	Increasingly impersonal, using technical/cost criteria	Increasingly impersonal, using market criteria (ROI, market share)
7. Rewards	Unsystematic and often paternalistic	Systematic with emphasis on stability and service	Systematic with variability related to performance
8. Control system	Personal control of strategic decisions	Personal control of strategic decisions	Indirect control based on analysis of "results"
9. Operating decisions	Personal control of operating decisions	Increasing delegation of operating decisions through policy	Delegation of market-product decisions within existing businesses
10. Strategic choices	Needs of owner versus needs of company	Degree of integration, market share objective; breadth of product line	Entry and exit from industries; allocation of resources by industry; rate of growth

SOURCE: Tuason [1973:37] as adapted from B. R. Scott [1973:137].

Typically, these stage II firms have adopted a strategy of attempting to protect themselves by dominating their industries and to the extent possible controlling their markets.

Companies at different stages of evolution tend to elicit different managerial and organizational styles. Often this means that those who have led the company at one stage may not be able to do so effectively at another; the probability that they will be replaced is high. In stage I a company requires a single guiding executive who basically operates a "one-man show." Such people tend to be rather authoritarian, to emphasize short-term thinking, and to have an operating orientation. They will be considered in greater detail in Chapter 16 on entrepreneurship.

At stage II a group of managers with functionally specialized duties replaces the entrepreneur. Thus, there is a requirement that the chief executive be able to work with other members of the management team and utilize their talents effectively. Otherwise, the additional overhead for salaries will yield no benefits to the company. Clearly a managerial style change is called for.

The move into stage III may be through internal development of new products or by acquisition. In any event the move to a divisionalized structure calls for a general office that maintains more or less loose-rein control over operating units while stressing overall corporate planning. Thus, "the key skills necessary to be an outstanding general manager . . . shift from short-term operating ability in stage I to product-functional emphases in stage II and broad management abilities in investment trusteeship, diversification, and management supervision and development in stage III" [Thain, 1969:43]. It is not surprising that relatively few managers can transform their styles to meet all these varied requirements and thus to develop the various types of strategies their companies require. Yet, if they do not change and are not replaced, the probability of company failure at the transition points from stage to stage is high [Clifford, 1973b].

Supplementary and Alternative Models

A number of writers have suggested stages supplementary to those of the three-stage model. Thus, Thain [1969] notes that stage IV may be a coalescing of major companies with government to formulate and implement national economic policy. Greiner [1972] moves one step further to five stages, each with its own management style to achieve growth—an emphasis on creativity, direction, delegation, coordination, and finally collaboration. Between each stage, and thus precipitating each style change, a particular crisis is posited. These crises involve first leadership, then autonomy, then control, and finally red tape. Except for his stage V, which involves a matrix of teams, a participative style and mutual goal setting, Greiner covers much the same ground as does the three-stage model. Whether stage V is in fact an evolutionary result or a desired alternative remains an open question at present; few if any examples exist.

Several of the organizational styles noted previously have been related to the life cycle concept. Thus within the Miles and Snow [1978] framework defenders approach the stage II company and prospectors have much in common with stage III. On the other hand, analyzers appear to be intermediate between these two, and reactors do not fit into the three-stage model, or any other model, at all. Overall, the match between the Miles and Snow [1978] concepts and life cycle stages is rough at best. Yet there are certain parallels.

Leontiades [1979; 1980] has extended the basic three-stage model to include unrelated business conglomerate forms of diversification as a separate stage. In this formulation he appears to be following closely Chandler's [1977] more recent thinking, and to be building upon the research dealing with strategy/structure relationships [Miner, 1982]. As a firm moves from single business to dominant business and then on to related business and unrelated business forms of diversification, evolutionary as opposed to steady-state management becomes increasingly important.

A number of similar formulations have been noted, almost always rooted in the Chandler [1962] theory [Galbraith and Nathanson, 1978]. In particular these formulations are concerned with stages beyond the basic three, which result from expansion into multinational markets. In general it appears that the relatively simple three-stage model holds up better than the more complex supplementary and alternative approaches. "The more detailed the specification of the stage, the less predictable the sequential movement. As long as we conceive of only three stages, with global forms considered to be a Stage III type, the stages of growth model holds. As soon as we consider other types of global structure or consider substages such as the international division phase, more alternate paths appear" [Galbraith and Nathanson, 1978:113].

Although varying in specifics, all of these models emphasize the style and strategy changes associated with growth and the problems resulting from these changes. A somewhat different concept of the corporate life cycle, developed by James [1973], focuses more on the problems faced at each phase of evolution and also introduces the matter of decline. There are five stages as follows:

1. *Emergence.* There is almost invariably a shortage of liquid cash, a need to create consumer demand, and a need to expand production to meet this demand. Administrative processes are loosely defined and a flexible use of labor reduces dependence on more costly specialized personnel.
2. *Growth.* A point is reached where major refinancing becomes necessary and there may be some acquisitions as well. Extensions are made to the basic product line and overseas markets are evaluated. At the same time as new plants and machinery are purchased, control systems are strengthened and formal personnel policies instituted.
3. *Maturity.* Initially investments produce high returns, but over time higher unit production costs and overheads cut in. There is a tendency to become very conservative in marketing and to sacrifice opportunities. Unit production costs are increasingly affected by declining economies of scale and obsolescence of equipment. Conformity rather than individuality are rewarded and labor problems increase.
4. *Regeneration.* If regeneration occurs, it may be internal or external. Internally a company may divest itself of unprofitable subsidiaries, sell off assets, resort to rigid cost cutting, reduce labor use, and close some production lines. There is an attempt to reverse the decline in sales and profits of existing products and introduce new,

profitable products. External regeneration may involve sacrificing a controlling interest, merger, being completely acquired, or government assistance.

5. *Decline.* As internal reserves are depleted, external financing becomes more difficult. The company is selling products that few want at excessive prices. Equipment becomes obsolete, production costs skyrocket, key personnel leave, and labor becomes increasingly militant.

Complete decline into liquidation is rare for the larger companies now, but in many cases external regeneration produces essentially the same result because the company does in fact lose its identity.

The Matter of Decline

Although the basic three-stage model does not concern itself with the final stages of the organizational life cycle, this latter period has been a matter of considerable discussion. Certain writers have argued that decline is not a basic characteristic of organizations, and that they typically tend to revive themselves by bringing in resources of a human, financial, and material nature from the environment, thus producing a state of negative entropy [Katz and Kahn, 1978]. Thus, it can be said that organizations lack the definite life cycle that their biological members possess.

Yet companies do decline and they do die, and experienced managers are characteristically concerned with warding off what they regard as the realistic possibility that this might happen. Their concern is entirely justified. An analysis carried out by the editors of *Forbes* [1967] reveals that of the top 20 companies in 1917 only 7 remained in that grouping 50 years later. Of the top 100, 43 dropped off the list and 28 of these disappeared entirely, either by merger or liquidation. Midvale Steel and Ordinance was number 8 in 1917, Cambria Steel was number 22, Central Leather number 24, Chile Copper number 29, Lehigh Coal and Navigation number 67, and so on. None exist today. Furthermore, a charting of the prior performance of companies that merge indicates that the great majority of the firms that have been taken over have been in a period of serious decline for some time [Vance, 1971].

Decline and death appear to be associated almost entirely with managerial failures [Adizes, 1979; Miller, 1977]. There is evidence that companies that decline and die tend to become involved in risks of such magnitude that alternative strategies are precluded. "Strategic decisions were undertaken for relatively large-scale activities even though potentially unsatisfactory performance would jeopardize the future viability of the complete enterprise" [Richards, 1973:42]. Overoptimism in forecasts was prevalent and contrary information tended to be suppressed, with the result that decisions were characterized more by dogmatism than rationality. Clearly the presence of managerial and organizational styles that were inappropriate to the demands of the environment and generated excessively risky strategies were crucial for failure.

Although organizations may not face inevitable decline in the manner of human beings, since they can revitalize themselves by taking in new members, regeneration and protection against decline are not automatic processes. They require active intervention [Hofer, 1980; Schendel, Patton, and Riggs, 1976].

CONCLUDING COMMENTS

The key requirement for coping with problems of decline just as with those of growth is that there be appropriate planning and effective implementation of these plans. By positioning itself in the corporate life cycle, a company can identify upcoming problems and take steps in advance to deal with them.

Planning of this kind has a life cycle of its own [Ringbakk, 1972]. Studies indicate that those firms that do such planning experience better growth and greater profitability, but to achieve this level of sophistication requires from four to six years of prior effort and preparation.

Furthermore, plans cannot focus entirely on financial matters and material resources. It is absolutely essential that what is known about requisite managerial and organizational styles at various stages in the life cycle be built into the planning process. Managerial manpower planning must be carried all the way to the top so that steps can be taken to have the right kind of people available when they are needed. This may be accomplished through planning for some type of management development activity, so that existing managers are transformed to meet the demands of new developmental stages, or through a planned pattern of succession in the management ranks, including the very top.

QUESTIONS

Discussion Guides on Chapter Content
1. How do the management process and managerial work roles approaches to understanding managerial jobs differ? What does the research evidence say with regard to the relation of each approach to managerial level?
2. Differentiate between managerial style and organizational style. What methods of categorizing each have been developed?
3. What is the office of the president idea? How does it work?
4. What are the different models of the corporate life cycle? How do they relate to organizational styles? Why is the number of stages an important consideration?
5. In what sense can it be argued that organizations are not subject to decline and death in the manner of human beings? How may organizational death be avoided?
6. Some argue that organizations rise and fall entirely as a consequence of external forces; others emphasize the roles played by individual managers and their strategies. Which position is more correct? Why?

Mind Stretching Questions
1. Imagine yourself as the chief executive of a large corporation in a highly competitive industry and describe in detail the managerial style you feel you *should* adopt. How

does this style differ from the one you believe you *would* adopt? Why the difference (if any)?

2. In marketing it is common practice to speak of a product life cycle. Is this the same thing as an organizational life cycle? What are the various possible relationships between the two? In what ways might each be influenced by organizational style differences?

Formulating Business Policy/Strategy

7

Systematic Planning in Strategic Management

INTRODUCTION

A central pillar of strategic management is, as was noted in Chapter 2, the strategic planning process or, more accurately, processes. Although the process can be and is done informally, more and more companies, particularly the larger ones, find it is best conducted within the framework of formal and systematic programs.

At the outset it must be emphasized that there is no one universally accepted way to introduce and do strategic planning. Every company is unique. Since each strategic planning system must fit the uniqueness of each company, if it is to be effective, no two planning systems are exactly alike. We do know, however, that there are fundamental principles and practices that are needed for success in planning. This chapter summarizes the nature of formal strategic planning systems, how they operate, their importance to managers, and the major pitfalls to be avoided in their operation. In the two following chapters policy/strategy identification and evaluation will be examined in detail. Later chapters will be concerned with policy/strategy implementation.

The literature in this field has been growing rapidly and now includes hundreds of articles and books. The more recent books about strategic planning, which also contain bibliographies, are as follows: Lorange [1980], Linneman [1980], Radford [1980], Abell and Hammond [1979], Allio and Pennington [1979], Naylor [1979], Steiner [1979a], Channon and Jalland [1978], Lorange and Vancil [1977], and Rothschild [1976]. Older books still recommended are Hussey [1974b], Ackoff [1970], and Steiner [1969b].

WHAT FORMAL STRATEGIC PLANNING IS AND IS NOT

Intuitive-Anticipatory Versus Formal Long-Range Planning

There are a number of different approaches to the strategic decision-making processes of a company, as will be pointed out in Chapter 12. Here it must be noted that there are two basic types of strategic corporate planning. The first is intuitive-anticipatory planning. Although no one really knows the precise mental processes by which it is done, intuitive-anticipatory planning has several discernible major characteristics. Generally it is the work of one person. It may or may not, but often does not, result in a written set of plans. It generally has a comparatively short time horizon and reaction time. It is based upon past experience, the "gut" feel, the judgment, and the reflective thinking of a manager. It is very important. Many managers have extraordinary capabilities in intuitively devising brilliant strategies and methods to carry them out.*

In contrast, the formal planning system is organized and developed on the basis of a set of procedures. It is explicit in the sense that people know what is being done. It is research based, involves the work of many people, and results in a set of written plans.

These two systems of planning often clash. A manager who has been successful with his intuitive judgments is not likely to accept completely the constraints of a formal system. He may be uneasy with some of the new language and methods incorporated by sophisticated staff in a formal planning system. Or, he may feel a challenge to his authority as those participating in the system engage in the decision-making process.

There should be no conflict, however. These two systems should complement one another. The formal system should help managers to sharpen their intuitive-anticipatory inputs into the planning process. At the very least, the formal system should give managers more time for reflective thinking. Formal planning cannot be really effective unless managers at all levels inject their judgments and intuition into the planning process.

Formal Comprehensive Managerial Planning Defined

The planning system that is the subject of this chapter has been given many names. We use synonymously: comprehensive corporate planning, comprehensive managerial planning, strategic planning, long-range planning, formal planning, over-all planning, corporate planning, and other combinations of these words. Strategic planning is the phrase most widely used today.

Corporate long-range planning should be defined in at least five ways, each of which is needed in understanding it. First, it deals with the futurity of current decisions. This means that long-range planning looks at the chain of cause-and-effect consequences over time of an actual or an intended decision that a manager is going to make. If he does not like what he sees ahead, he then will change the decision. Long-range planning also looks at the alternative courses of action that are open in the future, and, when choices are made, they become the basis for making current decisions. The essence of long-range planning is the systematic identification of opportunities and threats that lie in the future which, in combination with other relevant data, provide a basis for management to make better current decisions to exploit the opportunities and avoid the threats.

Second, strategic planning is a process. It is a process that begins with the development of objectives, defines strategies and policies to achieve objectives, and develops detailed

---

* We are using synonymously several words associated with creativity. Actually, there are differences among such things as intuition, judgment, hunch, instinct, invention, innovation, and entrepreneurship [see Steiner, 1969b:353–355].

plans to make sure that the strategies are carried out to achieve the objectives. It is a process of deciding in advance what is to be done, when it is to be done, how it is to be done, and who is going to do it. It is also a continuous process.

Third, it is a philosophy. It is an attitude, a way of life. It is an understanding that planning necessitates dedication to acting on the basis of contemplation of the future, a determination to plan constantly and systematically as an integral part of management. Strategic planning is more of a thought process, an intellectual exercise, than a prescribed set of processes, procedures, structures, or techniques. For best results managers and staff in an organization must believe strategic planning is worth doing and must want to do it as well as they can. "Not to do it well is not a sin," says Ackoff, "but to settle for doing it less than well is [1970:1].

Fourth, comprehensive corporate planning may be defined as a structure of plans. It is a structure that integrates strategic with short-range operational plans. In this structure are integrated, at all levels, major objectives, strategies, policies, and functions of an enterprise.

All these characteristics of corporate planning will be further examined. Before looking at them, however, it is important to make a few comments on what strategic planning is not.

What Strategic Planning is Not

Strategic planning does not attempt to make future decisions. Rather, planning involves choosing the more desirable future alternatives open to a company so that better current decisions can be made.

Strategic planning is not forecasting product sales and then determining what should be done to assure the fulfillment of the forecasts, with respect to such things as material purchases, facilities, manpower, and so on. Corporate planning goes beyond present forecasts of current products and markets and asks such questions as: Are we in the right business? What are our basic objectives? When will our present products become obsolete? Are our markets accelerating or eroding? For most companies there is a wide gap between a simple forecast into the future of present sales and profits and what top management would like its sales and profits to be. If so, comprehensive corporate planning is a system that managers can use to fill the gap.

Strategic planning is not attempting to blueprint the future. It is not the development of a set of plans that are cast in bronze to be used day after day into the far distant future. Indeed, much in long-range plans is obsolete when they are completed because the environment assumed in their plans has changed. On the other hand, long-range planning permits a company to "invent" its future. This means that a company, through the corporate planning process, tries to foresee the future it wants for itself. It then, very often, can fulfill the targets it sets for itself by the development of wise strategies and detailed plans.

Finally, formal strategic planning is not a single prescribed methodology, or flow chart, or set of procedures. As will be noted later it embraces a wide range of types of planning systems from that which is virtually informal and very simple to highly formal complex comprehensive structures. In the best managed companies it is inextricably interwoven into the entire management process (including thought and decision-making processes) and as a result displays many different variations among organizations. Furthermore, in any one organization, the design of the strategic planning system changes over time.

Corporate Planning Models

A conceptual model of the corporate planning process was presented in Figure 2-1. This model was developed over a number of years during which one of the authors examined and helped to establish many planning systems. Operational flow charts vary, depending upon differences among companies, but underneath, the basic elements of the model are found in the better systems. Conceptual models of leading authors in the field are quite comparable to Figure 2-1 [for example, Anthony, 1965; Gilmore and Brandenberg, 1962; Ringbakk, 1972; Stewart, 1963; Humble, 1969; Cohen and Cyert, 1973; Hussey, 1974b; Lorange, 1980]. For many conceptual and operational models see the following journals: *Long Range Planning, Planning Review,* and *Managerial Planning.*

In the following exposition we shall use Figure 2-1 to explain the planning process. It should be pointed out, however, that in actual practice the process is iterative and may begin at different points. Also, in practice there is much back-and-forth analysis before decisions are made. For instance, a tentative objective may be established; then strategies are examined to achieve this objective. Depending upon the analysis of the strategies, the objective may be changed, and vice versa.

When a formal long-range planning system is first introduced in a company, especially a large one, it is advisable to determine precisely how the organization intends to operate the system. Most companies that have planning systems, especially the larger ones, have manuals that lay out procedures to be followed. These are plans to plan, which will be discussed later.

THE STRATEGIC PLANNING PROCESS

As shown in Figure 2-1 the policy/strategy formulation part of the company-wide planning process includes five blocks to the left. We shall discuss each of these shortly, but before doing so a few characteristics of the strategic planning process should be mentioned.

First, it is quite obvious that the strategic planning process is the place where decisions of the highest significance to a company are made. Here is where the basic thrust and direction of the company is determined and the major approaches to proceeding along the lines set are decided.

Second, the time spectrum covered ranges from the very short range to infinity. Although the general thrust and content of strategic planning is long range, a decision can be made in this process to stop producing X product tomorrow or start to build tomorrow a new plant to produce Y product.

A third important characteristic is that, although the process may produce a written document on a periodic basis, such as once a year, the process is a continuous activity of top management, as illustrated in Figure 7-4. Top management cannot, of course, develop a strategic plan once a year and forget strategy in the meantime.

A fourth important characteristic of strategic planning, as compared with medium-range and short-range planning, is that the results are not usually neatly incorporated in a prescribed form. Medium-range and short-range planning result in numbers for specific functions for a prescribed period of time, as shown in Figure 7-1. Strategic planning covers any element of the business that is important at the time of analysis and embodies details that are of sufficient scope and depth to provide the necessary basis for implementation. The format for strategic plans is generally much more flexible and variable in content, from time to time, than for other type plans.

THE SITUATION AUDIT

The four blocks to the left of Figure 2-1 compose what has come to be called the situation audit. The activity covered is also sometimes called the current appraisal, or the planning premises, or the market/business audit. There is no concensus about the content of the situation audit. A more detailed discussion of the nature of the situation audit and methods to make it will be provided in the next chapter. At this point the discussion will be limited to the purposes of the situation audit and its general nature.

Fundamental Purposes of the Situation Audit

First, a major objective of the situation audit is to identify and analyze the key trends, forces, and phenomena that may have a potential impact of importance on the formulation of policies/strategies. This is a critical step for two reasons. There are and will be changes in the environment of business that will have a profound impact on the affairs of the enterprise. Obviously, it is to the advantage of a company to identify them before they occur rather than when or after they occur. Also, a moment's contemplation will make it quite obvious that no company, no matter how profitable, can examine in great depth every facet of the environment that may affect the company. Every company must identify specific elements in the environment that will be addressed. It also must specify the depth and nature of the examination. This problem becomes complicated because within the same company different managers at different levels will require different analyses of the same information or different types of environmental information.

Second, the situation audit serves to emphasize the importance of systematic assessment of environmental impacts. The search for and evaluation of environmental forces should be continuous and more or less systematic. The more systematically one surveys the environment the less likely is one to be surprised.

Third, the situation audit is a forum for sharing and debating divergent views about relevant environmental changes. Evaluations of the many forces operating in a company's environment will vary among managers and staff. The more open the debate about these forces, the more likely the planning system will be effective.

Fourth, and closely associated with the preceding paragraph, vague opinions about different parts of the situation audit can be made more explicit. Systematic attempts to appraise the environment should help individuals to sharpen vague amorphous attitudes about forces operating in the environment.

Finally, all of the information collected in the situation audit should provide a base for completing the strategic planning process in all of its phases, from reevaluating missions to formulating strategies and implementing them [Steiner, 1979a:122–126].

With these purposes in mind a brief description of the contents of various parts of the situation audit follows.

Expectations of Outside Constituents

As pointed out in previous chapters, especially Chapter 5, many people and groups are interested in what corporations do, especially the larger ones. These are constituents of the corporation. Many corporations systematically examine the attitudes, demands, and expectations of these people and groups and try to take them into appropriate consideration in the formulation of policies/strategies.

Expectations of Major Inside Interests

Similarly, as noted in preceding chapters, values, attitudes, and interests of individuals and groups inside a company must be understood and evaluated as significant premises for planning. The value systems of top managers particularly are basic and fundamental premises in any comprehensive corporate planning system. Sometimes executive values are written, but most of the time they are not written nor even articulated. Many of these values cannot be proven or disproven to be correct on the basis of numbers or even logic, yet they may determine basic long-range directions of a company. For instance, a chief executive may say, "I want my company to be the biggest in our industry in ten years." Or, he may say, "I want my company to be the technologically best in the industry." Or, he may say, "My goal is to make my company the biggest and the technically best company in my industry in the next decade." Each of these aims provides a very different frame of reference for doing corporate planning. Each is rooted in the value system of the chief executive officer in the company.

Not only do value systems influence objectives but they also influence all sorts of decisions made in the planning process. For instance, one executive may wish to do business with the Mexicans because he likes them. Another in the same industry may prefer not to extend his operations to Mexico. The reasons of both managers may have nothing to do with sales and profits but may be solely determined by the values each holds.

The Data Base: Past Performance

Data about past performance are useful as a base for assessing the present situation and possible developments in the future. For instance, if market share of product A has been declining over the past half dozen years, an appraisal of current performance as being satisfactory is hardly justified should the trend continue. Data about the past covers such matters as sales, profits, return on investment, productivity, marketing systems, and so on.

The Data Base: Current Situation

The volume of data in this part of the situation audit is understandably much greater than that concerned with past performance. Included here is anything management wishes to measure as being important in appraising the current position of the company. The current situation could include the financial position of the company, market share, competition, customers and markets, evaluations of managerial and employee skills, various measures of efficiency (for example, sales per employee, plant utilization, investment per employee), constituent demands, government regulations, general environmental setting, and so on.

The Data Base: Forecasts

Data about the future would certainly include forecasts of markets, sales, competition, and selected economic trends of prime interest to the company. These are traditional projections. More and more companies are adding estimates of future technological developments likely to affect the company, changing social expectations, anticipated political and regulatory forces likely to affect the company, and other trends of particular concern to the firm (for example, population, international political turbulence, military hardware demands, and so on).

WOTS Up Analysis

This is an acronym for weaknesses, opportunities, threats and strengths underlying planning. This is a critical phase of the situation audit. In this phase a company seeks to identify the principal opportunities that appear to exist in the environment of the future as well as the threats that may adversely affect the company. Included here, also, is an examination of the strengths and weaknesses of the company that will affect the formulation of strategy/policy and its implementation.

So significant is this step in the planning process that some companies begin strategic planning with a simple form that manager and staff use to identify opportunities, threats, strengths and weaknesses. The forms are sorted and planning begins with the evaluations.

MAJOR ELEMENTS OF MASTER POLICY/STRATEGY

Purposes

The fundamental purposes of an enterprise can be thought of in two ways. First are the basic purposes society establishes for enterprises. As noted previously, the business institution has been created and supported by society to achieve objectives that society establishes for it. If managers of businesses, especially the large companies, ignore these societal purposes, the results may be more government regulation, at a minimum. So, planning must consider larger societal purposes of the enterprise.

Second are fundamental purposes that managers of an organization implicitly or explicitly determine. These purposes can include a range of subjects—from economic to ethic. Purposes are stated in broad terms and tend to have long lives. For instance, one company identified a basic purpose as follows: "To strive for the greatest possible reliability and quality in our products." Another said its purpose was "To be recognized as a company of dedication, honesty, integrity, and service." When taken seriously such purposes have powerful influence over company plans and activities.

Missions

Mission statements identify the underlying design, aim, or thrust of a company. They may be expressed at different levels of abstraction. For example, they may be expressed as a grand design. Such was the most fundamental thrust of American Telephone and Telegraph Company for over fifty years—"Our business is service." Or the mission can be expressed in very specific and concrete terms, such as "Produce fabricated steel shapes and forms for the construction market."

The mission statement, however written, is very important. It determines the competitive arena in which the business operates. It determines how resources are to be allocated. It limits the search for opportunities, threats, strengths, and weaknesses. It can open up new opportunities, as well as threats, when rewritten.

Objectives

Objectives are the specific desired results to be achieved, usually in a specific time. They are important in the planning process because they are guides to developing specific actions to assure their fulfillment. Behavioral scientists also conclude they are important motivators of people in organizations because, generally, people in organizations like to try to achieve the objectives set for the organization. Objectives are also used, of course, as standards for measuring performance.

Objectives may be expressed for every element of a business considered important enough to be the subject of plans. There is no standard classification of objectives nor of the number of objectives a company should have. The common objectives found in long-range planning systems are sales, profits, margin, return on investment, and market share. These are usually stated in specific numbers and/or percentages of growth.

The number of possible objectives is very long, so each company must choose those it wishes to formulate. Objectives ought to be set for every activity that a company thinks is important and the performance of which it wishes to watch and measure. Peter Drucker [1954:63] says the following are such areas: market standing, innovation, productivity, physical and financial resources, profitability, manager performance and development, worker performance and attitude, and public responsibility. For a statistical distribution of objectives actually used in practice see Shetty [1979].

There are many different approaches to developing objectives, as will be shown in the next chapter. However derived, objectives should exhibit a few major characteristics. First, they should be able to lead and motivate, and the more concrete and specific they are the more likely are they to have directive power. To say that "Our company seeks to make a good profit," is far less powerful than to say, "Our objective is to make $4 million in profits three years from today." Second, objectives should be actionable. Goals that are far too high or far too low do not lead to action. Objectives should be a little aggressive and require imagination and hard work to achieve. Third, objectives should be understood by those who are to develop means to achieve them. Fourth, objectives should conform to ethical and social codes accepted by society and by the business. Finally, objectives should correlate and be mutually supporting, to the extent possible. For instance, if the objective is to achieve a return on investment of 15 per cent, after taxes, by the end of five years, the target is much more likely to be achieved if sub- and subsubobjectives are linked to it. For instance, subobjectives might be: increase sales to $10 million in 5 years, raise gross profits to $2.5 million in 5 years, build modern facilities and operate them at capacity over the next five years, and upgrade and maintain a skilled work force in specified ways. These objectives might also be linked to subsubobjectives. For example, an increase in sales might be sought by setting specific objectives for market share, advertising expenditures, market penetration, product redesign, and research and development in specific directions. Similarly, subsubobjectives might be set for achievement of the subobjectives of gross profits, facilities, and work force. If the sub- and subsubobjectives are achieved, the achievement of the dominant objective is inevitable.

Program Policies and Strategies

Conceptually, of course, the next logical step is to develop specific policies and strategies to achieve the preceding objectives, purposes, and missions. The general nature and significance of policies and strategies have been discussed previously. In the next two and later chapters, and in the readings, the reader will find details concerning the identification, evaluation, and implementation of policies and strategies. At this point it may be noted that there is no one way, no neat formula, by means of which program policies and strategies are formulated. We believe that a systematic strategic planning process in a formal planning system is a preferred approach to the development of effective policies and strategies. But there are many approaches, as will be noted later, that can be pursued within and independently of the formal planning system.

MEDIUM-RANGE PROGRAMMING AND PROGRAMS

Medium-range programming is the process where specific functional plans are related for specific numbers of years to display the details of how strategies are to be carried out to achieve long-range objectives and company missions and purposes. Typically, the planning period is for five years, but there is a tendency for more technically advanced companies to plan ahead in some detail for seven or more years. Generally, the medium-range plans cover only the major functions and are quantified on comparatively simple forms, as shown in Figure 7-1. In many companies, especially large decentralized ones, functional plans are prepared only for major strategic programs [O'Connor, 1976]. In most companies plans are translated into financial terms in the form of a pro forma profit and loss statement, as shown in Figure 7-2. Sometimes a *pro forma* balance sheet

Item	Last Year	This Year Forecast	Next Five Years				
			First Year	Second Year	Third Year	Fourth Year	Fifth Year
Sales							
Marketing Expenditures							
Advertising							
Distribution							
Unit Production							
Employees							
Total							
Direct							
Indirect							
R & D Outlays							
New Products							
Product Improvement							
Cost Reduction							
New Facilities (Total)							
Expansion Present Prod.							
New Products							
Cost Reduction							
Maintenance							

Figure 7-1   Division five-year plans.

DIVISION: _____

	This Year	19_	19_	19_	19_	19_
Sales — Units						
Gross Sales — Dollars						
Allowances						
Net Sales						
Cost of Goods Sold						
Gross Profit on Sales						
G & A Expense						
Selling Expense						
Advertising Expense						
R & D Expense						
Total Operating Expense						
Other Charges, Net						
Interest on Long Term Obligations						
Other						
Income Before Depreciation						
Depreciation						
Income Before Overhead allocation						
Allocation of General Overhead						
Net Income Before Taxes						
Rate of Return on Assets						

Figure 7-2   Financial summary.

is also prepared. Sometimes, depending upon its importance, detailed forms are prepared for selected elements. This is especially true for facility programs.

SHORT-RANGE PLANNING AND PLANS

The next step, of course, is to develop short-range plans on the basis of the medium-range plans. In about half the companies that do formal planning, the numbers for the first year of the medium-range plans are the same as in the short-range yearly operational budget summaries. Some companies believe that tightly linking budgets and medium-range plans will help to make long-range plans realistic. Others feel that a tight relationship will divert attention from the long-range to current matters, such as return on investment. This is especially so if a manager's compensation is based principally on yearly return-on-investment performance. If the linkage is very loose, the long-range plan still can be reflected in and be of high importance to current budget making.

The current operating budgets will, of course, provide very great numerical detail as compared with the medium-range plans. Many more subjects will also be covered. The numbers of subjects will depend upon what management wishes to control in the short run. Although strategic and medium-range plans may provide the framework within which short-range planning is done, the different types of short-range plans that can be affected cover a wide area. They can include plans for production, plant location, facilities, work methods, inventory, employee training, job enrichment, management education, and negotiations with unions. Space limitations prevent any further examination here of these types of short-range plans, their nature, or how they are prepared. That subject will be treated more fully in Chapter 14.

This obviously is a very important step in planning because here strategic plans and policies are translated into current decisions. This is a fundamental step, therefore, in assuring implementation of policies/strategies so as to achieve fundamental corporate aims.

IMPLEMENTATION, REVIEW AND EVALUATION OF PLANS

Following Figure 2-1, the next step is implementation of current plans. This is a major and essential step and one whose difficulty is often overlooked. The subject will be treated at length in Part IV.

Plans as well as the entire planning process should be reviewed and evaluated. There is nothing that produces better plans on the part of subordinates than for the top managers to show a keen interest in the plans, the results they bring, and in the entire planning process. When comprehensive formal planning was first developed some quarter century ago there was a tendency for companies to make written plans and not redo them until they become obviously obsolete. Now, the great majority of companies go through an annual planning process in which the planning process as well as the plans are reviewed and revised.

INFORMATION FLOWS AND DECISION AND EVALUATION RULES

The box on information flows in Figure 2-1 is shown simply to identify the obvious point that information flows throughout the planning process. Types of information, of course, differ significantly depending on the part of the planning process that are addressed and the subject of the information.

Feasibility testing takes place throughout the planning spectrum. For instance, when lower level managers are examining different alternative choices, one may comment, "Method A has great profit potential, but I do not think the top management would like to use this method." He is obviously applying a feasibility test by appraising an alternative against the values of top management, as he understands them. At lower levels the testing can become completely quantitative and sometimes very sophisticated, as for instance in the applicability of a linear programming model to testing distribution routes for products to their markets.

STEPS IN STRATEGIC PLANNING

Figure 2-1 is a conceptual model but the sequence of steps in it can be made operational. Table 7-1 presents four other models of steps in creating a strategic plan. They are conceptual but also operational in the sense that companies can and do follow the steps in practice. Each series of steps emphasizes a little differently some element in the planning process, but fundamentally they are all comparable. Like Figure 2-1 the steps in Table 7-1 can be tailored to fit the unique situation of every company. They can result in a comparatively simple planning process or in a very elaborate one. The planning process, whether it is formal or informal (that is, done only in the mind of one or a few managers), actually can start at many different points. This is illustrated in Figure 7-3 and needs no further elaboration here.

ORGANIZING THE PLANNING PROCESS

There is no single method, formula, or standard way to start and conduct a formal corporate planning system. What is done, to illustrate, is a function of such factors as managerial style, size of organization, whether the firm is centralized or decentralized, managerial authority extended to decentralized managers, types of problems the company faces, managerial knowledge, capital intensity, types of products, and services and managerial styles of top managers. So, each system is fitted to each company. There are no two exactly alike.

Before starting the planning process it is very important that top managers have a sound conceptual understanding of a long-range planning system (which we have tried to present in this chapter), an understanding of what a suitable system can do for them and their company, a clear concept of what they want the formal system to do for them and their company, and an understanding of how to set up the system and make it work effectively.

The Plan to Plan

There should also be a plan to plan, which should include first of all a strong statement of commitment of the chief executive officer. It should contain a glossary of terms to assure common understanding and avoid semantic debate. The information and documentation required should then be described. Time schedules should be included, such as that shown in Figure 7-4 (a typical illustration). Finally, the statement should specify policies and procedures needed by those doing the planning, such as depreciation policy, interdivisional transfer policy, assumed price inflation rates, and so on. Beyond this, firms making a "plan to plan" can and do include many other things such as "how we became committed," "history of planning in our company," and "why we need to do better planning."

Four Fundamental Approaches

There are four fundamentally different approaches to doing formal planning. The first is the top-down approach. Comprehensive planning in a centralized company is done at the top of the corporation, and departments and outlying activities are pretty much told what to do. In a decentralized company, the president may give the divisions guidelines and ask for plans. The plans are reviewed at headquarters and sent back to the divisions for modification or with a note of acceptance. If the division plans do not add up to what top management wishes, additional corporate plans are then prepared which may concern acquisitions, divestment, or refinancing.

The second is the bottom-up approach. Here, top management gives the divisions no guidelines but asks them to submit plans. Information such as the following may be requested: major opportunities and threats, major objectives, strategies to achieve the objectives, and specific data on sales, profits, market share sought, capital requirements, and number of employees for a specified number of years. These plans are then reviewed at top management levels and the same process as noted in the top-down approach is then followed.

A third approach, of course, is to develop a mixture of the top-down and bottom-up approach. This is the method used in most large decentralized companies. In this approach, top management gives guidelines to the divisions. Generally, they are broad enough to permit the divisions a good bit of flexibility in developing their own plans. Sometimes a top management may hammer out basic objectives by dialogue with division managers. Such objectives as sales and return on investments may be derived in this way, especially if the performance of the division manager is measured upon the basis of such standards.

Fourth, is the team approach. In smaller centralized companies the chief executive will often use his main line managers as staff in helping him to develop formal plans. In some very large companies the president will use his line managers in the same fashion. In many companies the president has a group of executives with whom he meets on a regular basis to deal with all the problems facing the company. In some

TABLE 7-1

Four Conceptual Models for Creating a Strategic Plan for Large, Medium, and Small Companies

A	B	C	D

1. Formulate the task
  • Define scope plan
  • Define results sought
  • Determine how plan is to be developed:
    • Who does what
    • Timing
    • Informational requests
2. Develop inputs
  • Past history
  • Major environmental trends
  • Opportunities and threats
  • Internal strengths and weaknesses
  • Present product sales forecasts
  • Values and judgments of managers
3. Evaluate alternative courses of action
	1. Define the kind of company we want
	2. Analyze our customers
	  • Who are they?
	  • How should they be classified?
	  • Why do they buy our product/service? Will this change? How?
	  • What market segments do we serve? Should this situation be changed?
	  • Etc.
	3. Analyze our industry
	  • Trends
	  • Pacesetters
	  • Competition
	  • Profit potential
	  • Etc.
		1. Develop pragmatic understanding of strategic planning in general and for a small company in particular
		  • Literature
		  • Management consultant
		  • Professional seminars
		  • Visit other companies doing planning
		2. Identification of WOTS UP
		  • Weaknesses
		  • Opportunities } Underlying
		  • Threats } planning
		  • Strengths
		3. Identification of strategies to exploit opportunities and avoid threats
		4. Evaluation and selection of strategies
			1. Where are we?
			  • Corporate philosophy, thrust, mission
			  • Financial situation
			  • Competitive situation
			  • Product reliability, acceptability, etc.
			  • Market served
			  • Etc.
			2. Where do we want to go?
			  • Preliminary redefinition of aims
			  • Strategic alternatives to achieve aims
			  • Evaluation of alternatives in light of strengths, weaknesses, constraints, and current momentum

4. Define major objectives
- Sales
- Profits
- Product development
- Manpower
- Etc.

5. Define major strategies and policies
- Markets
- Employees
- Products
- Prices
- Finance
- Technology
- Etc.

6. Develop medium-range detailed plans

7. Determine needed current decisions

8. Monitor performance

9. Recycle annually

---

4. Ask: What are the opportunities and threats for us?

5. Ask: What are our strengths and weaknesses?

6. Ask: What strategies are identifiable?

7. Evaluate alternative strategies

8. Develop objectives

9. Prepare detailed plans to implement strategies

10. Develop contingency plans

11. Translate plans into budgets

12. Monitor performance

13. Recycle annually

---

5. Implementation plans for priority strategies

6. Formulating major company aims
- Mission
- Purposes and philosophy
- Specific long-range objectives:
  - sales
  - profits
  - market share
  - other

7. Prepare other associated plans
- Manpower
- Financing
- Facilities
- Etc., as needed

8. Monitor performance

9. Recycle annually

---

3. Can we get there?
- Current momentum
- Organizational requirements
- People requirements
- Facility requirements
- Financial requirements
- Etc.

4. Which strategies will achieve which aims?
- Iteration among aims and strategies in light of managerial values and the situation audit
- Conclusions concerning aims
- Conclusions concerning strategies to achieve aims

5. What decision must be made now to get there?
- Short-term budgets
- Short-term organizations, personnel, managerial, etc., decisions and actions

6. Monitor performance

7. Recycle annually

SOURCE: From George A. Steiner, [1979a:24-25].

Figure 7-3   Starting points for formal strategic planning.

companies, part of the time of this group is spent on long-range planning. Over time the group will develop written long-range plans.

Ten Alternatives

Within each of these approaches there are many alternatives of which we shall note ten, as follows:

1. *Completeness of Cycle.* When the process is begun it is not necessary to go through a complete cycle such as that suggested by Figure 2-1. Some companies begin by asking departments and/or divisions to supply top management with perceived opportunities and threats and with the strategies they suggest to exploit the opportunities and avoid the threats. Of course, once the system is in operation over several cycles all phases of planning in Figure 2-1 should be covered.

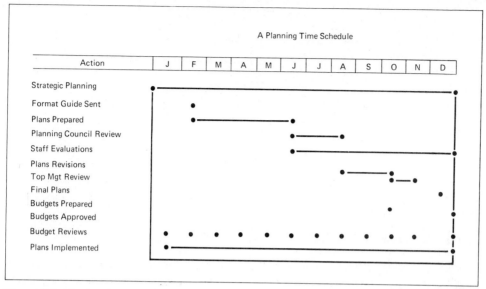

Figure 7-4   A planning time schedule.

2. *Depth of Analysis.* Again, when starting, it is not necessary to require deep analysis of all aspects of the planning process. Too heavy a research work load can sink the process. As experience is gained, however, analysis should be as deep as required for each subject.

3. *Degree of Formality.* There is a wide spread of formality among planning systems in the United States. Among the larger companies, those having centralized organizational structures, comparatively stable environment, and homogeneous product lines tend to have less formal systems than large diversified companies with decentralized and semiautonomous product division structures. High technology companies tend to have more formal systems than those employing low-level technology. Generally, the more flexible the system the better. But even in a system that is highly formalized it should be recognized that much informality in decision making and managerial activities associated with planning takes place. Figure 7-5 is designed to illustrate this point. For example, in the development of basic missions and important program strategies, the approach is often highly if not completely informal. Also, at the other extreme, for certain types of implementation, such as motivating personnel, the approach may be completely informal.

4. *Reliance on Staff.* Managers, of course, can determine how much planning they want to delegate to staff. Generally, the more managers do themselves the better.

5. *Corporate Planner or Not.* Larger corporations employ corporate planners to help top management with the planning process. Smaller companies cannot afford this luxury.

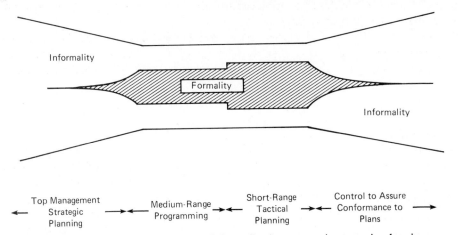

Informality

Formality

Informality

| Top Management Strategic Planning | Medium-Range Programming | Short-Range Tactical Planning | Control to Assure Conformance to Plans |

Figure 7-5 Comparative formality and informality in systematic strategic planning.

6. *Linkage among Plans.* As noted previously some companies use the numbers of the first year of the five-year plan for their annual budgets. Other companies prepare budgets in light of the five-year plans, but the numbers are not identical.

7. *Getting the Process Started.* There are many ways to get the process started. For example, strategic planning may begin with an effort to solve a particular difficult problem, such as obsolescence of a major product. It may begin with a situation audit, or it may begin with a review of current strategy. See Figure 7-3.

8. *Degree of Documentation.* A balance must be struck between too little and too much paper work.

9. *Participation of People.* Here, again, there is a choice. Top management can do the job itself, or it can elicit the help of many people.

10. *Role of the Chief Executive Officer.* The chief executive officer's role is critical and deserves a more extended comment.

The Chief Executive's Role

To begin with, the CEO (as used here this is shorthand for top management) should understand that the corporate planning system is his responsibility. What this means will vary much from case to case, but basically it means, as one CEO job description put it, "The CEO is the chief architect of the firm's future and the chief planner." In this role the CEO has several fundamental responsibilities, as follows: (1) make sure that the climate in the firm is congenial to doing effective planning; (2) make sure the system is organized in a fashion appropriate to the company; (3) if a corporate planner is employed, see to it that he is the right man for the job and he reports as close to the top of the firm as possible; (4) get involved in doing the planning; and (5) have face-to-face meetings with those who draw up plans for the CEO's review and approval.

The discharge of these responsibilities will vary much depending upon managerial styles. As noted in Chapter 6 there are different styles of managers. The permissive manager will operate differently than the entrepreneurial type. A manager who is a team leader will handle his responsibilities differently from the one who depends only upon his own council, and so on.

The roles of CEOs will vary over time. As the CEO and his staff become more experienced in planning, he may rely more on staff. Every company goes through a life cycle, as pointed out in Chapter 6, and the planning system reflects such change. CEO's tend to have different roles in complex organizations as compared with very simple ones.

Concluding Comment

Probably one of the most difficult problems in industry today with respect to formal planning concerns how the process is organized and pursued. It is an extremely difficult task for management, especially in a large corporation, to organize and implement a planning system that runs smoothly and fulfills its promise.

TYPES OF PLANNING SYSTEMS

As pointed out earlier in this chapter there are many factors that determine the nature of a planning system of a company. To illustrate, one important factor is size of firm. Smaller companies generally display characteristics considerably different from larger firms. Planning systems tend to be informal in small companies and more formal in larger companies. Table 7-2 illustrates some of the different dimensions.

Whether the planning system in a small company is formal or informal it generally is much less complex than in a larger company. Figure 7-6 illustrates a typical system for strategic planning in a small company. Figure 7-7 displays the types of plans generated in a large company.

Figure 7-7 identifies eight different types of plans. Posture plans concern the specification of basic company missions, purposes, philosophies, or underlying aims. Portfolio planning is concerned with resource allocation among divisions, affiliated companies, or projects. Ad hoc policy/strategy analysis identifies top management activities to aid in making policy/strategy decisions. These three types of strategic plans are the prerogative of the CEO. They sometimes are prepared only by the CEO; in other cases line managers and staff help the CEO in their preparation.

Decentralized planning is done in the company illustrated in the sense that the divisions are asked to prepare comprehensive strategic plans covering their operations. The result is the strategic business unit plan. Strategic business units (SBUs) are distinct businesses, with their own set of competitors that can be managed in a manner reasonably independent of other businesses within a company. The strategic plan, for example, for a General Electric Company SBU includes the following elements [Hall, 1978; Salveson, 1974]:

- A statement of the SBU's mission.
- Environmental assumptions including external environment and its opportunities and threats.
- Assumptions about key competitors.

TABLE 7-2
Some Organizational Characteristics of Small and Large Companies that Will Influence Planning

SMALL COMPANY	LARGE COMPANY
1. Chief executive is basically an entreprenuer.	1. Chief executive is a team leader and skilled at conflict resolution.
2. Most important decisions made at top.	2. Exceptional decisions made at top. Many important decisions and routine decisions made at lower levels.
3. Workers and top managers in frequent and close contact.	3. Middle managers stand between top and lower level managers and workers. Middle managers not often bypassed.
4. Lines of authority and responsibility loosely defined. Titles mean little. All top managers participate freely in decisionmaking.	4. Generally, authority flows from title, not personality. Jobs have defined responsibilities and duties.
5. Communications largely face to face, oral, and unspecified.	5. Communications more frequently in writing. Standard procedures are followed.
6. Few explicit policies and rules.	6. Many explicit policies and rules governing subordinate actions and freedom.
7. Staff functions are weak and poorly defined.	7. Staff function expanded and expertise respected.
8. Top managers personally check employee performance. Few statistical controls.	8. Formal, impersonal statistical controls established and used.
9. Operations not too complex.	9. Very complex operations.
10. No or little money to hire staff help.	10. Financially able to hire staff experts.

SOURCE: Adapted from Strauss [1974].

- Inside and outside constraints.
- Objectives that are sought.
- Strategy to be followed in achieving objectives.
- Development and investment programs critical to strategy.
- Specific time-phased events that must be met to attain objectives.
- Resources required to implement strategy.
- Contingency plans.
- Statement of financial plans that integrate the strategic and operational plans.

Following presentation of divisional plans, a company may prepare corporate strategic plans. There is no standard format for such plans but they might include basic policy/strategy for the company, plans to divest a division or acquire another company, and a financial resume of the divisional plans.

Planning within each of the divisions may be said to be centralized so far as the

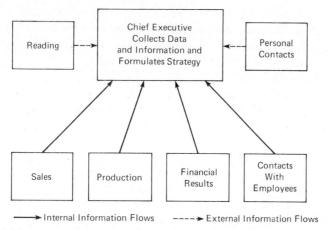

Figure 7-6 Strategic planning in a small company.

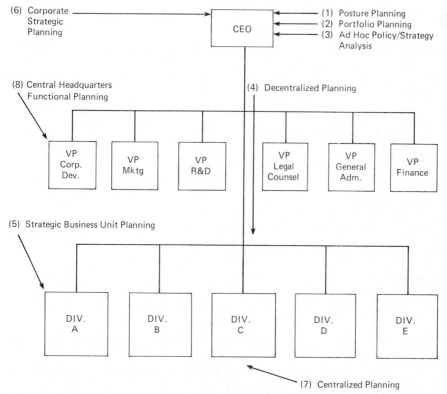

Figure 7-7 Types of business strategic planning systems.

division is concerned. As noted previously the division may act as an individual enterprise and have its planning done by line managers working together as a team with staff.

Finally, corporate headquarter staff offices may be asked to prepare strategic plans. In mind, for instance, would be staff offices for marketing, research and development, electronic data processing, and personnel.

This by no means exhausts the list of types of plans that may be found in a large company. Others will be discussed in later chapters. At this point it is in order to note contingency plans, since they are frequently associated with strategic planning systems. Strategic planning is done on the basis of the most probable events likely to occur. There are other possible events, however, that can open up great opportunities or pose serious threats to a company if they occur. Each company should ask itself some "what-if" questions and then briefly sketch out responses appropriate in the event the contingency takes place. For example, "What if a competitor suddenly drops his price 25 per cent?" "What if the government imposes an export tax on our product?" "What if a fire seriously damages our main plant?" The advantage of having such plans is obvious. Contingency plans are much briefer than those discussed previously.

THE VALUE OF FORMAL CORPORATE PLANNING

Comprehensive formal long-range planning has been growing in use throughout the world simply because managers find that it is valuable. There are many reasons why this is so, a few of which may be noted briefly.

As noted earlier in Chapter 3 long-range planning is essential to discharging top management's responsibilities. As companies become larger, the complexities of the task defy the capabilities of one or a few men to do it properly on an informal basis. System and formality are required, and the type of strategic planning process discussed in this chapter is employed.

The process is important because it asks and answers questions that good managers must address, such as: What is our basic mission and purpose? What are our competitors likely to do? What new product lines do we need? What opportunities are open to us to exploit? Where are the major threats to our business? What are our basic objectives? What strategies are best for us? Rapid environmental change alters answers to such questions as these rather quickly. That is why in most companies long-range planning is reviewed and revised on an annual cycle.

Planning enables a company to simulate the future on paper. If it does not like what it sees, it erases and starts over. This is much less expensive than letting the future evolve on an *ad hoc* basis. It applies the systems approach. It looks at a company as a system composed of many subsystems. Looking at the company in this way prevents suboptimization of parts. It forces a company to set objectives and clarifies future opportunities and threats. It links decision making between top and lower level managers. Lower level management decisions are much more likely to be made in conformance with the wishes of top management because plans are written and available to them. It sets standards of performance.

Long-range planning is a new and significant communications system. It permits people to participate in the decision-making process. People are more adaptable to change when they participate in making the change. It is a learning and mind-stretching exercise that increasingly is being recognized as a major tool for training managers [Camillus, 1975].

In sum, there are two types of values of comprehensive long-range planning—substantive and behavioral. Either set should be sufficient to convince management of the value of this new tool. When both are considered, it is easy to see why formal long-range planning has been introduced into most medium-sized and larger companies. More and more managers are agreeing with an old military assertion that says, "*Plans* sometimes may be useless but the planning *process* is always indispensable."

A few recent studies provide concrete evidence that long-range planning really pays off in cash. One study compared the five-year performance of firms that introduced formal planning with those that did not. It also compared the performance of the firms for the five years before introducing long-range planning with five years of long-range planning. Results were measured for sales, earnings per share, stock price, earnings on common equity, and earnings on total capital. In each instance those companies that did long-range planning had better performance in significant degree than companies in the same industry that did not formally plan. Also, in each case the record of the firms that did long-range planning was better after than before introducing the system [Thune and House, 1970]. Other scholars have confirmed that formal strategic planning pays off [Ansoff, *et al.,* 1970; Gerstner, 1972; Herold, 1972; Karger and Malik, 1975; Sheehan, 1975; Robinson, 1980; and Robinson and Glueck, 1980]. Some studies, however, cast doubt about the payoff of formal planning [Rue and Fulmer, 1973; Fulmer and Rue, 1973; Kudla, 1980; and Leontiades, 1980].

It is our view that, other things being equal, and especially for larger firms, formal systematic long-range planning will give a company an important edge over a competitor that does not have such a system. Our reason is that the success of a company is not due so much to the planning system as to the capabilities of managers. Our view is that better managers understand the significance to them of having an effective systematic planning system, and they devise a system to suit their needs. This is a view that other scholars have taken after a review of the evidence [for example, Hofer and Schendel, 1978:11].

One final point may be noted here. Some observers of managers claim that they do not plan [Mintzberg, 1973; 1976], but this view flies in the face of readily observable reality, as attested by a survey of Snyder and Glueck [1980] as well as the research cited above.

LIMITS OF FORMAL STRATEGIC PLANNING

Comprehensive strategic planning as described in this chapter is not, of course, without its shortcomings. There are intrinsic as well as imposed shortcomings of such planning. Among the more important intrinsic shortcomings is the fact that mere use of strategic planning cannot guarantee a company will produce the most appropriate policies/strategies. Policies/strategies are determined by people, and even the best formal system cannot make sure that people will always choose the "right" ones. Strategic plans also may not turn out as expected because of unexpected changes in the environment. Of fundamental importance, also, is the fact that planning requires a certain type of creative talent, which must exist in an organization for it to be effective. Strategic planning is intellectually difficult. It is also expensive.

Managers may also impose limitations on formal strategic planning by failing to recognize major pitfalls that experience teaches should be avoided. Steiner [1972b] developed a list of 50 pitfalls that empirical evidence showed were important to avoid if planning was to be effective. The list was confirmed by managers and corporate planners in an industry-wide survey. The survey also produced a list of the ten most important pitfalls to be avoided, as seen by experienced managers and staff. Many of the original list of most important pitfalls still are, of course, applicable. But the list needs updating. A current list of the most important pitfalls to be avoided, which is derived from empirical observation, probably would include the 14 traps presented in Table 7-3.

Despite the widespread use of formal strategic planning there is dissatisfaction with the systems being employed. A few studies on this subject are Hunsicker [1980], Warren [1966; 1980], Grinyer [1973], Kastens [1972], Pennington [1972], and Ringbakk [1971]. One of the important results of the study noted previously [Steiner, 1972b] was that companies showing high or above-average satisfaction with their formal strategic planning were those that avoided the major pitfalls experience said should be avoided if planning was to be effective. This is not meant to say that dissatisfaction with planning will disappear if the pitfalls in Table 7-3 are avoided. There is no doubt that there is a close correlation. However, causes of dissatisfaction are complex, as the authors who performed the studies cited point out, and more research is needed to identify more sharply what needs to be done in specific situations to improve strategic planning.

RATIONALITY AND IRRATIONALITY IN PLANNING

The Roman philosopher Seneca said, "Man is a reasoning animal." But Isaac Asimov [1975:46] commented, "What evidence he had for that assertion no one knows; certainly none has surfaced in the 19 centuries since his time." Asimov undoubtedly was referring to the large questions of man's governance. In our area of interest managers are rational and irrational—it is not always easy to decide which is which.

The planning system presented in this chapter is designed to try to inject more rationality into the decision-making process. It must be recognized, however, that many, and generally the most important, decisions made in this process cannot be settled on the basis of universal quantitative truths. The issues involve judgments, values, passions, and consequences that are very difficult to perceive. So, irrationality cannot be avoided no matter how carefully a formal planning system is erected. Anyway, the rationality or irrationality of any decision is often determined by who is looking. Nevertheless,

TABLE 7-3
Major Current Pitfalls in Corporate Strategic Planning

1. Failure to develop throughout the company an understanding of what strategic planning really is, how it is to be done in the company, and the degree of commitment of top management to doing it well.

2. Failure to accept and balance interrelationships among intuition, judgment, managerial values, and the formality of the planning system.

3. Failure to encourage managers to do effective strategic planning by basing performance appraisal and rewards solely on short-range performance measures.

4. Failure to tailor and design the strategic planning system to the unique characteristics of the company and its management.

5. Top management becomes so engrossed in current problems that it spends insufficient time on the strategic planning process, and the process becomes discredited among other managers and staff.

6. Failure to mesh properly the process of management and strategic planning, from the highest levels of management and planning through tactical planning and its complete implementation.

7. Failure to modify the strategic planning system as conditions within the company change.

8. Failure to keep the planning system simple and to weigh constantly the cost/benefit balance.

9. Confusing the extrapolation of financial and/or economic projections with strategic planning.

10. Management's failure to understand the analytical tools used in different parts of the planning process and thereby becoming captive to staff experts.

11. Failure to secure in the company a climate for strategic planning that is necessary for its success.

12. Failure to balance and link appropriately the major elements of the strategic planning and implementation process.

13. Failure by managers to understand the importance of implementation of strategy and how to make that process efficient and effective.

14. Blame strategic planning for failures in other managerial and staff procedures.

good formal planning does move a company *toward* rationality; that is why companies that have formal planning systems have generally been found to perform better.

CONCLUDING COMMENT

It is our contention that the basic fundamental concepts, principles, and practices set forth in this chapter and the readings to which it refers apply to all organizations in society. With nonprofit organizations as with individual business enterprises, the problem is one of determining what system of planning is most appropriate to the characteristics of the organization. However, there are many characteristics of certain types of nonprofit organizations that complicate the organization and operation of comprehensive formal planning systems. This subject is examined in Chapter 17.

QUESTIONS

Discussion Guides on Chapter Comment
1. Explain the difference between intuitive-anticipatory and formal systematic long-range planning. May they conflict in formal planning systems?
2. How do the authors define comprehensive managerial planning? What do they say it is not?
3. What is the "situation audit" made in planning, and of what significance is it to identifying and evaluating strategies?
4. What are the distinctions among an organization's missions, basic purposes, and long-range planning objectives?
5. "The name of the long-range planning game is to translate strategy into current decisions." Comment.
6. The authors make clear that there is no one way to do long-range planning. Identify different acceptable steps and approaches in doing it.
7. Identify the most important pitfalls that ought to be avoided in starting and doing long-range formal planning.
8. What differing characteristics do small and large companies have that cause differences in their strategic planning systems?
9. How does strategic planning in a small company differ generally from that in a large company?
10. What types of plans and planning systems would you expect to find in a large, decentralized firm?

Mind Stretching Questions
1. Can business long-range planning philosophy and practice be applied to a person's career plans? How about a person's life plans?
2. What research would you suggest in the area of formal long-range planning to advance the state-of-the-art?

8

Identifying Policies and Strategies to Evaluate

INTRODUCTION

In the strategic planning process the identification and evaluation of strategies/policies is, in many instances, a simultaneous activity. In other cases the identification of a strategy is a painful and time-consuming process to be followed by the equally painful and time-consuming process of evaluation. For purposes of exposition, however, we deal with identification in this chapter and evaluation in the next.

The range of alternatives open to managers in identifying policies and strategies is very wide. The range covers a spectrum from solely intuitive approaches to highly systematized processes. In smaller companies the process tends towards the informal intuitive end, whereas in large companies the process tends to become more formalized.

The choice of strategies is almost endless. For this reason some simplifying approaches must be developed. In this chapter are presented a number of approaches that should serve, for the most part, to narrow choice. No one approach is necessarily superior to others. The approaches are not mutually exclusive but may be subsets of one another, and they may be used in various combinations. All can be accommodated in a formal strategic planning system. They can be considered both thought processes and procedures.

THE SITUATION AUDIT

In Chapters 2 and 7 we noted the conceptual nature and basic purposes of the situation audit. In this chapter the focus is on a few significant dimensions of the situation audit as a base for identifying strategies. It is also a base for evaluating strategies, as will be discussed in the next chapter, as well as an aid in implementing strategy. This role is pictured in Figure 8-1.

Conceptual Versus Operational Content of the Situation Audit

Conceptually the situation audit should contain all information of importance to a company in formulating strategy and determining whether it can be implemented prop-

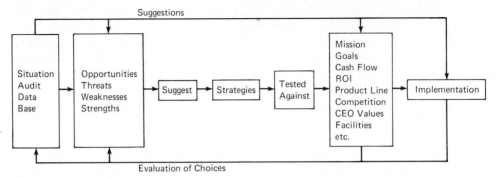

Figure 8-1 Strategies are derived from, but also tested against, analysis of opportunities, threats, weaknesses, and strengths.

erly. This involves, of course, both formally and informally accumulated information. Although there may be reasonable concensus about the conceptual content of the situation audit (for example, as expressed in Figure 2-1 and explained in Chapter 7), there is little concensus about what is and should be done in practice. A basic reason for this state of affairs is that the territory covered by a situation audit is so wide that no company can analyze it all. Every company must choose carefully what will be examined and how deep the analysis will be in any particular part of the audit. If a company does not go through this selection process, it may miss an important element in its environment or may become bogged down in staff reports and paper work.

Furthermore, it must be observed that what is developed in the typical organized situation audit is only a part, and sometimes not the most decisive part, of the knowledge managers bring to strategic decision making. Managers get much information from acquaintances, their own reflection about the environment and their enterprises, their own selection of reading materials, and their basic store of knowledge. In his classic study of 137 managers in 41 companies Aguilar [1967] found that managers generally relied more heavily on personal than upon impersonal sources of information.

The situation audit will differ from company to company and from time to time, depending upon many factors. For example, managers of a small company will rely for information much more on personal sources and published information than internally generated studies. In contrast, larger corporations will have voluminous reports and studies concerned with past performance, the current situation in which the company finds itself, and future prospects and environments. The more formal the strategic planning system the more formalized will tend to be the making of the situation audit. Much will depend upon the level at which the situation audit is made. A situation audit for a SBU will of course differ from one made by a centralized company. It will also differ from the situation audit made by central headquarters of a decentralized company.

Generally speaking a situation audit is not made by one staff group and accumulated in one package. Parts of it are developed by different managers and groups. For instance, a corporate planning staff of a large, decentralized company may make a general economic forecast that can be used as a frame of reference by all the divisions. The divisions will prepare economic forecasts of markets for their products. In this same company forecasts of changing social and political environments may be made by a public affairs staff. These may be introduced into the strategic planning process through the planning staff, directly by the vice president of public affairs, or in other ways.

Conceptually, as already noted, there should be an organized and systematic examination of all relevant information implicit and explicit in the four boxes comprising the situation audit in Figure 2-1. In practice, however, there are great variations in coverage, analysis, and methodology in accumulating and analyzing and using the data [O'Connor, 1976]. In general, only large companies have any organized activity analyzing expectations of major outside interests. Only large companies have any organized activity examining the expectations of major inside interests. This analysis is usually centered on the ways in which interests are focused and changing among employees. We know of no company that makes a systematic examination of values of managers, which are, as noted previously, so critical in strategic decision making. In preparing an organized situation audit, most companies concentrate on information in the data base—past performance, the current situation, and environmental forecasts. Many fewer companies analyze systematically opportunities, threats, weaknesses, and strengths. Even though this part of the situation audit may not be systematically addressed it is, of course, implicit in the strategic decision making process.

Table 8-1 presents an outline of a situation audit for a large tire and rubber producer. A comparison with Table 8-2 shows substantial differences between the conceptual situation audit and this operational outline.

TABLE 8-1
Situation Analysis Outline of a Tire and Rubber Producer

1. Key success factors:
   Secrets of success; break-even charts

2. Market characteristics:
   Segments; growth trends; customer identification; consumer attitudes; buying habits; geography; pricing

3. Competitive profiles:
   Identification; market shares; typical responses; specific comparisons

4. Product and market comparisons:
   Products; promotion; distribution

5. Manufacturing factors:
   Process descriptions; inputs; capacity; competitive comparisons; other uses; planning and control systems

6. Technological factors:
   Materials; processes, products, customers and others

7. Economic, social, political, governmental factors:
   Economic and demographic forecasts; likely effects of social and political changes; governmental expenditures and purchasing decisions; legislated controls and restrictions

8. Internal assumptions

9. Planning gaps now foreseeable:
   Life cycle analysis; size of sales, profits, assets gap; rationale of acquisitions versus internal development; divestment possibilities

10. Swopt items:
    *S*trengths; *W*eaknesses; *O*pportunities; *P*roblems; *T*hreats

SOURCE: Rochelle O'Connor [1976:32].

TABLE 8-2
Conceptual Classification of Information in the Situation Audit

1. Expectations from outside constituents
   Stockholders
   Suppliers
   Customers
   Government
   Community
   Creditors
   Intellectuals
   Etc.
2. Expectations from people inside the company
   Board of Directors
   Managers
   Staff
   Hourly employees
3. Past performance
   Sales
   Profits
   Return on investment
   Product development capability
   Managerial skills
   Labor relations
   Public relations
   Marketing capability
   Etc.
4. Current situation
   Financial
      Profitability, sales, debt, ROI, liquidity, etc.
   Resource use efficiencies
      Sales per employee, profits per employee, investment per employee, plant utilization, use of employee skills, etc.
   Managerial capabilities
   Staff capabilities

Evaluation of employees
   Skills, productivity, worker satisfaction, turnover, etc.
Products/markets
   Share, stengths, weaknesses, etc.
Technology assessment
   Impact on community, technical strengths, technical weaknesses
Competition
   Price, product/market, technology, etc.
Social policies
   Conformance with pollution standards, public image, social demands on company, evaluation of company voluntary programs, etc.
Organizational structure
   Suitability of, strengths of, weaknesses of, etc.
5. Forecasts
   Economic
      Projected sales, GNP, inflation rates, market potential, etc.
   Competition
      Products, technology, price, etc.
   Technology
   Social Forces
      Values, attitudes
   Political trends
   Other
      Population, international turbulence, etc.
6. WOTS UP analysis (external and internal)
   Opportunities
   Threats
   Weaknesses
   Strengths

An Organized Situation Audit in a Small Company

As noted previously smaller companies tend to prepare a minimum of formalized data concerning past performance, current conditions, and future prospects. That is a mistake. Small companies need carefully analyzed data as well as large companies. But how can small companies with limited resources acquire needed information? The answer, of course, is careful selection of questions asked and considerable reliance on published information.

A useful approach for a small company is to ask questions that are important in determining the situation of the company and where it should be going. Tables 8-3, and 8-4 pose sets of questions appropriate for small as well as large companies. Table 8-3 covers a wide range but does not deal as much as it should with changing environments. Table 8-4 focuses primarily on industry and competitor analysis. It needs to be

TABLE 8-3

Questions for a Small Firm's Planning Activity in Making a Situation Audit

(Each question should be answered in light of the firm's strengths and weaknesses).

ProductsServices (PS)

What are the PS for which customers come to us?

What are the most distinctive PS we offer?

What are the new PS? The fading PS?

What are our plans for developing new PS?

How do we compare with competitors?

What economic (value added) factor do we provide?

What are the most profitable PS we offer? The least profitable?

Customers

What business do we do with what customers at what profitability and investment?

What markets do we now serve?

What new markets should we serve?

How do our customers see us?

What do they think we do well or poorly?

Prices

How are our prices set?

When were they last reviewed?

How do they compare competitively?

Facilities (Plant and Equipment)

Do we have the facilities we need?

Do we know what is available in the industry?

Do we have controls over productivity? Over obsolescence?

Finance

What is our flexibility for growth? For recession?

What sources of funds do we use? What sources should we use?

What risks are we exposed to?

What controls do we have over cash, receivables, inventories, debt?

What controls should we have?

Information

What are our sources of information as to what's going on in the outside world?

What action do we take with the information we have?

What action would we take with additional information?

Do we know its cost-effectiveness ratio?

Where do we stand in relation to computerization?

Do we have adequate input from external sources?

Decision Making

What decisions are critical to our business?

Who makes what decisions on what bases? (a key question)

Profitability

How do we compare with the industry? With our own best period?

Are our decisions based on adequate information?

How can our decision making be improved?

TABLE 8-3 *(continued)*

People
   What do we know about our present management and technical staff in terms of age, skills, potential, turnover, and retirement?
   How does our fringe benefit program compare with that of other firms? With the expectations of our staff?
   How do our people feel about the company? About its prospects? About their own future?

Dangers
   What would we do if substantial changes took place in our products/services; customers; competitors; key staff; location/environment; sources of supply?

SOURCE: Theodore Cohn and Roy A. Lindberg [1974:52–53].

supplemented with information about other matters covered in Table 8-3 and also future environmental changes.

An Organized Data Base in a Larger Company

Divisionalized companies have two different approaches to data base information about past performance, the current situation, and future prospects. Some companies, on the one hand, simply ask divisions to supply headquarters with that basic information which the division finds important in developing its strategic plans. The divisions have a free hand in determining the information to be reported and how it is reported. On the other hand, other companies ask their divisions for information to be presented on prescribed forms.

For instance, Lear Siegler, Inc., asks divisions for very specific information to be presented on prescribed forms. "The purpose of the Market/Business Audit," says the planning manual, "is to lay the foundation upon which the division plan will be built." In addition, of course, the purpose is to tell central headquarters what base the divisions use in developing their plans.

The Lear Siegler Market/Business Audit consists of three parts. Part I is completed for each major product and requests, on a specified form, qualitative evaluations focused on identifying strengths and weaknesses of products and markets, as well as opportunities and threats inherent in the planning period. The evaluations are made for markets, competitive conditions, technical factors, operational considerations, financial considerations, and specific threats and opportunities.

Part II is a statement for each significant product and/or product line, presented on a prescribed form, of information concerning stage of life cycle, past and current information about sales, profits, assets employed, cash flow, market share, asset turnover, return on assets, total market served, market growth rate, and so on.

Part III is a qualitative evaluation of the entire division by functional area, also presented on a prescribed form. It consists of an assessment of the functional area of the division's business—finance, marketing, technical management, operations, and general management—in terms of the results of the product and market evaluations derived in the first two parts noted previously.

TABLE 8-4
The Situation Audit—Some Questions—An Exercise in Strategic Thinking

To evoke more substantial contributions to the planning process from the heads of the nine groups making up an industrial and consumer products company, a few years ago the firm's director of planning and market research prepared for the president a *list of 18 questions that group heads were to answer. The president pared the list to the nine set forth below.*

1. What steps can be taken to minimize effects of annual business cycles upon your profitability?
2. If you were to ignore the cost of entry, what new venture, new market, or new product line would you recommend entering, and why?
   (a) When you fully consider entry price, how does your answer change?
3. Are there competitive patents expiring that will enable you to take action previously denied to your group?
   (a) Are there new competitive patents issuing or likely to issue that appear to offer you problems? If so, are you considering requesting a license?
   (b) Are there company patents expiring in the five-year plan period that open doors for competitive action previously limited by our patent position?
4. As you ponder your competition and what action from each important competitor you might anticipate, what actions do you believe might occur in the next three years that would either hurt you or help you?
   (a) New technology or new product introductions?
   (b) Marketing programs or policies?
   (c) Pricing policies or practices?
5. Put yourself in your competitor's shoes. What market or product area in your group would you attack as the most vulnerable, and why? If you conclude that more than one warrants mention, do so.
6. What additional information or "intelligence" about your industry, competition, customers, trends, etc., would help your group be more effective in strategic or tactical planning?
   (a) If it might be possible to obtain any such information or intelligence from an outside source (Arthur D. Little, Stanford Research Institute, etc.), how much would you be willing to pay for it?
7. Consider the product life cycle as it applies to your key products.
   (a) Which do you identify as on the downgrade toward phasing out? Will any go out in the next three years?
   (b) Which do you identify as mature but still strong? Do they appear to be likely to remain for at least three more years?
   (c) Which do you identify as successfully introduced and on the upgrade toward a strong position in your industry? Are they enough to replace those in the first group?
   (d) Which have you recently introduced or are about to introduce that offer yet unproved promise?
8. In your opinion, are there unexploited opportunities for us to make more effective use of total division or total corporate strengths? If so, please describe.
9. Given freedom of action, would you increase your R&D budget beyond present levels? If so, how much and for what?
   (a) How about marketing?
   (b) If you did either of the above, how long would it take for results to show in increased profit and ROA? One year? Two?

SOURCE: Brown and O'Connor [1974:10].

The Lear Siegler planning manual observes that "the concept of the audit is to break your business down into its component parts and functions, and then to evaluate those parts and functions separately, in relation to each other, in relation to the whole, and in relation to the environment that affects them. The success of the audit as a basic tool for determining your business goals is dependent upon the perspective and objectivity you apply to that task" [1979:12].

To complete this task competently requires a great deal of thought and staff work.

Forecasting in the Situation Audit

In small companies, forecasts of environment are usually made by top management on the basis of general information acquired through readings and talking with acquaintances. In larger companies, vast expenditure of time and effort is made in preparing forecasts. Among larger companies four types of forecasts are made: economic, technical, social, and political. This clearly is an extremely important part of the situation audit and an important step in strategic planning. Space limitations make it possible to do little more than note the significance of these projections, comment briefly on methods for making them, and illustrate the relevant research concerning them.

ECONOMIC FORECASTS. Most large corporations make their own general economic forecasts covering such matters as gross national product, prices, employment, production, and so on. Depending upon their interests, they also will make their own forecasts of special types of economic conditions. A large public utility, for instance, will want a carefully prepared forecast of demands for electricity, gas, and water, in its area. The automobile companies make detailed forecasts of consumer disposable income. Companies with large borrowing requirements may make their own forecasts of interest rates. An agricultural implement company may make forecasts of agricultural income.

Large companies also make detailed forecasts of the markets for their products and competitive conditions within those markets. This obviously is a critical analysis, which is very important in helping a company to identify strategies, a fact that will be elaborated later in this chapter.

To illustrate the significance of economic forecasts it is only necessary to point to the disastrous situation in the autumn of 1980 of the automobile companies in the United States when those companies completely misjudged the changes taking place in consumer demands for smaller automobiles with better gasoline mileage. On the other hand, many American companies (including automobile companies) perceived an impressive economic expansion in the European market following World War II and profited significantly by extending their operations to that area.

There exists a vast literature on the methodology of economic forecasting as well as what companies forecast and how they do it (for example, Wheelwright and Makridakis [1980]; Armstrong [1978]; LeBell and Krasner [1977]; Hurwood, Grossman and Bailey (1978); Elliott-Jones [1973]; Hall [1972]; and Chambers, Mullick and Smith [1971].

TECHNOLOGICAL FORECASTING. To high-technology companies, technological forecasting is essential. But, because of the rapid increase in new technologies, it is important for more and more companies to be aware of technological opportunities as well as threats. A classic illustration of corporate failure because of lack of technology forecasts or appreciation of potential technology change is that of Baldwin Locomotive Works. More recently the Swiss watchmakers completely miscalculated the impact on them of the development of quartz crystals and digital watches.

Technology forecasts can take many forms. They can refer to developments with respect to existing technology, such as lazer beams or minicomputers. They can seek to identify new technological developments. They may be concerned, as in the aerospace industry, with new technologies likely to be demanded by a customer such as the Pentagon.

Here, too, the range of methodologies to be employed is wide. Bright has the standard book on this subject [1978], and the magazine *Technological Forecasting* is devoted to it.

SOCIAL AND POLITICAL FORECASTS. As was pointed out in Chapter 5, turbulent social and political environments are indeed changing the rules of the game under which business operates. Too many executives have been surprised and shocked at the impact of social and political changes on their businesses to support indifference to that environment. It is conceded, for example, that if in the 1960s the automobile companies had been more aware of the changes in social and political attitudes about the automobile (for example, emissions and safety standards), it is highly likely that that industry would not today be so controlled by the federal government.

One of the earliest companies to create a separate staff to examine social and political environments was General Electric Company [Wilson, 1974]. In the 1970s, GE derived from this staff work a series of challenges to a company like GE in the future business environment. For example, the most important challenges were identified in the areas of constraints on corporate growth, changes in corporate governance, changes in employee relations with the company, problems with government, and "politicizing" of economic decisions [Wilson in Steiner, 1976:30–31]. This provided a basis for the development of new strategies/policies by GE to meet such challenges and threats.

More and more companies are taking into consideration in their strategic decisions perceptions of changing social and political environments. Recently a food processor, for example, eliminated one product from its line because it anticipated that the government would require new information on the label and in order to comply the cost would make the product profitless. Regulatory agencies such as the FDA, FTC, ICC, and CAB shape the strategies of the industries they regulate. Any company these days is foolish to ignore potential regulatory changes of government agencies that may impact on it.

In recent years efforts to identify changing social and political trends have joined with older economic and technical projections, which sought to identify trends and issues, to form a new monitoring and forecasting analysis of a company's evolving environment. It is called environment scanning.

ENVIRONMENTAL SCANNING. There is a growing body of activity in business as well as in universities concerning the probing into the future environment of business [O'Connell and Zimmerman, 1979; Preble, 1978; Boucher, 1977]. Space does not permit any extended analysis of this activity here, but a few comments are necessary.

The environmental scanning in mind here differs from the typical GNP, sales, price, or technology forecast. The latter generally are done on the basis of well-understood quantitative formulations with appropriate judgmental inputs. Such scans are made to achieve a specific type of projection. Environmental scanning, rather, is an overview of a wide range of phenomenon in the environment made to identify to managers trends, issues, threats, opportunities, and so on. The effort, incidentally, is also made in many companies as a mind-stretching exercise. Environmental scanning generally is highly subjective in deriving conclusions. It may be formalized in the sense that some data are accumulated in a deliberate fashion, but most information and analysis is developed and analyzed on an informal and highly judgmental basis.

To illustrate the preceding statement, Sears Roebuck & Co. collects information concerning the external environment in these major categories: demographics, values and life styles, resources, technology, public attitudes, government, international, and the economy. These are divided into 130 subtopics. Internal information is collected in these major categories: sales, corporate income, capital expenditures, facilities, and other matters of internal significance. These are divided into 190 subtopics [Barmeier in Preston, 1980:184]. Information collected ranges from published sources to interviews with various experts. The final selection of trends and priorities for Sears is purely judgmental.

The approach to scanning can range on a scale from completely informal to highly formal. Most systems in use today tend towards the informal [Thomas, 1980]. Comprehensive, continuous scanning is done only by a comparatively few of the largest companies in the world (for example, AT&T, GE, Coca-Cola, Ford, DuPont, General Motors, Shell Oil, to mention a few). This does not mean, of course, that other companies and managers are not continuously scanning the environment. They certainly are. The distinction is that in the large company the process is ongoing and a staff has responsibility for developing, operating, and monitoring the system. In smaller companies the process is essentially informal. For a resume of the system in nine companies see Thomas [1980].

Nanus [1979] has devised a scanning technique called QUEST (Quick Environmental Scanning Technique). This is a four-step process. First, executives prepare a notebook containing their observations about major events and trends in their industry. Second, at a one-day retreat, the executives engage in wide-ranging speculation about important issues that might affect the future of their firm. An effort is made to scan the horizon broadly and comprehensively. Third, the QUEST director prepares a report summarizing the major issues and their implications. Also, from the discussion, the director prepares three to five scenarios incorporating the major themes of the discussion. Finally, at a half-day meeting, the report is reviewed and the group identifies feasible strategic options to deal with the evolving environment. The options are ranked and teams are designated to develop strategies.

A different approach is TAP (Trend Analysis Program) developed by the American Council of Life Insurance. More than 100 people are each given a specific publication to monitor and each is assigned a subject area to follow, such as science and technology, social sciences, politics and government, economics and business, and so on. Each person is to make an abstract of an article that meets two criteria: treats an idea or event that is indicative of a trend or discontinuity in the environment and has important implications for the life insurance industry. A committee meets each month to review the abstracts and summarizes the results. These are given to another committee that meets three times a year. This committee then selects themes for trend analysis reports, which are made available to the industry [Weiner, 1977].

RESEARCH ON ENVIRONMENTAL ANALYSIS. Scholars have given increased attention to research on environmental analysis in recent years [Utterback, in Schendel and Hofer,

1979:134–144; Klein, in Schendel and Hofer, 1979:144–151]. A few studies and conclusion of special interest for this chapter follow.

Klein and Newman [1980] have developed a system called SPIRE (Systematic Procedure for Identifying Relevant Environments) to help companies choose among a bewildering variety of phenomenon those which are of most concern to the company. Newgren and Carroll [1979] found that almost one-half the companies they studied had institutionalized social forecasting into their procedures. Anderson and Paine [1975] examined the way in which managers perceived environmental uncertainty and the need for internal change and identified the types of strategies that different perceptions appeared to determine. Ansoff [1975] developed a model to help a company detect and respond to what he calls "weak" signals in the environment that could, if not addressed, result in a strategic surprise. LeBell and Krasner [1977] have examined a variety of forecasting methods and have evaluated their appropriate use among a variety of subjects for forecast. An earlier comparable effort is that of Chambers, Mullick, and Smith [1971]. This resume does not do justice to the scholarly work of these and many others, but it does illustrate the range of activity in the field. Finally, the Center for Futures Research at USC should be noted for its long-standing series of research studies in this area [Nanus, 1980].

Identifying Opportunities, Threats, Weaknesses and Strengths

The WOTS UP analysis is of great potential value because, as pointed out in Figure 8-1, suggestions for strategies are derived from it. The WOTS UP analysis appears to be a simple and straightforward process, but it may encounter problems in its development. One reason is that there exists no standard measure for determining whether an opportunity, a threat, a weakness or a strength actually exists, and if it does how significant it is. A variety of measures may be applied, ranging from quantitative accounting data to personal judgment. In such a situation concensus may be difficult to achieve. Also differences may exist because managers at different levels may come to different conclusions even if the same measure is employed. For example, a division manager may see a significant profit opportunity in producing product ABC. A group vice president may see little value in it if it means allocating capital that might be put into a more profitable product in another division. For an excellent analysis of problems in defining strengths and weaknesses see Stevenson [1976].

OTHER APPROACHES TO IDENTIFYING POLICIES/STRATEGIES

If a company makes a complete situation audit, it will employ within that framework a wide range of approaches to policy/strategy identification. If it does not make a comprehensive situation audit, or makes only a partial audit, or prepares no audit on a systematic basis, it may use other approaches to policy/strategy identification. In the following sections we describe a number of the more outstanding approaches that can be employed within or separate from a broad situation audit described here. Many of the approaches overlap. Some are complementary. Some may conflict. They are not presented in any particular order of importance or interrelationships.

POLICY/STRATEGY PROFILE

A policy/strategy profile is simply a systematic examination of present company policy/strategy—implicit and explicit. In each major area the profile will register the principle policies/strategies of the company. In mind, of course, are master strategies as well as program strategies. Included would be competitive strategies, financial strategies, and so on. Once this is done, and it is not an easy task, the questions arise: Which policies/strategies should be changed? Where do we need new policies/strategies?

For example, the company may have a policy not to allow one customer to buy more than 15 per cent of the total sales of the firm. Excessive concentration of sales and profits in one customer can, of course, leave the firm vulnerable to a sudden drop in purchases of that customer. If the audit shows that one customer currently buys more than 30 per cent of the total output of the company, one of two things or a combination of both, must take place: (1) the policy should be revised, or (2) new policies and strategies should be devised to reduce the concentration. There are many possibilities: an acquisition of another firm will by itself reduce dependence on the customer, the development of a new product not sold to the customer will have the same result, a conscious reduction of sales to the customer may be decided upon, or an aggressive campaign to penetrate new markets to raise total sales may be undertaken.

GAP ANALYSIS

In this approach the stimulus is an examination of whether an end that has been established is likely to be achieved. If not, the question becomes "What strategies and policies must be adopted to reach the sought ends?" Or, "should we modify our ends?"

Suppose, for example, that the basic mission of an aerospace firm is to produce military and commercial aircraft. If it is not making commercial aircraft the question will arise in the situation audit: Should we produce a commercial aircraft? If the answer is affirmative the decision is a strategic one. If the answer is negative and the decision is made to delete commercial aircraft from the basic mission statement this, too, is a strategic decision.

There may be a gap between mission potential and aspirations of management. For example, Gerbers' stated mission several years ago was: "Babies are our only business." When population forecasts revealed that the baby boom was over the company deleted "only" from the mission and proceeded to add other products to its line.

In preparing the situation audit, a thoughtful forecast is usually made for sales of current products as well as those that are projected to be added in the future. If the forecasts are not equal to the desired objectives of management, there obviously is a gap. This sometimes is called the "planning gap." It either must be filled with new strategies and policies or the aspirations of management must be lowered.

COMPETITIVE STRATEGY

A company can be highly successful or in trouble by reason of the choice of a particular strategy in any number of areas—management, finance, organization, research and development, marketing, and so on—but in no area are the choices any more critical than in the competitive arena. If a firm is not competitive, it will fail. If it is a superior competitor, it will succeed.

A thorough analysis of the competitive forces operating in a firm's environment and alternatives in responding properly to the more important ones is, of course, a formidable task. Porter [1980] has simplified this task somewhat by, first of all, pointing out that there are five major forces that shape the competition in an industry and in turn shape company strategy. They are the bargaining power of suppliers, the threat of new entrants, the bargaining power of customers, the threat of substitute products or services, and jockeying of position among current competitors. He points out correctly that the goal of the strategist is to find a position in the industry where his company can best defend itself against these forces or influence them in his favor. In his book *Competitive Strategy: Techniques for Analyzing Industries and Competitors* [1980], Porter lays out the vast majority if not all of the really significant forces with which managers should be concerned in formulating their competitive strategies. The result is not only a frame of reference for managers but a check-off list by means of which strategies can be identified; and, once the strategies are identified, the list can serve as a basis for evaluating the suitability of a particular strategy. Porter's work, and that of others who will be mentioned later, narrow the search of strategists.

Porter [1980] identifies the critical data to be collected in Table 8-5. After assessing the forces operating in an industry, the strategist is in a position to protect the company from hostile environmental forces or to take advantage of them, whichever is most appropriate. Such a study, when carefully done, opens up all sorts of possibilities from which the strategist must choose. Porter's framework is not an automatic formula for strategic choice. It is an analytical approach, a framework, a device for narrowing the search, in industry analysis.

To illustrate but one potential in such an evaluation is the strategy of finding a niche in the market that no one else is filling. If a product can be developed and sold at a price that customers cannot resist, the result will be riches. A quarter century ago Baron Marcel Bich, for example, decided to make disposable ballpoint pens at a time when such pens were very expensive (around $12) and designed to last a lifetime. Societé Bic, the company built on this concept, has today captured a major share of the world market for pens. More recently Bic is battling Gillette in the sale of disposable shaving razors.

Of course, success is not automatically guaranteed when a niche is discovered. The Franklin Mint, for example, found an unfulfilled demand for coins and metals produced specifically to be collected, but it took a substantial marketing effort to convince collectors that they had this need. Also, a niche once filled successfully naturally attracts competiton,

TABLE 8-5
Raw Data Categories for Industry Analysis

DATA CATEGORIES	COMPILATION
Product lines	By company
Buyers and their behavior	By year
Complementary products	By functional area
Substitute products	

Growth
    Rate
    Pattern (seasonal, cyclical)
    Determinants	

Technology of production and distribution
    Cost structure
    Economies of scale
    Value added
    Logistics
    Labor	

Marketing and Selling
    Market segmentation
    Marketing practices	

Suppliers	
Distribution channels (if indirect)	

Innovation
    Types
    Sources
    Rate
    Economies of scale	

Competitors—strategy, goals, strengths and weaknesses, assumptions	
Social, political, legal environment	
Macroeconomic environment	

SOURCE: Porter [1980:370].

as Hugh Hefner of *Playboy* can attest. Lockheed found a niche in the commercial transport market that could be filled with a medium-range wide-bodied jet and decided to build the L-1011. Then Douglas decided to build the DC-10 in direct competition with Lockheed. At the present time the market is not large enough to yield profits for both companies.

Newman [1967] has described in detail a methodology to identify and exploit niches. Basically it involves a careful analysis of the market and the demand for a new product or service. Then, actual and potential competition is studied. Finally, potential for success in terms of company strengths and weaknesses is assessed.

There is a good bit of literature today on the analysis of market and competitive conditions. To note just a few different sources, we mention Abell and Hammond [1979], Luck and Ferrell (1979), Rothschild [1976; 1979], and Weber [1977].

PRODUCT/MARKET MATRIX

Figure 8-2 displays in a simple fashion major strategic alternatives that every company must choose among concerning its product line and/or its markets. A company, for instance, can choose to stick with its present products in its present markets. Or, it can decide to expand its line into either related or unrelated products. Similarly, it can choose to exapnd its present product line into other markets, or it can seek new markets for new products. Whatever it does will be a major strategic decision. The further the company moves from its present products and markets the more risky and expensive the move is likely to be. To illustrate the range of alternatives, suppose the company decides to increase penetration of existing markets with present products. Strategic choices are shown in Table 8-6.

Gutman [1964] found that 98 per cent of the companies he studied chose the sale of old products in old markets as the best strategy to growth. Morrison [in Mann, 1971] agrees but also observes that companies have shown outstanding growth by entering wholly new fields. In a study of Japanese companies Kono found that in the high-growth companies a major share of sales volume came from new products. Low-growth companies adopted a production-oriented strategy in contrast to the environment-oriented strategy of the high-growth companies [Kono, 1970]. Hofer's research takes him a step further. He concludes that, "the attempt to increase penetration of existing products for existing markets seems to succeed more often as a response to major increases in total demand than it does as a response to major changes in technology. By the same token, the development of new products for existing markets appears to be more successful as a response to major changes in technology than in horizontal diversification" [Hofer,

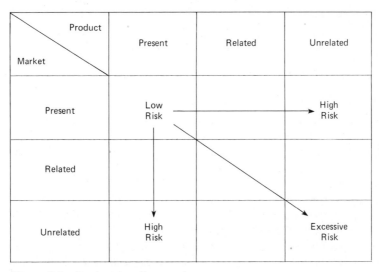

Figure 8-2   Product/market matrix.

TABLE 8-6
Alternative Strategies for Increasing Penetration of Existing Markets with Existing Products

1. Expand the product's rate of purchase by present buyers.
   (a) Make existing designs obsolete.—If owners or consumers of the product become increasingly dissatisfied with the current or "old" style of the product that they own, because new ones are much more efficient, attractive, etc., the total market is expanded, and the best innovator captures the best share (if he promotes his products as well as any competitor). Of course, there are many forms of such product improvement, and it is a favorite strategy of durable-goods manufacturers.
   (b) Obtain sharper brand differentiation.—This may expand the total market little, if any, but increase the share sold by the seller making his product most conspicuously different (in appealing and acceptable ways). New designs or packages that provide truly greater satisfaction in use or enjoyment are obviously safer and more effective strategies than those that seek purely psychological differentiation.
   (c) Make the product more widely or conveniently available.—An example, and a method hardly exhausted by all appropriate products, is offering one's brand in vending machines, always available. Displays or packaging suitable for outlets that have not hitherto carried the product would be another way. And, sometimes an industry has not noticed shifts in buying habits and the traffic of potential buyers in types of outlets through which they have not distributed. Packages or forms of product with longer shelf life and less perishability, institution of mail-order delivery, and many other forms of such strategies may be found.
   (d) Increase the unit of purchase.—The well known "6-pack" and other multiple-unit packaging, as well as variety packs are examples of strategies that bring more usage by existing buyers who tend to consume more because they have more on hand and because they run out of the product less often.
   (e) Increase knowledge and recognition of the brand.—Here is universal strategy that tends to be sought by every contending brand. One firm's superior promotional skill or power may suffice to increase its penetration of the existing market, but this is unlikely to be a strong strategy unless coupled with differentiations that give value to the buyer.
2. Induce new uses of the product.
   (a) Add features or qualities serving additional uses.—This may be done in many ways, such as snow removal attachments for power mowers, pocket-sized packages of tissues, etc. Greater number of utilities for the buyer spells more sales.
   (b) Educate the buyer regarding additional uses.—Whether one is selling mending tape, sardines, or home power tools, it is very possible that good uses are not known to present buyers.
   (c) Proliferate.—Putting out the product in new models or forms, involving just moderate changes in the existing product, may enable the buyers to use it in more ways or more often, e.g., soft margarine, mentholated tobacco, child-sized aspirin tablets.
   (d) Provide services to encourage or enable new applications.—These tend to be more appropriate strategies for sellers of industrial and office equipment, but their use in such diverse fields as telephone service, encyclopedias, and insurance indicates that many lines may use such strategies to expand their products' uses and purchase.

SOURCE: David J. Luck and Arthur E. Prell, *Market Strategy.* © 1968, pp. 177–178. Reprinted by permission of Prentice-Hall, Inc., Englewood Cliffs, N.J.

1973:51–52]. Rumelt [1974] found that companies that diversified into related businesses, on the average, were more profitable than other categories of firms.

Several researchers have devised classifications of product/market strategies. Foster [1970] suggests a set of preferred strategies Luck and Prell [1968] list types of alternative product/market strategies. Hofer [1973] classifies all strategies, including product/market strategies, that can flow from analysis of strategic challenges.

Clifford examined over 700 rapidly growing companies, which he called "threshold" companies, and concluded from their experience that the following were preferred product/market strategies [*passim,* 1973a:34–35].

1. Hold the expansion of product/market complexity to a pace and direction that can be managed effectively.
2. Obtain and hold niches in end-use markets where it is possible to maintain a profit performance superior to competition and to avoid retaliatory action from very large competitors.
3. Capitalize on the advantages threshold companies have over their giant competitors, such as ability to grow in small markets, to enter large markets without affecting profitability, to make and attract acquisitions, and to react quickly to market demands.
4. Avoid areas where a threshold company has disadvantages, such as markets demanding heavy capital investment for entry, products requiring high long-term research expenditures, and very large acquisitions.

PRODUCT PORTFOLIO APPROACH TO IDENTIFYING STRATEGIES

In this approach, probably first identified in its modern concept by Tilles [1966] and pioneered by the Boston Consulting Group, managers of companies with a variety of products in different life cycles, growth rates, and market shares, search for investment strategies to allocate resources among them to optimize company long-run profits [Moose and Zakon, 1971, 1972; Henderson, 1975; Day, 1975; Buckley, 1975; and Hedley, 1977].

The process begins with a distribution of company products in a matrix shown in Figure 8-3. Products having a high market share and prospective high market growth

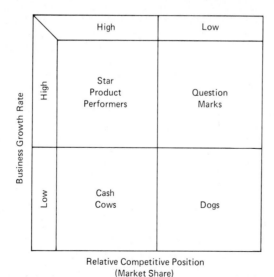

Figure 8-3   The business portfolio or growth-share matrix.

are likely to require capital over and above cash flow to maintain share. Eventually such products may become so-called "cash cows" with high share and low growth. In this category capital investment need not to be more than enough to maintain share, and cash spinoff can be great. When products fall into the category of low share and are in a high market growth area, they tend to create problems such as: Should the company increase capital expenditures to try to increase market share? Or, should the products be allowed to decline and disappear? Should they be sold? If nothing is done margins will be low and profits will be minimal or negative. Products that fall into the category of low share and low market growth are "dogs," which should be abandoned according to conventional wisdom.

Figure 8-3 is a highly simplified model, but the basic ideas generated considerable thought in the development of richer models. The best known model, and the one from which most derivatives have been developed, is the General Electric Company model, which is shown in Figure 8-4. It was developed by GE managers and staff with the aid of the Boston Consulting Group, and McKinsey and Company. Its basic

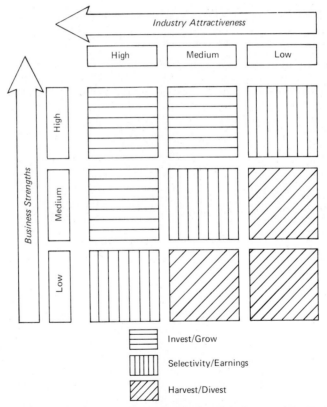

Figure 8-4 Business strength/industry attractiveness matrix. (Source: M. G. Allen, "Strategic Problems Facing Today's Corporate Planner" (speech before the Thirty-sixth Annual Meeting of the Academy of Management, Kansas City, Missouri, August 12, 1976).

purpose was to provide the GE SBUs with a better framework for formulating strategies and to permit top management to make a more informed review of the SBU strategies.

A firm with a number of products can identify each of them in one of the squares in Figure 8-4. Different strategies immediately will be suggested depending upon where the product is placed. Table 8-7 illustrates this point.

Although this matrix provides a valuable screen for narrowing selection, it still is highly simplified. One reason is that there are many dimensions to both market strengths and industry attractiveness. For example, major dimensions of market attractiveness are size of potential sales, annual rate of sales growth, pricing, competitive structure, industry profitability, customer purchasing patterns, government regulations, ease of entry, environmental concerns, legal situation, and technical characteristics. Dimensions of company strength are market share, profitability, image, technology, managerial capabilities, distribution system, sales skills, service capability, patent protection, product efficiency, raw material availability, and ability to meet government regulations.

TABLE 8-7
The Position on the Matrix Suggests "Natural" Strategies

| INDUSTRY STRENGTH | MARKET ATTRACTIVENESS | | |
	HIGH	MEDIUM	LOW
High	Premium: invest for growth • provide maximum investment • diversify worldwide • consolidate position • accept moderate near-term profits	Selective: invest for growth • invest heavily in selected segments • share ceiling • seek attractive new segments to apply strength	Protect/Refocus: selectively invest for earnings • defend strengths • refocus to attractive segments • evaluate industry revitalization • monitor for harvest or divestment timing
Medium	Challenge: invest for growth • build selectively on strengths • define implications of leadership challenge • avoid vulnerability—fill weaknesses	Prime: selectively invest for earnings • segment market • make contingency plans for vulnerability	Restructure: harvest or divest • provide no unessential commitment • position for divestment or • shift to more attractive segment
Low	Opportunistic: selectively invest for earnings • ride market • seek niches, specialization • seek opportunity to increase strength (e.g., acquisition)	Opportunistic: preserve for harvest • act to preserve or boost cash flow out • seek opportunistic sale or • seek opportunistic rationalization to increase strengths	Harvest or divest • exit from market or prune product line • determine timing so as to maximize present value

SOURCE: Monieson [1978].

To illustrate the importance of such dimensions, a company may locate a product in the upper left-hand corner of the matrix, presumably the strongest position. The company may decide, however, to reduce its investment in the product and gradually phase out of its production for many reasons, such as: government regulations are expected to increase with respect to the product; greater legal liabilities are expected to

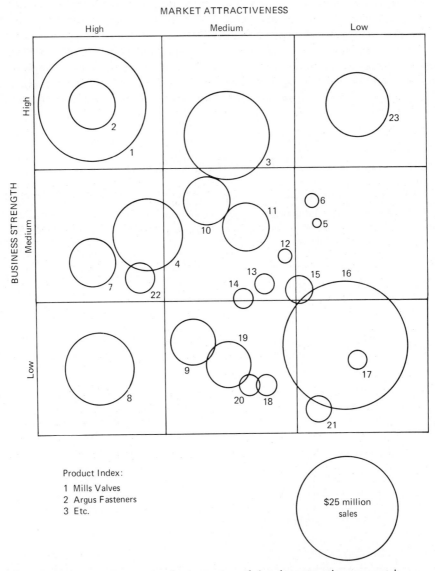

Figure 8-5   Stone Corporation business strength/market attractiveness matrix.

attach to the product; the product does not fit the company product line; or the company may wish to employ the facilities used to produce the product for other purposes.

There may be many modifications of Figure 8-4. Hofer has suggested a number of them [in Hofer and Schendel, 1978:29–35]. Figure 8-5 illustrates one useful modification. It shows products located in the matrix by subject and size of sales. Market share could also be shown in each circle as a slice of pie, with the whole representing 100 per cent. The model can also be used to show what constitutes strong and weak market strength or high and low attractiveness. For example low share might be set at 5 per cent; medium, 5 to 15 per cent; and high, over 15 per cent. It can also be used to show relative competitive position [Hedley, 1977].

Careful thought must be given as to where a product should be placed in either the BSG (Boston Consulting Group) or GE matrix. A much more difficult problem is to analyze precisely what the strategy should be once a product is located. There is nothing automatic in the matrix to tell a manager what is best [Porter, 1980: Appendix A; Palesy, 1980; Enis, 1980; and Hussey, 1978].

PRODUCT LIFE CYCLES

A number of writers have identified the fact that products pass through a distinctive life cycle [for example, Dean, 1950; Forrester, 1959; Patton, 1959; Levitt, 1965; and Clifford, 1965]. Polli and Cook [1969] examined 140 nondurable goods categories and reaffirmed the existence of the product life cycle. In identifying strategies it is important for managers to ask what stage in the life cycle each product has reached, because strategies that are successful in one stage can be disastrous in another. Figure 8-6 shows what may be a typical life cycle for a consumer durable good. (Life cycles of products

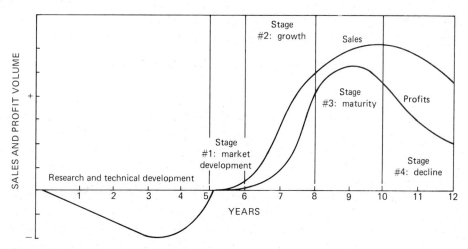

Figure 8-6   Product life cycle for an industry.

have been shortening at the same time research and development costs have been increasing and spreading over a longer period of time. This is one reason why long-range planning is expanding in usage.)

In those companies blessed with above-average strategists, the curves in Figure 8-6 occur up to stage 4, at which time a product modification or a new product replacement is introduced, and a new life cycle is begun. In companies with the poorest strategies the classical life cycle does not occur because the life line never gets beyond stage 1, and the product is dropped.

In the research and development stage, strategies relate to the precise product and technology to be developed, the timing of introduction of the product, the expenditures

TABLE 8-8
Alternative Strategies for Stage 3 (Maturity) in the Product Life Cycle

1. Intensify brand promotion.
    (a) Use more intensive and brand-stressing advertising.
    (b) Make heavier point-of-sale effort.
    (c) Design more attractive and functional packaging.
    (d) Vary advertising messages and media for different market segments.
    (e) Offer more services with product.
    (f) Increase weight of expenditure on sales promotion rather than advertising, to hold customer loyalty rather than seek out new buyers.
2. Trade down.
    (a) Enter a "fighting brand" on the market at a lower price, to avoid jeopardizing an established premium brand.
    (b) Introduce lower priced models of an established brand.
    (c) Lower prices of the entire line, preferably as temporary promotions rather than imply line is worth lower value. Keep prices close to private labels.
    (d) Produce for private labels.
3. Proliferate (extensively or radically).
    (a) Offer more variety in features, flavors, designs, etc.
    (b) Seek more exclusive and innovative features.
    (c) Create more radical and distinct package designs.
    (d) Make more options available in accessories, designs, etc.
4. Trade up (strategy opposite to item 2).
    (a) Improve quality, appearance, etc. to offer better product.
    (b) Use prestige packages, brand names, etc.
    (c) Increase prices to cream market levels (to increase penetration of markets willing to pay higher prices, earning more margin on possibly lower sales and keeping greater differentiation over competitive products).
5. Increase product availability and point-of-sale service.
    (a) Use longer channels to make more available at wholesale level.
    (b) Open more distribution centers closer to point of use or sale.
    (c) Get into more outlets and different channels (e.g., vending machines).
    (d) Improve service offered by dealers (where applicable) or establish manufacturer-operated service centers.

SOURCE: David J. Luck and Arthur E. Prell, *Market Strategy.* © 1968, pp. 186–187. Reprinted by permission of Prentice Hall, Inc., Englewood Cliffs, N.J.

to be committed, and who is going to develop the prototype and lay plans for introducing the product on the market. In each case strategic decisions must be made.

Stage 1 is characterized by difficult problems in getting the product accepted and in achieving a break-even profit position. In stage 2 the product's sales take off and rise sharply. So do profits. Competitors then jump into the market and the originator, instead of trying to induce customers to try his product as he did in the early phases of stage 2, now faces a problem of getting consumers to prefer his brand. In stage 3 the market becomes saturated, price competition intensifies, manufacturers step up services, and the rate of sales growth slows down. Intense competition tends to turn down profits in the later parts of this stage. Then, in stage 4 sales decline and the drop in profits accelerates [Levitt, 1965]. Michael [1971] has concluded that products decline in different ways, which suggests different strategies for them.

As a product moves through the different stages of its life cycle, it has an impact on all areas of management strategic decision making: for example, company missions, long-range strategic objectives, product design, pricing, packaging, distribution systems, production, promotion, information systems, personnel, facilities, cash flow, organization, and planning [Wasson, 1971; Fox, 1973; Hofer, 1975, 1977]. We cannot here display alternatives in all areas, but to indicate the richness of possibilities an extended list is shown in Table 8-8 covering only the marketing and distribution strategic choices.

PIMS

PIMS (profit impact of market strategies) was begun at General Electric Company to answer a question raised by then chairman of the board Borch, namely: Why is it that some of our businesses fail and others succeed? The PIMS project, now in the nonprofit Strategic Planning Institute, has built a massive statistical data bank from over 1500 product and service businesses among its 200 present members. PIMS has used statistical regression analysis to correlate over 30 factors, which are claimed to have unusual predictable influence on profitability. For example, there is according to the PIMS data a close relationship between market share and pretax return on investment (ROI). With a 7 per cent market share, ROI in general registers 9.6 per cent. It rises progressively to over 30 per cent with market share of 36 per cent [Schoeffler, Buzzell, and Heany, 1974]. Although this basic proposition stands, there are many reservations shown in other correlations. For example, rapid rates of new product introduction in well-growing markets damage ROI, low market share is less damaging to ROI when selling customized products, expensive marketing of new products reduces ROI, as investment intensity rises ROI declines, and high R&D plus high marketing depresses ROI. There are many other relationships of importance. Here are just a few to illustrate the richness of the PIMS data: productivity is most important in high-growth markets; in slow-growth markets quality is very important; low quality, early in product life cycles, is unprofitable; market share is most profitable in vertically integrated industries; high capital intensity and small market share equals ROI disaster. Most of these conclusions are what thoughtful observers would reason themselves, but some are counterintuitive (Schoeffler, 1975; Hofer, 1976; and Gale, 1978). PIMS does not stop with generalization, however, it puts specific numbers on its conclusions.

THE LEARNING CURVE

The so-called "learning curve" was identified a half century ago in the aircraft industry by T. P. Wright, then commanding the Wright-Patterson Air Force Base. Since then it has been important in aircraft contractual matters between the aerospace industry and the Pentagon. The Boston Consulting Group studied the curve in depth in a number of industries and has come to some useful conclusions about identifying strategy.

The rule of thumb for a long time has been that there is a 20 per cent reduction in hours for each doubling of performance in a production run. Boston Consulting Group has moved beyond costs of direct labor hours and says: "Costs of value added net of inflation will characteristically decline 25 to 30 per cent each time the total accumulated experience has been doubled" [Henderson, undated]. There are differences in learning curves, of course, but this is a general trend.

Knowledge of the learning curve suggests a number of different strategies. For example, if you can predict a lower cost curve than a competitor, you can displace the higher cost competitor by aggressive pricing. The learning curve suggests that the higher the market share the greater the production and, hence, the lower cost per unit. PIMS, of course, has demonstrated well the truth of this conclusion. Learning curve experience says that the first company in a new business is likely to reap the benefits of the learning curve first. Hence, a major strategy is to jump into the market first [Henderson, 1979; The Boston Consulting Group, 1972].

COMPUTER MODELS

There are all types of computer models from which information is gathered to help identify strategies. Simulation modeling, for example, is widespread. An increasing number of companies are building computer simulation models of various degrees of complexity and comprehensiveness. The insurance industry, for instance, has developed a comprehensive computer simulation model that includes functional relationships among all significant factors involved in decisions such as rate structures, reserves, and demand elasticities. With such a model, managers are in a position to ask "what-if" questions of the computer and come to informed strategies with the answers [Life Office Management Association, 1970]. One of the earliest comprehensive simulation models was that of Rapoport and Drews [1962], made for the oil industry. A well-publicized early financial model made for the Sun Oil Company was reported by Gershefski [1968], its creator. Today, computer-based models are used throughout the strategic decision-making process, such as forecasting, diversification, marketing, production, finance, and so on [Naylor, 1979].

INVENTION

The creation of a new and better product or service is a superb strategy. The success of companies such as DuPont and 3M stems from the strategy of these companies of emphasizing research to produce new products that give them a commanding lead position in a market. There are few if any better strategies than to invent a new product that becomes a generic name, such as Coca-Cola, Smith Brothers cough drops, or Dixie Cups. Not all such inventions, however, were instant successes [Campbell, 1964]. Chester Carlson patented his xerography process in 1937 and tried without success to interest over 20 companies in the process, including such firms as Remington Rand and IBM. Finally, in 1944 he was supported by the Battelle Memorial Institute, but it was not until 1950 that the first machine was marketed. This machine became the strategic factor in the spectacular growth of Xerox.

INTUITION

By intuition we mean innate or instinctive knowledge, a quick or ready apprehension, without obvious recourse to inference or reasoning. Many managers depend upon their intuition to a surprising degree in identifying the right strategy. For instance, Alfred Sloan said of Will Durant: "He was a man who would proceed on a course of action guided solely, as far as I could tell, by some intuitive flash of brilliance. He never felt obliged to make an engineering hunt for the facts. Yet at times he was astoundingly correct in his judgment" [1941:104]. Mihalasky [1969:23] suggests in his experiments that "some executives have more 'precognitive' ability than others—that is, they are better able to anticipate the future intuitively rather than logically and thus, when put in positions where strong data support may not always exist, will make better decisions." Although there probably is some truth to this statement, it is our view that the apparently "intuitive flash" is more the result of digestion of masses of information blended with experience, insight, and an intellectual capability of a manager to sift through the irrelevant and focus quickly on the critical. In some people this can be done very quickly in "the computer between the ears." There is no superior approach to superb strategy identification than a brilliant intuitive mind.

CONCEPT OF SYNERGY

Synergy is the process of putting two elements together to achieve a total greater than the sum of the individual parts. This has been called the "2 + 2 = 5" effect. A simple illustration would be a motel owner who decided to build a restaurant close by. Each could contribute to the business of the other and net a total greater than they would achieve if operated independently.

There are many possibilities for identifying strategies that have a potential synergistic effect. The purpose in mentioning the subject here is simply to observe that the manager who is thinking about synergy is more likely to achieve it than one who is not.

ASK WHAT ARE THE STRATEGIC FACTORS IN BUSINESS SUCCESS

Clearly, managers can narrow the range of strategy identification by asking themselves what are the handful of strategic factors determining the success of their firm in their particular environment and then identifying those strategies capable of meeting the requirement. There is help for them in narrowing choice from research that has been done, but the predictive nature of most of the research is far from certain.

There are strategic factors that will determine the success of any company in a particular industry and at a given stage in its life cycle. The economics, technology, and sociopolitical setting of the industry will determine what they are. One study identified 85 strategic factors that businessmen across all industries considered to be of major importance in company success. There was surprising consensus among survey respondents about the 10 to 15 factors that were most important across all industry. Respondents to the survey revealed close agreement about strategic factors governing success in particular industries [Steiner, 1969a]. There may be a question as to how applicable are these specific strategic factors today, but the principle confirmed in the study is as true today as when the study was made: there are indeed strategic factors needed for the success of a business and they can be identified.

Cohn and Lindberg [1974:5] identified the following factors as bearing critically on the survival and growth of small businesses: "A cautious attitude toward growth. A concern for liquidity. A focus on providing wanted products or services and satisfying work while keeping costs lean. Establishment and maintenance of an open system of communication and decision making. Creation of a rational organization. Control over certain functions. Economical use of time. Control of owner-manager subjectivity." A more comprehensive list of strategic factors responsible for the growth of larger firms was prepared by Guth [1972].

Henderson says that any businessman who can answer certain basic questions better than his competitors has a strategic advantage. These questions are

What are my competitor's costs?
Why do I make money on one product but lose money on an equally good one?
How shall I price this new product?
How much is more market share worth for a given product? Alternatively, what are *all* the
    costs of losing market share?
Should I lower prices? When? By how much?
How much capacity shall I add? When?
What will prices be next year? Five years from now?
Why have my prices broken so sharply? When will the decline stop? [Henderson, 1979:15].

Ross and Kami examined in depth a number of companies that were in crisis situations or went bankrupt and concluded that, had they not overlooked the following "Ten Commandments of Management," they would not have failed.

1. Develop and communicate a *strategy . . . a unified sense of direction* to which all members of the organization can relate.
2. If you want to achieve plans, programs, and policies, then *overall controls* and *cost controls* must be established.
3. Exercise care in the selection of a *Board of Directors* and require that they actively *participate in management*.
4. Avoid *one-man rule*.
5. Provide *management depth*.
6. Keep informed of change and *react to change*.
7. Don't overlook the customer and the *customer's new power*.
8. Use but don't misuse computers.
9. Do not engage in *accounting manipulations*.
10. Provide for an *organizational structure* that meets the *need of people* [Ross and Kami, 1973:21].

Rothschild has set forth a somewhat different set of questions that he concludes must be answered appropriately for success. They are

1. What kind of business do you wish to have in the future?
2. Are there any unique factors in the micro-, macro-, or competitive environment that may have contributed to your past successes or failures? What are these factors, and do you believe that they will continue in the future?
3. What are the criteria that you have used and plan to use in the future to set investment priorities? Have they been sales- or profitability-based, or do they include other qualitative criteria?
4. How have you segmented your business in the past and how do you plan to do so in the future?
5. For each segment, what is your current assessment about its position and attractiveness? What will it be if you continue the same strategy? Where do you wish to be in the future?
6. What will be the leading thrust or driver that will enable you to achieve your investment goals and objectives?
7. What must be done in engineering, marketing, and manufacturing to successfully implement the strategy?
8. What must be changed in order to satisfy the guidelines?
9. How will changes be achieved?
10. Will management and management systems fit the strategy, or must additional changes be made? [Rothschild, 1979:224–226].

In recent years there has been a welcome growth of research concerning preferred strategies in different situations. We cannot do justice to all of this research here, but most of the important work is cited in Schendel and Hofer [1979]. To illustrate the richness of this research we mention a few studies (many more will be mentioned in later chapters). Woo and Cooper [1980] have set forth strategies that have proven to be effective for low-share businesses. Harrigan [1980a] has examined the effect of exit barriers on strategic flexibility. She has also set forth in detail strategies for declining businesses [1979, 1980b]. Strategies for political action have been discussed by Gram and Crawford [1979]. Kotler [1978] describes harvesting strategies for weak products. Clifford [1977] studied 1800 companies with sales in the range of $30 million to $300 million and identified the strategies that permitted the successful ones to outperform giant corporations in their industries in both good and bad economic times. From a study of 21 companies, Pitts [1977] developed strategies and structures for effective diversification. Schendel, Patton and Riggs [1976] have identified preferred strategies to turn a company around. Cooper and Schendel [1976] have pointed out strategic responses to technological threats. Bloom and Kotler [1975] examined strategies for high market share companies and pointed out dangers in getting high shares. A comprehensive listing and description of pricing strategies was prepared by Bailey and others [1978]. Porter (1980) has developed an exhaustive list of competitive strategies as noted previously. Fisk (1975) has set forth product strategies to react appropriately to social sanctions. Textbooks in the functional fields are increasingly dealing with preferred strategies. To pick out just two, we note Abell and Hammond, *Strategic Market Planning* [1979], and Weston and Brigham, *Essentials of Managerial Finance* [1981].

THE ART OF ASKING THE RIGHT QUESTIONS

The art of asking the right questions runs throughout all of the preceding approaches. The simplicity of this approach should not distract one from its great power. The graveyard of unprofitable products is strewn with brilliant mechanical wonders that could not find a market. The reason is that managers asked whether a product could be produced rather than whether it would sell at the price required to make a profit.

Sven Lundstedt underscores the value of asking questions in the following passage:

Initial scientific questions, like first impressions, carry a great deal of weight in shaping the direction of a system of thought. Past experience suggests that more emphasis ought to be upon questions than upon method. If one discovers how to ask good questions (a substantive issue) and if one also learns how to determine if they are in fact also logical ones (a formal issue), the pursuit of scientific discovery in psychology in general is likely to be advanced [Lundstedt, 1968:229].

This is equally true for those managers seeking to derive the very best strategies and policies for their organizations.

OTHER APPROACHES TO IDENTIFYING STRATEGIES

The procedures mentioned in the preceding sections by no means cover all useful approaches to identifying strategies. Others that might be discussed include brainstorming, Delphi, dialectics, luck, and game playing [see Grant and King in Schendel and Hofer, 1979:104–122].

CONCLUDING COMMENT

Strategy identification reflects other considerations not examined in this chapter, such as cognate thought processes, managerial values, organization structures, company life cycles, and interpersonnel relationships. These aspects of the process of strategy/policy formulation and implementation will be examined in detail in other chapters.

Strategy identification is not a single and discreet step in management. It is iterative with other parts of the strategic decision-making process which will become clearer in the next chapter.

QUESTIONS

Discussion Guides on Chapter Content

1. The president of General Motors Corporation asks you to tell him what information he should gather to make a situation audit prior to developing strategy. What would you suggest?
2. How can the WOTS-UP analysis help in identifying strategies? Illustrate?
3. Why is there no concensus in industry about what precisely should be included in the situation audit?
4. How does environmental scanning differ from traditional economic-type forecasts?
5. How does a policy/strategy profile differ from the gap approach in strategy/policy identification?
6. Explain and illustrate the crucial role of analyzing competitive strategy for a company's successful strategy.
7. What is the role of the product/market matrix in identifying strategies? Illustrate.
8. What are the strengths of the product portfolio approach to strategy identification? What are some of its weaknesses?
9. Illustrate how strategies may differ as a company's product goes through a normal life cycle.
10. Is the learning curve useful in identifying strategies? Illustrate.
11. Do you think the concept of strategic factors in business success is useful in strategy identification? Explain.

Mind Stretching Questions

1. You are asked this question by the president of a medium-sized corporation: "Out of all the research that has been done on identifying strategies, state ten major hypotheses that have been tested and found to be true and would be of the most importance to me in helping me to identify the right strategies for testing and evaluation." What would you reply?
2. Name several corporations that found successful strategies by finding niches in the market place and explain the strategies.

9

Evaluating and Choosing Among Policy/Strategy Alternatives

INTRODUCTION

Approaches to identifying major policies and strategies were presented in the last chapter. Here, we address the question of their evaluation and choice.

In recent years there has grown up a body of literature concerning this process called "decision theory" [Harrison, 1981]. Decision theory itself is not new. The "economic man" concept of the economist, for instance, was for generations the core of normative economic decision making. However, today's decision theory has broadened considerably beyond this narrow range. Some writers refer to the process as policy science [Dror, 1971]. Others speak of policy analysis [Wildavsky, 1979]. The words decision theory are used more often among management scholars, and policy analysis or science among those studying public policy decision making. They are both, however, referring to the same phenomenon—the making of strategic decisions in organizations.

It should be noted here that decision theory falls today into two broad classifications—normative and descriptive. Most relevant current research is of the normative type, and most of that is concerned with quantitative optimization models in monetary terms. One reason for the slow growth of research about decision making is that the real world is a very messy place. The processes are extremely difficult to unravel and trace, and universal generalizations of cogency are difficult to discover. This is truer the higher in an organization's hierarchy one probes and, generally, the more significant the decision is to the organization.

The purposes of this chapter are to examine the conceptual and operational processes of evaluation and choice of dominant policies and strategies; to illustrate the variety of disciplines focused on the strategic decision-making process; to illustrate the types of tools available for analysis, their strengths and weaknesses; and to present major overall tests for strategy evaluation and choice. Much more will be said in later chapters about strategic decision making. Indeed, the next three chapters are devoted to this topic.

SOME MAJOR CHARACTERISTICS OF THE OPERATIONAL STRATEGIC DECISION-MAKING PROCESS

Evaluation Does Not Always Follow Identification

It is worthwhile to point out that, when managers individually or in their planning processes identify alternative policies and strategies, the conceptual process of decision making calls for evaluation and choice. This does not always happen. Many managers fail to see that the end result of strategic planning is current decisions not just "plans." Some of the reasons why they do not leap to decisions once they have identified policies and strategies are as follows.

Decision-making is risky. A major decision demands that executives take a stand. If they are wrong, their careers may be at stake. Making major decisions requires courage, and executives may prefer the safety of no decision.

Strategic decision making is fundamentally a creative process that is difficult. It demands a type of thinking and breadth of knowledge that many executives who have arrived at top management levels have neglected as they rose in the ranks because they devoted themselves to solving short-range problems in their narrow functional areas of expertise.

Most major strategic decisions are controversial and demand leadership to implement. How many times has one heard in corporations a statement such as this: "We ought to get out of that business." But nothing is done. Leadership is needed to decide to act and see that action is taken.

Finally, the promotion and evaluation systems in many corporations work against the making of significant decisions. Managers that show the best short-run profit results tend to be promoted rapidly, which means that they may not be obliged to live with the medium- and long-range impacts of their decisions [Salveson, 1974]. As Gerstner notes [1972:9] ". . . incentive compensation is often tied either to short-term earnings performance or to stock-price movements, neither of which has anything to do with strategic success."

The Uniqueness of the Process

The decision-making process for the most significant decisions made by top executives will vary from organization to organization. Each process is unique because involved in the decision making will be managerial value systems and judgments; internal political forces; interpersonnel relationships; and individual managerial skills, capabilities, motivations, and values. In no two organizations will these be identical. Furthermore, major strategic decisions tend to be, but may not always be, unique to each organization.

The Decision-Making Process Is Very Complex

One of the authors had an opportunity to make major policy decisions in government organizations and concluded, after careful consideration, that even immediately following a top policy decision he could not reconstruct the detailed processes by means of which the decision was made. The forces, events, information flows, and thought processes were much too complex. Former White House Press Secretary Moyers undoubtedly felt the same way in responding to an inquiry about how a particular decision had been made. He said: "You begin with the general principle that the process of decision making is inscrutable. No man knows how a decision is ultimately shaped. It's usually impossible even to know at what point a decision is made" [*Los Angeles Times,* January 23, 1966:1]. Efforts to describe the decision-making process from which major decisions have come underscore this point [Allison, 1971; Hitch, 1966; Bryan, 1964; and Bailey, 1950]. Mintzberg and his students studied 25 decision-making processes in companies over a five-year period of time and concluded that descriptions of the 25 decision processes suggest

. . . a strategic decision process is characterized by novelty, complexity, and open-endedness, by the fact that the organization usually begins with little understanding of the decision situation it faces or the route to its solution, and only a vague idea of what that solution might be and how it will be evaluated when it is developed. Only by groping through a recursive, discontinuous process involving many difficult steps and a host of dynamic factors over a considerable period of time is a final choice made. This is not the decision making under *uncertainty* of the textbook, where alternatives are given even if their consequences are not, but decision making under *ambiguity,* where almost nothing is given or easily determined" [Mintzberg, Raisinghani and Théorêt 1976:250–251].

The Interdisciplinary Framework of Decision Making

There is no simple analytical model upon which basis strategic choices are made. Figure 9-1 is presented to show that at least six classifications of phenomena can have significant influence on strategic decision making in organizations. This diagram also shows that a large number of disciplines relate to the detailed forces in the phenomenon classes. The decision-making process is obviously complicated by the fact that different disciplines apply to different strategic problems. The student of strategic decision making must understand that there are no neat formulas to determine how much of each discipline will apply to a particular problem nor how much weight a decision maker should give the discipline.

The Decision Making Process Is Iterative and Fluid

Major policy/strategy decisions are typically made only after long discussions among managers and staffs, reevaluations, checking and double checking, and jumping from one point in a conceptual decision-making process to another. This is undoubtedly what Marion Folsom, a top executive in business and government, had in mind when he said, "Decisions generally are the result of a long series of discussions by both line and staff people after the staff has collected the pertinent material. It is often hard to pinpoint the exact stage at which a decision is reached. More often than not, the decision comes about naturally during discussions, when the consensus seems to be reached among those whose judgment and opinion the executive seeks" [Folsom, 1962:4].

From company to company, and within the same company, the decision process is

Figure 9-1   An interdisciplinary framework of decision making. [Adapted from Harrison, 1975, p. 41.]

constantly changing. It alters with subject matter but also because of different individual and group involvements in the process.

Although there may be a certain amount of formality to a planning process in a company, there can be and usually are informal communication and decision processes also at work. Grinyer and Norburn [1974:86] in their study of British corporations concluded that ". . . those involved in the real process of strategic decision making recognized that it is ultimately a political process in which power and influence of individuals change with the nature of the challenges to the company, with changing personal relationships, and with other factors like the health of top managers . . . informal political processes constitute the system by which decisions are really made." They go on to conclude that ". . . financially more successful companies tended to use more *in*formal channels of communication . . ." [Grinyer and Norburn, 1974:86].

Dominance of Nonquantifiable Element in Decision Making

Much of the literature of decision making emphasizes quantitative decision measures, and quantitative models and techniques to reach conclusions. This includes such measures as return on investment, maximization of output per unit of input, least cost, and profit maximation. For any major decision a manager will have available enormous quantities of factual information. Despite this quantitative emphasis in decision making, the facts are, as observed by Greiner, Leitch, and Barnes [1970], that informed managers rely much more on qualitative than quantitative criteria in appraising performance, even when quantitative information is available and in use. Former Secretary of Defense McNamara validated this conclusion for a large and complex decision, that of the TFX airplane, in testimony before the Congress, as follows:

Fundamentally, we are dealing with a question of judgment. Granted there are specific technical facts and calculations involved; in the final analysis, judgment is what is at issue. . . . In this case we are faced with a situation in which judgments are pyramided upon judgments. . . . There is only one way I know to minimize the compounding error . . . and that way is to apply the judgment of the decision maker not only to the final recommendation but also to the underlying recommendations and factors [*TFX Contract Investigation,* 1963:387].

This conclusion of the Secretary is even more significant given the fact that, for the first time in the history of the Department of Defense, he had established in the Office of the Secretary a large and distinguished staff of mathematicians and quantitative science experts specifically to help him make such decisions.

Why is the preceding statement true? Fundamentally, it is because the "right" type of quantifiable information is not available; what is available is not convincing or creditable; but, more importantly, there are overriding considerations in decision making with which quantitative data cannot deal. Many major decisions must be made by managers that cannot be proven to be correct or incorrect by quantitative methods. An outstanding illustration is the definition of an organization's mission and purpose.

One of the most fateful strategic decisions a chief executive will make is to answer the question: "What is our business?" As Drucker [1974:79] points out, there never is one right answer and the answer, when derived, is seldom if ever the result of logical conclusions drawn from a set of "facts." The evaluation of alternatives and final choice is made solely on the basis of judgment.

No other strategic decision is as important as this one. This is so because, as described in Chapter 7, the mission establishes the lines of business and markets in which the firm will engage and the purposes will establish the main policies and standards of conduct for all employees both for economic and ethical activities. This is the foundation for determining specific objectives, resource priorities, strategies, plans, work assignments, organizational structure, and managerial tasks [Abell, 1980].

Strategies and policies may also be determined at lower levels, which spring from a manager's judgment rather than any set of facts that lead to the decision. For instance, irrespective of financial conditions an executive may decide from among one of the following strategies: invest for future growth, manage for earnings, or manage for immediate cash. Each of these choices will have a different impact on such decision areas as market share, pricing, promotion, existing product line, and new products. Kirchhoff's studies [1980] show that if a manager values short-run ROI over long-run ROI the strategies he chooses will differ considerably than vice versa.

Conceptual Versus Operational Models

The preceding discussion makes quite clear the fact that the strategic decision-making process in practice is by no means standardized. The literature on decision making is filled with conceptual models. Virtually every writer on the subject has created his or her conceptual model. (See Lang, Dittrich, and White [1978] for a comparison of many models.) The simplest ones usually follow a few fundamental steps, such as: (1) recognize the need for decision making, (2) consider and analyze alternatives, (3) select an alternative or strategy to attain a goal, (5) communicate and implement the decision, and (6) evaluate and review. The more complex conceptual models are variations on details in these basic steps.

Despite the vast differences in steps in strategic decision making in industry our empirical observations, as well as scholarly studies, reveal that there are patterns of decision making that have broad application to and are used in practice. Mintzberg's empirical research suggested to him a basic framework that described unstructured, strategic decision processes [Mintzberg, Raisinghani, and Théorêt, 1976]. Quinn [1977] interviewed 100 top managers and found that, in practice, executives followed a sequence of steps in strategic decision making, which he called "logical incrementalism." First, Quinn said, they recognized a need for change. Second, they sought to encourage the organization to acknowledge this need by commissioning study groups, staff members, or consultants to examine problems, options, contingencies, or opportunities posed by the sensed need. Third, they tried to broaden support through unstructured discussions, probing of positions, definition of differences of opinion, encouraging concepts favored by the chief executive, discouraging ideas not favored by top management, and so on. Fourth, they created pockets of commitment by building necessary skills or technologies within the organization, testing options, and taking opportunities to make decisions to build support. Fifth, they established a clear focus either by creating an *ad hoc* committee to formulate a position or by expressing specific ends that top management desired. Sixth, they obtained real commitment by assigning someone who would champion the goal and be accountable for its accomplishment. This last step can be expanded, for example, by including specific commitments in budgets and by making short-range operating plans. Finally, the chief executive must insure that the organization is capable of responding to new opportunities and threats; in other words, that once a decision is made, the firm will not become locked in a fixed position. Quinn concludes:

. . . most strategic decisions in large enterprises emerge as continuous, evolving political consensus-building processes with no precise beginning or end. Managing the generation and evolution of this consensus is one of the true arts of management, calling for the best practices of both behavioral and decision scientists [Quinn, 1980:205].

Strategic Decisions Are Made Throughout Organizations

In virtually all normative models of strategic decision making the final choices are made by top management of organizations. In fact, strategic decisions are made at different levels in organizations [Hofer and Schendel, 1978; Lorange and Vancil, 1977]. Kinnunen offers eight hypotheses in this connection which are worthy of thought and research for confirmation.

1. CEOs in large divisionalized corporations tend to ratify strategic investment proposals sent to them by managers heading operating units.
2. Executives heading fairly autonomous operating units in large divisionalized corporations are the primary formulators of company strategy.
3. Operating units in large divisionalized corporations develop strategy for their business, and the strategy of the corporation is the sum of the strategies of the operating units.
4. As one proceeds from large divisionalized corporations to corporations of smaller size (as indicated by sales) and complexity (as indicated by product diversity), the CEO will do more formulating and less ratifying until the point is reached where the CEO is the chief strategist of the corporation.
5. Clear articulation of strategy from the CEO to various operating units is seldom a characteristic of the formulation process in large divisionalized corporations.
6. CEOs of large divisionalized corporations ratify strategic investment proposals because they have chosen to approve rather than dictate the strategic direction of individual operating units.
7. The absence of a clear articulation of strategy by the CEO forces executives heading operating units to choose the direction they feel is best for the unit they govern.
8. Whether or not strategic investment proposals from operating executives are ratified (as opposed to being thoroughly examined for appropriateness with total company objectives) will depend on the competence of executives of the operating units as viewed by the CEO [Kinnunen, 1976:9–12].

These hypotheses add additional insights into our discussion of the strategy formulation processes. It must be remembered, however, that even in highly decentralized companies there are certain strategies that are distinctly the prerogative of the CEO. These were pointed out in Figure 7-7 and its discussion.

RATIONALITY IN THE DECISION-MAKING PROCESS

Types of Rationality

In theory, managers are the most successful stewards of their organizations when they make rational decisions either upon the basis of intuition, logical evaluation of facts, or both. But, when is a decision rational? In the simplest of terms, a decision is rational when it effectively and efficiently assures the achievement of aims for which the means are selected. If a man is cold and wants to get warm, it is rational for him to get close to a fire. If a man is in business, it is rational to satisfy consumer wants at a profit.

Such simple concepts get complicated in organizational life. When Consolidated Edison of New York passed its dividend in 1974 for the first time in decades, the action was considered to be rational by management but the stockholders did not think so. The fact is that many individuals and groups are interested in every action a manager takes. Each has different aspirations, needs, and interests and views rationality in different ways. Even top managers of a business often disagree upon the rationality of a decision.

This suggests that rationality may be defined as the best selection of means to achieve an objective that is acceptable to the value system of the evaluator. The test of which means is best is, of course, determined by the same value system. For example, if the evaluator is a stockholder, his system of values may establish maximum rate of return on his investment as the desired objective. He can determine over time whether his objective has been met, but he will find it difficult to determine whether any particular decision is rational since its influence on the rate of return may be obscure. Suppose, for instance, management decided to maximize stockholder investment by building a new productive facility but the investment turned sour because a competitor got to the market first. Was the decision rational?

Different disciplines also look upon rationality in diverse terms. Rational action to the economist is that which maximizes profit. Chester Barnard [1968] defined rational decisions as being those which assured the communication, coordination, and motivation necessary to weld the organization into a cooperative effort to reach common ends. Quantitative scientists think of rational decision making as that which optimizes output per unit of input. Behavioral scientists look upon decision making as being rational when it meets certain human psychological needs. Environmentalists look at decisions in terms of impact on environment.

Simon suggests one way to avoid, or to clarify, complexities in determining whether a decision is rational or not is to think of different types of rationality. He says:

. . . a decision may be called 'objectively' rational if *in fact* it is the correct behavior for maximizing given values in a given situation. It is 'subjectively' rational if it maximizes attainment relative to the actual knowledge of the subject. It is 'consciously' rational to the degree that the adjustment of means to ends is a conscious process. It is 'deliberately' rational to the degree that the adjustment of means to ends has been deliberately brought about (by the individual or by the organization). A decision is 'organizationally' rational if it is oriented to the organization's goals; it is 'personally' rational if it is oriented to the individual's goals [Simon, 1976:76–77].

It is obvious that there is no universal standard for judging rationality of managerial decisions. What is rational depends upon the evaluator. Much is to be said, however, for determining the rationality of managerial decisions in terms of the decision makers' own frame of reference [March and Simon, 1958]. Of course, frames of reference vary among individuals and organizations, as will be shown shortly.

Theories of rational behavior, rooted in classical economic theory, use the concept "comprehensive rationality." According to it a goal is established and rationality involves the choice of best alternatives, taking into account probabilities and utilities. Such choice requires knowledge of all possible alternatives, complete assessment of probabilities and consequences of each, evaluation of each set of consequences in achieving the objective, and choice of those alternatives that optimize goal achievement. Because a decision maker cannot comprehend all that this process would require, he forms simplified models of the real world and uses them to make decisions. Simon calls this "bounded rationality" [1976]. Theoretically, this process is not likely to produce as rational a decision as the first, but in practice it probably does and is much easier.

Organizational Models and Rationality

One's theory of the organization has much to do with his concept of what is rational behavior. Until the publication of *Organizations* by March and Simon [1958] and later *A Behavioral Theory of the Firm* by Cyert and March [1963], classical economic theory dominated organizational theory. A core concept of classical economic theory is that firms operate rationally when they seek to maximize profits under conditions of comprehensive rationality. Cyert, Simon, and March, on the other hand, view organizations as coalitions of participants with different motivations and limited ability to solve all problems simultaneously. Goals are formed in light of such constraints and achieved through a bargaining process.

The most complete description and differentiation of major organizational models, especially with respect to decision making, is that of Allison [1971]. He explains the differences between what he calls "The Rational Actor," "Organizational Process," and "Governmental Politics" models. The first is patterned after the classical economic model, the second sees organizations as composed of different organizational units that have their own ways of doing things, and the third views organizations as institutions that get things done through political processes. The third encompasses the Cyert, Simon, and March model.

In sum, rational behavior as perceived from inside and from outside an organization depends upon the model that best explains the functioning of the organization.

Rationality of Profit Maximization

Central in decision making in "rational" business organizations is the goal to achieve profit maximization. Any decision is irrational in classical economic theory that does not serve to achieve this result. Hence, in economic theory, profit maximization is *the* goal of the firm.

There are many who challenge this notion of maximization. Anthony [1960] suggests the more usual objective is satisfactory return on capital employed. Alchian [1950] says the objective of firms is "realized positive profits." Steiner [1969b; 1971] says the goal is "required and steadily rising profits," and Simon [1976], whose phrase has been most widely used, says it is "satisfactory profits."

Others challenge the idea that profit maximization is *the* goal of a firm. Mason [1958] quotes Keynes as saying the general stability and reputation of an institution is a higher goal. Baumol [1967] maintains that sales, subject to a profit constraint, is the objective. Clark [1961] says firms have many objectives, a fact that is amply clear from what has been said previously in this book.

Transition Comment

As noted, much more will be said about the theory and practice of decision making. This discussion at this point is designed as a frame of reference in building a bridge between scholarly research and actual practice. It dramatises the role of these two approaches in identifying policies/strategies, analyzing and evaluating policies/strategies, and making of a final choice. Again, this is not a sequential but an iterative and continuous process.

ANALYTICAL TOOLS FOR EVALUATING POLICY/STRATEGY

The palette of analytical techniques for helping managers to decide upon policies/strategies is indeed rich. Since most readers of this book are familiar with the major ones, we shall not attempt to describe them in this section. Those who are not familiar with them can readily find descriptions in the literature references in this book. Our purpose in this section is to help the reader get a feel for the richness of the palette of analytical tools available for evaluation; to look at the strengths and weaknesses of some of the tools, especially those presented in Chapter 8; and to relate the use of analytical tools to managerial requirements and responsibilities.

The Spectrum of Analytical Tools

The many tools available for evaluation may be divided into four major categories. First are older nonquantitative techniques. Included here, for illustrative purposes would be individual creativity, judgment, hunches, intuition and reliance on experience. Also in this category would be such techniques as brainstorming, project teams, and Delphi.

Second, are older quantitative methods. In this class would be accounting systems and models in the accounting system, such as balance sheets, profit and loss statements, cash flows, accounting ratio analysis, break-even analysis, budgets, cost control models, and so on. Quantitative forecasting methods are numerous, such as trend extrapolation, correlation analysis, econometric models, input-out analysis, and multiple regression analysis. Another class in this area would be tracking models, such as milestone charts, decision trees, and critical path models like PERT/Time.

Third are new computer based models. Included here are newer mathematical techniques and the adaptation of older techniques to computers. Computer-based simulation models are the most extensively used models in strategic planning today. The most popular ones are financial models [Naylor, 1979]. Older techniques of forecasting, such as correlation analysis, are frequently used in computer-based models to project future trends. PIMS is a new computer-based model and is fundamentally a correlation analysis. Cost-experience curves can also be classified here, since they frequently involve computer modeling. Most of the computer-based models are deterministic as distinct from probabilistic. A major exception is risk analysis as developed by Hertz [1969].

Finally, there are various complex techniques that combine many different tools. In mind, for example, are elaborate cost-benefit analyses, social science research, formal strategic planning systems, and program budgeting.

This short classification by no means exhausts the list of analytical tools available in formulating policy/strategy. As brief as it is, however, it should make clear the wide range of available tools. Each tool has its own strengths and weaknesses and relevance to particular policy/strategy problems. This, too, is a very large subject, and space limitations permit only illustrations of the point.

Strengths and Weaknesses of Selected Techniques

INTUITION. As was mentioned before but it is worth repeating: There is no more powerful method to evaluate and choose the best policies/strategies. However, as far as we know there is no record of any individual who depended upon this technique with an infallible record.

THE ACCOUNTING SYSTEM. There are few if any more important analytical tools for policy/strategy analysis in industry than found in the typical accounting system of a company. Ratio analysis, for example, is a powerful tool of analysis with predictive value. The reading in Appendix B describes in detail the more important ratios useful in analysis. In a longitudinal study of 221 firms and 48 financial ratios, Pinches, Eubank, and Mingo [1975] identified the following as having the highest predictive value: earnings before interest and taxes/total assets, net income/total assets, earnings before interest and taxes/sales, net worth/sales, sales/working capital, debt/total capital, and debt/total assets.

Observe, however, that accounting data can be manipulated in many ways to produce a variety of results, all within standard accounting principles and practices. William Casey when chairman of the Securities and Exchange Commissson lamented:

The public has lost more money through the use of permissible variations in accounting to exaggerate earnings and growth than through the whole catalogue of things which we have made impermissible [Quoted in Andrews, 1973].

Even with consistent and well-understood accounting practices, accounting ratios must be used very carefully. Reservations even about the widely used and powerful return-on-investment ratios have been raised [Dearden, 1969]. Weston [1972], however, says ROI has powerful applicability at all levels of decision making.

THE PORTFOLIO MATRIX. This is, of course, a powerful tool for identifying strategies as well as evaluating them, as explained in the last chapter. The matrix must be used with great care, however, if errors in strategy are to be avoided. Managers must not assume that because a product lands in one of the squares on the matrix that the decision about strategy is made. For example, if a product falls in the upper left corner—strong market position and strong industry attractiveness—it is not a foregone conclusion that the strategy should be "invest for growth." Even for a product in such an enviable position, careful analysis of its situation might lead to the conclusion that the company should sell the product or phase it out of its line.

Location of a product on the matrix can be influenced by manipulation or judgment. For example, forecasts of market growth rates can be manipulated by managers. Managers may also define a market to achieve a desired location of a product on the matrix.

For example, what is the market for General Foods' Country Time brand of lemonade powdered soft drink? Is it the cold refreshment beverage market? Is it the lemonade soft drink market? Is it the powdered soft drink (PSD) market? Is it the sugar-sweetened PSD market? Or, is it the presweetened PSD market for canister products? The market share of this product will vary from 2 to 51 per cent depending on the operating manager's selection of market served [Palesy, 1980].

THE PRODUCT LIFE CYCLE (PLC). The PLC is a simple and powerful analytical tool but it does have significant limitations in policy/strategy formulation. Dhalla and Yuspeth [1976] have admonished managers to "forget the product life cycle." Their position is that simplistic use of the PLC has led managers to take actions that have been contrary to the best interests of their companies. They certainly are correct in underscoring the fact that, actually, the PLC is a very complicated phenomenon. Hofer [1975], for example, has observed that the PLC must be examined and defined in more specific contexts and with more variables than a simple sales and profit curve. Variables that he has in mind include purchase frequency, nature of the buyer's needs, rate of technological change, the ratio of distribution costs to value added, price elasticity of demand, marginal plant size, and so on. Note also that there are many different PLCs. Shin and Wall [1979] have identified nine different life cycle curves. It should not be forgotten, too, that the PLC depends very much upon management decisions. Its shape, direction, and time span can be influenced by strategic decisions.

PIMS. There is no question about the fact, as noted in the last chapter, that PIMS is a potent model for formulating strategy/policy. But, it too, has weaknesses that must be understood if the technique is to be used effectively. Anderson and Paine [1978] and Naylor [1978] have set forth the major limitations of PIMS. Gale [1978] replied to Naylor's criticisms. Space limitations prevent any full analysis of PIMS's shortcomings. But, to illustrate, the quantitative correlations of PIMS must not be taken without reservations for there is high potential for management controllability among the many independent variables used by PIMS. For example, PIMS says that high R&D plus high marketing depresses ROI. Hewlett-Packard did not find this to be true. Also, although there is general acceptance to the PIMS conclusion that high market share and profitability are closely related, there are also significant exceptions. High market share has sometimes been unprofitable [Fruhan, 1972]. On the other hand, Burroughs Corporation, Crown Cork & Seal Co., Inc., and Union Camp Corporation do not enjoy dominant market shares in their industries and yet they are highly profitable [Hammer-mesh, Anderson, and Harris, 1978]. As a correlation analysis of past activity PIMS deals with the past, not the future. Those relationships of the past that resulted in one conclusion can change in the future and bring a far different conclusion. Despite these and other limitations of PIMS, the data are valuable in policy/strategy formulation; however, they are not substitutes for careful managerial analysis and creativity.

THE LEARNING CURVE. Here, as in the preceding discussion, the relationship between cost and output is a powerful analytical tool; however, it has serious shortcomings if used without careful analysis. Like the PLC there are many variables that affect the relationship, and many of them are controllable by management. An increase in productivity, for example, can be produced by the introduction of new capital investment. However,

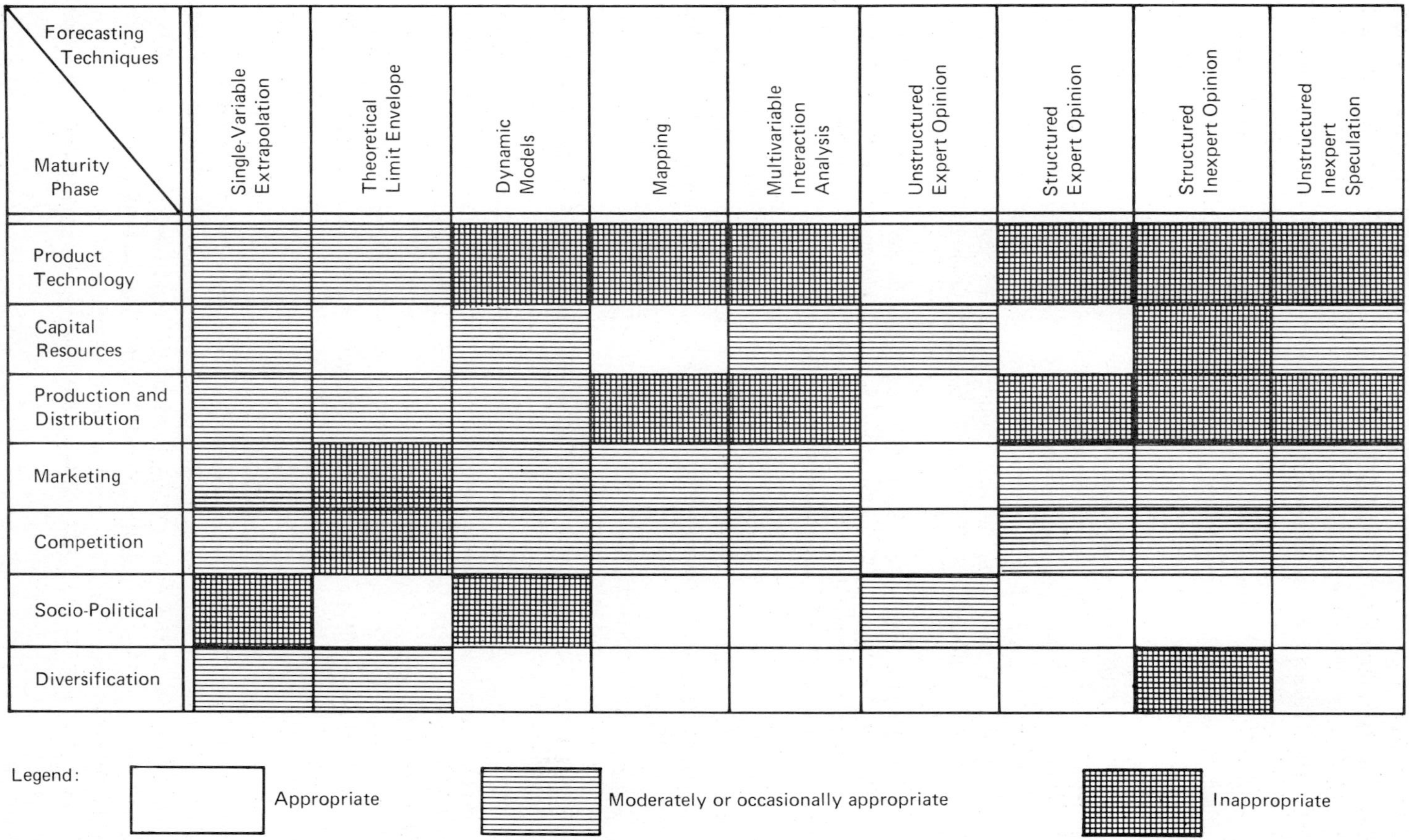

Forecasting Techniques / Maturity Phase

Forecasting Techniques (columns):
- Single-Variable Extrapolation
- Theoretical Limit Envelope
- Dynamic Models
- Mapping
- Multivariable Interaction Analysis
- Unstructured Expert Opinion
- Structured Expert Opinion
- Structured Inexpert Opinion
- Unstructured Inexpert Speculation

Maturity Phase (rows):
- Product Technology
- Capital Resources
- Production and Distribution
- Marketing
- Competition
- Socio-Political
- Diversification

Legend:
- ☐ Appropriate
- ⦀ Moderately or occasionally appropriate
- ▦ Inappropriate

Figure 9-2 Relationship between enterprise's development phase and forecasting techniques at policy/strategic planning level. (Source: Lebell, Don, and O. J. Krasner, "Selecting Environmental Forecasting Techniques from Business Planning Requirements." *The Academy of Management Review,* July 1977:379.)

if the investment is too great and results in excess capacity, the net impact may be a cost increase. For an analysis of major limits to the learning curve see Abernathy and Wayne [1974].

FORECASTING. There are a vast number of forecasting techniques available for policy/ strategy analysis. Each has its own strengths and weaknesses. Space limitations prevent any analysis of the uses of different techniques, but the point is illustrated in Figure 9-2. This chart shows that different techniques have different applicabilities for different subjects of analysis in policy/strategy formulation.

The Manager Is His Own Best Analytical Technique

The preceding illustrations of strengths and weaknesses of selected analytical tools makes clear that thought must be given to when and where each technique is applicable and how much of it is appropriate. Decisions such as these should be made by managers not staff specialists. Staff specialists can and should advise managers, but the decisions are for the managers. A biographer of Winston Churchill observed on this point:

He was always deeply interested in techniques of all kinds and listened avidly to experts and professionals, imbibing all they told him with a rare accuracy and grasp. But he never fell a victim to the black magic of specialist infallibility. It was the task of specialists and experts to supply the weights and measures: it was for him to assess them and to reach conclusions [Carter, 1965:36].

In developing the needed assessment capabilities of diverse disciplines focused on the policy/strategy-formulation process the manager becomes his own best analytical tool.

KEY QUESTIONS TO TEST STRATEGIES/POLICIES

Tilles [1963] first suggested a set of overarching tests for strategies, an evaluation approach that we think is most significant. Following are our seven major overarching criteria, following Tilles, with comments and illustrative questions. It is our view that, if questions such as these are forthrightly asked and answered, the result will be the formulation of superior strategies and assurance of their implementation. The history of business, on the other hand, is filled with instances where a company failed to ask and answer one or another of these questions and, as a result, disappeared.

Is the Strategy Consistent with Environment?

If it is to perform well, a firm must adapt to its environment. We mean the total environment, as described in Chapter 4. The policies/strategies of a firm must reflect not only the current but the evolving elements in the environment, which open up major opportunities and pose potentially lethal threats. For example, as noted in the last chapter, the strategies of a firm must make it competitive for survival. Also, as noted in Chapter 5, a large, exposed company that ignores changing social values will create difficult problems for itself. The current plight of the automobile companies is witness to the truth of this observation. Illustrative of the questions that suggest themselves in this category are the following:

- Is your strategy acceptable to the major constituents of your company?
- Is your strategy in consonance with your competitive environment?
- Do you really have an honest and accurate appraisal of your competition? Are you underestimating your competition?
- Does your strategy leave you vulnerable to the power of one major customer?
- Does your strategy give you a dominant competitive edge?
- Is your strategy vulnerable to a successful strategic counterattack by competitors?
- Are the forecasts upon which your strategy is based really creditable?
- Does your strategy follow that of a strong competitor?
- Does your strategy pit you against a powerful competitor?
- Is your market share (present and/or prospective) sufficient to be competitive and make an acceptable profit?
- If your strategy seeks an enlarged market share is it likely to be questioned by the Antitrust Division of the Department of Justice or the Federal Trade Commission?
- Is it possible that other federal government agencies will prevent your achieving the objectives sought by your strategy?
- Is your strategy in conformance with moral and ethical codes of conduct applicable to your company?

Is the Strategy Consistent with Your Internal Policies, Styles of Management, Philosophy, and Operating Procedures?

A living organization is a composite of policies, procedures, values, work habits, aspirations of people, communications, interpersonal linkages, and so on. Obviously, the better policies/strategies are in congruence with the most effective workings of this mechanism the more likely they are to be successful. No strategy will succeed, for instance, if it is contrary to the strongly held values of top management. Mighty General Motors Corporation found out at Lordstown that it had to be concerned with worker attitudes. Some questions that arise in this classification are:

- Does the strategy/policy really fit management's values, philosophy, know-how, personality, and sense of social responsibility?
- Is your strategy identifiable and understood by all those in the company with a need to know?
- Is your strategy consistent with the internal strengths, objectives, and policies of your organization?
- Is the strategy under evaluation divided into appropriate substrategies that interrelate properly?
- Does the strategy under review conflict with other strategies in your company?
- Does the strategy under review exploit your strengths and avoid your major weaknesses?

- Is your organizational structure consistent with your strategy?
- Does your policy/strategy make the greatest overall contribution to the performance of your company?
- Is the strategy likely to produce a minimum of new administrative problems for your organization?

Is the Policy/Strategy Appropriate in Light of Your Resources?

Resources are those tangible and intangible assets a company has that are important contributors to its viability and success. This, of course, includes a wide range of assets from money to managerial competence and employee loyalty. A few illustrative questions in three classes of assets follow:

Money
- Do you have sufficient capital, or can you get it, to see the strategy through to successful implementation?
- What will be the financial consequences associated with the allocation of capital to this strategy? What other projects may be denied funding? Are the financial substrategies associated with this funding acceptable?

Physical Facilities
- Is your strategy appropriate with respect to existing and prospective physical plant? Will the strategy utilize plant capacity? Is equipment obsolete for the proper implementation of the strategy?

Managerial and Employee Resources
- Are there identifiable and committed managers to implement the strategy?
- Do we have the necessary skills among both managers and employees to make the strategy successful?

Are the Risks in Pursuing the Strategy Acceptable?

There are all types of risks associated with strategic decisions. The spectrum ranges from no risk, which might be the case where a company decides to stick with its current products rather than diversify, to a situation where the very survival of the company may be at stake. Broadly speaking, a policy/strategy is a higher risk where amounts of capital involved are great, the payout period is long, and the uncertainty of outcome is significant, than just the reverse. But there are other risks, such as, for example, a risk that skilled managers and workers may not be acquired in time to perform as required to make the strategy/policy successful. Appropriate questions in this area would include:

- Has the strategy/policy been tested with appropriate analysis, such as return on investment, sensitivity analysis, the firm's ability and willingness to bear specific risks, etc.?
- Does your strategy balance the acceptance of minimum risk with the maximum profit potential consistent with your company's resources and prospects?
- Do you have too much and too large a proportion of your capital and management tied into this strategy?

- Is the payback period acceptable in light of potential environmental change?
- Does the strategy take you too far from your current products and markets?

Does the Strategy Fit Product Life Cycle and Market Strength/Market Attractiveness Situation?

- Is the strategy appropriate for the present and prospective position in the market strength/attractiveness matrix?
- Have you considered all the characteristics in the matrix that are pertinent to evaluating properly your strategy?
- Is your strategy in consonance with your product life cycle as it exists and/or as you have the power to make it?
- Are you rushing a revolutionary product to the market?
- If your strategy is to fill a niche not now filled in the market, have you inquired about the niche remaining open to you long enough to return your capital investment plus a required profit?

Can Your Strategy Be Implemented Efficiently and Effectively?

Many of the questions raised previously pertain to implementation of policy/strategy, but the subject is so important that it deserves separation. The ability of a company to implement a policy/strategy involves a great many conditions. A strategy is not implementable, of course, if insufficient capital is available to make it work, or if managers and employees are indifferent to its success. It will not work if there are absent the necessary coordination and control mechanisms to assure that strategic plans are indeed fulfilled. Probably the most neglected area in scholarly treatment of policy/strategy rests in the implementation of it. A few illustrative questions in this area are:

- Overall, can the strategy be implemented in an efficient and effective fashion?
- Is there a commitment, a system of communications and control, a managerial and employee capability, that will help to assure the proper implementation of the strategy?
- Is the timing of implementation appropriate in light of what is known about market conditions, competition, etc.?

Are There Other Important Considerations?

This final grouping is, of course, a catchall to identify other pertinent considerations not dealt with in the preceding classes. A few questions here could be

- Have you tried to identify the major forces inside and outside the organization that will be most influential in insuring the success of the strategy and/or in raising problems of implementation? Have you given them the proper evaluation?
- Are all the important assumptions realistic upon which your strategy/policy is based?
- Has the strategy been tested with appropriate analytical tools?
- Has the strategy been tested with appropriate criteria such as past, present, and prospective economic, political, and social trends?

This is indeed a formidable list of questions. Not every question will be most relevant in every situation. So, managers have the responsibility for determining which is the most pertinent question. Any one might turn out to be the core question. For instance, Rolls Royce could answer affirmatively most all of these questions but it failed to ask this one: Are your rushing a revolutionary product to the market? It did indeed rush the RB-211 jet engine designed for Lockheed's L-1011 to the market. Technical problems and enormous cost overruns pushed the company into bankruptcy in 1971. For any particular situation questions other than those posed or narrower versions of those raised above may be more appropriate.

There is no implication here that every one of the preceding, or other, questions must be answered in depth. In many cases, merely to ask a question will quickly yield an acceptable quick response. For others, of course, a good bit of rigorous analysis will be appropriate.

A CONCLUDING OBSERVATION

Alfred Sloan in his book *My Years With General Motors* said, "No company ever stops changing. Change will come for better or worse. I also hope I have not left an impression that the organization runs itself automatically. An organization does not make decisions; its function is to provide a framework, based upon established criteria, within which decisions can be fashioned in an orderly manner. Individuals make the decisions and take the responsibility for them. . . . The task of management is not to apply a formula but to decide issues on a case-by-case basis. No fixed, inflexible rule can ever be substituted for exercise of sound business judgment in the decision-making process" [Sloan, 1964:443].

Clearly, at the strategic decision-making level each case is unique. Yet, there are underlying approaches to identifying preferred strategies, to evaluating the strategies, and to making the final choices. Research is no more than ankle deep in the search for tested theories applicable to this process

QUESTIONS

Discussion Guides On Chapter Content
1. Why does not policy/strategy evaluation always follow identification?
2. Discuss the complexity of decision making in a firm.
3. Identify a major strategic decision of a company of which you are aware and hypothesize about the many different disciplines that probably influenced the decision.
4. How do conceptual and operational models of decision making differ?
5. Do you think it would be correct to say that the higher in an organization a decision is made, and the more important the decision, the less likelihood the decision will be made upon the basis of quantitative analysis and/or a single discipline? Explain.
6. Where in an organization are policy/strategy decisions made?

7. "Any important decision in an organization is irrational to someone." Do you agree or disagree? Explain.

8. Economic theory asserts that profit maximization is a completely rational goal of an enterprise, but there are many scholars who say that profit maximization as the single goal of an operating firm is irrational. Where do you stand and why?

9. Comment on the outstanding strengths and weaknesses of these analytical tools for formulating policy/strategy: a company's accounting system, the portfolio matrix, the product life cycle, PIMS, the learning curve, and major forecasting techniques.

10. The authors have set forth in this chapter seven overarching questions, with a number of subquestions, as criteria for testing and evaluating policies/strategies. Do you think this is a valuable list? Explain. Pick out one of the questions and explain in detail why it might have great power in determining whether a manager chooses the right or wrong strategy.

Mind Stretching Question

1. Return to "Mind stretching question" 1 in Chapter 3. Can you relate the strategy or strategies you found in response to this question with one or more of the tests for policy/strategy in this chapter in such a way as to draw a conclusion about the correctness of the strategy?

10

Individuals in Policy/ Strategy Formation

INTRODUCTION

Although individuals in policy-making positions are required to make decisions, this does not mean that policy formulation and decision making are identical. Policies are developed in an organizational context and thus evolve out of a political process that extends well beyond the boundaries of mere decision making. Bauer [1968] even goes so far as to argue that bargaining, not decision making, is at the heart of the policy/ strategy process. In any event, when the general managers in charge of the product divisions of a company are vying for limited financial resources to expand production of their particular products, it is apparent that something more than is usually implied by the term decision making is involved.

Yet a knowledge of decision making, how it occurs and the factors that influence it, can contribute a great deal to understanding the policy/strategy process. This chapter focuses on the individual as a decision maker and the ways in which cognitive, emotional, and motivational factors may affect decisions. The prototype for this discussion would be the corporate chief executive officer laying down policy on a unilateral basis. Actually this does not happen as often as one might think. There is good reason to believe that it is most typical, within larger firms, of those who have put together and operated multiindustry conglomerates [Vance, 1971]. In many more-established firms, decision making often takes on something of a shared character. It is for this reason that the following chapter takes up the influences that groups such as boards of directors, executive committees, finance committees, and less formal coalitions of company officers and even consultants, may exert on top level decision making.

What Is Decision Making?

Decision making has been defined as follows:

A conscious and human process, involving both individual and social phenomena, based upon factual and value premises, which concludes with a choice of one behavioral activity from among one or more alternatives with the intention of moving toward some desired state of affairs [Shull, Delbecq, and Cummings, 1970].

The crux of this definition as with the definition given in the previous chapter, is the idea of choice. When a manager decides to introduce a new product in one area rather than another or to accept certain union demands and not others during contract negotiations, he is making a choice. Putting it somewhat differently, he may also be said to be exercising judgment or attempitng to solve a problem. What seems to be required for decision making to occur is that there be

1. A gap between the existing state of affairs and some desired state.
2. A focusing of attention on this praticular gap.
3. A desire to reduce the gap.
4. Some possibility that the problem can be solved and the gap reduced.

It is apparent that policy formation does involve this kind of problem solving or decision making. Policies are developed to solve a problem or reduce a gap. If no one perceives the gap, or no one cares about reducing the gap, or no one believes it is possible to reduce the gap, then policy formation does not occur. If this happens with regard to a large number of problems or gaps, the company involved becomes very much like a rudderless ship. It simply drifts on a sea filled with treacherous and often-conflicting currents, constantly buffeted by the winds of uncertainty.

COGNITIVE FACTORS IN DECISION MAKING

Decisions and policies are expected to be, and usually are to a certain degree, rational—rational in the sense of contributing to organizational objectives or goals. This kind of rationality implies a clear logical link between what the company wants to do and what it decides to do; a decision maker who can make decisions with knowledge, intelligence, in an appropriate manner, and without distortions induced by values or motives that might lead him or her away from implementing such corporate goals as profit, growth, survival, and the like. Individual differences on a wide range of factors thus become important to decision-making effectiveness [Beach and Mitchell, 1978; Connolly, 1977].

The Role of Knowledge
There is very little question that decisions require knowledge. This knowledge may reside in a person as a consequence of education and prior experience or it may have to be sought out. Search of this kind requires time, and managerial decision situations may not permit time. Thus, all in all, there would appear to be a clear advantage if production decisions were made by production people, marketing decisions by marketing people, and so on. That way the search for relevant information can be conducted in one's own mind, rather than over an extended landscape, and accordingly can be completed much more rapidly.

This becomes a problem primarily for those in general management. For such people the amount of knowledge needed and revelant to their work is tremendous, and the prospects for information overload overwhelming. Given the complexity inherent in such positions as chief executive officer, general manager, executive vice president, project manager, and the like, it is almost essential to resort to some kind of knowledge search, and in most cases this means relying on the judgments of staff specialists.

But people such as marketing research managers, research and development managers, and lawyers have quite different commitments, values, responsibilities, and personal objectives than general managers. They may well have the needed knowledge and still lack the loyalty or motivation to use this knowledge strictly for the accomplishment of company goals. In other words, their knowledge may not be brought to bear on the real problems of the company in a rational manner because of distortions introduced by functional, professional, and personal considerations.

This is the dilemma of the general manager or any manager whose responsibilities extend over multiple specialties and diverse expertise. He trusts his own knowledge, but he does not have enough of it; he rightly distrusts the knowledge of others, but this is where he can compensate for his own intellectual lacks. The possible solutions are to accumulate a great deal of the kinds of knowledge required by the job or to surround oneself with people he can trust. But without the knowledge to evaluate what one hears from advisors, how can trust be maintained? It follows that being an effective decision maker and policy maker requires a great deal of knowledge. The primary question is: What kind of knowledge is crucial?

BACKGROUNDS OF GENERAL MANAGERS. There is no simple solution that would permit us to sift the alternatives and say that some limited set of knowledge is all that is required of a policy maker. Studies of the academic backgrounds of top executives have consistently indicated a diverse array. The major trends appear to be some shift to the various areas of business administration and away from the liberal arts, and a greater prevalence of advanced degrees. More, and more relevant, information is increasingly in demand.

There is good reason to believe that the ranks of the MBAs are furnishing an increasing proportion of chief executive officers and that college majors such as accounting and production are declining in numbers, whereas finance majors are increasing [Steele and Ward, 1974]. Yet Livingston [1971] argues convincingly that much of the kind of learning that occurs in MBA programs is irrelevant to managerial decision making and executive success in any event. Nothing in the shifting trends of educational specialization appears to offer the prospect of identifying the knowledge required for policymaking.

Table 10-1 indicates that in the functional experience background of chief executive officers, one finds much the same diversity as in college majors [Boone and Johnson, 1980]. It seems apparent that relevant knowledge is important and that having it is a lot better than not having it. There is no one functional area of experience or type of major that will provide this knowledge. At the general management level at least, and to some extent below that level, better decisions will be made when the breadth as well as depth of knowledge is greatest. In any specific situation, at a point in time, however, some particular kind of knowledge may be crucial.

TABLE 10-1
Functional Background Experience of CEOs

Finance	20%
General Administration	16%
Marketing	14%
Law	12%
Production/Operations	11%
Banking	11%
Technical	9%
Other	7%

KNOWLEDGE DOES MATTER. That having knowledge within oneself, and thus being in a position to conduct an information search within, makes for greater competence in decision making may seem self-evident. If it is not, there are data to support this viewpoint. Whybark [1973] found that on a standardized set of business decisions, fifth-year business students with a knowledge of forecasting and inventory theory came much closer to the criteria of success produced by an adaptive decision model than did second-year students without such knowledge. One fifth-year student did practically as well as the model; no second-year students did.

In another study Moskowitz compared graduate business students and experienced R&D managers on a similar standardized decision task:

Although both groups were highly motivated to perform well . . . , R&D managers were found to be more rational decision makers, superior information processors, and more risk-inclined than students, notwithstanding that [they] had no formal training in decision theory. R&D managers also appeared more interested, devoted more time . . . and *could better relate underlying concepts to actual decision problems as faced in practice* [Moskowitz, 1971:324]

Other research indicates that experienced managers are particularly likely to face their work decisions with a logical style "characterized by objectivity, by lengthy consideration in terms of objectives, evaluation of alternatives and final choice on the basis of which alternative is best in objective terms" [Arroba, 1978:221]. Decision making of this kind requires an extensive search, either within or outside the self, for information and knowledge.

One might argue that the advent of computerized information systems makes it less necessary to hold knowledge in one's own head and thus reduces the need for personal knowledge. At the present time the best answer to this argument appears to be that decisions at the top levels are less programmed, or programmable, and thus less susceptible to solutions based on computer information alone [Simon, 1977]. Computers can contribute a great deal in terms of reducing the difficulty of search for information, but it still takes a great deal of knowledge to combine and utilize this information effectively to make the kinds of decisions required at the policy/strategy level.

All in all it seems evident that the more one knows, which is relevant to on-the-job decisions, the better one will do. The problem is that a large amount of what is learned in school may not be very relevant to the managerial policy decisions against which the students may be gauged some 20 years or more later.

The Role of Intelligence

Intelligence refers to the degree or extent to which an individual is ready to learn new things rapidly and solve problems correctly. It is the developed capacity to grasp, relate, and use concepts, and thus to reason effectively. This is the type of capability needed to make rational decisions in pursuit of company goals, and there is good reason to believe that where the decision-making process does utilize such a rational mode an organization is more effective [Price, 1968]. It would seem to follow that intelligence is an important ingredient of decision making; in part because it permits the accumulation of relevant knowledge more rapidly; in part because it facilitates making effective choices among multiple alternatives.

The available evidence reinforces this expectation. Studies have repeatedly shown that more successful managers and executives are typically more intelligent [Ghiselli, 1973, Campbell *et al.,* 1970]. In fact, it is practically impossible to arrive in the competitive world of top-level corporate decision making without a high level of intelligence. And those unintelligent few who do arrive are unlikely to remain long. Table 10-2 contains information on 39 company officers, mostly from the larger United States corporations. Their intelligence is compared with data for the total United States population age 10 and above [Miner, 1973]. Roughly three quarters of the presidents are in the top 3 per cent of the population and all are in the top 10 per cent. The company officers at a somewhat lower level score almost as well.

Although intelligence may contribute to other aspects of managerial performance, it definitely is a primary factor in decision making. On a standardized decision task, more intelligent managers were found to process information more rapidly, to make more accurate decisions, and to be less willing to shift away from these accurate decisions on reevaluation [Taylor and Dunnette, 1974]. Intelligence appears to be particularly important in evaluating information, integrating this information to make a correct choice, and judging the potential impact of adverse consequences.

TABLE 10-2
Intelligence Level of Company Presidents and Company Officers Below the Level of President Compared With the General Population

INTELLIGENCE TEST SCORE LEVEL	PER CENT OF GENERAL POPULATION SAMPLE AT GIVEN LEVEL OF INTELLIGENCE OR ABOVE ($N = 1500$)	PER CENT OF COMPANY PRESIDENTS AT THIS LEVEL OF INTELLIGENCE OR ABOVE ($N = 23$)	PER CENT OF COMPANY OFFICERS BELOW THE LEVEL OF PRESIDENT AT THIS LEVEL OF INTELLIGENCE OR ABOVE ($N = 16$)
20	0.4	26.1	12.5
19	0.9	65.2	18.8
18	2.9	73.9	68.8
17	5.3	95.2	75.0
16	10.1	100.0	81.3
15	15.1		93.8
14	22.1		100.0

The Role of Cognitive Style

In addition to knowledge and intelligence, the policy or strategy formulator should benefit from possessing a certain kind of what has come to be called "cognitive style." One approach in this area has stressed the importance of cognitive complexity [Schroder, Driver, and Streufert, 1967]. Cognitively complex people tend to search out and use a great deal of information in their thinking and to develop a variety of alternatives or choices based on this information. They are able to differentiate between aspects of a complex problem and to integrate these different aspects in achieving a solution.

This sounds very much like what is involved in developing policies and strategies. Certainly policy problems are typically complex and many faceted. One has to be aware that solving one problem in a particular way often only creates another problem. Preventing a strike by giving the union what it wants may well commit the company to costs in terms of wages and benefits that have major implications for production output, pricing, marketing, and practically every other aspect of the business. People who use a cognitively simple style may well not be able to cope with these interrelated problems effectively. At least, they do not perform as well on a standardized top management decision simulation as more cognitively complex individuals [Lundberg and Richards, 1972]. There is also good reason to believe that the ability to think using a complex style can be developed in business students through appropriately structured courses [Johnson and Werner, 1975].

A closely related view of cognitive style has been developed by McKenney and Keen [1974]. The most important distinction they make is between systematic and intuitive thinkers. Although both styles are viewed as appropriate under certain circumstances and in particular types of jobs, the manager engaged in policy formation should benefit most from using the more rational, less emotion-based systematic style. Such a style involves

1. Looking for an explicit method of problem solving and making a plan of approach.
2. Defending solutions primarily in terms of the method used to reach them.
3. Defining constraints on what can be done at the beginning and discarding alternatives quickly.
4. Moving through a process that involves increasing refinement of analysis based on a systematic search for relevant information.
5. Not leaving things hanging, but rather completing all analytic steps that are begun.

Such a systematic style appears closely allied with cognitive complexity. There is also a possible parallel with certain ideas that have emerged from brain research. Mintzberg [1976] argues that when the brain is more fully developed on the left side, planning is facilitated; when the individual has a more developed right hemisphere, this contributes to managerial effectiveness. Taking this idea one step further, left hemisphere activity appears to have much in common with the systematic style, and right hemisphere activity with the intuitive [Steiner, 1979a]. Relationships such as these are hardly proved by the data currently available, but this type of theorizing does point up the desirability of linking research on policy/strategy to physiological concepts and evidence wherever possible.

The Impact of Age

The preceding discussion provides some insight into how effective decision makers at the policy level think—how their minds work. A question might be raised, however, as to whether very many people are thinking this way by the time they get to policy level positions. Within the larger companies the average member of top management is in his or her early 50s, and it is very rare indeed for anyone to move to this level before age 35. If cognitive capabilities tend to decline with age, this could mean that the very people who need such capabilities most are least likely to have them; the frequently heard criticisms by the young of "irrational" decision making at the top might have some justification in fact.

It was indeed thought for some time that intelligence did decline with age in the adult population. However, this conclusion turned out to be an artifact of faulty research design. A review of more recent research in which the earlier deficiencies have been corrected indicates that, in the intelligence range characteristic of managers, there is a rise in average intelligence level at least to the age of 50. After that there appears to be some leveling off; however, there is *no decline,* at least through to the usual retirement age in the mid-60s [Carroll and Maxwell, 1979].

Analyses that focus directly on decision making lead to much the same conclusion. In a study using a standardized personnel decision-making situation, older managers (up through their late 50s) were at least as capable as younger managers; in some respects they were more capable [Taylor, 1975]. Probably the reason younger people often *perceive* top management as acting irrationally is that the information available to them is not the same as that available to those at the top. A merger agreement that ultimately results in extensive personnel changes and layoffs (as most such agreements do), simply cannot make sense to anyone who is not privy to all the details of the company's financial position. Yet making such details available might well hinder the merger discussion and thus eliminate the possibility of choosing this alternative; many people would not fully understand them in any event.

VALUES AS INFLUENCES ON DECISIONS

A study conducted some years ago reported that United States business managers tend to have values that place strong emphasis on the economic, the political, and the scientific, as opposed to social, religious, and aesthetic considerations [Guth and Tagiuri, 1965]. It is apparent that such value orientations can influence the way in which decisions are made [Badr, Gray and Kedia, 1980]. A manager with predominately religious values would be much more likely to be responsive to pleas for corporate contributions to a church-supported college than would a manager whose values were overridingly economic in nature.

The term *value* is often used in a loose manner without a clearly specified meaning.

As a result, considerable confusion frequently exists as to what is really meant. The following definition, although somewhat cumbersome, does have the advantage of being comprehensive:

To say that a person has a value is to say that he has an enduring prescriptive or proscriptive belief that a specific mode of behavior or end-state of existence is preferred to an opposite mode of behavior or end-state. This belief transcends attitudes toward objects and toward situations; it is a standard that guides and determines action, attitudes toward objects and situations, ideology, presentations of self to others, and attempts to influence others [Rokeach, 1973:25].

The Role of Values

The most extensive analysis of managerial values currently available has been conducted by England [1975]. This research has clearly established the role that values play in decisions. Managers who value profit maximization strongly will not decide to commit funds to such things as cafeteria and rest room facility improvements if they can possibly help it. Managers who hold compassion to be an important value do, in fact, try to avoid the strategy of withholding part of a prospective employee wage increase when faced with the need to finance a research and development effort.

As these examples imply, certain kinds of values appear to contribute to executive success: Successful managers appear to favor pragmatic, dynamic, achievement-oriented values, whereas less successful managers prefer more static and passive values, the latter forming a framework descriptive of organizational stasis rather than organizational and environmental flux. More successful managers favor an achievement orientation and prefer an active role in interaction with other individuals instrumental to achievement of the managers' organizational goals. Less successful managers have values associated with a static, protected environment in which they take relatively passive roles [England, 1975:72–73].

It appears that what makes certain managers successful in policy positions is that they possess values that foster making decisions when decisions need to be made and taking risks when risk taking is called for, rather than passively doing nothing. On the other hand, there remain major differences between those in leadership positions in different types of organizations; Table 10-3, which lists strongly held value objects among business and labor leaders, attests to this conclusion.

One might anticipate that turbulent value climates such as those of the late 1960s, both on campus and elsewhere, might have produced major changes in the values of business managers. A comparison of data over time refutes this hypothesis, however [Lusk and Oliver, 1974]. The values of business managers have remained as pragmatic as ever.

Managerial Values in Different Countries

Although there are major similarities among countries in the values of their managers, there are differences also [Whitely and England, 1980]. In the United States tactful acquisition of influence and due regard for others are valued; in Japan deference to superiors and company commitment; in Korea personal forcefulness and aggressiveness

TABLE 10-3
Value Objects of Leaders in Different Organizations

Business Managers	Labor Leaders
Owners	Blue-collar workers
Stockholders	Laborers
High productivity	Employee welfare
Organizational stability	Social welfare
Organizational growth	
Organizational efficiency	
Industry leadership	
Ambition	Trust
Ability	Loyalty
Skill	Honor

with low recognition of others; in India a highly centralized, personal, and rigid social structure; in Australia a low-keyed approach to management with a high concern for others. Even at a more global level of analysis there are distinct differences, as a study of chief executive officers around the world demonstrates [Peterson, 1972]. In terms of decision making the Latin American and Asian CEOs value participative processes highly, but when it comes to directing, and thus implementing decisions, their values support a very close type of supervision (see Table 10-4). United States chief executives, on the other hand, reject this type of leadership style completely. One would expect from these data that the processes through which policy is made and the way in which it is implemented in various parts of the world would differ considerably.

Furthermore those values that are culture-based seem to have the capacity to carry over into new cultural contexts. Thus Japanese-American managers in Hawaii value long-term employment commitments to the company, respect for the formal authority of a position, team performance as opposed to individual superiority, and paternalism in dealing with subordinates, just as Japanese managers in Japan do [Kelley and Reeser, 1973]. What kinds of values are actually best in terms of effective, rational, goal-oriented decision making is not entirely clear. However, it does seem apparent that values that mesh with the existing culture are needed to gain the rewards of that culture, and that a degree of pragmatism of the kind United States managers value is needed to maintain flexibility in the face of varied cultural expectations.

Values and Business Ethics

Obviously values have much to do with ethics in business decision making and with social responsibility concerns as considered in Chapter 5. There are those who raise serious questions about the values of business managers and prospective managers, and indeed about the values of American society as a whole [Cavanagh, 1976]. The emphasis on pragmatism appears to suggest a shallowness and lack of commitment to strong values; additional considerations indicate a lack of concern for others. Taken together this value pattern can be interpreted as reflecting a willingness to do whatever will turn a profit, and thus something less than an ideal level of ethical behavior.

TABLE 10-4
Values of Chief Executives in Various Parts of the World

AREA	MEAN VALUE SCORE FOR*	
	DIRECTING SUBORDINATES IN EXACTLY WHAT THEY SHOULD DO AND HOW TO DO IT	INVOLVING AS MANY PEOPLE AS POSSIBLE IN IMPORTANT DECISIONS
United States	6.5	4.0
Western Europe	4.7	4.1
Latin America	3.6	2.3
Asia	2.8	2.9

* Scored on a 1-7 scale, where 1 is "strongly agree" and 7 is "strongly disagree."
SOURCE: Adapted from Peterson [1972:112].

Against this background a study by Sims and Hegarty [1977] has considerable significance. MBA students participated in a simulation that, at certain points, required them to make decisions as to whether they would or would not pay kickbacks to purchasing agents in order to guarantee the continued profitability of the business. Although theoretical, political, aesthetic, social, and religious values were unrelated to the decisions made, those with strong economic values were particularly likely to decide in favor of kickbacks. However, the foreign nationals within the sample were also more likely to select the unethical alternative than the United States citizens. The introduction of a clearly stated company policy opposing unethical behavior, including "giving or accepting gifts or money," served to reduce sharply the incidence of decisions to permit kickbacks.

The study clearly supports the view that values can play an important role in decisions that have an ethical component. Strong concern for economic achievement, profits, and competitive success can lead an individual to make decisions that, at least within the United States, are viewed as unethical. On the other hand, these same decisions appear to be made even more frequently by individuals from certain other parts of the world, perhaps because the behavior involved is more fully condoned in those cultures.

PERSONALITY FACTORS IN MAKING DECISIONS

In addition to values, three other aspects of human personality have received considerable attention as they relate to making managerial decisions. These are a willingness, or perhaps even desire, to take risks, the tendency to hold dogmatically onto preexisting beliefs, and the level of an individual's self-esteem, or belief in his or her self-worth. As far as can be determined these three factors are not related to each other. All have implications for policy formulation.

The Role of Individual Risk Propensity

Whether a propensity for taking risks is desirable in a policy maker depends very much on the situation. Because risk taking is presumably allied to entrepreneurship and founding or investing in new enterprises, it has tended to take on very positive connotations in our society. Yet risk takers may not be the best decision makers. They tend to limit the amount of information they bring to bear on a problem and to reach decisions very rapidly [Taylor and Dunnette, 1974]. This is impressive if they are right, but the failure to search out needed information and consider multiple alternatives can be very costly; it all depends on the situation.

In situations where decisions should be made quickly, as in adapting price levels to those of competitors, risk takers can be expected to do well simply because high costs may be associated with decision delay. But the same approach to developing a corporate long-range plan can be disastrous; there are risks enough in such planning efforts without compounding them at the personal level. We find, for instance, that public school administrators are much less likely to take risks than business managers [Brown, 1970]. This seems entirely appropriate to the demands of the two decision environments. A risk-taking school administrator can quickly get in trouble with his school board, city government, and the parents, to the point where he is prevented from accomplishing his objectives. Thus, whether a high risk taker should make policy depends on the nature of the organization, its stage of development, the uncertainties inherent in its environment and a host of other considerations.

There is evidence that older managers tend to be less prone to take risks [Ebert and Mitchell, 1975]. This is probably because they have more to lose and less to gain than younger managers. It is also true that companies differ in the extent to which their managerial ranks are staffed with risk takers. One would think that older, large companies, which are firmly established in their industries, would benefit most from the low propensity for risk associated with an older policy level group. Young companies without an established industry position, like young managers with few assets, may need to resort more to risk taking.

The Role of Dogmatism

The assumption underlying much of the research on dogmatism is that this characteristic will serve to distort decisions to make them conform to preexisting beliefs; thus policy makers should not be of a dogmatic nature. Yet existing data do not support this conclusion. Managers who tend toward dogmatism do make decisions more quickly and they do have considerable confidence in their decisions once made, nonetheless their decisions are not less accurate; if anything the reverse is true [Taylor and Dunnette, 1974; Muldrow and Bayton, 1979]. Also dogmatism has no impact on decisions when the problem is unambiguous and the information clearly establishes the superiority of one choice over others; it does not override clear-cut, rational choices [Brightman and Urban, 1974].

How important dogmatism really is as an explanatory variable in executive decision making remains to be established; it may well have been overrated in the past. Almost certainly it is not a negative factor, as originally assumed. On certain kinds of problems, it appears to yield more accurate decisions. Beyond this there is very little that can be said at the present time, without additional research. Yet the manager who dogmatically and rigidly sticks to certain views cannot be assumed to be wrong; quite the contrary, he, and particularly she, is often likely to be right.

The Role of Self-Esteem

There is considerable evidence that in many areas of endeavor those who are characterized by high levels of self-esteem exert more effort and do better. Yet an emerging conclusion from some recent research is that such is not the case for all decision-making situations [Weiss and Knight, 1980]. In fact, under certain circumstances a low level of self-esteem appears to contribute most to decision effectiveness. Individuals who lack self-esteem tend to seek out more information before making a decision, presumably because they are unsure of their current knowledge. Because they obtain more relevant information, they do a better job in making their decisions. Obviously not all decisions require extensive information search, but many at the policy/strategy level do. Under such circumstances it appears, strangely enough, that a lack of belief in one's own self-worth and competence is an asset.

What comes out most strikingly from the research on personality factors is the variation in relevance of various characteristics, depending on the nature of the decision problem. Risk-taking propensity (or the lack of it), dogmatism, and self-esteem level can all be important, but whether they are depends very much on the nature of the decision to be made.

CREATIVE MANAGEMENT DECISIONS

There is little question that creativity can be important in such scientific research areas as new product development and manufacturing equipment design. Studies conducted in the R&D context indicate that the scientist who is creative performs better when the job calls for and facilitates originality and innovation. But even in R&D, creativity can be a detriment; scientists who are creative tend to do poorly in the more restricted and controlled work situation, often of a development engineering nature, where innovation is difficult [Pelz and Andrews, 1966].

This conclusion, that creativity is not universally good, has important implications for management, especially at the policy level. It raises a distinct question as to whether creative people do contribute more effectively to the formulation of corporate policies and strategies and, if so, under what circumstances.

What Is Creativity?

For a plan, or a policy, or a managerial decision to be creative it must be original and different. But a unique idea is not necessarily a creative idea; it may merely be eccentric. Thus, a policy of paying employees only once a year to hold payroll preparation costs down would certainly be unusual, but in the world of today it is not very realistic. Insofar as policy making is concerned at least, creative means original *and* realistically related to achieving company objectives.

The kind of person who is creative in this sense can make a tremendous contribution to a company. However, this contribution may carry with it certain unexpected and undesired consequences. If these side effects are too marked and the situation is such that they assume considerable importance, then the costs of creative decision making may outweigh the benefits. To understand how this can happen it is necessary to know something about the characteristics of creative people [Barron, 1969; Suler, 1980].

For one thing, the creative manager must know a good deal about the particular area in which the decision making is to occur. To reinvent the wheel, not knowing that the wheel is already in widespread use, accomplishes nothing. Thinking at the forefront of knowledge requires knowing where the forefront is. Creative thinking is not a substitute for learning; it is a supplement. Accordingly, the creative manager has to want to learn and to have in fact done so.

Furthermore creativity appears to involve a feeling of excitement. Creative people do in fact get "wound up" over their ideas; thinking of this kind is exciting. As a result they tend to stick to problems they are trying to solve with a tenacity, even stubbornness, that may frustrate others. While other managers want to move on to new concerns, the creative member of a group may well refuse to leave the topic of his efforts. He may, over time, become quite unpopular because of such behavior.

There are other bases for unpopularity, also. Being creative often involves rejecting or ignoring the more conventional or stereotyped thinking of others. Creative people may appear hostile, conceited, contentious, domineering, nonconforming, and emotional, as well as having a tendency to live in the future and ignore the present and past. All of this implies a considerable potential for discord. Creativity is not merely an intellectual ability; it has major emotional and motivational facets as well. These latter seem to provide the necessary conditions for the creative problem-solving process to work. They also have a great capacity to disrupt the smooth functioning of a top management team. Thus, if such a team badly needs smooth functioning or its members cannot tolerate conflict and dissension, the creative ingredient in company decisions may well not be worth the cost [Summers and White, 1976].

Creative Managers and Creative Climates

There is a considerable body of research and writing that stresses the view that creative pontential will not come to fruition in a context that is inhibiting, restricting, and highly controlled [Taylor, 1972]. Among other things those who might *want* to stifle creativity should:

1. Stress that there is only one best way of doing things.
2. React quickly and negatively to any expression of new ideas.
3. Oppose anything they do not understand.
4. Emphasize that creativity brings only trouble.
5. See that rewards never go to creative people.
6. Keep creative individuals under tight control and, if that does not work, ostracize them.

Much of the writing on this subject deals with the climates that teachers create for their students and managers create for their subordinates. In general the thrust of this writing is that teachers and managers *should* foster learning and working environments that stimulate creativity. All of this might appear to have very limited relevance for creativity at the policy level where there are no teachers and the policy makers are at the top level of management.

Yet there is a sense in which the findings regarding creative climates have considerable relevance. Company policies are made in a context of governmental laws and regulations. These provide the climate within which companies solve problems and make decisions. If this governmentally imposed climate acts on a whole industry, or on companies of a particular size or configuration, or on an individual company in certain ways, creative planning and policy making will be stifled just as surely as with school children or subordinate workers. Such a climate would include the following:

1. A stress on doing business one way and not any other way.
2. A proclivity for reacting quickly to suppress new approaches.
3. A tendency to oppose business strategies that are not clearly understood.
4. Indication that new business approaches can only lead to trouble.
5. Procedures that deprive creative managers of rewards for their ideas.
6. Close control over innovative companies or, if this fails, mechanisms for making it impossible for them to do business in the country.

Without much imagination one can easily think of many ways in which the legislative process and the executive enforcement agencies can serve to produce such consequences through the medium of antitrust laws, regulation of rates and profits, taxation, tariffs, labor legislation, and the like. Where such an unfavorable climate for creativity exists, introducing a creative element into the policy process may very well do more harm than good. Just as creative scientists can be expected to fail in highly restricted, controlled work situations, so too will creative policy makers.

Given this impact of climate, one would expect companies in the more controlled industries such as the utilities, transportation, and insurance to benefit very little if at all from creative management; the alternatives available are too limited or the incentives for seeking new alternatives too few. Similarly, creative approaches may only introduce problems in companies that have been under continued antitrust scrutiny, Securities and Exchange Commission investigation, and the like. For creative managers to develop plans and introduce policies that are new and different and effective, they must be, and feel, free to create.

DEVELOPING CREATIVITY. Creativity can help a company's decision-making processes when the conflict engendered is not too debilitating and when the external environmental climate serves to foster rather than inhibit creative ideas. This raises a question as to whether companies can do anything to increase the creative capabilities of those managers for whom this might appear to be an appropriate course of action.

The answer appears to be that techniques are available for this purpose and that they do seem to work well in most situations where they have been tried [Tyler, 1978]. On the other hand, very little is known about their application to policy formulation. In general, it appears that the various approaches to creative training are effective because they induce values indicating that creative thinking is good and worth doing, foster a group attitude favorable to creativity and new ideas, and require participants to spend considerable time in searching for alternatives.

In many situations such an approach should facilitate decision making at the policy level, but not in all. Where the alternatives realistically available are sharply circumscribed and the situation calls for quick and unified action at the top, creativity training could well prove detrimental. Such might be the case if a company were faced with a determined take-over attempt or with drastic price cutting by a competitor. Planning activities, on the other hand, should be facilitated. In fact, it is in the planning sphere that the creative contribution seems most likely to be essential.

CONCLUDING COMMENTS

The evidence is strong that individual decision-making capability may be influenced by knowledge levels, intelligence, cognitive styles, values, risk propensity, dogmatism, self-esteem, and creativity. These are the factors that have been studied in some depth. No doubt there are many other such factors that can assume a significant role that have not been studied as yet. The major implication of the existing studies is clear, however.

Relevant knowledge, intelligence, and certain kinds of values, particularly those in a pragmatic vein, appear to be essential to effective decision making in any policy context. But there are also a multitude of individual factors that may or may not be important depending on the situation. There are certainly policy makers who are better than others, and no doubt this is why some companies succeed and others do not. But it is also true that one organization may require a very different type of policy maker than another given its environment, existing top management, and other constraints.

The important conclusion that emerges from this analysis is that individual differences do matter. Some people are better at making a particular company's decisions than others, and it is in the interest of a specific company to find and develop such individuals. This leads to the question of how such individuals should be organized and how their thinking should be combined to produce the most effective result. This is the topic of the following chapter.

QUESTIONS

Discussion Guides on Chapter Content
1. What is decision making? How does it relate to policy?
2. What is known regarding the effects of knowledge and intelligence on decision making? What particular kinds of knowledge and intellectual abilities appear important at the policy level?

3. How may computers influence top-level decision making?

4. What are some of the different ways of formulating cognitive styles? How might these relate to physiological factors?

5. How may values influence decisions? Give some examples. How might values differ in different types of organizations and in different cultures?

6. In what way do values relate to business ethics and social responsibility?

7. What are some of the personality factors that have been shown to have a role in decision making? For what kinds of decisions does each have the greatest significance? What are the effects involved?

8. It has been said that managing is not a creative art. Comment and document your answer. How might the legal texture of a society be involved?

Mind Stretching Questions

1. A number of characteristics of an individual have been discussed in this chapter as they relate to decision making. What other characteristics do you feel are worthy of research investigation in this regard? Why?

2. It has been suggested that the values of the key decision makers in a company should be included in the assessments made by financial analysts. Does this make any sense? Why would anyone suggest this?

11

Group Aspects of
Policy/Strategy Formation

INTRODUCTION

In the business world, and elsewhere, decisions related to policy formation and strategy typically are products of group interaction. Generally this group contains one person, perhaps the company's chief executive officer, who is in charge of the meeting, and the other members are individuals who report to this person on the organization chart. Thus the policy-making group has an inherent structure that is determined by the company's organization structure.

Although there are certainly many variations from company to company and situation to situation, it is common practice for such a group to utilize some type of staff work on a policy issue as a starting point. This report, which may be presented orally or in writing or both, usually spells out certain alternative choices and the pros and cons of each. However, in most cases the report concludes with a recommended decision. Not infrequently such reports are structured from the beginning so as to facilitate a particular choice, in spite of their seeming objectivity.

In any event, the report forms the basis for a group discussion in which members participate to varying degrees. The person in charge may act only in the role of a facilitator or catalyst for this discussion, but more often than not he is an active participant. He may very well be the most active participant. The final decision usually is made by the person in charge, but it may well be predetermined by a consensus within the group; decisions by voting tend to be rare, at least in the business world.

Although the staff reports may be primarily individual efforts and certain members of such a policy group may have given considerable individual thought to the issues, the decision-making process described is strongly interlaced with group interaction. This is even more true where a problem arises in the context of such a discussion and a decision is reached without benefit of staff input or individual investigation—a not uncommon occurrence.

The point is that decision making at the top levels of many organizations is very much a group process. This raises a question as to whether this is a desirable state of affairs and, if so, how this group process might best be carried out. Is the typical approach described here the best approach?

INDIVIDUAL VERSUS GROUP DECISIONS

Not all decisions are alike. Although typologies of decisions abound, one that appears particularly useful for understanding policy making differentiates between creative, programmable, and negotiated types [Shull, Delbecq, and Cummings, 1970]. Creative decision making is needed when there is considerable uncertainty surrounding the problem and new and original approaches are required. Programmable decisions are those to which a given technology may be applied and which are capable of some definite, clear-cut solution. Negotiated decisions imply the existence of conflicting factions, cliques or power centers, all of which must be to some degree satisfied in the final decision. A special case of negotiated decision making occurs when those who will implement the decision must get a decision they can "live with" in order for implementation to occur.

Creative Decisions

It does appear that the usual group discussion or meeting has the effect of inhibiting creativity; the group context simply does not permit realization of the full idea-producing potential of all the people participating. This is true for a number of reasons [Delbecq, Van de Ven, and Gustafson, 1975]:

1. Interacting groups often become focused on one train of thought for long periods of time, to the exclusion of other alternatives.
2. Individuals tend actually to participate in the discussion only to the extent they view themselves as equally competent with others.
3. Even though more expert group members may not express criticism, others tend to expect that they will and thus hold back their ideas.
4. Lower level managers often are inhibited and go along with the ideas of their superiors, even though in their own minds they have better solutions.
5. Group pressures for conformity with the implied threat of some kind of punishment are almost inevitable.
6. More dominant individuals tend to monopolize and control the group with the result that the ideas of others are lost.
7. Groups as such tend to devote time to their own maintenance and survival and to the members' getting along with each other; this takes away from decision effectiveness.
8. Groups have a tendency to move to quick decisions, thus shortcircuiting the search for relevant information.

In meetings people tend to evaluate others and to expect to be evaluated, both in terms of their expressed ideas and in terms of their social skills. This can well create a less than optimal climate for creativity. As a result, the number of ideas dwindles and the quality of what ideas are produced tends not to be the best. It seems likely that these tendencies become particularly pronounced in well-established managerial groups where the existence of superior-subordinate relationships, competition among members, and the potential for long-term consequences all should militate against idea expression.

A STUDY COMPARING INDIVIDUALS AND GROUPS. An interesting example of this group inhibition process, insofar as idea production is concerned, is provided by a study in which the participants were to offer ideas for "defining the job description of part-time student dormitory counselors who reside in and supervise student living units of university owned or approved housing." This is a difficult practical problem, producing considerable emotional involvement and controversy, that has no clear-cut solution. The participants in the study were student dormitory residents, student housing administrators, faculty members, and academic administrators [Van de Ven and Delbecq, 1974:605–607].

Three decision-making approaches were compared as follows:

Nominal Group Technique. Individual members first silently and independently generate their ideas on the problem or task in writing. This period of silent writing is followed by a recorded round-robin procedure in which each group member presents one of his ideas to the group without discussion. The ideas are summarized in a terse phrase and written on a blackboard. After all individuals have presented their ideas there is a discussion of the recorded ideas for the purposes of clarification and evaluation. The meeting concludes with a silent independent voting on priorities by individuals through a rank ordering or rating procedure.

Delphi Technique. A questionnaire designed to obtain information on a topic or problem is distributed by mail to a group who are anonymous to one another. The respondents independently generate their ideas in answering the questionnaire, which is then returned. The responses are then summarized into a feedback report and sent back to the respondent group along with a second questionnaire designed to probe more deeply into the ideas generated in the first questionnaire. On receiving the feedback report, respondents independently evaluate it and respond to the second set of questions. They are requested to vote independently on priority ideas included in the feedback report and to return their second responses by mail.

Discussion Group Technique. Interacting group meetings begin with the statement of the problem by the group leader. This is followed by an unstructured group discussion for generating information and pooling judgments among participants. The meeting concludes with a majority voting procedure on priorities, or a consensus decision.

The result obtained when 20 separate groups of seven people each worked under each procedure are given in Table 11-1. The nominal and delphi groups, where people generated their ideas free of the inhibiting effects of group interaction, both produced a greater number of unique ideas for job activities that should be included in the job description. The nominal technique, in addition, yielded a more positive evaluation of the decision-making process. The delphi approach has been found to be of special value

TABLE 11-1
Relative Effectiveness of Nominal, Delphi and Discussion Groups in Defining the
Job Descriptions of Student Dormitory Counselors

EFFECTIVENESS MEASURES	NOMINAL GROUPS	DELPHI GROUPS	DISCUSSION GROUPS
Mean number of ideas per group	33.0	29.0	18.0
Mean perceived satisfaction level per group	21.1	19.1	18.8

SOURCE: Adapted from Van de Ven and Delbecq [1974:616].

in planning with a diverse group of experts, particularly when the latter are geographically dispersed [Tersine and Riggs, 1976].

The finding that creative thinking is more likely to flourish where individuals work independently of each other is typical. On the other hand, there is no implication that a single individual is likely to do better than many. Having more minds brought to bear on a problem does help, but it also makes a great deal of difference how those minds are organized and utilized.

MAKING CREATIVE DECISIONS. Say a manager is faced with the need to develop certain new products and to plan for the introduction of these products in the marketplace. He has a sizable staff of people who are familiar with those technologies that might be considered reasonably available to the company for producing new products. Instead of bringing these people together in a series of large meetings designed to hammer out the new product ideas, the manager would do much better to set his staff members working on the problem independently. What is needed initially is a large pool of potentially feasible ideas. When people work independently, more and better ideas can be expected to emerge. When the same number of people operate in a discussion group setting, it is as if there were half as many people involved, or less.

This superiority of individuals alone over groups extends to the use of subgroups as well. One might think that setting up three or four subcommittees or small project teams would generate more ideas because each subgroup would go off in a different direction and thus largely overcome the inhibiting effects of group discussion. This turns out not to be the case. The same number of people working alone do much better than the pooled result of subgroup efforts [Bouchard, Drauden, and Barsaloux, 1974].

When individuals work alone along the lines established by the nominal group procedure, there appear to be major advantages to utilizing a large number of individuals [Burton, Pathak, and Zigli, 1977]. The quantity and uniqueness of the ideas generated increases with up to at least 17 people, but quality does not benefit beyond 13. If for some reason it is not possible to avoid group meetings to deal with creative problems, the level of trust among the members becomes an important consideration. A lack of trust tends sharply to depress the number of ideas generated [Klimoski and Karol, 1976].

Once an idea base has been generated, the major need is for good, hard-headed arguments regarding the feasibility and profit potential of the proposed product. This kind of evaluative input to the decision process can be effectively developed through discussion.

Group members may well stimulate each other and a general searching out of new information tends to occur; members can facilitate each other when the major goal is judgmental rather than creative [Rohrbaugh, 1979].

Programmable Decisions

How much decision making of a policy nature really fits the requirements for a creative designation is an open question. In many cases there are so many constraints and restrictions operating that attempts to generate a list of new and original options are pointless. What is needed is to determine *the* best solution to the problem within the limited options available.

Research on these kinds of programmable problems, where there is an answer if it can only be found, does not indicate the same inhibiting effects of group interactions as with creative decisions. A person can be wrong in such a situation; but as long as he stays within the reasonable bounds established by the problem, he does not risk being labelled a "nut" by others. And these bounds are relatively easy to determine, in contrast with the creative decision situation where the high level of uncertainty involved makes it much more likely that one might burst forth with an "absolutely idiotic" idea.

Where the decision is one of making an economic investment under known constraints, such as deciding where among several alternatives to locate a new plant, or whether or not to manufacture a particular product batch [Schoner, Rose, and Hoyt, 1974], or involves troubleshooting an existing operation [Green, 1975], group discussion is at least as effective as a more individualized approach and it may be more so. These are cases where the alternatives are relatively clear. The real needs are to develop an appropriate method for coming to a decision, to apply sufficient judgment to know when a reasonably correct decision has been worked out, and to avoid adopting a poor decision. In these respects group discussion and interaction can be very helpful, and the more traditional business decision-making approach appears to be entirely appropriate.

A question arises in such cases regarding the role that the person in charge should assume. Most of the research has utilized unstructured groups with any leadership being emergent at best. Recently, however, some research has begun to address this issue. The conclusion is that leadership does make a difference, especially when acceptance of the final outcome by the members of the group is an important consideration. Under such circumstances good results are likely to be obtained with an essentially nondirective style [Miner, 1979:83–84]:

1. State the problem in such a way that the group does not become defensive but instead approaches the issue in a constructive way.
2. Supply essential facts and clarify the area of freedom without suggesting a solution.
3. Draw members out so that all members will participate.
4. Restate expressed ideas and feelings more briefly, accurately, pointedly, and clearly.
5. Ask questions that stimulate problem-solving behavior.
6. Summarize as the need arises.

Negotiated Decisions

Negotiated decision making is by its very nature at least partly a group process. In general, we tend to view this type of decision situation as being limited to collective bargaining between union and management, purchasing negotiations, bargaining over conditions of sale, and certain similar activities. There is a tendency to consider negotiated decision making as something that only occurs across the boundaries of an organization. This impression is misleading. It is precisely the fact that so much decision making within organizations is of a negotiated nature that accounts for the widespread use of meetings and group discussions. Perhaps there is a greater use of this approach than there needs to be; perhaps even many negotiated decisions should not be considered as involving decision making in the usual sense of the term at all, being more in the nature of conflict reduction or coordination efforts. Be that as it may, negotiation does imply a group rather than an individual approach to the decision process.

One might expect in companies, where authority generally resides at the top and is typically accepted as such, that there would be little need to negotiate decisions. This would seem to be particularly true at the policy level. Do top level executives really need to negotiate, say, with the somewhat lower level managers who will implement the policies? Within a relatively wide band of acceptable alternatives they probably do not, but one can imagine instances where this would not be true.

A company may, for example, be considering a pricing policy that involves a certain amount of implicit collusion with competitors or an arrangement with a union that is not specifically stated in the formal contract. Such strategies and policies can involve some personal risk to the managers who implement them. If these managers should not wish to assume these risks and, in fact, might consider resigning before doing so, then the decisions at issue had best become negotiated decisions. There is little point in establishing policies that no one is willing to implement.

Perhaps these are extreme cases, but negotiating decisions among managers at the same level is a common practice and, where implementation is a major concern, there must inevitably be some implicit, if not explicit, negotiation. Furthermore, the terms of the employment contract, what the organization will give to the individual and what the individual will give to the organization, typically provide a continuing basis for negotiated decision making.

Although research on bargaining and negotiation is still in its infancy, a certain amount has been learned that can be translated into guidelines for action [MacMillan, 1978; Miner, 1978; Rubin and Brown, 1975]. As in other group decision contexts, attention from others tends to be viewed as evaluative and, accordingly, those doing the negotiating often try to please those who are watching. A manager who represents his department can become very intransigent when the views of the department are widely known. Thus, separating negotiators physically from constituencies and minimizing representative loyalties often help to make a generally acceptable decision possible.

Bargaining on one's own ground is an asset. If a manager wants to get his view across, it does help to have the meeting held in *his* office and to sit behind *his* desk. Intangible issues, such as the self-esteem of individuals or past animosities, often tend to deflect the decision-making process. Generally those who introduce them and feel strongly about them win on the intangible questions only at the expense of loss on the immediate tangible issue; getting off into intangibles is not a wise strategy. Since decisions in many areas result from a series of gradual concessions by those involved, it is in one's self-interest to start with as extreme a position as possible, without being so outrageous as to antagonize everyone.

One of the most important considerations, if negotiated decision making is to be effective, is that those involved get a clear picture of what each wants and what the attached utilities are. This may require considerable initial discussion and sparring. It is important to learn what the value of any concession might be. Within stable management groups much of this process has already occurred in the past. But new issues and circumstances can upset the existing balance of utilities drastically. Thus, it is important to let the negotiation process expand in time to the extent necessary and possible. Negotiated decision making at its best is not a means to quick action.

DO GROUPS TAKE MORE RISKS?

It is apparent that a great many business decisions are made in groups, whether or not they should be. Given this fact it becomes important to identify any special problems that may be associated with group decision making. Perhaps if one is aware that such problems are potentially present, it might be possible to avoid them.

One such problem is a tendency for groups to shift, beyond the degree individuals would, to risky decisions—or under certain circumstances to more cautious decisions. The latter appears to be less common, but it does occur. In both cases, although explanatory theories abound, the phenomena are much more clearly in evidence than the reasons for their occurrence [Davis, Laughlin, and Komorita, 1976; Ebert and Mitchell, 1975].

The Nature of Risky Shift

A sizable number of studies have demonstrated that there is a tendency for individuals to be more willing to accept high-risk decisions after participating in a group discussion— decisions they would not have made previously. When this process appears, and it is by no means universal, the following phenomena seem to occur [Clark, 1971]:

1. The average preferred decision for the group as a whole shifts in a risky direction.
2. There is greater agreement in the group, converging on this more risky position.
3. No individual moves to a decision any more risky than that preferred by the riskiest group member before the discussion began.
4. The preponderance of comments in the discussion tend to favor risk.

Although much of the research establishing this phenomenon has utilized decision situations far removed from the economic sphere and the policy-making context, there are more immediately relevant findings also. Risky shift has been found in making decisions about investments in new business projects, and the degree of risk taking tends to increase with the length of time spent in discussion [Streufert and Streufert,

1970]. Risky shift was also found in a study of stock market investment decisions made by business students majoring in the finance area [Deets and Hoyt, 1970].

Policy Implications

There is nothing in all this to indicate that risky decisions are necessarily bad; certain firms at certain points in their development need to take risks, even though they certainly would be expected to do all they could to minimize adverse consequences. Nor can it be assumed that discussion, among a group of top-level executives for instance, will invariably yield a high-risk decision. There are clearly many conformity pressures operating in any group situation, and a group composed of very cautious and conservative managers is unlikely to move very far in the direction of risk; in fact, many managers in this situation may move in the opposite direction after discussion. But given at least one advocate of a high-risk course of action, the potentiality for risky shift becomes real [Roberts and Castore, 1972].

This means that group composition becomes an important consideration. The potential for risky shift is only as great as the most risky position taken by a member going into the discussion, and the probability of occurrence is clearly related to the number of high-risk advocates involved. Thus the risk level of policy recommendations from a committee, for instance, can be controlled by knowing something about the initial views of potential members and constituting the committee accordingly [Cecil, Cummings, and Chertkoff, 1973].

This type of outcome is not limited to the situation where a true group decision is made as with committee recommendations. A manager may become engaged in a discussion with a number of subordinates and subsequently shift to a riskier alternative than he would have selected without the discussion. This becomes increasingly true to the extent the subordinates favor high-risk alternatives. The decision to fire an inefficient employee, who also happens to be the son of a major customer, is much more likely to occur after discussions with other managers at least some of whom favor the separation or some other such punitive action.

GROUP COHESION AND GROUPTHINK

In the case of risky shift the major concern is with group processes. However, groups can also produce a temporary loss of conscience; stable groups such as the top management of a company can maintain such an effect over a considerable period of time.

This effect tends to occur in the presence of a cohesive group; a group whose members experience a sense of emotional closeness that makes them stick together even when external pressures are working to break them up. The phenomenon has been labelled "groupthink" by Irving Janis [1972], who has documented it primarily with reference to decisions at the top levels of the federal government—the Bay of Pigs invasion of Cuba, the escalation of the Korean War, Pearl Harbor, and the escalation of the Vietnam War. He later extended his analysis to the Nixon administrations' decisions *vis à vis*

Watergate. Corporate examples of the same process abound, although reduced visability makes them harder to document [Janis and Mann, 1977].

Janis' point is that the more friendly and close the members of an in-group, the greater the chance that independent critical thinking and realistic moral judgment will be suspended in favor of group norms and conviviality. The result is groupthink, with the following consequences:

1. A belief in the group's basic morality so strong that ethical consequences of decisions are ignored.
2. A stereotyped view of some outside enemy (a competing firm) as evil, weak, or stupid.
3. A sense of invulnerability that encourages optimism and risk taking.
4. Efforts to rationalize so that warnings from outside are discounted and assumptions are not reconsidered.
5. Direct pressure on members not to express arguments against group positions under threat of being considered disloyal.
6. Self-censorship to the point where doubts regarding the wisdom of the group consensus are suppressed.
7. A shared sense of unanimity born out of the self-censorship and a view that silence must mean agreement.
8. The emergence of certain members who protect the group from information that might interfere with the cohesion-induced irrationality, irresponsibility, and immorality.

In addition to high cohesiveness, several other conditions tend to foster groupthink. These include some degree of insulation of the group from the outside world, a lack of methodical procedures for searching out and evaluating alternatives, a highly directive leader, and a sizable amount of stress surrounding the decision [Janis and Mann, 1977]. The result is a failure fully to examine alternatives, objectives, and risks, a general tendency to defensive avoidance, and in the end a defective decision on both rational and moral grounds.

The overlap between risky shift and groupthink is obvious. Most important, both represent major threats to the integrity of decisions arising out of a group context. There are dangers inherent in a group approach above and beyond those noted in our consideration of the inhibitory effects on creative thinking. These dangers may not be insurmountable, but they often have not been surmounted. Perhaps with full knowledge of their potential impact, policy makers of the future can take steps to see that they do not emerge or that their consequences are minimized.

CONSTITUTING A MANAGEMENT TEAM FOR DECISION MAKING

Selecting the members of a group to control and adjust risk-taking propensities is not the only way in which decision outcomes may be influenced by group composition.

At least three other considerations appear to have an influence. One is the extent to which the members of a group are similar to each other, another is the degree of social skill possessed by the various people, and a third is the number of individuals involved. Although in many instances it is not possible to manipulate such factors, as in the case where those who are in certain positions must be included in a given discussion, there are other occasions when one has more discretion. This is true of many committees and project teams constituted for a specific purpose.

The Effects of Similarities and Differences

Groups may be constituted to contain people whose abilities, knowledge, attitudes, values, and personality characteristics are very similar or, on the other hand, sizable differences between members may be introduced. A considerable amount of attention has been given to such considerations in the research that has been done on group decision making [Ebert and Mitchell, 1975; Huber, 1980].

It is apparent that the more similar the members, the easier it is for them to work together, to understand each other, and to get right at the task at hand. Diversity is almost certain to bring on some conflict and misunderstanding. Groups in which there are large differences between individuals have a difficult time getting organized; sometimes they never do settle their differences sufficiently to get on with the job.

On the other hand, diversity brings varied abilities, information, viewpoints, and approaches to a problem. Where everyone has roughly the same background, knowledge, values, and the like, even if these are well focused in terms of the requirements of the specific problem, there is a paucity of resources for generating alternatives. It is like having a single individual rather than many.

In fact, there is a strong parallel between the similarity versus difference question and the individual versus group one. This parallel extends to the solution. Where the decision is essentially of the programmable type, similar individuals can easily get down to programming it. Alternatives are limited in any event, and people who think alike can usually find the right or best answer relatively quickly because they can focus their energies on the problem rather than on conflicts within the group.

Where the problem requires a creative decision, however, diversity has its value for the same reason that the average group is superior to the average single individual— more worthwhile alternatives are generated. Even the inhibitory impact of group discussion and the almost inevitable conflict between individuals are not usually sufficient to offset the advantages of greater resources. Thus, on creative decisions, constituting the group out of quite dissimilar people, even if the situation is such as to require initial and continuing face to face discussion, appears desirable. In particular, diversity in the degree to which members like to dominate or direct others is needed.

SIMILARITIES AND DIFFERENCES IN THE REAL WORLD. Typically the research in this area has not been conducted with ongoing groups in real organizations. A question arises as to how applicable it really is. Policy-making groups, for instance, are usually made up of people who have worked together for a long time and the company structure itself produces an inherent organization for the group. Thus, diversity may not have as much negative impact as in the newly formed groups used in the research. Once conflicts are ironed out and procedures for working together are established, they can remain in that status while the group tackles many problems over a considerable period of time.

In addition, there are often more pressing considerations than similarity and diversity that condition assignment decisions. Take for instance an engagement team in a management consulting firm. Such teams can number from three to ten or more consultants. They are put together to serve a particular client. One might think that similarity would be a helpful feature for an engagement team working on a routine cost reduction study, whereas diversity should be stressed in assigning consultants to a complex marketing strategy study. Perhaps this is the case, but it is in fact, difficult to accomplish. Consultants must be assigned in terms of what they know, engagements must be started as soon as possible after the client requests them, and consultants must be kept busy so that as much of their time as possible is chargeable to a client. This means that as soon as a person frees up some time due to the completion or changed requirements of one engagement he must be assigned to another team where his skills are needed. One cannot wait to put together teams of similar or dissimilar people; the firm would quickly go out of business.

The same situation arises in the corporate setting where prior assignments, travel commitments, the nature of positions, and the like, all may influence the way in which groups are constituted. Yet a familiarity with the results of research into the effects of group similarities and differences can be useful in the limited number of cases where the results can be put to use.

THE DIALETICAL APPROACH TO STRATEGY FORMATION. One instance in which homogeneous groups have been utilized, apparently effectively, is described by Mason and Mitroff [1979] and Mitroff and Emshoff [1979]. It involves the use of a dialectical debate between groups advocating different positions to establish strategy. It is applicable to ill-structured problems on which agreement regarding appropriate strategy solutions cannot be obtained; nor can those involved agree on a methodology for developing a strategy or even clear formulation of the problem.

Two or more homogeneous groups are formed reflecting alternative viewpoints within the company. These groups are established so as to contain "maximum interpersonal similarity and affinity." This would involve a desire to work together, a desire to work on the same kind of tasks, and/or similarity in personality makeup [Kilman, 1977]. At the same time an effort is made to maximize differences, especially in knowledge and perspectives on the problem, between the groups.

The steps involved in developing a strategy are outlined in Figure 11-1. In the first stage there is an attempt to argue back from the existing strategy (or the closest thing to one) to the underlying assumptions behind this strategy. The opposites to these assumptions are then used in the second, dialectic phase to develop alternative new strategies. In step three the diverse range of options is considered with a veiw to obtaining agreement between the groups on a specific set of assumptions (but not at this point necessarily on strategy). Finally working forward on a logical basis from the set of acceptable assumptions a "best strategy" is defined.

This approach utilizes both within-group homogeneity and across-group heterogeneity

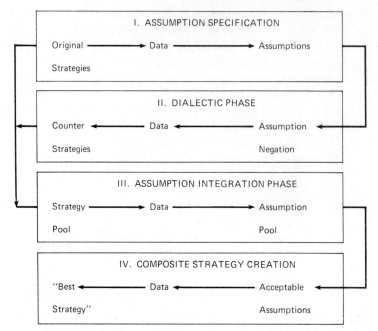

Figure 11-1 The steps in utilizing a dialectical approach to policy and planning. (Source: Ian I. Mitroff and James R. Emshoff: "On Strategic Assumption-Making: A Dialectical Approach to Policy and Planning." *Academy of Management Review,* January 1979, p. 5.) Reprinted by permission of the Academy of Management.

on the same problem; it may very well combine the advantages of both. On the other hand, solid empirical tests comparing the approach to others that might be used are lacking. There is a need for such research as a next step.

The Effects of Social Skill

There is good reason to believe that managers with highly developed social skills do better in group decision making. This has been demonstrated in creative decision contexts and with standardized simulations of managerial decision situations. Such people can be characterized as outgoing, self-assured, somewhat dominant and aggressive and enthusiastic. They are probably least likely to be inhibited in their expression of ideas before a group. On the other hand, they are not necessarily people who prefer making decisions in groups; quite the contrary may well be the case [Karmel, 1972].

The implication of these findings is that, where possible if group decisions are to be made, the groups should contain people with the social skills that facilitate interaction among members and the expression as well as effective utilization of ideas by the group. This sounds self-evident, yet in practice a sufficient number of decision-making groups are constituted of individuals who are uncomfortable, perhaps even quite anxious, in the group context to make the idea worth some repetition. There is no point having group decisions made by those who function at their worst in this type of social setting. Accordingly, if a top management group is to place heavy reliance on group decision making, social skill should be a criterion for selection to a position as an officer in the company.

The Effects of Group Size

The question of group size is of particular interest, not only in its own right but because it provides an indirect approach that can be used to deal effectively with the similarity-dissimilarity issue. There has been a continuing debate as to how large committees should be, how many people should serve on boards of directors, how large a group of subordinates should report to one superior, and similar problems [Cummings, Huber, and Arendt, 1974; House and Miner, 1969]. It is apparent that the answers in this regard are closely tied to both the nature of the decision to be made and the effects of similarities and differences among group members.

As a group gets larger, the range of any particular characteristic expands so that with eight people present it is almost triple that with only two. Thus larger groups are likely to contain sizable differences, with both the greater resources for problem solving and the greater potential for conflict that this implies. Second, as groups get larger, a member is more likely to find at least one other member who is quite similar to himself. As a consequence, there is an increasing probability of splintering and clique formation.

If the decision making required is at all complex, as many policy decisions are, small groups of up to four members tend to do poorly [Huber, 1980]. On the other hand this does not mean that size can be increased indefinitely with favorable results. Ultimately, the problems of coordination become overwhelming and decision quality suffers [Zander, 1979] as does the feeling of satisfaction with the group. Probably in most policy settings something in the range of from 8 to a maximum of 11 people is best. Such groups may find it difficult to come to complete agreement, but this should not be required if the person in charge takes responsibility for the final decision or even if a vote is employed. A group of this size is much more likely than either smaller or larger groups to develop an effective policy. Such limitations do not apply to contexts where interaction is restricted as with the nominal and delphi procedures, however. In these latter instances increased numbers are much more easily tolerated.

DECISION MAKING IN BOARDS OF DIRECTORS

At one time corporate boards functioned largely to legitimize decisions made elsewhere. Increasingly, however, as a result of external legal and social forces, this situation has changed so that boards have come to make a sizable number of important decisions that require a wide range of information inputs [Boulton, 1978]. The result is that decision making within the board of directors, long a neglected and perhaps also hidden matter, has now become a major topic of concern.

Constituting the Board for Decision Making

A question arises as to whether boards as currently constituted are suited to the new and expanded decision-making roles they now face. Insofar as size is concerned, it would appear that many firms are either below or above the optimal range [Miner, 1978]. The number of directors may range from a legally required three up into the 30s. The median size would appear to be 12 or 13, but the medians in banking and insurance are well above this. Board size tends to increase with company size, particularly in the manufacturing sector.

In general the problem of excessive size outweighs that of too few members. A great many boards are sufficiently large so that they inevitably foster clique formation and internal conflict. This tendency is exacerbated by an increasing tendency to structure board actions along committee lines. These committees, which typically include executive, compensation, stock option, audit, and finance among others, may be rather effective decision-making units within themselves, but at the whole board level they foster divisiveness. Coordinating decision making toward pursuit of corporate goals in such boards is no easy task.

This problem of coordinated action is compounded by the rapid growth in recent years in the proportion of directors whose primary employment is outside the company [Business Roundtable, 1978; Estes, 1977]. Among the larger companies now approximately 85 per cent have a majority of outside directors who are not officers of the company. Furthermore, as Table 11-2 indicates, these outside directors are themselves a diverse lot, coming from a wide range of occupational settings. This heterogeneity, although potentially functional as a source of ideas and knowledge (if it could be harnessed), may well prove unmanageable when injected into a board that is already of excessive size. If we add to this the fact that these outside directors tend to be rather independent people, have relatively little time to devote to board business, and often are not well informed regarding the particular company involved, it becomes apparent that many boards are not constituted so as to maximize decision-making effectiveness. Rather they are constituted to maximize internal conflict.

TABLE 11-2
Affiliations of 1103 Outside Directors in 156 Firms

AFFILIATION	PER CENT
Commercial banks, bank holding companies, savings banks	8.9
Investment banks, securities dealers, and underwriters	7.8
Pension and investment funds, foundations	1.5
Insurance companies	2.1
Consultants including accountants, professors, representatives of nonprofit institutions	9.6
Lawyers	7.9
Retired executives	13.8
Private investors and professional directors	3.0
Corporate executives (nonfinancial)	45.4

SOURCE: Adapted from Schmidt [1977:679].

Cooptation and Constituencies

Why, then, do companies place large numbers of outsiders on their boards? The answer appears to be that they wish to gain a degree of control over, and thus manage, their environments. By coopting significant representatives of groups and organizations in that environment, and thus bringing them inside the company, they hope at the very least to neutralize potentially threatening forces [Pfeffer and Salancik, 1978]. Business organizations would be expected to resort to cooptation in this manner:

1. With very large organizations, which would be costly to acquire.
2. With financial institutions, where total absorption is frequently forbidden by law.
3. With political bodies important to the organization, where merger is not feasible.
4. With special interest groups, which are temporarily politically potent.

Data indicate that indeed cooptation does occur along these lines. It appears to be most pronounced in the larger corporations, where the proportion of debt in the capital structure is sizable and when the firm is in a highly regulated industry. Failure to coopt outside forces to the necessary degree is associated with less effective financial performance. Thus, the use of cooptation through the placement of outsiders on corporate boards is not only a widely used method of coping with the organization's environment but an entirely appropriate one as well. Unfortunately, however, the prescribed cure for one malady—vulnerability to environmental threat—produces another problem—conflict-laden decision making—in the face of increasing pressures for a more significant board role in corporate decisions.

The difficulties associated with cooptation become especially pronounced where the individual joining the board does so to represent some constituency, rather than to foster the interests of the company itself. Examples would be representatives of labor unions (a legally mandated procedure in many parts of the world outside the United States), public interest directors, and members of pressure groups. In general the business community is opposed to the concept of constituency directors [Business Roundtable, 1978], but it has not been totally immune. Where constituency representation does become a factor in board selection, the decision-making process tends to shift to a negotiated form with some loss in organizational rationality and an escalation of conflict and controversy.

A major factor involved appears to be the degree of trust existing among board members. Where certain members represent outside constituencies and view it as their role to do so, others may naturally mistrust their commitment to company goals. Such a lack of trust within a group can seriously interfere with decision-making effectiveness when dealing with the type of problems with which boards of directors are concerned. This has been demonstrated in a study where groups of managers from the same company worked together to solve the joint problems of [Zand, 1972]:

1. Developing a strategy to increase short-term profits without undermining long-term growth of a medium-sized electronics company with a very low return on investment, outdated manufacturing facilities, whose labor force has been cut 25 per cent and

whose top management personnel had been changed and reorganized two years before.
2. Obtaining commitment to implement such a program despite strong managerial disappointment because expectations of immediate investment for expansion and modernization would not be met.

In dealing with these problems the managerial groups with lower trust were much less effective in clarifying their goals, in using realistic information, in searching for solutions, and in obtaining commitment to implement solutions. It seems safe to assume that constituting boards to include individuals who do not have the interests of the organization as a major concern can only create just this lack of trust among those who are primarily committed to the organization; decision making will suffer accordingly.

DECISION MAKING INVOLVING CONSULTANTS

Many important decisions in corporations, including those of a strategic nature, involve inputs from outside consultants; in some cases the degree of influence from this source is sizable. This involvement may occur through direct incorporation of consultants in company decision-making units, or groups of consultants (engagement teams) may be hired to make recommendations on certain issues. In either case consultant contributions tend to focus primarily on decision making rather than decision implementation, and the decision making is of a group nature.

General Management Consulting

The greatest influence on corporate, and probably also governmental, policy making comes from the general management consulting firms, many of whom have offices throughout the world. The typical procedure, when a firm of this kind is engaged, is for a group of consultants to work together on the assignment. This engagement team may also include representatives of the client company [Higdon, 1969; Hunt, 1977; Kubr, 1976].

Generally there is an initial diagnostic phase involving considerable interviewing of managers at various levels in the company and perusal of company data, particularly financial data. In addition, efforts are frequently made to relate the company's current position to other companies in the industry or industries in which it operates. In essence what is done is a situation audit of the kind described in Chapters 7 and 8. Ultimately, recommendations are developed that are presented to top management in both oral and written form. In many instances these recommendations represent some form of strategic planning.

As indicated in Table 11-3 the duration of an engagement varies considerably, depending on the depth of the analysis undertaken, the degree of consultant involvement in the implementation phase, and the availability of individual consultants. Since one person may be working on a number of engagements at once, availability may be an important consideration. On the average an engagement typically runs seven or eight months, but the amount of consultant time billed within that period can vary sharply.

TABLE 11-3
Duration and Number of Consultants Involved for 133 Engagements

DURATION	PER CENT	NUMBER OF CONSULTANTS	PER CENT
3 months or less	16	1 or 2	13
4 to 6 months	29	3 or 4	37
7 to 9 months	23	5 or 6	25
10 to 12 months	12	7 or 8	12
13 to 15 months	8	9 or 10	4
16 to 18 months	3	11 or 12	4
19 to 24 months	6	13 or 14	4
Over 24 months	3	Over 14	1

Similarly the number of consultants assigned to an engagement may range from one to fifteen or more, depending upon the specific circumstances. The typical engagement involves four or five individuals at some time during its course. Some of these may spend as little as an hour, providing advice on a particular aspect. But billings to a single engagement for one individual covering as much as 300 work days are not unheard of either; there is tremendous variability.

A frequently heard criticism of consultants is that they tend to view problems too narrowly through the prism of their own particular expertise and orientation, or, as Leavitt [1966] puts it, through their own "rose-colored blinders." On the other hand, the narrowness of some consulting recommendations may not be so much a function of the limitations of the consultant's perspective as of the way in which the problem is presented by the client and the limits placed on investigation. In any event the great majority of decisions with which general management consultants deal appear to be of a programmable nature—a solution utilized elsewhere on a previous engagement is applied. This does not necessarily mean that the consultants start with a solution and then reconstruct the problem to fit, although that can happen. Much more likely is that they select a solution from among those they have used in the past which fits the demands of the existing situation. Thus, the consultant role is to transfer technology and expertise to a new context. Given the noncreative nature of such decisions, the use of group decision-making procedures appears entirely appropriate.

Organization Development Consulting

A considerable amount has been written in the past decade about the use of organization development in changing organizations; recently several books have focused more directly on organization development consulting [Abramson and Halset, 1979; Blake and Mouton, 1976; Lippitt and Lippitt, 1978]. These latter books make it clear that the external consultant role is an important one, but matters of corporate policy and strategy are not always given much attention. When organization development consultants do deal directly with policy matters, their approach leads them to involve people at lower levels in the organization more than the general management consultants do.

As described by Paine and Naumes [1978] the organization development approach to policy and strategy formation has five major characteristics. Several of these are not unlike those of approaches considered previously in this book. Thus, the effort involves a systematic diagnosis aimed at identifying relevant factors, and then the establishment of action steps that can be expected to lead to improved strategies and their implementation. In short the organization-development process is planned, just as many other policy formation efforts are.

Second, the organization-development approach to policy formation has organization-wide ramifications or, at the very least, ramifications for a major segment of the organization. This too is characteristic of other approaches to policy formation, but it is not nearly as characteristic of organization-development efforts that do not focus directly on policy matters.

Third, as in other approaches to policy development, top management involvement and commitment are important. Although top managers may be the analysts on certain occasions, it is more common for top management to endorse the combined efforts of external consultants and lower level groups.

Fourth, the approach achieves its ends through planned interventions using particular analytical and developmental tools. Here the organization-development approach to policy formation tends to part company with other policy formation approaches; it is more like other kinds of organization-development efforts. However, there is a somewhat greater emphasis on market, economic, and financial factors. The approach to problems is one of sharing information and attempts at solutions widely throughout the firm.

Finally, the approach focuses on coalitions and groups in the decision context rather than on individuals. There is a major concern with establishing problem-solving processes involving group and intergroup interactions out of which corporate strategies will emerge.

The important point here is that the consultant does not serve primarily as an advocate for a particular policy, such as expansion through acquisitions, or promotion from within, or a major emphasis on leasing. His advocacy is generally limited to a particular approach to the policy-formation process characterized by widespread involvement throughout the organization and a group emphasis in problem solving. "Outside advisors, assessors or consultants often share the responsibility with managers for the problem-solving and development process, but they also work with managers toward increasing the organization's own capacity to diagnose the external and internal environment and to develop and carry through strategic plans of action" [Paine and Naumes, 1978:163].

What has already been said makes it clear that organization development, whatever its central concern, tends to advocate a participative, democratic approach to the management of organizations. The values are humanistic rather than pragmatic, egalitarian rather than hierarchic, democratic rather than authoritarian. These values serve to establish premises for the decision-making process such that the decisions themselves tend to become programmable. Certain kinds of decisions, policies, and strategies are consistent with organization-development values; others are not. Furthermore, there is a tendency to draw from an established bag of approaches and techniques just as the general management consultants do. Thus, the strong group decision-making emphasis in organization-development consulting appears appropriate to the task at hand. Once again, as with general management consulting, programmable decisions are combined with group discussion as a major approach to the decision process.

Leading Edge Consulting

The discussion to this point would suggest that consulting is primarily a matter of applying known solutions to previously defined problems—and thus highly programmable in its decision processes. To a very large extent this is true. What is involved is not so much problem solving, in the sense of producing creative solutions, as the transportation of existing solutions from other contexts. Yet this is not the whole story. There are consultants who offer highly creative services, but not within a group framework.

Typically these are individuals located either in university settings, or sometimes within general management consulting firms, or within small, highly specialized consulting organizations. They are themselves researchers and developers of new knowledge, and they consult in the areas they research. Because of their research, and perhaps teaching and theoretical interests, they may be informed about certain areas well in advance of other consultants. In this sense they are at the "leading edge" and in a position to offer truly creative solutions to corporate problems.

Such individuals tend, appropriately enough, to do their consulting on an individual basis. Although they may offer their solutions to a group of managers, their decision making does not occur in a group context. For very important decisions, which would warrant the cost, several consultants of this kind should be hired to develop their own separate solutions to a problem, in a manner comparable to the nominal group process. Then these solutions should be combined by bringing the leading edge consultants together, or by delphi procedures, or by having management members argue the various positions in a discussion context. What is important is that consultants of this kind be allowed to make their decisions originally on an independent basis, rather than within the group framework that characterizes most consulting decision making.

CONCLUDING COMMENTS

This chapter and the one preceding have considered a great range of factors that may operate within the organization to influence the effectiveness of policy decisions. It is apparent that the capabilities and characteristics of individuals make a sizable difference and that in many cases it might be advisable for individuals to work on problems more independently than they normally do.

It is also apparent that, if groups are to be used in connection with the decision process, they often can be used more effectively than they usually are. Such considerations as the risky shift phenomenon, groupthink, similarities and differences, social skills, group size, and trust can have a profound impact on the way in which organizational decisions are made and on the policies and strategies that are developed. With a knowledge of the ways in which these effects occur, it should be possible to upgrade policy and strategy decisions considerably. There are a wide range of individual, group, and decision-related factors at work, and sorting them out in a given instance is not easy. Our knowledge at this point does not permit the presentation of a series of simple, easily applied normative statements. But it does provide a framework within which sizable advances in decision capability can occur.

QUESTIONS

Discussion Guides on Chapter Content
1. How do creative, programmable, and negotiated decisions differ? Give examples of each.
2. What is the relative effectiveness of nominal group, delphi, and discussion group approaches to decision making? When would each appear to be called for? Define these approaches and cite the evidence.
3. What is risky shift? What are its policy implications? How might it be avoided if that seemed appropriate?
4. What are the consequences of groupthink? Why would they not occur in a noncohesive group? What factors other than cohesiveness contribute to groupthink?
5. What is the evidence regarding the effects of similarities and differences within a group on decision effectiveness? Why might it be difficult actually to utilize what is known in this area to improve decisions?
6. What is the dialectical approach to strategy formation and how does it work? How does it relate to the homogeneity-heterogeneity research?
7. How does the size of a group affect its decision-making processes and capabilities? Compare nominal and discussion group procedures in this regard.
8. What factors often contribute to making boards of directors much less effective decision-making units than they could be? How does cooptation relate to this problem?
9. Differentiate among general management consulting, organization-development consulting at the policy level, and organization-development consulting more generally? How does each relate to group decision making?

Mind Stretching Questions
1. This chapter presents a great deal of evidence regarding the effectiveness of various group and individual decision-making approaches, but there are many loose ends as well. What additional questions need to be answered? What research is called for? How might this research be conducted?
2. If you were constituting an ongoing decision-making group, such as the executive committee of a major corporation, how would you do it? What factors would you take into account?
3. You are the chief executive of a large corporation and feel that you need assistance in strategy planning. What considerations would you take into account in deciding whether or not to use a consultant and in selecting a consultant? What would your decision regarding a consultant be? Why?

12

Alternative Approaches to Decision Making

INTRODUCTION

Given all the discussion about planning and decision making that precedes, it seems paradoxical to raise a question as to how important such activities are in the day to day life of top level managers. Yet this question has been raised, and there are a number of early studies that appear to indicate that, although managers often spend considerable time searching for information, they typically spend much less time actually making decisions [Dubin, 1962; Sayles, 1964]. This viewpoint has been affirmed by Mintzberg [1973:38].

The pressure of the managerial environment does not encourage the development of reflective planners. . . . The job breeds adaptive information manipulators who prefer the live, concrete situation. The manager works in an environment of stimulus-response, and he develops in his work a clear preference for live action.

Yet there are a number of studies that indicate planning and decision making require considerable time of many executives, particularly those at the highest levels [Holden, Pederson, and Germane, 1968; Mahoney, Jerdee, and Carroll, 1965; Miner, 1971]. The conflicting conclusions appear to reflect variations in methods of study and in the samples of managers considered. Direct observation of managers at work in their offices is not an approach conducive to revealing how much time these managers spend making decisions; one cannot see them think and, in any event, they may well do much of their thinking and planning outside the office. Only self-reports by the managers themselves can provide an indication of the time spent in decision making and planning, and when this approach is used many do emerge as devoting considerable time to such activities [Stieglitz, 1969; Heidrick and Struggles, 1972; Quinn, 1981].

Yet there clearly are other top level executives who perform their jobs quite differently. They spend relatively little time in decision making; either they do not make many decisions, or they use approaches to their decisions that are not very time consuming.

When studies utilize a rather small number of executives, there is always a good chance that a disproportionate number of those who spend little time on decisions will be included. This, too, appears to have contributed to the finding in some studies of a relatively low level of involvement in planning and decision making.

VARIATIONS AMONG MANAGERS

If nothing else the studies of managerial work point up the fact that major differences exist in the time managers devote to decisions. This is, of course, in part a consequence of the nature and consequences of the particular decisions to be made, a matter that will concern us later in this chapter. But it is also a consequence of the way in which specific executives and companies approach the decision-making process. One financial executive faced with the need to come up with a method of financing a projected expansion project may spend days evaluating the pros and cons of various alternatives; another, faced with the same problem, may hardly hesitate before attempting to work out details with a bank with which he has dealt on numerous occasions in the past.

The Formal Structured Approach

Planning and decision making that is formally structured follows procedures that have been laid down beforehand. Structured planning usually involves a number of people and an extensive search for information. Above all else it strives to be rational and systematic. When applied to the planning process, this formal approach is usually referred to by some such terms as long-range planning, comprehensive planning, comprehensive corporate planning, integrated planning, overall planning, or corporate planning. In such cases it almost always eventuates in a written document.

However, a similar formal approach can be applied to any decision of consequence, including the development of policies. Staff reports may be prepared and a standard sequence of individual analysis followed by group analysis may be employed, especially if the decision is creative in nature. The crucial point is that the attack on the problem follows some systematic and explicitly stated procedure.

The Intuitive-Anticipatory Approach

In contrast to formally structured planning, the intuitive-anticipatory approach does not follow any explicitly stated process [Steiner, 1979a]. In fact, no one really knows the precise mental processes and steps introduced. Generally only one person is involved, such as the chief executive officer. Although written documents may result, this tends not to be the case. Typically, the decision plan or strategy applies to events within a short time horizon. Executives who stress the intuitive approach are not usually prone to engage in long-term projections and planning for the far-distant future. Basically, what occurs is that the executive has a "gut" feeling that a particular alternative is the right one, based on past experience. How he got to this feeling and why this particular choice is the best one are things the manager cannot specify with any degree of certainty.

He simply has a hunch that this is the thing to do, and he has deve
confidence in his hunches over the years.

Such an approach can involve a telescoping of years of observatioi
Many managers have a great capacity to learn from their past failur
and to apply this knowledge to new, but similar, situations. If one can
is compressed into a single intuitive decision, a highly complex analytic pi
Attempts to do this and represent the thinking involved in the form c
program attest to this fact [Simon, 1979]. The result can be a brilliant
very insightful decision. However, because there is no way of checking (
and rationality of the various steps in the decision process, the potentiality ⌐ı error is
also very high. Furthermore, managers who have experienced some success with the
intuitive approach often find it extremely personally satisfying, with the result that they
may utilize it to the exclusion of other approaches more appropriate to a particular
decision.

The Entrepreneurial Opportunistic Approach

There is also an approach that stresses finding and utilizing opportunity. The focus
is on opportunity identification rather than problem solving. Such a manager is constantly
searching for new types of business ventures, new products, and new markets. In many
respects this approach is prototypic for the entrepreneur, and it usually involves the
assumption of high levels of risk.

However, as Mintzberg [1973] emphasizes, the entrepreneurial role is not limited to
the small business enterprise. Managers in large organizations can become extensively
involved in a variety of improvement projects—self-initiated change efforts designed
to exploit opportunities. Again, this is an approach that may be totally alien to one
manager, while representing the major thrust of another manager's efforts. As with
the typical entrepreneur, such a manager is constantly on the alert to identify new
opportunities both within the organization and outside and to develop methods of exploit-
ing them.

The Incrementing Approach

The incrementing approach is best illustrated in the writings of Charles Lindblom
[1959, 1965], who uses the term *disjointed incrementalism* to describe it. It is characterized
as follows:

1. Rather than attempting a comprehensive survey and evaluation of alternatives, as
   in the formal structured approach, the decision maker focuses only on those policy
   alternatives that differ incrementally from existing policies.
2. Only a relatively small number of policy alternatives are considered.
3. For each policy alternative only a restricted number of consequences considered important are evaluated.
4. The problem is continually redefined, allowing for countless ends-means and means-
   ends adjustments, which make the problem more manageable.

Thus, it is assumed that there is no one right decision; there is a never-ending series of attacks on the issues at hand through serial analyses and evaluation.

6. As such the incrementing approach is remedial, geared more to the alleviation of present concrete imperfections than to the promotion of future goals.

Lindblom has referred to this approach as "muddling through." It is heavily concerned with obtaining agreement and seeks to simplify the decision process to make it more manageable or even manageable at all. Such an approach tends to result in decisions that are typically of the negotiated type.

The Adaptive Approach

The adaptive approach takes a somewhat different form as described by different authors. However, it has in common the idea of adapting or changing one's strategy depending upon the way existing circumstances are perceived. The adaptive search approach of Ansoff [1965] involves the following:

1. A successive narrowing and refining of decision rules depending upon the circumstances.
2. Thus, a cascade of decisions with feedback between stages.
3. A process of gap reduction within these stages. This involves:
   (a) Establishing a set of objectives.
   (b) Estimating the gap between the current position of the firm and the objectives.
   (c) Proposing one or more courses of action.
   (d) Testing these courses of action for their capacity to reduce the gap.
4. Adaptation of the objectives and the starting point evaluation.

Ackoff [1970] elaborates upon this adaptive approach with reference to the states of certainty; uncertainty, as ignorance regarding the future, resides in the decision maker's mind. Where near certainty exists, one can commit oneself to a given course of action consonant with the anticipated future. Where there is uncertainty, but it is possible to be relatively sure regarding the available possibilities, contingency planning is required; thus it is possible quickly to exploit the opportunities once the future becomes evident. Finally, where there is ignorance regarding an aspect of the future, responsiveness must be built into the system so that it can detect deviation from the expected rapidly and respond accordingly.

Under uncertainty and ignorance this adaptive approach involves relatively less attention to search and choice activities. Rather, there is more stress on building up a capacity to respond quickly when action is called for [Ackoff, 1970]. A manager utilizing such an approach needs to monitor his company's environment very closely to detect the first signs of change. He must then have the contingency plans or the capacity for response available, ready to bring to bear when the occasion calls for it; he must have the resources to implement the appropriate contingency plan or simply to respond in some manner.

Although such an approach does not require forecasting as such, it substitutes extensive monitoring and data collection. It is also costly in terms of planning costs (because many of the contingency plans may never be needed) and it often requires considerable stockpiling of resources. An example would be an approach that attempted to respond to any sign of a build up of competition in any local market area with a direct head-to-head challenge in kind to the particular strategy employed by the competitor. To be effective, this would require a very rapid response and, thus, a standing inventory of money, people, and products. Yet it is Ansoff's [1979a; 1979b] firm belief that the turbulent environments of the future will introduce increasing amounts of uncertainty and ignorance, thus requiring a high degree of adaptive capacity.

Variations in the Ways Problems Are Perceived

The variations in approaches reflected in designations such as formal structured, intuitive-anticipatory, entrepreneurial opportunistic, incremental, and adaptive occur in terms of the way decisions are approached. These five do not exhaust all such possibilities, but they do serve to illustrate the great variability among managers. However, there is another source of variability that appears to be at least as important. This is a function of the way in which a problem is perceived.

An instructive example of how variable these perceptions may be is provided by a study of how different teams of individuals approached a simulated top management decision [Norman, 1967]. The teams had to react to a major reduction in materials requirements, which produced a reduction of 25 per cent in direct manufacturing costs. Each of the nine teams tended to focus on a different aspect of the problem. The nine results were as follows:

Team 1 structured its decisions around its estimates of the changes in the total industry market.
Team 2 searched for an efficient level of sales in a given market.
Team 3 geared its decisions to a desired percentage of the market.
Team 4 focused on an efficient level of production and operating efficiency.
Team 5 tried to make and sell just as many units as possible.
Team 6 attempted to copy successful competitors.
Team 7 concentrated on pricing procedures that would yield the maximum revenue.
Team 8 established and held to a top industry price.
Team 9 focused on inventory and inventory control.

Each of these teams was faced with the same problem; yet each saw that problem differently and developed strategies accordingly. It is little wonder that the profitability of competing firms often varies so widely.

THE CONTROVERSY OVER DECISION APPROACHES

There has been much controversy over the years regarding how managers should and do make decisions. The position with the longest history is the one that emphasizes organizational rationality and the maximization of expected utility—the concept of *economic man.* This position, as noted in Chapter 9, has been attacked as unrealistic by both the incrementalists and advocates of so-called *administrative man,* who consider satisficing rather than maximizing as more characteristic of the real world of managerial decisions. These latter two positions have in turn come under attack on a variety of grounds including the view that both "muddling through" and satisficing settle for too little, and thus do not permit major change. Further confounding this picture is a considerable amount of uncertainty as to whether a given viewpoint is intended to be normative or descriptive or both.

Problems with the Maximizing View

The initial attacks on the maximizing concept by Herbert Simon [1976] are well known. Essentially Simon felt that maximizing is not what managers actually do; rather they make the choice that occurs to them first and is at the same time good enough for the intended purpose (satisfice). These views seem to have evolved at the present time into the following three criticisms of the maximizing concept:

1. Although it is appropriate to consider firms and the individuals in them as having objectives, it is not true that these objectives are pursued in the maximizing mode.
2. The idea that firms or their decision makers have objectives for which a preference ordering of the states of nature always results in the choice of the most preferred alternative is unrealistic.
3. Mazimizing is virtually impossible because the information required and the time and money to obtain it are limited.

All this does not necessarily say that some kind of mazimizing is not, and should not be, what managers *strive* for. Thus, *good* decision making might be gauged in terms of the degree of approximation to, or effort expended to attain, the maximizing ideal. On the other hand, a normative theory of satisficing or muddling through would argue that all this effort to mazimize is not worth the expenditure of energy and money involved.

Problems with Not Maximizing

Concerns over the incrementalist and satisficing approaches take both a normative and a descriptive tack [Etzioni, 1967; Michael, 1973]. Many feel that both approaches set only minimal standards for decision making, at least in terms of decision quality, and are to a large degree directionless. Even if decisions have been made this way in the past, they should not be in the future. Approaches of this kind are considered to be inconsistent with effective long-range planning and a structured formal approach to the planning process. Settling for satisficing and incremental change comes very close to encouraging nonrational and irrational decision making.

Furthermore, neither approach (satisficing or incrementing) seems adequate to the task of explaining how decisions in favor of major change occur. The incrementalist approach as such virtually precludes this possibility. The satisficing approach makes it very unlikely. Yet the annals of business history are full of instances where decision makers have instituted fundamental and far-reaching changes in their organizations [Chandler, 1962; 1977]. In view of the uncertainties that emerge from so much of the writing in this area, it is not surprising that solutions have increasingly been sought in research.

Studies of Real-Life Decisions

Although research on decision making has not always focused on top management policy making, there are a number of studies of the decision process in a context where the consequences are real and the incentive to do well sizable. This research clearly reveals that the alternative approaches previously considered are not sufficient to explain all of what actually happens when decisions are made. In particular, many people appear to be neither maximizers or satisficers, but rather are best described as confirmers or validators [Cecil and Lundgren, 1975; Soelberg, 1966].

Such individuals continue to search for information for some time after they have already located a satisfactory alternative, but they do not truly attempt to maximize. They tend to establish a preferred choice early in the decision-making process and then rapidly reduce the number of possible choices to two—the preferred alternative and one other. From then on the search process is devoted largely to validating or confirming the preferred choice.

The data seem to indicate that, where a decision makes several approaches feasible, some people will seek to maximize, some will satisfice, and some will validate or confirm early choices. Information on these three approaches as related to the decision to accept a job after graduating from college is given in Table 12-1. It is important to note that the maximizing mode is approximated by a sizable proportion of the students, although of course their search for alternative companies is ultimately limited by time constraints. Furthermore, those students who have had more, and more diversified, work experience are the ones who are most likely to resort to maximizing [Glueck, 1974]. This would suggest that experienced policy makers may well be more likely to attempt to maximize than to settle for less demanding approaches.

TABLE 12-1
Alternative Approaches to a Job Choice Decision

DECISION APPROACH	CHARACTERISTIC SEARCH PATTERN	CHOICE PROCEDURE	PER CENT OF INDIVIDUALS
Maximizing	Comprehensive—talk to as many companies as possible	Choose the company offering the most of what is wanted in a position	47
Validating or confirming	Moderate—continue searching until have two acceptable offers	Validate initial choice so as to justify it	30
Satisficing	Restricted—stop looking as soon as first satisfactory offer is received	Accept first satisfactory offer	23

SOURCE: Adapted from Glueck [1974:80].

Analyses of top-level decisions related to major investments and to acquisitions indicate that extensive search extending over multiple levels of the organization can occur, but that there is a certain amount of negotiated decision making as well [Carter, 1971]. Furthermore, it is clear that top-level decisions may be made with reference to goals other than profit maximization and that on occasion estimates of marginal costs and profits are only roughly made at best. Yet there is reason to believe that those firms which more nearly approximate a formal, structured, rational approach to decisions are more likely to be profitable [Stagner, 1969].

Data derived from this study of top-level decision making in over 100 firms are given in Table 12-2. From these data it would seem that, to the extent a firm can approximate the formal structured approach on most decisions, it will benefit accordingly. However, the goal pursued may not be profit at the expense of all else. At least one other goal is of considerable importance and that is the public image of the company. However, the data in this regard may well be reflecting the fact that such a concern for the realities of the social environment can contribute indirectly to profits. Always making decisions solely in an attempt to maximize the direct profitability of a particular decision may not always return the greatest profits overall.

Organized Anarchies

In certain situations, such as universities [March and Olsen, 1976] and some research and development contexts [McCaskey, 1979], rationality may be very difficult to attain in any form; in fact it has been argued that in such contexts a goodly dose of foolishness and acting before one thinks is to be desired [March and Olsen, 1976]. The contexts considered are characterized by very fuzzy concepts of the organization's goals, with objectives typically being discovered in the course of action rather than determining action; a heavy reliance upon trial-and-error, with little real understanding of organizational processes; and a fluid type of member participation, where people join and leave

---

TABLE 12-2
Characteristics of Decision Making in More Profitable Firms ($N = 109$)

There is a concern over formal steps in decision making at the top level including regular meetings, written records, and attention to formal routines.

Estimates of costs and anticipated profits to results from a decision are always carefully computed.

Discussions at the top level include all executives affected by the decision.

A top-level policy committee or operating committee is actively used in the decision-making process.

Social interaction among top executives outside office hours and for nonbusiness purposes is frequent.

The chief executive is concerned about having detailed information on which to base decisions and wants substantial detail.

There is concern for going through channels and this communication pattern is always observed.

The preferred style of the chief executive is to talk with all interested managers together.

There are clear lines of authority that everyone knows and respects.

Importance is attached to the company image as seen by the public in making decisions and this often outweighs cost factors.

There is a high degree of satisfaction with the way in which decisions are handled.

SOURCE: Adapted from Stagner [1969:10].

the organization often and where the attention paid to the organization even by members may be fleeting. In decision situations of this type, which have been labelled *organized anarchies,*

Organizational participants arrive in an interpretation of what they are doing and what they have done while doing it . . . . An organization is a collection of choices looking for problems, issue and feelings looking for decision situations in which they might be aired, solutions looking for issues to which they might be the answer, and decision makers looking for work . . . . A key to understanding the processes within organizations is to view a choice opportunity as a garbage can into which various problems and solutions are dumped by participants [Cohen and March, 1974:81].

Despite its apparent cynicism, such a picture of decision making as it occurs within university faculties, for instance, does have a certain amount of face validity. Things like this do appear to happen. They even appear to happen sometimes at the top levels in corporations. However, there is a question as to whether these situations are as random, and devoid of reason, as they appear; they may very well not be and, if they are indeed comparable to the garbage can, they may not need to be [Miner, 1982]. There is increasing evidence that many "unstructured" decisions do in fact have an underlying structure if one looks hard enough for it [Mintzberg, Raisinghani, and Théorêt, 1976]. In the same manner seeming irrationality and almost random choice is in all probability simply a reflection of our as yet insufficient capacity to identify the inherent logic of the decision situation. If so, organized anarchies may not actually be quite what they seem on the surface, and attempts to maximize rationally may not be as fruitless as they would appear in these situations.

THE INFLUENCE OF ENVIRONMENTAL FORCES

Of the various approaches to decision making, the incrementing alternative and the adaptive are the most explicit in dealing with environmental forces. To a very large extent this environment outside the organization is negotiated, and thus to understand how strategic decisions are made it is necessary to understand how negotiation across the organizational boundary with other firms, with government, with pressure groups, and the like occurs.

Dealing with Governments

There is a philosophy of corporate-government relations that views government as unilaterally establishing a set of constraints within which company decision making must operate. Realistically, however, this is not what happens. Companies do exert influence on the constraint structure that flows from government, and they often induce government to introduce regulations that facilitate the conduct of business. In all such instances a negotiated, highly political process is at work. Although companies may have a clear picture of what they want their strategies to be, they may not find out what they really are until many years of negotiating with regulatory agencies, environmental pressure groups, and even the courts.

This type of strategic decision making has been studied in considerable detail in the context of a utility company's efforts to develop new electrical capacity:

Although management's strategy and supporting plans were intendedly rational and comprehensive at the outset, they were subject to resistance and revision through a protracted process of negotiation and bargaining with numerous external parties and emerged as more nearly incremental and disjointed actions than integrated and large ones . . . . Corporate strategies, or at least plans related to issues of major strategic importance, are not only formulated within the firm, but also negotiated (implicitly if not explicitly) by the firm with external parties [Murray, 1978:967–968].

In this instance the construction of a nuclear power plant and the development of various alternative sources of power were negotiated not only with federal agencies but with environmental groups who, through their access to the courts, were able to exericse influence equal to that of the government agencies. Many similar examples could be cited. It has been found, for instance, that sensitivity to equal employment opportunity pressure from the government is closely related to the amount of business done with the government and to the amount of enforcement pressure experienced [Pfeffer and Salancik, 1978]. When the pressure is high, companies that get the most business from the government respond by giving considerable attention to equal employment opportunity; in small firms, which are less visible and subject to less pressure on such matters, this relationship does not hold.

Corporate negotiations with government often relate to mitigation of potential constraints, but they may also serve to facilitate the goals of the companies involved. A number of benefits to a company can be obtained from government [Pfeffer and Salancik, 1978]:

1. Government can provide direct cash subsidies or a guarantee of loans; this is typically done in times of difficulty.
2. Government can restrict the entry of rivals into an industry, as it did for many years in the airline industry.
3. Government can operate to influence the emergence of substitutes and complements to existing products and services; the long-standing restrictions on the sale of margarine as a substitute for butter provide a case in point.
4. Government can fix prices legally, thus reducing the effects of competition and guaranteeing profits.

To achieve such results, companies typically must engage in protracted negotiation, either individually or in concert. It is clear that whether such efforts succeed or fail can have major impact on the directions strategic decision making takes.

Dealing with Other Firms

We have already noted (in Chapter 11) the role that cooptation onto a board of directors may play in reducing unpredictability in the environment that stems from the actions of other relevant organizations. A number of other approaches, which have the same purpose, and require negotiation with other organizations and their members can be noted. One is merger of a kind that reduces competition, assures access to resources or markets, or spreads risk. Mergers typically occur with firms in industries that create problems [Pfeffer and Salancik, 1978]. They are intended to make the environment more maleable or predictable; they result in a negotiated environment.

Much the same argument can be made for joint ventures, where firms pool their efforts and create a new organizational entity subsidiary to the partners. Such efforts are often negotiated within the same industry, to drill for oil for instance. They, too, are concentrated where interorganizational problems exist, in particular competitive problems.

There are numerous other structures, both formal and informal, through which information flows and negotiations are carried on—negotiations that are central both to the formulation of strategic decisions and to carrying them out. Club memberships, consultant relationships, trade associations, industry-wide collective bargaining structures, and cartels (in those parts of the world where they are allowed to exist) are examples. There is no question that many established firms in an industry would like to stabilize the industry, thus restricting entry, assuring raw materials, eliminating price competition, and the like. Government, through its antitrust laws, may limit these efforts, but it can also intervene to facilitate them. Thus, there is a continuing attempt to establish channels of communication with government and with other organizations in the environment through which negotiations can take place, and hopefully a more predictable world be achieved.

VARIATIONS IN APPROACH AS A FUNCTION OF THE NATURE OF THE DECISION

Several recent studies have made it increasingly clear that a single manager may vary considerably in his decision-making approach, depending on the nature of the decision and the situation surrounding it. In fact such variability from decision to decision within the context of a manager's job tends to be at least as great, if not greater, than the variation in characteristic approach among a group of managers [Vroom and Jago, 1974]. To date these studies of variability in the approaches of individual managers, with very few exceptions, have been concerned with the degree to which subordinates are included in the decision-making process. There is a need to extend this type of research to other aspects of the decision process, such as the degree of formal structuring, the total amount of search for information, and so on, and indeed some work of this kind is now beginning to appear [Beach and Mitchell, 1978; McAllister, Mitchell, and Beach, 1979; Stumpf, Freedman, and Zand, 1979]. However, the findings are still too scattered to reach definite conclusions.

Leadership Styles and Power Sharing Among Senior Managers

The major initial study of decision-based variability was conducted by Frank Heller [1971] using data provided by 260 senior managers in 15 large and successful companies.

As indicated in Table 12-3 certain consistent preferences in style were found, with consultation being the approach most frequently used. However, when managers had large spans of control they tended to use the timesaving approaches at the extremes (own decision and delegation) more frequently. Managers in the personnel area and in general management were more prone to use decision approaches involving power sharing, whereas those in the finance and production functions more frequently kept power to themselves. More experienced managers shared decisions more. The primary rationale for sharing a decision was to improve its technical quality.

Behind these general trends, however, was considerable variation dependent on the nature of the decision and those involved. The managers did not use one preferred personal style irrespective of the nature of the situation. Senior managers gave their immediate subordinates considerable latitude in making decisions having an impact down the line; much less latitude when the decision involved only the senior manager and his subordinate. When the decision was of great importance to the company and a clear commitment to company goals was required, the senior managers typically made the decisions themselves; otherwise, they shared more power. If the senior manager perceived a sizable skill difference, such that the subordinate involved was less knowledgeable and experienced, there was little sharing in the decision process. More experienced subordinates were more likely to be included in decisions when appropriate.

Studies of Decision Quality, Acceptance, and Speed

A second series of studies has provided additional information on decision-based variability and on the factors that may influence this variability [Vroom and Yetton, 1973; Vroom and Jago, 1974]. Here also the major concern was with the degree to which the senior manager made the decision himself or involved subordinates. The alternative approaches considered were much the same as those used by Heller (Table 12-3). However, a greater variety of situational factors that might influence the choice of an approach was investigated. These were [Vroom and Jago, 1974].

1. The quality requirements of the decision and thus the need for rationality.
2. The manager's own level of knowledge relative to the decision.

TABLE 12-3
Use of Various Decision-Making Approaches as Reported by Senior Managers

Approaches to Decisions	Percentage of Time Used
The manager makes his own decision alone	15
Having made his own decision, the manager adopts some formal method of communicating the result to others	21
Prior consultation is used, but the final decision rests entirely with the manager	37
The decision emerges as the result of joint boss-subordinate discussion in which both take an approximately equal share	20
The senior manager delegates the decision to his subordinates	7

Source: Adapted from Heller [1971:xvi and 74].

3. The degree to which the problem is structured.
4. The need for acceptance of the decision by subordinates in order to implement it.
5. The extent to which subordinates would in fact accept a decision made unilaterally by the manager.
6. The probability that subordinates share the organizational goals to be attained in solving the problem.
7. The likelihood of conflict among subordinates with regard to a preferred solution.
8. The availability of information needed for a high-quality decision among subordinates.

As in the Heller research it was found that when the managers had the needed information they tended to make decisions themselves; the major reason for consulting subordinates was to obtain needed technical information to improve decision quality. Also managers do not share decision making with subordinates when there is reason to distrust the subordinates' commitment to organizational goals and thus to believe that they would favor decisions that would serve their own interests at the expense of the company.

The studies indicate that decision sharing tends to occur when quality is important, when the problem is unstructured (creative) in nature, when subordinate acceptance is crucial to implementation and the likelihood of acceptance of a unilateral decision is low, and when conflict among subordinates is absent. Time constraints do not appear to play a particularly important role in the choice of an approach.

This approach is complex in that a sizable number of variables enter into the decision to utilize participation, perhaps more than most managers would normally keep in mind. Furthermore there are several problems with the research done to date that lead one to question whether the normative guidelines for making decisions regarding participation can be fully trusted [Field, 1979; Miner, 1980a]. Nevertheless the Heller and Vroom studies do appear to have identified some very important factors in the choice of a decision strategy.

The Role of Perceived Expertise and Power

One problem in utilizing the results of these studies is that managers may believe that are sharing decisions, and their subordinates may even believe it too, when this is not actually the case. Within decision-making teams, if one member is considered to be more expert, that person's views are very likely to prevail [Mulder, 1971; Mulder and Wilke, 1970]. Others will often change their positions to that of the expert, even though ostensibly the decision-making process is open and joint in nature. It does not matter whether the expert is really the best informed or not; the mere fact that he is believed to be tends to inhibit the expression of alternative views when creative decisions are to be made.

The consequence is that a senior manager may go into a meeting with his subordinates in search of information and alternatives for dealing with a problem that he poses and come out with nothing more than the solution that he had in mind himself originally. The mere fact that he poses the problem and elaborates its nature, coupled with the relative power inherent in his position, may be sufficient to bar any real sharing of the decision or even the presentation of realistic alternatives. Yet all those present may interpret the situation as one in which some sharing of decision making has occurred.

An antidote to this outcome seems to be introduced, however, when one or more of the subordinates is generally considered to have a major stake in the decision. Heller [1971] notes that senior managers tend to share decisions when these decisions are likely to affect not only the subordinate manager but those who work for him as well. Vroom and Yetton [1973] indicate much the same thing when they discuss decision sharing under conditions of a need for acceptance to facilitate implementation, and concomitant uncertainty regarding acceptance without sharing. Patchen [1974] found the same tendency in studying varying influences on purchasing decisions; those who had a major stake in the decision were given an opportunity to influence it, and they did. What is involved in all of these instances is negotiated decision making occasioned by the existence of the power to withdraw commitment or contributions on the part of those at lower levels, combined with an implicit or explicit recognition that this could occur and introduce new problems of its own. Under such circumstances real decision sharing does appear to occur.

CONCLUDING COMMENTS

Taking a clue from the fact that managers tend to vary their approaches widely, depending on the demands of the situation, it is now possible to gain further insight into the use of the various approaches to organizational decision making discussed at the beginning of this chapter. It would seem likely that, as companies face different types of decisions in different contexts, the same decision-based variability would occur. But it also seems probable that the environment one organization faces need not be the same as that another faces; in fact, we know this to be true. Thus one would expect the predominant decision approach of organizations to vary, depending upon variations in the environments in which they operate.

The formal structured approach, although probably desirable wherever it can be applied, seems most likely to be used in large companies that can exert at least some influence over their environments (suppliers, customers, governments, and so on) and thus stabilize them for purposes of planning.

The intuitive-anticipatory approach seems almost inevitable in very uncertain situations where the external world is changing rapidly and unpredictably and quick, risky decisions are better than nothing at all. To take an extreme case, many businesses face this kind of situation in wartime with the ebb and flow of the fortunes of battle. The use of the intuitive approach may not be highly desirable, and there are situations where it offers little hope of warding off failure, but it can on occasion be all there is.

The entrepreneurial-opportunistic approach appears most likely to emerge in the case of small firms faced with a need to make frequent changes in products or services because of rapid obsolesence or changes in profitability. Many small electronics firms lose their markets almost as soon as they develop them because the larger firms are attracted to these expanding markets and can achieve economies of scale that the smaller companies cannot. The need to seek new opportunities constantly is an almost inevitable consequence. Also there are certain entrepreneurs who are strongly oriented to the future and to the growth of their companies who appear to utilize the opportunistic approach consistently [Smith, 1967].

The incremental approach is generally associated with governmental organizations exposed to strong political pressures, that is, those operating in a democratic system. However, any organization that is highly institutionalized may resort to this approach frequently—utilizes and regulated transportation companies for instance. Any organization that needs agreement among its multiple publics more than it needs rationality or decision quality is likely to resort to incrementalism.

The adaptive approach does not appear to be used widely or at least to be used widely in an effective manner. A number of companies do play "follow the leader" and attempt to adapt quickly to the strategies of an industry leader or a price leader. But they typically lack the resource reserves needed to utilize this approach competently, even if they do monitor industry changes correctly. The more such an adaptive decision maker lags behind in responding to the first cues that a change is needed, the less effective the approach. Furthermore, it is implicit in the adaptive approach that one does attempt to "zero" in on the more certain situations and exploit them to the utmost. This may require considerable ingenuity; it is very difficult to do well.

It seems apparent that there is no "one best way" for all companies, but there are better decision approaches given the constraints and characteristics of the situation. Even so, to the degree a formal, rational, structured approach can be used, the company will be likely to benefit.

QUESTIONS

Discussion Guides on Chapter Content

1. Define and describe each of the approaches in decision making considered at the beginning of the chapter. How does each relate to environmental forces?
2. What are the arguments pro and con on the maximizing approach to decision making? How are individual differences involved?
3. What are organized anarchies? How does decision making in such contexts relate to rational maximization?
4. What is a negotiated environment? How does negotiation influence decision making across organizational boundaries? Give examples.
5. What methods do companies use to reduce unpredictability in the environment? What legal problems exist here?
6. What factors influence the degree to which managers share their decisions with subordinates?
7. Why might a desire to share a decision with subordinates fail to achieve that result? Is this likely to be a special problem at that very top of an organization? Explain.

Mind Stretching Questions

1. Describe the decision-making approaches you would expect to find in each of the following organizations and indicate what aspects of their environments lead you to that conclusion.

   (a) U.S. Department of Labor

   (b) Princeton Manufacturing (a small R&D based firm)

   (c) IBM

   (d) AT & T

2. Think about some major decision that you have made recently. How did you go about it? How long and thoroughly did you search? Describe your search efforts and indicate when you made your decision. What do you think your characteristic decision approach is?

Implementing
Policy/Strategy

13

Organizational Structures and Processes for Implementing Policies and Strategies

INTRODUCTION

President Kennedy once said that "Our responsibility is not discharged by the announcement of virtuous ends." He spoke often of the problems he had in moving the huge bureaucracy of government to act when he made a decision. For instance, even during the crucial events associated with the Cuban missile crisis, several times he ordered the withdrawal of United States missiles from bases in Turkey, in the clearest language, yet they were not removed [Allison, 1971]. To formulate policies and strategies without assuring their implementation is an exercise in futility.

The implementation of policies and strategies is an extremely complex problem in all organizations, especially larger ones. Ackerman [1975a], for instance, concluded after in-depth studies of two organizations that it took six years to assure effective implementation of top management policies associated with social programs. When George Romney was Chairman of the Board of the American Motors Corporation, he made the decision to produce a small compact automobile. It took him seven years and involved some dramatic personnel changes in the company before he succeeded in implementing his strategy.

Implementation of policies and strategies is concerned with the design and management of systems to achieve the best integration of people, structures, processes, and resources, in reaching organizational purposes. The scope of managerial activities associated with implementation is virtually coextensive with the entire process of management.

Obviously, space does not permit an examination in any depth of the range of theory and practice that is embraced. Our focus in the text will be limited to three major aspects of implementation: organization structure and processes; major coordinating, control, and motivating systems; and the role of people in implementation. The present chapter will deal with organization, the following with systems, and the next with people. Obviously all three interrelate but they are segregated here for purposes of exposition.

PERSPECTIVE ON IMPLEMENTATION AND STRUCTURE

Since implementation encompasses all functions of management, of both strategic and operational management, no simple statement of what is involved can be sufficient. To narrow the focus and establish a framework for the discussion, Table 13–1 presents major responsibilities of managers in implementing policies and strategies. The list is not intended to describe procedural steps for implementation. Rather, the list is designed to present major considerations involved in designing and managing implementing systems.

A quick glance at the list reveals a number of important characteristics of policy/strategy implementation. First, it is clear that the focus is on design and integration of major mechanisms, philosophies, structures, and personal interrelationships. Second, many different disciplines are involved in the design, operation, and use of integrating systems. Third, conflicts inevitably arise and must be resolved. Conflict resolution is a key consideration in implementing about which there has been much research [Miner, 1978]. Fourth, the discharge of the responsibilities listed requires the exercise of almost every aspect of management.

Problems of implementation differ, depending upon many variables. Among these variables are the stage of organization development as considered in Chapter 6, stability

TABLE 13-1
Major Managerial Responsibilities in Implementing Policy/Strategy

1. Divide the key tasks and sequences of steps to be performed to carry out policies and strategies in a fashion required to achieve objectives.
2. Determine who is responsible for major specific tasks that must be discharged, steps that must be taken, and decisions that must be made.
3. Determine the major organizational structures within which implementation will take place, e.g., functional departments or decentralized product divisions.
4. Determine the resources (physical and human) necessary to implement policies and strategies and assure their availability when needed.
5. Determine types of performance required by organizational units and individuals and the dates when specific activities must be accomplished.
6. Determine the personal motivation and incentive systems to be employed.
7. Analyze the key interrelationships among people, organizational units, and activities within units that require coordination and determine the appropriate systems to assure their proper coordination.
8. Assure the proper degrees of participation in the formulation and operation of implementing systems and processes.
9. Establish appropriate information systems to assure accurate measurement of performance against standards so that corrective action can be taken when required.
10. Adopt training programs to develop the technical and managerial skills needed in implementation.
11. Assure that managerial leadership is effective in motivating and leading the organization in implementing policies and strategies in such a way as to achieve organizational ends in the most effective and efficient fashion.

or instability of environments, types of organizational structures, interdependencies among organizational units, personnel interrelationships, environmental competitive conditions and cultural forces. These and other factors introduce many contingencies into the implementation process.

Actually implementation is important not only in its own right but as a constraint on strategic decisions. In this latter context the term *strategic capability* is often used to refer to what a company can meaningfully do to implement a given strategy, and thus to the strategic alternatives that are realistically available to it. Lenz [1980] has described the components of strategic capability as follows:

1. The knowledge-technique base for value creation, including both the number and type of technologies and their level of sophistication.
2. The capacity to generate and acquire resources, including the ability to dominate competition and to assess resources for operations, as well as the level and quality of support available in the environment.
3. The general management technology, including managerial knowledge and experience and the effectiveness of structure.

Although one might question whether such a concept of strategic capability is sufficiently comprehensive, it does illustrate the point that a variety of factors related to implementation must be considered in evaluating the feasibility of a given strategy. Thus, strategy formulation and strategy implementation involve a continuing dynamic interplay.

The Role of Structure

In defining the components of strategic capability Lenz [1980] notes that the effectiveness of structures, both formal and informal, is important to the total implementation process. Although differing views exist, organizational structure generally refers to the more or less fixed relationships of roles and tasks to be performed in achieving organizational goals, the grouping of these activities, utilization of authority, and informational flows vertically and horizontally in the organization. Implementation of strategy, however, includes more than this. It involves various mechanisms to coordinate, influence, and control these activities, such as planning, interpersonal relationships, and incentive systems; managerial styles; and control mechanisms. These are called organizational processes. Each of these elements relates to the design problem and the mixture of all elements must not be inconsistent. Our emphasis in this chapter is primarily on structure, but we shall also touch upon organizational processes.

Interdependence of Structure with Strategy

In summarizing the long experience of his consulting firm in devising strategies and organizing companies Cannon [1972:30] said: "The experience of McKinsey supports the view that neither strategy nor structure can be determined independently of the other. . . . If structure cannot stand alone without strategy, it is equally true that strategy can rarely succeed without an appropriate structure. In almost every kind of large-scale enterprise, examples can be found where well-conceived strategic plans were thwarted by an organization structure that delayed the execution of the plans or gave priority to the wrong set of considerations . . . good structure is inseparably linked to strategy. . . ." He then goes on to say that structure must reflect an organization's basic mission as well as goals and strategic programs of top management.

Contingency Views

In the past there have been schools of thought that claimed to have had the correct prescription for the best organizational structures and processes. The classical writers on management, for example, felt that over many years there had been developed a set of principles which, if properly applied, would determine the structural design best suited to achieve the purposes of the organization [for example, Gulick and Urwick, 1937]. Early behaviorists insisted that better results would be achieved when organizational structure and process followed certain prescribed concepts about individuals [for example, Likert, 1961; McGregor, 1960]. More recent research supports the thesis that there is no one "right" or "best" way to organize for effective results. This is called "a contingency theory of organizations." These words to describe the theory were first used by Lawrence and Lorsch [1967], but the ideas underlying the concept have been supported by many others.

"The basic assumption underlying the theory," say Lawrence and Lorsch [1967:157], "is that organizational variables are in a complex interrelationship with one another and with conditions in the environment." Organizations must be designed according to the tasks they are trying to perform.

Although many observers agree with the basic theme of the contingency theory, they concur from different perspectives. For example, Clifford examined 103 rapidly growing companies and concluded that "The 'right' structure for each company at any point in time is a function of five determinants: corporate objectives and plans . . . the number of distinct businesses making up the company . . . the key factors for success in each major line of business . . . organizational principles (adopted by the company) . . . and management capabilities, style, and personality . . ." [Clifford, 1973a:26–27].

A major difficulty with many of the contingency approaches is that they fail to include top-level decision making and strategy formation in their formulations. Yet it is now clear that, whatever one's perspective on the problem, the strategic variable needs to be built into the equation [Miner, 1982; Thorelli, 1977]. Without some concept of how the decision processes involved work, it is not possible even to understand organizational structuring [Pfeffer, 1978], let alone how structuring operates in the implementation of strategy. For these reasons little attention is given here to contingency approaches that derive organizational structures and processes directly from differing technologies [Perrow, 1967; Woodward, 1965], or from variations in environmental uncertainty [Lawrence and Lorsch, 1967; Lorsch and Allen, 1973], or from combinations of these two [Burns and Stalker, 1961]. At best such theories have not been adequately tested; at worst they have been found to be in substantial error [Miner, 1982].

A second type of approach does incorporate decision making and strategy formation in an effort to understand organizational structure and process, but still fails to provide useful information for the present purposes. Thus, Thompson's [1967] sociological open systems formulations, although developing a major new theoretical thrust for organizational science, have never been utilized to develop an applied technology of organizational design. The same conclusion holds for the related views of March and Simon [1958] and Cyert and March [1963]. These approaches are important because they stress varying contingencies related to organizational decision making, but they do not provide specific guidance for strategy implementation. Nonetheless, there are theories and lessons from experience that are helpful both in explaining the interrelationships between strategy and organization structure and in predicting success or failure with different structures. We now proceed to presenting some highlights of the research undertaken in this area.

EVOLUTION OF MAJOR ORGANIZATIONAL STRUCTURES

The first comprehensive analysis of the interrelationships among environment, strategy, and organizational structure was made by Chandler in 1962. He compared the history of organizational change among 50 large companies during the century following the Civil War. His major conclusions were as follows:

The comparison emphasizes that a company's strategy in time determined its structure and that the common denominator of structure and strategy has been the application of the enterprise's resources to market demand. Structure has been the design for integrating the enterprise's existing resources to current demand; strategy has been the plan for the allocation of resources to anticipated demand [Chandler, 1962:476].

Chandler also found that our present-day large companies evolved through four stages. They all tended to move sequentially through these stages, but the timing differed among companies in different industries with different environments.

He found that the large American industrial enterprise was born and grew in the post-Civil War years. The rapid industrialization and urbanization of the nation of that period opened up new opportunities, and enterprises began to acquire new productive facilities, a labor force, and trained supervisory personnel to exploit them. Consolidations of companies permitted the new firm to produce higher volume at lower costs per unit. This was a period of great growth for such companies.

The second stage began when these vertically integrated companies found it increasingly imperative to coordinate better their activities in order to meet customer needs and maintain profits. The old organizational structures and administrative methods could not meet these needs. A new centralized, functionally departmentalized administrative structure was therefore created. Technical specialists were trained to coordinate various functional activities, and the central headquarters installed control mechanisms to assure the integration that was needed to meet customer needs. This was a complex communications network that linked together all the activities in the industrial process to customer demands.

The third stage began when large companies found that opportunities for expanding their markets with their present products were declining, as were possibilities for reducing costs per unit. So, these companies began to increase the number of products in their product line, to expand their overseas activities, and to produce new products for new markets.

The fourth and final stage began when these companies discovered that their old functional organizational structures and processes were inadequate to coordinate the activities involved in the production and sale of diverse products in different markets. They established new divisions in which all activities associated with a major product or product line were placed under the authority of a division manager. A central headquarters remained, of course, to assure the necessary coordination among the divisions and to make those strategic decisions that were required to assure a strong growing enterprise. The product-division structure was first introduced in the early 1920s.

The timing of these stages varied from company to company and industry to industry. By and large, however, the fourth stage began in the early 1920s after DuPont established (in 1921) the product-division structure. Many companies continued with functional organizations until recent years, and the substantial increase in the product-division structure among large companies did not take place until the post-World War II period.

There were often delays between the acceptance of a strategy and the emergence of the appropriate structure. Barring a severe crisis, typically it was necessary to wait for the retirement of top management before change occurred. Such a lag between strategy and structure produced inefficiency.

Recent Elaborations

Although often referred to as the theory of strategy and structure, these ideas actually are more limited than that title implies. They deal only with one type of strategy— that of growth. However, in recent years the theory has been fleshed out in a number of respects [Chandler, 1977; Chandler and Daems, 1979]. The following propositions deal with the role of administrative coordination in implementing a growth strategy:

1. Modern multiunit business enterprise replaced small traditional enterprise when administrative coordination permitted greater productivity, lower costs, and higher profits than coordination by market mechanisms.
2. The advantages of internalizing the activities of many business units within a single enterprise could not be realized until a managerial hierarchy had been created.
3. Modern business enterprise appeared for the first time in history when the volume of economic activities reached a level that made administrative coordination more efficient and more profitable than market coordination.
4. Once a managerial hierarchy had been formed and had successfully carried out its function of administrative coordination, the hierarchy itself became a source of permanence, power, and continued growth [Chandler, 1977:6–8].

Administrative coordination as a method for structuring and facilitating transactions between independent divisions resulted in economies of speed. It was followed very shortly by monitoring systems to check on the divisions and reward them accordingly.

Somewhat later, companies evolved various resource allocation procedures when increased cash flow created sizable internally generated funds as sources of capital for expansion. Thus, an essential element in the implementation of growth strategies, in addition to the adoption of a multidivisional structure, was the creation of accounting procedures for coordination, monitoring, and allocation.

It is important to recognize that these ideas about strategy and its implementation grew directly out of the historical data that Chandler collected. Thus, it is not appropriate to turn back to exactly the same data to test out the ideas [Miner, 1979]. Such tests have been conducted using different samples of companies at different points in time and in different parts of the world.

Studies with Multinationals

Stopford and Wells [1972] studied United States firms that had expanded into international markets. Here the initial structure tended to be a single overarching international division, comparable to the functional form and suitable for single-product firms. At the other extreme, with diversification, came an increasing shift to multiple, world-wide, product divisions. When firms that did and did not have structures appropriate to their strategies were compared, it appeared that an appropriate fit was associated with growth in foreign sales and that the best results in this regard accrued to multiproduct firms with world-wide product divisions. Strategy-structure fit was also related to return on investment in the expected manner, but the superiority of the diversification strategy per se was not demonstrated in terms of profit; single-product firms with international divisions did at least as well.

European Studies

Analyses of British [Channon, 1973], French and German [Dyas and Thanheiser, 1976], and Italian [Pavan, 1976] firms generally show the expected patterns, although sizable differences in rate and extent of change exist between countries. In all cases there was a shift toward diversification strategies and a comparable increase in multidivisional structures. However, in Europe the lags between the adoption of the strategy and the introduction of a revised structure were so long as to raise some question whether the structural change was in fact intended to implement the strategy.

A study of European multinationals by Franko [1976] indicates similar lags. In particular a structure labelled "mother-daughter" tended to remain in place long after the move to a diversification strategy. Mother-daughter firms had an informal, personal relationship between the parent company president and subsidiary presidents in each foreign country. The type of decentralization with extensive use of accounting controls emphasized by Chandler was not in evidence. The predominant organization in the home country was functional.

With increasing competition in the European Economic Community, structure has moved to align itself with strategy; but the process has been slow. Unfortunately data to indicate whether, during the period of lag, inefficiencies were pronounced are not available.

Fortune 500 Studies in the United States

Several studies have dealt with large United States firms since World War II. The first conducted by Wrigley [1970] generally supported Chandler's thesis, although it dealt only with strategy and structure, not with the consequences of relationships between the two. Another more comprehensive study by Rumelt [1974] surveyed companies from 1947 to 1969 and found that those having product-division structures rose from 20.3 per cent to 75.9. per cent of the total. Those that were functionally organized fell from 62.7 per cent to 11.2 per cent of the total. Most of the decrease was due to the fact that previously functionally organized firms became product-division firms, rather than dropping from the top 500 list. These are very substantial changes.

Rumelt also reached valuable conclusions about performance. He divided firms into the following classes, depending upon strategies employed [Rumelt, 1974:29–32]:

1. Single Business: those whose revenue comes from one business.
2. Dominant Business: those for whom 70 per cent or more of revenues comes from one business.
   (a) Dominant-Vertical: vertically integrated firms for whom 70 per cent or more of total revenue comes from one business.
   (b) Dominant-Constrained: those nonvertical firms that have expanded by emphasizing a dominant original strength, skill, or resource and whose activities are related one to another and to a dominant business (the constraint).
   (c) Dominant-Linked: nonvertical firms that have expanded by building upon several skills, strengths, or resources and where the preponderance of activity is not directly related to the dominant business but is related to different activities of the firm.
   (d) Dominant-Unrelated: nonvertical firms whose diversified activities are not related to the dominant business.
3. Related Business: nonvertically integrated firms whose dominant business produces less than 70 per cent of total revenue and whose other activities are related to the dominant and other businesses.
   (a) Related-Constrained: related business firms that have diversified by relating new businesses to a particular skill or resources but where each activity, as a result, is related to almost all other activities.
   (b) Related-Linked: related business firms that have expanded by relating the new business to an old strength or skill but not always the same one.
4. Unrelated Business: nonvertical firms that have diversified into unrelated businesses.
   (a) Acquisitive Conglomerates: firms that have aggressive programs for acquiring unrelated businesses. Criteria for aggressiveness are (1) average growth rate in earnings per share of over 10 per cent annually in the past five years, and (2) issued new equity shares with total market value at least as great as the total amount of common dividends paid during the period.
   (b) Unrelated-Passive: those conglomerate firms that do not qualify as acquisitive conglomerates.

Rumelt [1974] came to the following major conclusions about the financial performance associated with these strategies:

- Related Business firms, on the average, have higher profitability, higher rates of growth, and higher price-earnings ratios than other categories of firms.
- Related-Constrained firms outperform Related-Linked firms on these (previously mentioned) measures.
- The Related-Constrained and Dominant-Constrained firms are top performers on almost all measures—growth, return on equity, earnings per share. (Controlled diversity pays off. It may be that controlled diversity itself is not the cause of high performance but rather that high performance eliminates the need for greater diversification.)
- Both the Acquisitive Conglomerates and Unrelated-Passive firms had average returns on capital not much different from the overall averages of all firms.

Perhaps the most significant finding of Rumelt [1974:121] was that "the [preceding] categories did separate firms into groups that displayed significant and consistent differences in financial performance." However, attempts to relate strategy-structure fit to profitability did not achieve much success. Thus, although those related business firms that had adopted a divisional structure showed a greater sales growth than those that had retained the functional form, they did not show greater profitability on any of the measures employed.

British Research

A recent study conducted in Great Britain yields results very similar to those of Rumelt. Single business firms were typically functionally organized, dominant businesses showed great variation, related businesses tended to use some type of product division (but 30 per cent remained functional), and unrelated businesses generally employed the product division structure [Grinyer, Yasai-Ardekani, and Al-Bazzaz, 1980]. When the firms in each strategy group that had the appropriate structure were compared with those that did not (based on Chandler's expectations) there was no evidence of any difference in profitability. What did differ, however, was growth (in sales and in number of employees). On the evidence it would appear that using a divisionalized structure to implement a multiproduct growth strategy is a very effective method of obtaining the desired growth, but it does not guarantee more profits.

THE ROLE OF INTEGRATION

Integration and Decentralization

Firms that have introduced the product-division structure of organization have had difficult problems in determining the degree of integration that should be maintained between the divisions and central headquarters. In commenting on this question Sloan, for many years the top executive of General Motors, said: "Having . . . established techniques of control in the particular areas of appropriations, cash, inventory, and production, the general question remained: How could we exercise permanent control over the whole corporation in a way consistent with the decentralized scheme of organization? We never ceased to attack this paradox; indeed we could not avoid a solution of it without yielding both the actual decentralized structure of our business and our philosophy of approach to it" [Sloan, 1964:139–140]. He went on to say that the solution was to review the effectiveness of divisionalized operations on the basis of return on investment. But subsequent analysis has shown that this standard has significant weaknesses [Weston, 1972].

The issues in integration between headquarters and decentralized divisions cover a broad spectrum of managerial philosophy, tasks facing both areas, interpersonnel relationships, integration mechanisms, and environments (internal and external). In this light there can be no universal solution.

Aside from the research noted there has been other work that throws light on preferred courses of action in designing organizational structures and processes. Lorsch and Allen [1973] concluded that the better the integration between corporate headquarters and divisions the higher the performance of the company. They also identified the mechanisms that managers in the companies surveyed considered to be the most significant in achieving desired integration. Planning systems were among the more prominent integrating mechanisms. Greiner examined 58 companies and concluded that the more the planning is systematized into the organizations the more effective it is; the more explicit goals are for an organization the higher is the estimate of effectiveness for the organization [in Aguilar, *et al.,* 1970:98]. Dearden concluded that "a decentralized profit center system . . . requires a more sophisticated and expensive budgeting and planning system to overcome the problems of communication, coordination, and evaluation that profit decentralization creates" [Dearden, 1962:147].

There have been a number of contributions of a very specific nature to this general question, only a few of which can be illustrated. Solomons' [1965] research has detailed the methods used to measure and control the performance of decentralized divisions. Lorange and Vancil [1977] have described an allocation of funds methodology to assure better planning and control of product development. Soden [1972] has described causes of failure and their solutions in establishing computerized information systems linking headquarters with divisions.

The mixture of integration devices is as important as the mechanisms chosen. A number of companies, for example, have experienced grave problems in, first of all, making the decision to decentralize and, having made the decision, in managing properly the decentralized firm. On the first instance management, not used to delegating authority and responsibility, may not make the transition. Many entrepreneurs who built a company have not been able to do so and, as a result, have had the traumatic experience of being asked to resign by their boards of directors. Once decentralization has been undertaken, there are factors that must be considered in designing and employing integrating mechanisms. Many companies have lost the effectiveness of decentralization because their design and management of integrating mechanisms was faulty.

Program Structures and Business Units as Integrating Forms

Corey and Star [1971] conclude that the greatest single influence on business organizational structures is the market environment. To exploit strategies for that market, most companies have created program structures. In their survey of over 500 companies they found 77 per cent with such structures. "A program is a total strategic plan for serving a particular market segment. It provides for product design, pricing, channels of distribution, advertising, promotion, and field selling; for product supply and customer service" [Corey and Star, 1971:2]. Those firms that produce a diverse product line for homogeneous markets generally use a product-market program manager. Those that have a homogeneous product line to sell in diverse markets typically have market program managers. Those with both diverse lines and markets are likely to have both types of managers. Companies generally form divisions, product departments, or business units to house one or more programs.

Coordination of activities is accomplished principally through product managers, who integrate marketing and production programs; interface managers, who guide the allocation of resource efforts to programs; resource scheduling activities; and planning. Among all the areas of responsibility that different product and market managers assume, planning is dominant above all others. Indeed, the central integration and resource allocation device is annual and long-range planning. Corey and Star [1971:53] found that "the type of program structure (product, market, or both) which a business has is a function of the type(s) of diversity with which it is faced." They also found that "businesses with program organizations seem to have been considerably more successful in developing and introducing new products than businesses without program organizations."

Steiner and Ryan [1968] examined the managerial attitudes and techniques employed by 18 project managers in the aerospace industry who were given a responsibility for producing a new high-technology product to meet a new requirement. Each manager was given a rather free hand by the government and his own top management. It was found that each had the same fundamental management attitudes and employed similar managerial methods. Furthermore, they were able to produce a prototype product at a time and cost that was one third that of project managers who operated under conditions of greater control and supervision from top managers.

Matrix Structures

Program, product, or project managers often do not have their own resources and draw upon outside sources for this purpose. The key aspects of this structure are a project manager, decentralized resource support, and centralized planning and control. In the matrix structure, on the other hand, there is a permanent dual authority relationship. The power of the product component becomes coequal to that of the functional. The key roles are top leadership, which is outside the matrix; matrix managers, who share subordinates with each other; and subordinate managers, who have two bosses.

Matrix structures are recommended when there are two or more critical sectors, such as products and functions, that are important to achieving the organization's goals; when a sizable information processing capacity is required to accomplish complex and interdependent tasks; and when it is important to utilize scarce human resources effectively [Davis and Lawrence, 1977]. They are seen as a means to coping with highly uncertain environments through the addition of increased structural flexibility. Thus, they would appear to be most suitable for implementing strategies involving rapid change—perhaps a new technological advantage or the rapid introduction of new products into the marketplace.

Unfortunately there is little solid evidence regarding the value of the matrix structure in implementing strategies. What little is known relates to program, product or project forms where, typically, the structure is a temporary one and relationships are not fully power balanced [Knight, 1977; Miner, 1978]. Davis and Lawrence [1978] note a number of things that may go wrong within matrix systems, suggesting that effective matrix functioning may be a very vulnerable and unstable state. There is evidence that, even under project management conditions, role conflict and ambiguity, with resultant increases in anxiety levels and reductions in effectiveness, may occur. Under the full two-boss concept of matrix management, this seems much more likely. Thus, at the present time it is not possible to say whether or not matrix structures are an appropriate method of implementing strategies demanding high flexibility. However, they are being advocated for this purpose, and used with this end in mind.

EXTENDED CONCEPTS OF ORGANIZATIONAL FIT

The Chandler [1962] formulations posit certain fits between growth strategies and structures as necessary for organizational effectiveness. In Chapter 6 aspects of these views were elaborated in relation to various stages of the organizational life cycle. Another extension of Chandler's theory carries the fit concept beyond strategy and structure so that it covers the whole spectrum running from the environment on the one hand to individual organizational members on the other [Galbraith and Nathanson, 1978]. This approach draws heavily on research by Lawrence and Lorsch [1967], Lorsch and Allen [1973], and Lorsch and Morse [1974]—particularly on the last.

A basic schema for this extended fit concept is contained in Figure 13–1. That product/market strategy must fit with structure and information and decision processes is consistent with Chandler. But the present model moves beyond this to deal with aspects of tasks, reward systems, and people (organization members). In so doing, it becomes considerably less specific and at the same time much more complex.

Galbraith and Nathanson [1978] advance some hypotheses regarding the necessary relationships among task, structure, process, reward, and people variables if various strategies are to be implemented, but the theory is admittedly incomplete in this regard and research support is at a minimum. Lorsch and Morse [1974] utilize cognitive complexity, tolerance for ambiguity, independence in authority relationships, preference for working alone, and feelings of competence as aspects of people that may be important in extended fit formulations, but problems in interpreting this research make it impossible to say whether these are the key variables [Johnston, 1975; Miner, 1979].

Yet, just as evidence is developing regarding some of the key relationships involving strategy and structure toward the environmental end of the continuum, there is also a

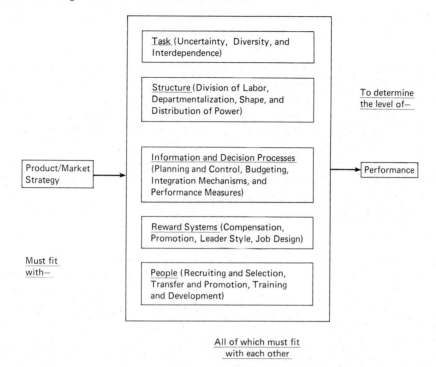

Figure 13-1   Relationships involved in the extended concept of organizational fit. (Source: Adapted from Galbraith and Nathanson [1978:95–96].)

body of knowledge building up from the opposite direction relating people and structure. Thus, considerable evidence exists relating the following characteristics to the managerial component of bureaucratic (hierarchic) systems [Miner, 1977]:

1. A favorable attitude toward people in authority positions generally.
2. A desire to exercise power over others.
3. A desire to assert oneself.
4. A desire to compete.
5. A desire to assume a distinctive, differentiated role.
6. A desire to perform routine administrative duties in a responsible manner.

There is also reason to believe that there are distinctive personality characteristics that fit with professional, group (such as sociotechnical), and task (entrepreneurial) structures [Miner, 1980c], although the evidence in these three instances is less focused. The apparent fits are as follows:

Professional Structures
1. A desire to learn and acquire knowledge.
2. A value-based identification with the profession.

3. A desire to acquire status in the eyes of others.
4. A desire to help others to achieve their best interests.
5. A desire to act independently.

Group Structures

1. A desire to interact with others and to do so effectively.
2. A desire for continuing group membership.
3. A favorable attitude toward peers and coworkers generally.
4. A desire to work with others in a cooperative or collaborative fashion.
5. A desire to participate in democratic group processes.

Task Structures

1. A desire to achieve through one's own efforts and to be able to attribute clearly any success to personal causation.
2. A desire for some clear index of the level of performance.
3. A desire to introduce novel, or innovative, or creative solutions.
4. A desire to take moderate risks that can be handled through one's own efforts.
5. A desire to think about the future and anticipate future possibilities.

The idea that there are appropriate fits extending through almost all aspects of organizational functioning is intriguing and, at the same time, probably valid. However, evidence regarding what specific kinds of fits make for success is only beginning to accumulate, and even then on a piecemeal basis. Perhaps this is inevitable in view of the size and complexity of the task. In any event, the needed beginnings, at both a conceptual and empirical level, are in evidence.

CONCLUDING COMMENTS

This review has touched only the most dominant conclusions of research dealing with organizational structure and processes concerned with implementation of policy and strategy. Although there has been research, there are few prescriptive guides that managers may employ to be assured they have the "right" structure and mix of procedures. Each case must be designed in light of the unique circumstances surrounding it. It is clear from much of the research, however, that long- and short-range planning is a major integrative methodology. We now turn to how planning implements policy and strategy.

QUESTIONS

Discussion Guides on Chapter Content

1. Discuss important problems that you think managers in most companies have when trying to be sure that strategies are implemented. Generally, how are the problems overcome?

2. Identify some of the key factors in organizations that will influence the manner in which strategies are implemented.

3. What is strategic capability and how does it relate to strategy formulation and implementation?

4. What are the interrelationships among top-level strategy formulation, aspects of structure, and contingency concepts? Why do many of the theories in this area fail to provide useful guidelines for strategy implementation?

5. What is the current status of strategy-structure theory as formulated by Chandler? Cite specific evidence.

6. In what ways is integration important to strategy implementation? How might integration be achieved?

7. What do we know about the value of matrix structures for strategy implementation? What can we surmise from related evidence?

8. What is the extended fit concept of Galbraith and Nathanson? Discuss the evidence as it relates to components of this concept.

Mind Stretching Questions

1. You have been asked to design the implementation effort of a single-product, functionally organized company which has just adopted a highly diversified, multiproduct strategy. What would you recommend? Why? What if the company went world-wide in this new strategy?

2. What are the key questions for practice that have not yet been answered insofar as the utilization of structures and processes for strategy implementation are concerned? What kinds of studies might serve to answer these questions?

14

Formal Systems for Implementing Policies and Strategies

INTRODUCTION*

No company ever made a nickel of profit by making plans; plans must be effectively implemented if a firm is to be profitable. As was pointed out in the last chapter, the implementation of strategic plans involves the entire process of management. A major step in this process is the translation of plans into current decisions. The core of formal systems in this process is the preparation of operational plans and budgets. This, therefore, is the focus of this chapter. However, there are other formal systems important in this process, two of which will be discussed in this chapter, namely, management by objective and management control systems. As a backdrop for the discussion of these systems the chapter begins with a few comments on integrating and implementing systems.

INTEGRATING AND IMPLEMENTING SYSTEMS

Design Tailored to Each Company

It is worth repeating here what was said previously, that integrating and implementing systems must be tailored to each organization. There are many ways to organize, introduce, and use each of these systems, and the "right" design must be found for each situation for best results. The forces that influence design are the same as those discussed in connection with organizational structural design, plus many more.

The influence of one dimension—interdependence of subunits of an organization—

---

* This chapter draws substantially from George A. Steiner: *Strategic Planning: What Every Manager Must Know.* New York, Random House, 1979, Chapters 13 and 16.

will illustrate the point. Thompson [1967] identified three major types of interdependence, as follows:

Pooled interdependence—units having virtually no needed contacts, such as a conglomerate with unrelated divisions.

Sequential interdependence—an organization where the output of one major unit is the input for other units, such as is the case in vertically integrated companies.

Reciprocal interdependence—instances where outputs of each unit are the inputs for other units, such as single product companies that produce components for their end item.

The design, introduction, implementation, costs, problems, and usage of major systems will vary depending upon which type of the preceding interdependence exists.

The Spectrum of Systems

Lorsch and Allen [1973], in their study of four companies with decentralized organization structures, identified the major integrating devices that were perceived by managers as playing the most significant role in corporate-divisional relations. They were an annual budgeting system, an approved system for capital and expense items, a formal goal-setting system, performance evaluation, an incentive compensation system, group vice presidents, direct managerial contact, monthly budget reviews, and a five-year planning system. Other devices that managers in this study identified as of importance, but did not cite as frequently, were a quarterly budget forecast; monthly operating reports; a cash management system; an approval system for hiring, replacement, and salary changes of key division personnel; divisional "specialists" in corporate controller's office; annual meetings between corporate and divisional general managers; group management committees; a technical evaluation board for capital projects; permanent cross-divisional committees; line management task forces; and *ad hoc* cross-divisional meetings for functional managers. This is a long list of systems for integrating and implementing plans. It is by no means an exhaustive list. But the point is made, we believe, that there is a very wide spectrum of systems for implementing plans; these systems are both formal and informal, and they touch upon virtually all aspects of management.

Coordination Takes Place Throughout the Planning Process

Integrated corporate planning has two significant dimensions. First, plans are coordinated, more or less, from the top levels of an organization down through the lower levels. Second, plans are coordinated at different levels. Both dimensions were explained in Chapter 7. One result of a conscious effort to perfect such coordination is that the formulation of strategy takes place with some reference to circumstances surrounding its implementation, even at low levels of an organization.

To illustrate the first dimension of coordination, the Monsanto Chemical Company decided several years ago to enter the detergent field with a branded product. This strategy was well timed and in line with the company's resources. It was not implemented, however, because it aroused strong opposition from consumer product companies who were major customers for Monsanto's detergent materials. To illustrate the second dimension of coordination, Rolls Royce did not interrelate properly its marketing planning for the RB-211 engine, designed for the Lockheed L-1011 airplane, with research and development engineering and, as a result, went bankrupt [Ross and Kami, 1973].

Typically, in most organizations that have a formal planning system, there are three sets of plans, as described in Chapter 7—strategic, medium range, and short range. In theory, each relates to the other and each has some degree of internal coordination. Complete and detailed coordination and integration within and among these sets of plans would be extremely difficult. As a consequence managers are wise when they coordinate only that which is necessary to the achievement of the major organization aims. This will, of course, vary from case to case.

Nature of Implementation Plans

Implementation plans translate strategic plans into current decisions. The process is that of making medium-range functional plans and using them as bases for making short-range plans and decisions. In this section our focus is on medium-range plans.

Figure 14–1 shows how different medium-range plans may be interrelated. Each company must decide for itself whether plans will be prepared for each of the subjects shown in the chart, in what detail, and with what coordination with other plans. There is no rule or formula governing such decisions. There are some minimums, however, that each company should consider. For example, a medium-range marketing plan of a manufacturing company should interrelate, at a minimum, with production and product development plans. Depending upon circumstances it might be wise to extend the interrelationship to other functional plans, such as facility plans. The medium-range marketing

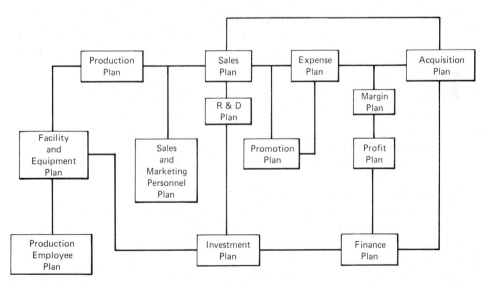

Figure 14-1 Medium range programming of the strategic path.

plan should be developed within the overall objectives and strategies of the company and in relationship to other functional plans at the same level of planning.

The objectives, strategies and detailed plans will depend upon the functions of the marketing manager. Functions of marketing managers vary much from firm to firm, but if the job descriptions of a number of them were aggregated the range of activities would encompass the four P's identified by McCarthy [1964:36] to classify marketing functions—product, place, promotion, and price. Each of these, of course, covers a wide range of possible detailed activities. For instance, under product might be included plans for adding, dropping, or modifying product lines; branding, packaging, standardizing, and grading. Place refers to distribution channels to get the right product at the right place at the right time. Promotion is concerned with communicating with customers, such as through advertising, developing salesmen, etc. Pricing involves not only the actual price of a product but costs, volume, product mix, promotion, and so on.

Similarly, other medium-range program plans will cover different details, depending upon the company. Diversification plans, research and development plans, personnel plans, facility plans, and so on, will vary from company to company and time to time.

It is worth repeating here what was said previously about the comprehensiveness of medium-range plans. Empirical observation indicates that companies prepare such plans in a much less comprehensive fashion than in the past. The reason is that preparing comprehensive five-year functional plans is extremely difficult and not really necessary to translate strategic plans into current decisions. Some integration of medium-range functional plans is, however, valuable in the translation of strategy to current decisions.

In some divisionalized companies a strategy will be formulated and medium-range programs will be prepared to implement the strategy. In such cases, of course, the functional relationships associate only with the implementation of the strategy. Some programs center on three major categories of funds—development expense, plant and equipment, and working capital. Selected plans are prepared for priority items in each of these categories for appropriate numbers of years. Current budgets are then linked to these programs. In some companies this is called Strategic Funds Programming [Stonich, 1980; Stonich and Zaragoza, 1980]. The completeness of programming to implement specific strategies will vary, of course, from company to company [Vancil and Lorange, 1975].

Linkage Among Plans

Before discussing short-range operation plans and budgets it is important to comment about linkages among plans. Practice varies concerning the relationship between medium-range and short-range plans and budgets. One study of 137 companies revealed that about half said the long-range plans applied directly to the budget, 36 per cent said the long-range plan provided guidelines for current budgets, and 14 per cent said the long-range plan was not applicable to current budgets [Said and Seiler, 1978]. It appears, according to this study, that small, young, rapidly growing companies tended to have very loose relationships between long-range plans and short-range plans and budgets. Mature, cash generating, corporations tended to have tighter linkages. It is informative to note that this study asked companies whether they were satisfied with their long-range planning. The great majority of those who rated their long-range planning below normal were among those who said their long-range plans were not too applicable to their operating budgets.

When speaking of linkage between medium-range plans and current plans and budgets, the connection usually in mind is in terms of numbers. There is a tight linkage when the numbers used in plans and budgets are identical with the numbers in the first year of multiple-year medium-range plans. There is a loose linkage when medium-range plans are only used as a frame of reference for preparing short-range plans and budgets.

When the linkage is tight the top management of a firm in effect is saying to managers that the long-range planning process is serious and not a game. There are disadvantages, however. If the focus is sharp and intense on short-run plans and budgets, the manager whose plans and budgets are under survey naturally will pay attention to the short run and neglect the long run. This is especially so if his performance is measured on short-run criteria. In addition, short-run orientation tends to induce risk aversion. For such reasons about half the firms in the United States have a loose linkage between plans and budgets and medium-range plans.

Another reason for not using a tight linkage is that, between the time the medium-range plans are made and the actual short-range plans and budgets are prepared, basic assumptions upon which plans rest may have changed. The first draft of the plan and budget may reveal relationships unforeseen at the time the strategic guidelines and subsequent medium-range plans were prepared. Wisdom would, of course, suggest appropriate adjustments.

Although linkage is generally discussed in terms of specific numbers, especially financial numbers, there are many other connections between multiple-year and short-range plans. In mind are such matters as organizational relationships, the inevitable iteration in the development of medium-range functional plans with current prospects and expectations, management and staff discussions between company headquarters and divisions, and so on.

OPERATING PLANS AND BUDGETS

From Medium-Range Plans to Operating Plans

Figure 14-2 shows that corporate strategies can be reflected immediately in current plans or used as a basis for the development of medium-range plans which, in turn, are the basis for annual or shorter plans. It will be noticed that the details of the one-year plans are considerably different from the main categories of the five-year plans. The two can be the same, but the short-term plans are more concerned with coordination and control of critical internal flows of resources. The subject matter of the short-range plans, therefore, will be focused on these concerns rather than on the more aggregative functions in the medium-range plans. The aggregates of the short-range plans, however, can relate to medium-range plans, as noted previously.

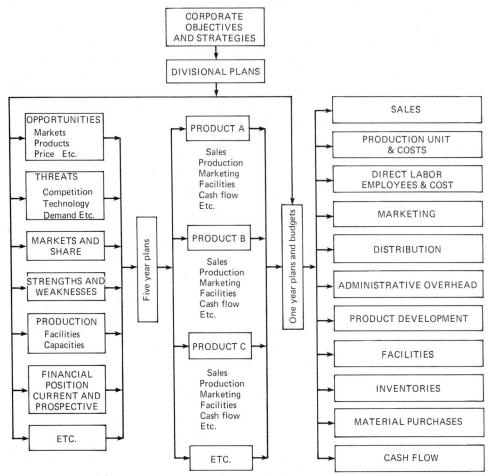

Figure 14-2   Relationship between strategic and tactical plans.

Detailed Tactical Plans

Figure 14-3 is presented to show how detailed current plans may become in a company. The illustration is, of course, only for marketing, and the figure details only specific plans for sales. The same sort of detail can be developed for other plans, such as production, research, facility expansion, product modification, channels of distribution, managerial training, pricing, and so on. All, of course, in some degree need to be integrated.

Key Operational Questions to Implement Strategy

The interrelationships among functions to implement a strategy is illustrated in Table 14-1. The strategy here is to enter the multiple-speed bike market for the reasons given. To implement that strategy requires the resolution of many key questions, as noted.

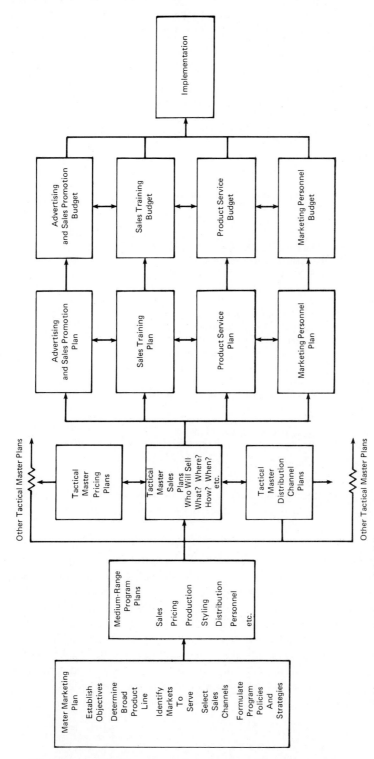

Figure 14-3 Marketing plans and budgets.

TABLE 14-1
Key Operational Questions to Implement Strategy

Strategy decision?
- Enter multiple-speed bike market
- Why?
  - Market expected to expand four times in next five years
  - We have technical capabilities to exploit this market opportunity
- We should have 14 per cent of market in five years
  - With this share our pretax ROI should be 30 per cent

Illustrative operational questions
- Research and development
  - Develop better clutch and gear mechanism
    - We need this to gain competitive advantage
    - What R&D and technical skill is needed?
    - How much will a new design cost?
    - How long will it take to be operational?
- Production
  - Do we need new manufacturing process abilities?
  - Will fiberglass replace metals for frames?
  - What schedule of production will be required?
  - What model mix is needed?
- Marketing
  - What changes are needed in distribution system?
  - What should be the promotion campaign?
  - What services should we provide?
  - Must we provide customer financing?
- Financing
  - Do we need outside financing?
  - What is our financial outlook for each year of the next five years for this product?
- Management
  - What new managerial training is required?
  - What new managers will we need?

The answers, in turn, of course, will result in decisions. If there is a multiple-year functional planning program, the decisions will be reflected there. If not, the decisions will be reflected directly in the short-range plans of the company.

Budgets

Budgeting translates organizational plans into concrete terms. Operational plans, for example, can be translated into operating budgets, such as production budgets, budgets for the purchase of raw materials, and so on. Facilities planning is translated into capital budgets; financial planning is translated into cash budgeting, and so on.

NATURE AND PURPOSE OF BUDGETS. Peter Drucker once observed: "The test of a plan . . . is not how good the plan is itself. The test is whether management actually commits resources to action which will bring results in the future. Unless this is being done, there is no plan. There are only promises and hopes" [in Ewing, 1972:5]. A dominant method to make commitments to assure action is a budget.

Budgets are formal statements of policies, plans, and goals that are designed to assure

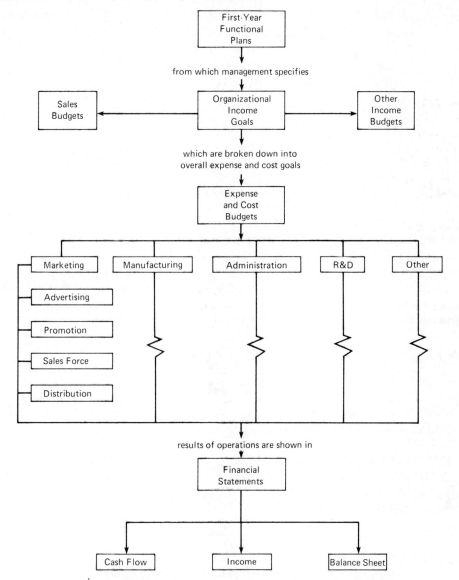

Figure 14-4 A simplified development and structure of operating budgets.

that actions are taken within specified boundaries laid down by top management and upon the basis of which performance can be measured. Three basic purposes are expressed in this definition. Budgets are based upon plans, as explained previously, and are plans in themselves. Budgets conceptually express detailed plans that interrelate various functional activities in such a fashion as to assure the most effective and efficient utilization of resources to achieve the objectives sought. This means that budgets interrelate such activities as production, raw material purchases, inventories, facilities, labor requirements, and so on. Budgets are vehicles for assuring the proper coordination of activities. Budgets set standards for performance and when management monitors activities there will be control over performance. Budgets not only facilitate but force integration of functional activities to achieve predetermined objectives.

TYPES OF BUDGETS. Although budgeting is universal in usage, there is no uniform pattern of budgets in use in industry. Budgets can be prepared for virtually anything managers wish to try to control. Typically, most companies have some types of financial budgets. A coordinated structure of financial budgets is presented in Figure 14-4. Notice the dominant position of the cash budget, which is typical in industry.

FLEXIBILITY IN BUDGETING. Jerome [1961:109] observed that: "To freeze a plan and to put a dollar sign on it is the essence of budgeting. But as soon as plans are frozen, the attitude and behavior of everyone concerned with the plans have a way of freezing too." Managers adopt a number of methods to assure flexibility in budgets. Among these are supplemental budgets, which provide funding above budget ceilings; alternative budgets, which may be applied when different environmental conditions occur; and variable expense budgets, which relate such elements as raw material purchase, inventory, direct labor, and supervisory costs to fluctuations in customer demand and production runs. In addition to such budgets, top management injects flexibility into budgeting through its own activities and by instilling flexible thinking in the minds of all managers.

THE MANAGEMENT CONTROL PROCESS

The word control is used here in the sense of managerial control that seeks to insure that performance conforms to plans. This process, of course, is the final step in translating strategic plans into current actions in such a way as to implement the strategic plans to achieve the objectives for which they were set. This process, as depicted simply in Figure 14-5 involves three basic steps—establishing standards, measuring performance against standards, and correcting deviations from standards. If this process does not meet the satisfaction of management then, as shown in Figure 14-5, plans should be changed.

Types of Controls

The following type controls may be classified by use on the basis of their controls to standardize performance, to conserve assets, to standardize quality, to limit authority without top management's approval, to measure performance, and so on. Newman classified controls into three basic types. First are steering controls, which are designed to detect deviations from a standard and to permit corrective action before an operation is completed. For example, trajectory measurements were made immediately after the moon spacecraft takeoff and corrections were made long before the vehicle reached the moon. Quality controls in the production process may also be of this type. Second are yes-no controls, which specify that approval is required before a next step can be

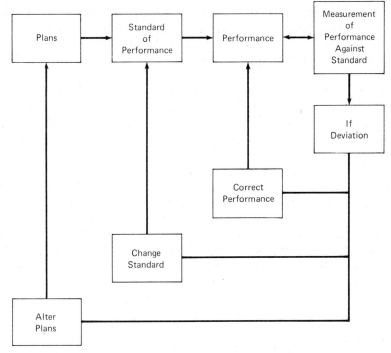

Figure 14-5 A model of the management control process.

taken. Steps in the development of a new product may be monitored with this type control system. Finally, there are postaction controls, which measure results after an action is completed. Annual ROI reviews of managerial performance are of this type [Newman, 1975]. Most of what is said in the following analysis concerns the first type, steering controls.

Establishing Standards

The key to determining what standards will be set is the answer to this question: What is it that management wishes to measure? Standards cannot be set for everything, so choices must be made about those key activities that managers wish to monitor continuously.

The more concrete and specific the standard is, the easier it will be to measure performance against it. This is not to say that all standards must be specific. Actually, not all activities that management wishes to monitor can be expressed in concrete terms. For example, a plan to improve managerial training is not readily expressed in numbers.

Measuring Performance Against Standards

There are many important facets to the measurement of performance. First, how much variation will constitute a reason for taking corrective action?

Second, managers must be on the alert to determine whether standards should be altered. As changes in environment take place it may be necessary to correct standards before looking at performance. Variable budgets are designed to do precisely this.

Third, management must develop the proper type of reporting and information system to appraise, compare, and correct performance. This aspect of control opens up a vast subject because it concerns not only control but all other aspects of management as well. So far as control is concerned, the management information system must identify certain points in a manager's area of responsibility. Surveillance of these points will permit the manager to exercise the appropriate control over employee performance to achieve the targets for which the manager is responsible. This is a complex design problem because it must be responsive to a manager's needs, knowledge, preferred methods to get and use information, the standard under review, and so on. The less concrete the standard against which performance is measured the more difficult is the information system design problem.

Control reports will vary much at different levels in the organization. The chief executive officer, for instance, will want reports concerned with whether the missions and objectives of the company are still adequate, whether critical parts of the strategic plan are being implemented (e.g., acquisitions, divestment, new product development, and progress of new facility construction), and whether current operations are satisfactory.

The executive vice-president will want much more penetrating details about the operations of the enterprise. The focus of lower level managers will be still narrower.

Finally, getting reports that compare actual results with desired results may be useful for certain types of information but quite inadequate for others. When managers are appraising the overall performance of other managers, a comparison of financial results of their area of operation with predetermined objectives is a needed base for evaluation. For many other types of activities, however, what is required is advance warning, or predictors of results. This is future oriented, feedforward, control [Koontz and Bradspies, 1972]. Managers do not want to find out that sales last month were 10 per cent under what was desired. They want to know today that sales next month may be 10 per cent under standard unless some action is taken to counter the trend. Really effective control requires accurate prediction.

Much ingenuity is needed to find useful predictors. Forecasts provide one type of forewarning. Networks, such as scheduling flows of activities, may serve to flag future difficulties when a particular milestone is not reached. A sales manager may use a composite of field visits, customer inquiries, complaints, returned merchandise, and so on, to foresee future deviations from plans.

Evaluating Performance and Taking Corrective Action

Measurements of past performances and predictions of things to come alert management to what is going on or likely to happen but do not determine what should be done. There are two phases to this activity. The first concerns the evaluation of the warning signals, and the second relates to managerial decision about any remedies for correcting deviations from standards.

Proper evaluation of signals is important. Some methods to predict future events may not be entirely reliable, and considerable judgment may be required to prevent precipitous action. For example, a sudden increase in the sale of a product may indicate a fad and not a long-lived increase in consumer demand. To take action on the current jump in sales could lead to excessive overcapacity, rising costs per unit, and declining profits.

Once a manager decides that corrective action is required, the issue then joins the entire process of management. Revision of plans may be required. New standards may be needed. New leadership may be in order. Better motivation of employees may be desired. And so on. Although control may be identified as a key function of managers, it cannot be performed without simultaneous actions among other functions.

MANAGEMENT BY OBJECTIVE (MBO)

Drucker [1954] is widely credited with first publicizing the MBO approach. Today MBO is widely used in industry, has been used in the federal government, and is widely found in many nonprofit organizations.

There are almost as many definitions of MBO as writers in the field. McConkey defines the system as follows:

MBO is a systems approach to managing an organization—*any* organization. It is not a technique, or just another program, or a narrow area of the process of managing. Above all, it goes far beyond mere budgeting even though it does encompass budgets in one form or another.

First, those accountable for directing the organization determine where they want to take the organization or what they want it to achieve during a particular period (establishing the overall objectives and priorities).

Second, all key managerial, professional, and administrative personnel are required, permitted, and encouraged to contribute their maximum efforts to achieving the overall objectives.

Third, the planned achievement (results) of all key personnel is blended and balanced to promote and realize the greater total results for the organization as a whole.

Fourth, a control mechanism is established to monitor progress compared to objectives and feed the results back to those accountable at all levels [McConkey, 1975:10–11].

The operating systems found in practice vary considerably from very simple systems, where superiors and subordinates agree upon a simple set of objectives to be achieved by the subordinates, to very complex systems, which seek to integrate many management processes and activities in a logical and consistent manner. In some companies with very elementary budget systems, MBO may carry an important responsibility for implementing strategies to achieve the overall objectives of a company. In companies with well-established and sophisticated budget systems, MBO may be a vital complement to budgets in implementing strategies.

MBO is a system that can facilitate planning and the implementation of plans. It should be observed, however, that it can have wider purposes, such as to motivate people to help achieve organizational aims, to improve problem solving and decision making in a company, to facilitate performance appraisal, and, in general, to improve management so as to achieve more efficiently and effectively the aims sought by an organization. A number of studies support the view that MBO can be a significant process in improving implementation of plans [Carroll and Tosi, 1973; Howell, 1970]. Other benefits are also claimed for the system. Thus McConkey [1973:27] in a 20-year reassessment of reported company experience concluded that " . . . practicing MBO in depth does result in improved communication, coordination, control, and motivation of managers. These desirable ends are considered the minimum an organization should expect from its MBO efforts. . . ."

Like formal strategic planning, however, MBO is conceptually simple but deceptively difficult to do well. There are many pitfalls to be avoided for successful application of an MBO system to occur, and sizable numbers of companies have indeed fallen into them [Mines, 1980a]. Carroll and Tosi [1973:107] in their assessment of MBO experience, concluded that " . . . unless the various organizational systems are tied into MBO, it will be very difficult to carry out the MBO process." They also noted that there is a tendency for MBO programs to become less effective after the first year or so of application. Ford [1979] says there are so many things that can go wrong with MBO that it is an idea whose time has gone. This view is not universally shared [Odiorne, 1978, 1979; Richards, 1978] but does warn managers and scholars that major pitfalls must be avoided if MBO is to be valuable. But that is true of most all managerial tools and systems.

Because of the many problems associated with MBO, it is not as likely to facilitate efficient and effective implementation of strategies as will a well-conceived system of budgets and tactical plans. Nevertheless, an appropriate MBO system may complement a well-conceived short-range planning system in insuring superior implementation of strategies and more effective achievement of overall aims.

CONCLUDING COMMENT

To repeat what was said at the beginning of this chapter, there is a wide range of formal systems for implementing policy/strategy. A few of the most important ones were examined. Of equal if not greater importance in implementation is the role of people in implementation. This is the subject of the next chapter.

QUESTIONS

Discussion Guides on Chapter Content
1. Identify what you believe to be the most significant managerial devices for integrating activities in organizations to assure the implementation of strategies.
2. How do you visualize differing integrating systems among Thompson's three types of organizational interdependence?
3. Specify how a strategic planning system can assure the proper implementation of policies/strategies.

4. What is meant by linkage in plans? Do you favor a tight or loose linkage? Explain.
5. What are the principal purposes of budgets?
6. How do budgets differ from tactical plans in the implementation of policy/strategy? Are they similar?
7. How would you define "the management control process"?
8. Discuss some key considerations in establishing standards to measure performance, actually measuring performance, and correcting deviations from standards.
9. Explain how MBO can improve the implementation of policy/strategy.

Mind Stretching Questions
1. Identify four or five different managerial styles that might be adopted by the chief executive officer of an organization and explain how implementation systems may vary depending upon the style.
2. How do you think formal systems for implementing policy/strategy might differ as between a very small company making bakery products and a company like General Electric Company.

15

The Role of People
in Implementation

INTRODUCTION

When policies are formulated, strategies are developed, and plans are established, there is a definite assumption that what is decided will in fact be done. To the extent such decisions are clearly and effectively stated, they can be translated into specific organizational structures and formal systems for implementation. Each individual member of the organization who is touched by a policy is in effect provided with information as to how he or she is expected to act so that the policy may be carried out. These role prescriptions or implementation plans vary from individual to individual, depending on the particular nature of the job; but, when all are put together in the end, it is intended that they add up to effective policy implementation.

Unfortunately, effective implementation is not entirely a matter of decision-making factors; concrete, clear, explicit, and comprehensive role statements do not guarantee that policies will be implemented. The people who make up an organization vary widely in terms of their motives, values, capabilities, and so on. Often they cannot or simply do not wish to implement a policy, or do what is required to implement it. There is no certainty that job behavior will match the requirements that have been established. It is this problem introduced by the people who work in a company, rather than problems inherent in the policy formation process itself or in the organization structures and formal systems introduced to implement policy, that will be of concern in this chapter.

PARTICIPATION AND POLICY/STRATEGY IMPLEMENTATION

Human behavior on the job is a complex result of many factors, and all of these can contribute to job behavior that departs from role expectations and thus to failures of implementation. One analysis identified 35 types of factors that might contribute to this result [Miner, 1975].

However, those factors falling in the broad area of motivation have been very much at the forefront insofar as discussions of policy implementation are concerned. Thus, the desires, wishes, needs and values of those who must implement policies will provide the primary focus in the ensuing treatment.

Participation and the Acceptance of Decisions

For a number of years a group of very productive and widely read authors have been advocating participation as the answer to the implementation problem. Among them are Argyris [1970], the Likerts [1976], and McGregor [1960]. According to this view, the way to get people to accept a decision and have a desire to implement it is to involve them in the decision-making process itself, so that they can come to view the decision as at least in part their own. The basic assumption is that people will *want* to do what they themselves have *decided* to do. The argument is a cogent one, so much so that many people tend to think of participation almost automatically whenever questions regarding problems of implementation are raised.

Furthermore, a number of well-conducted research studies tend to support this argument [Maier, 1970]. Consistently in these studies of small-group decision making, acceptance has been higher for participative decisions, or where the individual made his own choice, as opposed to the condition where outsiders did the planning or chose the problem solution.

Managers clearly do vary their styles as they are exposed to real implementation problems of various kinds (see Chapter 12). In addition, they report using participation more, and thus engaging their subordinates in the decision-making process more, when they foresee problems in getting a decision actually carried out. On balance, there is sufficient evidence available to recommend the use of participation when, for some reason, the individual manager foresees trouble in getting his subordinates to accept a decision in a particular area.

Participation at the Policy Level

However, there are a number of considerations that raise questions regarding the widespread use of participation at higher levels, on policy issues. For one thing top-level managers are very loath to resort to participation when the decisions are of great importance to the company, presumably because they tend to suspect the motives of subordinates and believe the recommended policies may be more in the self-interest of the recommenders than in the interest of the company [Heller, 1971]. Also, there is consistent evidence that top-level decisions are likely to be implemented somewhat more than lower level decisions, and that even participative decisions benefit from top-level support; role prescriptions accepted at high levels and promulgated with the idea that sanctions will be mobilized behind them do tend to gain greater acceptance [Bell, 1968]. Thus, there may be less need to use participation on top-level policy issues. In any event it is evident that widespread resistance to the use of participation is characteristic where the decision is one that is usually made at upper levels in an organization and the decision sharing involves individuals with low job status (Rosen and Jerdee, 1977). This reluctance to share appears to be associated with concerns about competence and about commitment to organizational goals.

All this suggests that hierarchy never does totally disappear, even when widespread participation in policy making is the accepted norm. Data from studies of conventional American business firms as well as socialist organizations in Yugoslavia and Israel support this conclusion [Tannenbaum *et al.,* 1974]. Top managers may be willing to coöpt other members of the organization to the extent necessary, but they do not go all the way to power-equalization. Presumably there are good reasons for this fact.

The problem appears to be that findings regarding the value of participation in small groups, or with reference to specific decisions where implementation by the particular individual consulted is crucial, do not appear to be as applicable to policy issues at the top levels of large organizations. Thus, a chief executive who shares decisions with his "cabinet" may gain support for implementation at that level but no further.

However, implementation requires support at many levels further down. Should all these levels participate in the decision to gain their acceptance? Is it even possible for them to participate really? Do they have the expertise to participate or even to feel they are participating? Does not the sheer weight of large numbers create a situation where each individual's influence on a decision is so small that there is little incentive to implementation? In short, can the implementation advantages of participation be obtained throughout large groups and organizations, and is real participation possible under such circumstances?

The data available suggest that the answer is a very qualified yes at best [Miner, 1982]. Top level policy inplementation problems cannot be fully solved through participation. Expertise differentials and influence diffusion are simply too great for the advantages of participation found in small-group or in one-to-one situations to apply in most cases. Attempts to solve this problem by viewing the company as a series of interlocking small groups (the linking-pin concept proposed by Likert) seem to misrepresent the facts. When a chief executive shares decisions with his vice presidents and policy is established, there is no possibility that managers at the next lower level can either make these decisions themselves or share them with their subordinates. Large organizations and the managerial hierarchies they produce preclude a total reliance on participation to achieve effective implementation.

THE LARGER ISSUE OF ORGANIZATIONAL COMMITMENT

The underlying principle in the use of participation is that a person who is involved in making a decision will feel committed to it and will want to see it implemented. In small homogeneous groups this seems to work in the sense that decision acceptance does occur, although greater productivity or output need not occur [Locke and Schweiger, 1979]. The point is that resistance to implementation is defused. In large organizations, where policies apply to very sizable numbers of people and where certain individuals are likely to exert undue influence on decisions because of their relevant expertise, the use of participation in policy making does not appear to work as well.

Yet the idea of commitment is an important one for policy implementation. What seems to be needed is for the members of the organization to be committed to it and to its objectives so that they will accept policies, strategies, and plans that appear to be in the organization's interest. The concept of organizational commitment draws upon the principles inherent in participation, but broadens them to apply to the organization as a whole, rather than to each decision separately. This broadened perspective makes organizational commitment a very important factor in policy implementation.

The Nature of Organizational Commitment

Although definitions of organizational commitment tend to vary, a common theme is clearly in evidence. Buchanan [1974, 1975] notes the following components:

1. A sense of identification with the organization's objectives such that individual and organizational goals are closely aligned.
2. A sense of involvement and psychological immersion in one's work resulting in considerable enjoyment.
3. A sense of loyalty, perhaps even affection, toward this particular organization as a place to spend one's time and work.

Another formulation takes a similar approach [Porter, Crampon, and Smith, 1976; Morris and Steers, 1980]:

1. A strong belief in and acceptance of the organization's goals and values.
2. A willingness to exert high levels of effort on behalf of the organization.
3. A strong desire to remain a member of the organization.

These definitions were developed with corporate and governmental organizations in mind, but the type of organization appears to matter very little. Thus a study of commitment to a union identified union loyalty, responsibility to the union, willingness to work for the union, and belief in unionism as major components [Gordon *et al.,* 1980]. Again the aspects of organizational commitment emerge as very much the same.

Such a commitment tends to be present in older, more senior employees, who are at higher levels in the organization; also in those who basically trust their organization, who have a clear understanding of what they are expected to do, and who desire to exert influence [Hrebiniak, 1974]. Trust is a particularly strong concomitant of organizational commitment, especially as reflected in faith in management [Cook and Wall, 1980]. The basic pattern involved appears to be as follows:

Individuals come to organizations with certain needs, desires, skills, and so forth, and expect to find a work environment where they can utilize their abilities and satisfy many of their basic needs. When the organization provides such a vehicle . . . the likelihood of increasing commitment is apparently enhanced. When the organization is not dependable, however, or where it fails to provide employees with challenging and meaningful tasks, commitment levels tend to diminish [Steers, 1977:53].

As might be anticipated changes in commitment levels are closely associated with a propensity to leave the organization [Porter, Crampon and Smith, 1976].

Further data on factors associated with organizational commitment are given in Table 15-1. The four organizations described there are taken from a total of eight that were studied—five federal government agencies and three large corporations. As Table 15-1 indicates, managerial commitment was consistently higher in the private sector than in government.

Given the conceptual ties between participation and organizational commitment, one might expect a direct relationship between the two. Actually, however, the association is more complex. Employees having a high level of organizational commitment do feel satisfied with the extent of participation they experience [Alutto and Acito, 1974]; they also tend to be employed in more decentralized organizational contexts [Morris and Steers, 1980]. But the key factor appears to be something labelled *political access*—being able to raise issues and to secure serious attention to these issues [Mohrman, 1979]. It is not actually being able to participate in a wide range of decisions that makes for trust, commitment, and ultimately a more effective organization, but rather the capacity to gain an appropriate forum on issues that are important to the individual.

Professional Commitment

A question arises regarding commitment as a means to policy implementation in organizations that employ a large number of professionals. Studies indicate close relationships among various kinds of commitments—to one's job, career, and organization [Wiener and Vardi, 1980]. Yet there is also a widely held view that professional commitment draws people away from the organization, to a more cosmopolitan world outside. The evidence indicates, however, that professionalism and professional commitment is positively related to organizational commitment; thus, it, too, appears to provide a base for the more effective implementation of policy [Bartol, 1979]. Individuals with strong professional commitment tend to do well in terms of the external criteria of success utilized by the profession, but they also tend to receive greater organizational rewards in the form of promotions and salary increases [Miner, 1980b].

Inducing Organizational Commitment

Knowledge of how to create commitment, whether organizational or professional is not as extensive as might be desired, and this of course is the really crucial consideration. Furthermore, we know little about any side effects of commitment that might yield detrimental consequences for the organization, in spite of the positive implications for policy implementation [Salancik, 1977].

There clearly are major differences among people in the propensity for feeling a strong sense of commitment to an organization. Some people are averse to any such feeling with regard to any organization. Others hold certain values that conflict with a particular organization's mission so strongly that identification with that organization may be impossible. Strong environmentalists do have problems in the wood products and coal industries, vegetarians find identification difficult in meat packaging firms, and so on. The answer in these cases is to try not to hire people who have little chance of developing commitment in the first place.

TABLE 15-1

Average Scores for Factors Differentiating between Two Organizations Having Managers with High and
Two with Low Levels of Commitment (Out of a Total of Eight Organizations Studied)

FACTOR	LOW COMMITMENT LEVELS		HIGH COMMITMENT LEVELS	
	GOVERNMENT AGENCY	GOVERNMENT AGENCY	LARGE CORPORATION	LARGE CORPORATION
Commitment score	101.5	99.2	141.3	142.3
Feeling that present job is accepted as important	18.9	19.4	29.4	29.3
People worked with during first year had mostly positive attitudes to organization	16.5	18.5	22.8	21.8
Feeling that organization has fulfilled initial expectations	16.3	14.4	24.3	28.0
Managers are *expected* to be personally committed to organization	13.8	12.9	16.3	17.3
Given challenging work to do during first year with organization	12.7	13.9	17.6	15.4
People currently working with have mostly positive attitudes to organization	16.2	19.0	19.7	22.5
People currently working with friendly and close-knit	12.7	12.2	22.4	22.6

SOURCE: Adapted from Buchanan [1974:539–540, 1975:72].

NOTE: The factors noted are the seven out of the thirteen studied that clearly differentiated between high- and low-commitment organizations as defined by the overall Commitment Score.

Another important consideration appears to be to avoid overstaffing, so that job challenge may be maintained and organizationally meaningless make-work avoided. People should be told about the relationship between what they are doing and organizationally relevant ends, even if this seems obvious. Furthermore, attention should be given to their work, and responsibilities expanded at periodic intervals. Above all it is important not to induce unrealistic expectations that may result in later disillusionment with the firm. Companies should convey the message that organizational commitment is expected, and top-level managers should be very careful not to act in their own self-interest at the expense of the firm. A poor model at the top will almost guarantee it at lower levels.

All this does not imply that organizational commitment is a panacea for all policy implementation problems. Some organizations do not appear to be able to use this approach effectively, and it is not entirely clear why. Certainly there are large numbers of employees with whom this method of achieving policy implementation simply will not work.

On the other hand, the consistent finding that trust is an important concomitant of commitment bears attention. If organizational members are given every opportunity to air their concerns and have reason to believe they will receive fair treatment, this can contribute considerably to commitment. Often this means no more than taking the time to explain in detail why a certain policy action has been taken, rather than arbitrarily noting that "this is the way it is." In any event it means keeping promises once they are made and openning up channels of communication, so that people can actively explore methods of satisfying needs within the organization.

LEGITIMATE AUTHORITY AND THE INDUCEMENT-CONTRIBUTION BALANCE

The traditional approach, should other approaches either fail or appear to have little chance of succeeding, has been to implement policies through the use of hierarchic authority and by varying positive and negative sanctions. The use of hierarchic control in this manner to get policies carried out has continued to receive widespread usage [Miner, 1978] in spite of its general unpopularity even among many managers who apply it [Haire, Ghiselli, and Porter, 1966], and a long-standing attack by human relations advocates. Argyris [1964], for example, has argued that exposure to hierarchic control in this manner is debilitating to the individual and stunts psychological growth. Certainly writers in this area have produced convincing evidence documenting their view that the use of formal authority often elicits a response from the informal organization that effectively serves to undermine policy implementation.

Yet the fact that the use of authority continues to be a major, if not the major, method of implementing policies does bear some testimonial to its effectiveness. There are occasions when there appears to be no alternative available, and at such times effective managers will use all the authority they can bring to bear rather than see important policies go unimplemented. Certainly experienced managers do view the use of authority as an effective way of getting policies carried out, while recognizing that there are certain negative side effects and that total implementation is unlikely. Studies have repeatedly demonstrated that changes initiated by top management and promulgated down through the managerial hierarchy do produce results [Dalton, Barnes, and Zaleznik, 1968; Guest, 1962; O'Connell, 1968].

It should be recognized, however, that in any society which protects the rights of individuals, hierarchic organizational control can never be complete and total [Lee, 1977]. Top management cannot get people to do anything; only what those people are willing to do without taking some counteraction that is definitely not desired by the company, such as leaving employment, bringing suit against the company, engaging in sabatoge, or enlisting strong union support.

In this sense the response to authority is to some degree negotiated. A lower level manager may have the weight of support from higher authority behind him, but his subordinates have the weight of society's laws and values to call on also. Thus, the views regarding the upward flow of authority, expressed originally by Barnard [1968] and Simon [1976] do fit the realities of the organizational authority situation.

Companies must offer inducements to get people to do the sorts of things necessary to have policies implemented, and the use of authority must be viewed as legitimate in terms both of its source and of its nature. The organization gives something; in return it obtains a willingness to contribute in a manner specified by legitimate authority up to a certain maximum. Beyond that the organization will have to give more.

One major thing that companies give as an inducement is money; there is no question that in doing so they can motivate people and get them to contribute [Lawler and Rhode, 1976]. The problem is that in building the inducement-contribution balance primarily around money one is forced to rely largely on authority to implement policy. Organizational commitment appears to be a contribution that is elicited more by other types of inducements, such as a feeling that one's work is important and challenging.

Also, the effective use of sanctions to implement policies requires that the rewards be firmly placed behind behavior that is desired. All too often, as Haire [1964] and more recently Kerr [1975] have pointed out, the behavior actually rewarded turns out to be different from, if not directly antithetical to, that which the policies imply. Table 15-2 contains data taken from one division of a large manufacturing firm concerning the extent to which lower level employees perceive that rewards are placed behind risk taking and nonconformity. In this particular company it is the policy to encourage employees at all levels to take appropriate risks and to think originally and creatively about developing new approaches to the work. In fact the reason for collecting the data of Table 15-2 from employees was to determine if this policy approach was being effectively implemented [Kerr, 1975].

Clearly, it was not. Sizable proportions of the employees indicated that taking risks was, in fact, disapproved by their supervisors rather than being rewarded and that conformity was a source of positive reward. In no case did a majority describe their work situation as one where risk taking was definitely rewarded and the nonconformity required for creative, new decisions fostered. Somehow the reward system had become disengaged from the policy system. This appears to be a rather frequent occurrence; the contributions induced by rewards are not those the policies presuppose.

IMPLEMENTING AFFIRMATIVE ACTION POLICIES: AN EXAMPLE

In the past few years one of the most active areas of policy formation and implementation has been that of equal employment opportunity. Under pressure from various government agencies and the courts, which are in turn backed by a variety of newly enacted laws and executive orders, many companies including practically all of the large ones, have introduced staffing policies revised to foster affirmative action in the hiring and upgrading of women and/or minorities [Miner and Miner, 1978]. These policies have presented some very difficult implementation problems and thus provide fertile ground for illustrating implementation approaches.

As evidence that this is a policy issue that companies will have to deal with for some time in the future, data from a recent Delphi study of experts in the area can be cited [Fry, 1980]. Full equality of employment for minorities was not anticipated on the average until 2040; however, a concensus was not achieved, and many of the experts

TABLE 15-2
Extent to Which Lower Level Employees Expect Approval or Disapproval for Certain Risk and Conformity—Related Behaviors ($N = 127$)

	PER CENT EXPECTING		
BEHAVIOR	DISAPPROVAL	NOT SURE	APPROVAL
Making a risky decision based on the best information available at the time, but which turns out wrong.	61	25	14
Setting extremely high and challenging standards and goals, and then narrowly failing to make them.	47	28	25
Setting goals that are extremely easy to make and then making them.	35	30	35
Being a "yes man" and always agreeing with the boss.	46	17	37
Always going along with the majority.	40	25	35
Being careful to stay on the good side of everyone, so that everyone agrees that you are a great guy.	45	18	37

SOURCE: Steven Kerr: "On the Folly of Rewarding A, While Hoping for B." *Academy of Management Journal,* December 1975. Reprinted by permission of the Academy of Management.

did not expect the problem to be resolved for another 100 years or more. For women agreement was greater, and the average date for full integration was 2024. General integration in the *larger* companies was anticipated long before this result is achieved in smaller firms.

Problems and Methods of Implementation

Affirmative action policies typically establish certain goals for hiring minorities and women so as to create employment percentages roughly comparable to appropriate labor force statistics. Those statistics may be for the local labor force, the national labor force, the proportion of college graduates in the labor force, and so on, depending on the occupational and geographical groups involved.

These policy goals often have proved difficult to achieve for a variety of reasons, among them a lack of job qualifications on the part of minorities and women, a lack of requisite motivation in these groups, and the existence of strong stereotypes and prejudices among those currently employed. On the latter score for instance, it has been found that white supervisors are more likely to resort to firing, suspension, written warnings, and formal disciplinary actions for the same infractions with black subordinates than with whites [Kipnis, Silverman, and Copeland, 1973].

Yet a number of companies have achieved some success in implementing affirmative action programs. They have done this in part by instituting a variety of special recruiting, selection, training, counseling, and other services through the personnel department. Personnel managers have generally been very sensitive to the negative consequences for a company associated with a lack of compliance with governmental regulations in the equal employment opportunity area. Many have worked hard in support of these special programs out of a strong sense of organizational commitment and a feeling of responsibility for protecting the company against the sizable financial costs that may accrue if affirmative action goals are not met.

Within the line organization some companies such as General Electric have achieved success in implementing affirmative action policies by establishing specific goals for every manager in the company who has responsibility for hiring and firing [Miner and Miner, 1978; Purcell, 1974]. Rewards and punishments then are tied to these goals through management appraisal and compensation systems that give specific attention to the affirmative action implementation factor.

The results of a survey conducted among equal employment opportunity compliance officers in the federal government as given in Table 15-3 provide some insight into the kinds of implementation actions that are likely to be viewed as representing a good faith effort on the company's part [Marino, 1980]. Doing these things can be expected to minimize the risk of governmental action against the company and thus achieve at least one objective of affirmative action policies.

The Use of Authority, Participation, and Commitment

Policy implementation in the affirmative action area may require that the top managers who introduced the policy maintain a continuing close tie between inducements, such as pay and promotions, and contributions to the end of facilitating the hiring and retention of minorities. Given the existing laws and the effects that penalities may have on company profits, the area of affirmative action is clearly one where the use of managerial authority is an appropriate method of inducing change.

The extent to which such authority may be needed appears to vary, depending on the extent of resistance generated by existing prejudices and stereotypes. One large firm reports a successful introduction of blacks into sales and repair positions involving considerable customer contact, which had previously been considered very sensitive on this issue. The managers responsible for actually implementing the change were in fact highly supportive and acceptance by fellow employees and customers was good. Subsequent performance levels for the blacks were equal to those of whites and retention rates somewhat better [Kraut, 1975].

Yet it is apparent that affirmative action policies, like many other policies, are not easy to implement. There are often major sources of resistance at lower levels, and these may manifest themselves in many different ways. Where such resistances exist their manifestations must be identified and dealt with, usually through appropriate use of legitimate authority and inducements. To the extent organizational commitment can be mobilized, it can make a useful contribution to implementation in the affirmative action area, as in any policy area. The important need is that the relevance of affirmative action for company goal-attainment be clearly spelled out and understood. Participation has not been widely utilized in this type of policy implementation, but there is some evidence that it might prove useful in gaining acceptance for changes in the composition of work groups [Marrow and French, 1945].

Problems of implementation in this area are at present increasingly being compounded

TABLE 15-3

Actions That Federal Compliance Officers Consider Evidence of Good Faith in Implementing Affirmative Action Policies

GENERAL CATEGORIES OF ACTIONS AND SPECIFIC EXAMPLES	MEAN IMPORTANCE SCORE (1–7 SCALE)
Seeking community support	
Evidence that a formal EEO (Equal Employment Opportunity) compliance procedure has been established	5.9
Sponsoring a formal on-the-job training program	5.8
Institution of a transportation program or car pooling service	5.3
Appointment of key management personnel for service on community relations boards	4.8
Informing the employees	
Posting of promotion opportunities within work areas	6.5
Explanation of the company's EEO policy during new employee orientation	5.9
Discussion of EEO matters in company publications	5.4
Display of company EEO policy statement in work areas	5.0
Internalizing the EEO policy	
Evidence that the company treats violations of EEO policy as severely as other policy violations	6.7
Inclusion of affirmative action progress in management performance evaluations	6.4
Evidence that minority employees are encouraged to refer other minorities for employment	6.1
Direct notification of all eligible employees regarding promotion opportunities	6.0
Enhancing advancement opportunities	
Evidence that the company EEO coordinator has authority to review all hiring and promotion decisions	6.5
Institution of minority-oriented training programs	5.9
Availability of tuition-refund benefits	4.8
Increasing minority applicant flow	
Personal contact by the EEO coordinator with agencies such as the Urban League or Job Corps	6.1
Inclusion of predominantly minority colleges in campus recruiting	6.0
Retention of applications from unhired minorities for review as future vacancies occur	5.9
Participation in Job Fair and Career Day programs at area high schools	5.0
Demonstrating top management support	
Evidence that the CEO is seriously committed to EEO policy	6.7
General awareness of the EEO coordinator regarding matters related to compliance	6.5
Involvement of line supervisors in establishing affirmative action hiring goals	6.3
Frequency of preparation of written reports evaluating progress toward affirmative action goals	5.8

SOURCE: Adapted from Marino [1980:348–349].

by affirmative action backlash. White males who have been passed over for promotion solely because of affirmative action goals may well react with strong feelings of inequity. Feelings of this kind as regards perceived preferential treatment of women have been found to exist in roughly 20 per cent of employed white males [Rosen and Jerdee, 1979]. Similar findings as regards minorities would be anticipated.

The result is that management can become caught between pressures from the government and female or minority groups on the one side, and a sizable proportion of the company's employees on the other. Such a situation argues for some possible moderation in the use of unilateral authority to enforce affirmative action goals. Commitment and participation become more attractive alternatives. In this connection the following approaches have been recommended:

1. Reassessment of affirmative action guidelines to identify inequities . . . to insure that guidelines established to create more opportunities for minorities are not in themselves unfairly discriminatory against other groups.
2. Survey of employee reactions to affirmative action . . . to identify areas where improved communication about the rationale behind a specific affirmative action policy is needed.
3. Education and awareness . . . to correct misunderstandings and change negative attitudes toward the program.
4. Employee participation in implementation of affirmative action goals . . . to facilitate both creative solutions to complex problems and greater commitment to the implementation of these solutions [Rosen and Jerdee, 1979:19–20].

EXCEPTIONS TO POLICY AND IMPLEMENTATION

The discussion to this point has concentrated entirely on the implementation of existing policies, strategies, and plans. However, there are instances where, in spite of cogent arguments for maintaining a policy in general, there do appear to be good reasons for making specific exceptions. Thus, a company having a basic policy of expansion through acquisitions, and with a very small research and development investment, might still make an exception to the standard expansion policy should an extremely promising product emerge unexpectedly from internal research efforts. Similarly, an exception to a policy of promotion from within might be made should a situation arise where the best internal candidate for a position was an unlikely prospect at best, and highly qualified alternative candidates were readily available in the industry.

The argument against making exceptions to policy is that they may undermine implementation of existing policy where that policy is entirely appropriate. If people can point to exceptions, they may use these as a basis for arguing against implementation in other instances, or they may simply not implement because they feel the policy has limited validity due to past failures to implement. Such an undermining of policies can occur; the threat is real. Yet the need for some mechanism to permit exceptions so that capitalizing on special circumstances is not precluded is just as real [Miner, 1975].

Exceptions to policy should be made only in the presence of convincing evidence in their favor. They should be made only at the highest levels or by special units or committees to which such powers have been delegated. They should be recorded in writing and if a number of exceptions to a particular policy are required this very fact should serve as a basis for reevaluating the policy. To the extent exceptions are limited in number, obtained only with high-level, formal approval, and based on explicit, rational considerations, undermining of policy implementation on a general basis should not be a problem. Otherwise, there is a distinct possibility that implementation may be gradually eroded over time.

CONCLUDING COMMENT

There are many other aspects of the role of people in implementation, but space prevents examination of them. Managers are giving more and more attention to implementation. Strategy implementation is a big hole in research in the area, especially with respect to the role of people in implementation.

QUESTIONS

Discussion Guides on Chapter Content

1. What problems are involved in using widespread participation to facilitate implementation of major corporate decisions? Why might top-level managers resist this approach?
2. What is organizational commitment, and how does it facilitate implementation? What are some of the components of organizational commitment?
3. Where and when would one expect to find high levels of organizational commitment?
4. What relationships exist among various types of commitment? Is professional commitment a bar to organizational commitment?
5. How does the inducements-contributions balance relate to implementation? What are the theoretical origins of this concept?
6. What are some of the limits on managerial authority in the United States?
7. Why is affirmative action policy difficult to implement? What are the roles of authority, participation, and commitment in this area?
8. Discuss the matter of exceptions to policy. What are the arguments pro and con?

Mind Stretching Questions

1. We have considered the matter of implementing affirmative action policies. Select some other major policy and discuss the implementation problems you would foresee and the methods you would use to deal with them.
2. What are the various things that those at lower levels may do to impede the implementation of top management policies? Why would they do these things? Is such behavior irrational?

Policy/Strategy in Varied Contexts

16

Entrepreneurship

INTRODUCTION

This and the following chapters deal with policy/strategy considerations outside the framework of the established business corporation, which has been the major focus of the discussion to this point. There are two particular types of organizations that require consideration, each of which is treated in a separate chapter. The first is the new business venture headed by, and in the early stages almost synonymous with, a single entrepreneur or a small entrepreneurial group. The second is the not-for-profit organization, of which government is the prime example.

Chapter 6 raised the issue of entrepreneurship briefly in several connections. One involved the concept of a corporate life cycle. Entrepreneurial organizations are at stage I and are in a state of emergence; they are led by a certain type of individual, who may have to be replaced by a different kind of person in later stages of the firm's development. It is this type of person, who founds an organization, and the company thus created that concerns us here.

Chapter 6 also introduced the term entrepreneur in describing a managerial role involving the initiation and design of organizational improvement projects [Mintzberg, 1973]. Other writers have also tended to identify entrepreneurship with managing to varying degrees. Thus, Anyon [1973:49–50] says ". . . an entrepreneur and a general manager may become almost synonymous. Entrepreneurship remains, however, only one aspect of the total of management challenges involved in the running of an organization." Palmer [1971] defines entrepreneurship with reference to decision making under conditions of great uncertainty and thus makes it as much a part of managing any large corporation in an erratic and unpredictable environment as it is of managing a new business venture.

Certainly the parallel between entrepreneurship and certain kinds of general managerial activities, such as initiating improvement projects and coping with uncertain environments, cannot be denied. However, for the present purpose a definition that focuses directly on the emerging business is more to the point. The discussion will be concerned with established firms only in the case of new businesses that are funded by an existing corporation—the special field known as *venture management*.

Entrepreneurship and the Policy Discipline

The inclusion of the topic of entrepreneurship within the broad rubric of business policy reflects a growing trend. In fact, the founding of new businesses has become the primary focus of some business policy courses. Popp and Hicks [1973] describe an experiential business policy course in which groups of students either started new businesses or conducted feasibility studies preliminary to doing so. The new businesses included an arts and crafts dealership, a tutoring service, a company selling packaged pecans to school groups, a car pool matching service, and an automobile shopping service. Although the companies experienced varying degrees of success, student reaction to the emphasis on entrepreneurship in a "living case" was overwhelmingly positive.

Courses such as this appear to be proliferating at a rapid rate in business schools across the country. Topics covered include new venture initiation, management of small companies, entrepreneurial development of emerging economies, minority entrepreneurship, psychology of the entrepreneur, economic and social impact of entrepreneurship, and entrepreneurial history. Although objectives such as building knowledge about the legalities of incorporation, learning from the experiences of current entrepreneurs, and inspiring interest in becoming an entrepreneur are prevalent, many courses focus directly on the design of specific venture projects by student teams.

CHARACTERISTICS OF THE SUCCESSFUL ENTREPRENEUR

Although characteristics of individual managers and in particular the style with which they approach their jobs exert important influences on policy formation and implementation generally, these individual characteristics become crucial in the case of the entrepreneur. In the small emerging firm, typically lacking both financial and human resources, if the talent needed for survival and growth is not inherent in its entrepreneurship, success is unlikely. In the early years the person and the organization are very much as one.

Achievement Motivation and the Entrepreneur

A sizable amount of study has been devoted to the question of the relationship between entrepreneurship and the desire to achieve. The data consistently indicate that people who found new businesses where none existed before and make them survive have high levels of achievement motivation [Hines, 1973; Hornaday and Aboud, 1971; Hornaday and Bunker, 1970]. Table 16-1 contains data from the Hines [1973] study, which was conducted in New Zealand. Achievement motivation was measured by a questionnaire which assigned scores in terms of the following characteristics:

1. A tendency to have difficulty relaxing on holidays.
2. A tendency to become annoyed when people are late for appointments.
3. A dislike of seeing anything wasted.
4. A dislike of getting drunk.
5. A tendency to think about work matters outside working hours.

TABLE 16-1
Achievement Motivation Levels of
Entrepreneurs Compared With Other Occupational Groups

OCCUPATIONAL GROUP	NUMBER	MEAN SCORE	PER CENT LOW	PER CENT HIGH
Entrepreneurs	80	5.5	14	36
Engineers	74	4.7	19	24
Accountants	68	4.6	25	29
Middle managers	93	4.0	37	15

SOURCE: Adapted from Hines [1973:314–315].
NOTE: Achievement scores can vary from zero to eight. A low score is defined as falling in the range zero through three; a high score in the range six through eight.

6. A preference for competent but difficult work partners over congenial but incompetent ones.
7. A tendency to become angry over inefficiency.
8. A long standing pattern of working hard to be at the top in one's area of endeavor.

Endorsing six or more of these items was interpreted as indicating high levels of achievement motivation, whereas endorsing three or less was considered indicative of low levels. The entrepreneurs endorsed these statements significantly more often than any of the other occupational groups and were particularly high on achievement motivation relative to the middle managers.

This finding, that achievement motivation is related to entrepreneurship, extends not only to those who found businesses but to other managers in whose jobs the entrepreneurial role predominates. Furthermore, entrepreneurs who have high levels of achievement motivation tend to head firms that grow more rapidly in terms of such indexes as sales volume, number of employees, and total investment in the business than do companies headed by entrepreneurs with lesser achievement needs [Hundal, 1971; McClelland and Winter, 1969; Wainer and Rubin, 1969].

It is even true that higher levels of achievement motivation are found in those who obtain financing for a new business from lending agencies as opposed to those who are rejected [Pandey and Tewary, 1979]. These links between achievement motivation and entrepreneurship appear to take the following form:

1. Individuals differ in the degree to which achievement is a major source of satisfaction.
2. Highly achievement motivated people have certain characteristics:
   (a) They are more concerned with achieving success than avoiding failure and thus do not concentrate their energies around warding off adversity.
   (b) They tend to give close attention to the realistic probabilities for success associated with different alternatives.
   (c) They much prefer situations where they themselves can influence and control the outcome rather than having success depend on chance factors.
   (d) They are strongly future-oriented and are willing to wait for rewards.

(e) They prefer situations where there is a clear criterion of whether they are succeeding.

(f) They prefer situations involving clear-cut individual responsibility so that if they do succeed that fact can be attributed to their own efforts.

3. These characteristics are inherent in the entrepreneurial job, and thus people with high achievement motivation will be attracted to this type of work and, because they fit its requirement more closely, will be more likely to achieve success (business growth).

Achievement-oriented people of this kind should be highly rational decision makers, and in this respect one would expect them to make good corporate managers as well. However, their strong need for individual credit may make it difficult for them to cooperate with others in their activities. This and other considerations to be taken up in the next section make it unlikely that most effective entrepreneurs will make effective corporate managers. It is for this reason that most expanding companies require changes at the top as they move through the various stages of their development.

The Enterprising Man

In addition to the work related to achievement motivation, another major program of study dealing with the characteristics of entrepreneurs is one initiated at Michigan State University by Collins and Moore. Their major publication, entitled *The Enterprising Man* [1964], dealt with the results of interviews and psychological tests obtained from 150 entrepreneurs in the state of Michigan whose firms have survived the first trying years.

The most striking finding from this research was that the entrepreneurs "had difficulty throughout their lives in playing the role of employee and subordinate. . . . These men came to realize that they can never adequately measure up to the demands placed on them by other people's organizations . . . they cannot go on accepting situations in which their security is dependent upon forces outside themselves . . . they cannot adjust to older and superordinate figures." [Collins and Moore, 1964:133] As a consequence of this inability to handle authority relationships effectively, the entrepreneurs drifted from one organization to another experiencing a number of failures enroute. Finally they solved this problem by going into business on their own, where they would be accountable to no one but themselves. In this sense founding a company represents an escape, but is also a creative act which does in fact appear to provide a satisfying and rewarding solution to their personal problems.

Collins and Moore [1964:245–246] sum up their findings as follows: "Our study suggests that the 'carriers' of the basic entrepreneurial values of our society tend, paradoxically enough, to be those who are marginal to the established social networks. They are those who for social, psychological, ethnic, or economic reasons, cannot make a go of it in existing social structures." Interestingly enough this picture coincides in a number of respects with that presented by Vance [1971] in his portrayal of the men who have been the dominant force in putting together large conglomerates. He says, "Tracing the education and experience backgrounds of these eminent leaders, it is rather astounding to note that they, as a group, are definitely not in the pattern prescribed by James Burnham's *Managerial Revolution* . . . the heads of major nonconglomerate firms . . . tend toward the high image, well-educated, socially prominant, civically active, scientific, and professional managerial types. The new conglomerators, relatively speaking, are not of that ilk. They do, however, bring to mind the almost forgotten breed of entrepreneurs, the Henry Fords, John D. Rockefellers, J. P. Morgans—the men who built our enterprise system" [Vance, 1971:62 and 70].

The picture that Collins and Moore present is also consonant with another finding in the research literature. Entrepreneurs have been found to have a low level of need for support from others [Hornaday and Aboud, 1971]. They care litttle about being treated with understanding, receiving encouragement from others, and being treated with kindness and consideration. One can assume that when it comes to authority figures such as superiors in a company not their own, they may even feel acutely uncomfortable about receiving this kind of support. Certainly the lonely world of the entrepreneur is no place for the person who requires constant encouragement from other people.

Although research on entrepreneurs often has failed to differentiate subtypes, there are some data on this point derived from a further analysis of the Collins and Moore interview materials [Smith, 1967]. Two types of entrepreneurs were identified, as follows:

1. *Craftsman.* Characterized by narrowness in education and training, low social awareness and social involvement, a feeling of having little competence in dealing with the social environment, and a limited time orientation.
2. *Opportunistic.* Characterized by breadth in education and training, high social awareness and involvement, high confidence in his ability to deal with the social environment, and an awareness of and orientation to the future.

These types of entrepreneurs were found to head very different kinds of firms. Characteristically the craftsman entrepreneurs had introduced few changes. The firm's customer mix, product mix, and production methods were much the same as when the company started. Production is concentrated at one location, sales are restricted to the company's own state, and plans for change and growth are lacking. Such a firm was defined as *Rigid.* In contrast *Adaptive* firms, most commonly headed by an opportunistic entrepreneur who perceives and reacts to a much broader range of his culture, had undergone considerable change and diversification and there were plans for even more.

The nature of this relationship between type of entrepreneur and type of firm is set forth in Figure 16-1. The conglomerator described by Vance [1971] provides a good example of the opportunistic entrepreneur who heads an adaptive firm. In the Smith study, firms of this kind under an opportunistic head had 12 times the sales of the rigid companies under a craftsman entrepreneur.

Although many of the cases included in Figure 16-1 do serve to substantiate the hypothesized fit between individual and firm and there are no cases where the craftsmen had highly adaptive firms and the opportunistic had very rigid ones, there is a clustering concentrated slightly to the left of the center of the figure which suggests a possible third type of entrepreneur. Further analysis reveals that the 10 circled cases do have a

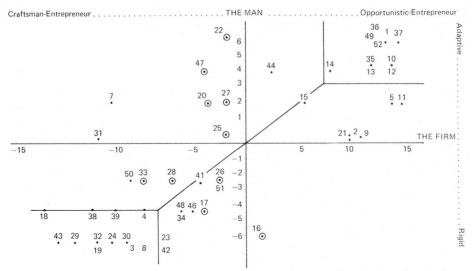

Figure 16-1 The relationship between type of entrepreneur and type of firm (as indicated by the positioning of their numbers) $N = 52$ entrepreneurs and their firms. [From Norman R. Smith, *The Entrepreneur and His Firm: The Relationship Between Type of Man and Type of Company.* © 1967. Reprinted by permission of the publisher, Division of Research, Graduate School of Business Administration, Michigan State University.]

great deal in common. Smith [1976] suggests the name *Inventor-Entrepreneur* for them. All had taken out a large number of patents. Such an entrepreneur is described as follows: "It appears that his orientation is not to attempt to build a business or to turn out the best product. Rather, his major concern seems to be to develop an organization, not as an end in itself, but rather as a vehicle to allow him to invent and produce various products" [Smith, 1967:89]. Whether this organization turns out to be rigid or adaptive depends on the nature and number of products involved.

It thus appears that there are distinct differences among entrepreneurs. Probably it is the opportunistic type who is most likely to found a company that grows sufficiently to have a life cycle of the kind described in Chapter 6. It is likely also that achievement motivation is a particularly relevant consideration among opportunistic entrepreneurs.

In recent years the idea that entrepreneurs are not all of one kind has received increasing attention, and a number of typologies have been proposed both for individuals and for entrepreneurial organizations. Filley and Aldag [1980] classify small organizations as craft, promotion, and administrative in type, thus paralleling the Smith [1967] proposal in many respects. Vesper [1980] sets forth a much longer list containing solo self-employed individuals, team builders, independent innovators, pattern multipliers, economy of scale exploiters, capital aggregators, acquirers, buy-sell artists, conglomerators, speculators, and apparent value manipulators. Other approaches have been proposed as well [Cooper, 1979; Webster, 1977]. The important point is that entrepreneurs and their organizations differ considerably, and, accordingly, the strategic approaches that might be expected to work for various entrepreneurs will cover a wide range as well.

St. Louis Entrepreneurs

A third program of study has utilized data on a sample of entrepreneurs in the St. Louis area, which were collected both as these individuals started their firms and again three years later [Brockhaus, 1980a; 1980b; Brockhaus and Nord, 1979]. Comparisons were made with managers who had also changed positions at essentially the same time as the entrepreneurs.

One of the most striking findings was that, contrary to popular lore, the entrepreneurs as a group were not particularly disposed toward risk taking in any generalized sense; nor did they show any strong tendency to view events in their lives as largely subject to their own influence, as opposed to being at the mercy of fate, luck, and more powerful individuals. This latter characteristic has been found to be closely allied to achievement motivation [Pandy and Tewary, 1979]. What did emerge among the entrepreneurs was a certain lack of success in their previous employment and a feeling that their opportunities there were not very good.

When the data were utilized to compare those who were still in business three years later with those who had failed in the intervening interval, a pattern more consistent with previously considered results was obtained. Risk-taking propensity still failed to differentiate the groups, but the successful entrepreneurs were those who viewed the world as more subject to influence through their own efforts. Furthermore, those who had succeeded were particularly likely to have failed in their previous job; they were more disatisfied with that job and they had been more insecure in it, in that they feared dismissal. In short, success seemed to be associated with strong pressure to make a go of the new business because alternatives were unattractive, if, in fact, they were available at all.

INITIATING A NEW BUSINESS

With some knowledge of what kind of people start new businesses and why they do it, it is now feasible to look into what is involved and some of the problems that may arise.

Factors to be Considered

The entrepreneur's job is indeed that of a generalist. Depending on the circumstances, he may be called upon to make decisions in any area of business expertise. Since he rarely possesses all the knowledge he would like to have, typically does not have the time to acquire this knowledge, and either does not have access to or cannot afford the advice of specialists in the area, a truly systematic approach to decision making can only be approximated at best.

Some idea of the complexity and the diversity of the decisions an entrepreneur faces may be obtained from the following list of factors that must be considered in starting a business [Grieco, 1975:32]:

· Determining the capital requirements.
· Obtaining legal assistance.
· Researching the market.
· Locating the business enterprise.
· Securing personnel.
· Providing physical facilities.
· Creating a profit plan.
· Determining accounting procedures.
· Determining risk and insurance coverages.
· Determining information needs.

Generally, in order to obtain financing for his business, an entrepreneur must develop a detailed business plan [Brockhaus, 1976]. Such a plan must cover the areas noted in considerable detail; normally, it will project the company over a three- to five-year period. Among the questions such a business plan must answer are the following:

· What are the objectives of the business?
· What is the precise nature of the market?
· What competitor firms now exist and what are their strengths and weaknesses?
· What are the anticipated selling prices and how do these compare with current prices?
· What are the exact specifications of the product or service?
· What patents are held?
· What are the key technologies and skills required?
· What alternative distribution channels are available?
· What capital equipment is needed?
· When and how will additional funds go into the venture in the future?
· What staffing and space requirements will exist at various points in the future?
· What business locations are proposed and why?
· What cash flow positions are projected for various points in the future?
· What profit and loss positions are projected at various points in time?
· What ownership position is anticipated and how might this change over time?

Preparing such a plan well and implementing it with some degree of success, requires that a tremendous amount of energy be focused on the new enterprise. Presumably it is the function of a high level of achievement motivation that it does in fact bring this needed energy to bear.

Decision Approaches in Small Business
In general, planning of a systematic, formal nature is much less prevalent in small firms than in larger ones. As a result, approaches such as the intuitive-anticipatory and the entrepreneurial-opportunistic are more characteristic, although variants of the

incremental and adaptive approaches are also found. Yet even in the smallest organization it is important that the chief executive officer be engaged in planning, establish policies and strategies, and make decisions with planned objectives as well as realistic appraisals of the future in mind (see Chapter 12).

Given that examining future consequences of present decisions, as well as choosing bases for making current decisions from among future alternative courses of action, are important to all managers and organizations, irrespective of size, a strong argument can be made for utilizing a more formal structured approach even in small firms [Steiner, 1967]. Because the small business has less capacity to control its environment and therefore is often at the mercy of events, truly long-range planning may not be fruitful; however, middle-range efforts extending to two years or so can pay off. Many of the techniques of formal systematic planning and structured decision making are applicable in organizations of any size.

Problems of Survival

New firms rarely fail in the first year, but after that the proportion of all failures runs at least 10 per cent a year up through the fifth year [Van Voorhis, 1980]. After the fifth year the chances of survival improve considerably with only about half as many failures per year occurring in the second five years as in the first. Roughly two thirds of all new business fail within the first four years [Hosmer, Cooper, and Vesper, 1977].

Survival appears to be strongly influenced by the initial choice of industry [Vesper, 1980]. High technology firms tend to have a good chance of survival; consumer products manufacturers do not. Retail failures are particularly likely to occur in the early years. Crowded, highly competitive industries simply are not an appropriate place for an entrepreneur to begin.

Yet, given this fact, opinions regarding the most frequent causes of failure tend to vary sharply depending on whose opinion is obtained. As noted in Table 16-2 those

TABLE 16-2
Rank Ordering of Causes of Business Failure
as Indicated by Entrepreneurs and
Their Creditors

CAUSE OF FAILURE	RANKING OF NUMBER OF FIRMS AFFECTED	
	BY ENTREPRENEURS	BY CREDITORS
Business depression	1	3
Insufficient capital	2	2
Competition	3	5
Decline in value of assets	4	6
Bad-debt losses	5	4
Inefficient management	6	1
Poor location	7	7

SOURCE: Adapted from Baumback and Lawyer [1979:21].

who actually own the businesses that fail tend to attribute their difficulties to external environmental problems, which probably could not have been predicted, rather than to themselves and their own poor decisions. Yet their creditors say the major cause of failure is inefficient management. Truly objective data on this point are lacking. However, the fact that in almost 60 per cent of the cases creditors attribute failure, at least in part, to inefficient management is a striking statistic [Baumback and Lawyer, 1979].

Problems of Growth

Assuming that a new business survives, growth will inevitably bring with it new problems even in the early stages. Many of these problems relate more to the implementation of policies and strategies than to their formulation. As the business grows it becomes increasingly difficult for the entrepreneur to supervise all employees directly and maintain personal relationships with them. This changing relationship with employees is disturbing to many entrepreneurs, a feeling that becomes accentuated as informal organization develops among employees and in many cases as organizational commitment declines. Ultimately, the work force may be unionized. The shift from owner to manager that occurs with growth introduces a whole host of implementation problems.

A second problem area relates to partners. In the early period when it is crucial to obtain customers, get production moving, purchase supplies, and pay off short term notes, many entrepreneurs tend to lose or trade away considerable control over the firm. Partners may be brought in for purposes of obtaining their skills or their money. However, once the firm has hurdled the problems of getting started, the need for these individuals is less and the primary entrepreneur typically tries to get rid of them in order to reassert control over his business. "At the interpersonal level, he must get rid of those people who have, during this transitional phase, either supported him or used his temporary position of weakness to intrude upon him. He must get rid of these figures for two reasons. At the interpersonal level he must get rid of them because they block the further development of the entrepreneur's own career and the development of the firm. At the level of internal dynamics, he must get rid of them because they inhibit him, restricting the autonomy for which he constantly searches" [Collins and Moore, 1964:196].

Multiple partners tend to eat into profits and to restrict the amount of money available for reinvestment in expansion. Furthermore the achievement-motivated entrepreneur wants to be able to attribute success to his own efforts and he wants no restrictions on his authority and opportunity to achieve personally.

This process of getting rid of partners can be a difficult one, and the resulting turmoil can pose a major threat to the survival of the business. Personal enmities are almost inevitable, although when provisions for buying out partners are included in the agreements establishing the business, they may occasionally be avoided.

A final problem area related to growth involves legal and governmental requirements. When a firm is small it is typically exempted by statute from many regulations, especially with regard to personnel practices, which apply to larger firms. Furthermore, governmental enforcement agencies characteristically have limited financial and manpower resources and, accordingly, focus their efforts on larger companies where a greater return on the investment of their efforts can be anticipated. Small companies being less visible simply are not held to the same stringent compliance requirements that larger ones are, and, knowingly or not, many entrepreneurs do ignore regulations that apply to them.

With growth, however, this situation changes. Increasing numbers of laws do apply, and restrictions and red tape escalate. Many of the restrictions are costly. Furthermore, anonymity is no longer possible; compliance becomes necessary. All this poses many problems for expanding businesses because of costs, because of the need for know-how, and because of the increased staffing required to process forms and meet reporting requirements. This kind of government control is onerous to most entrepreneurs. In their efforts to avoid it as their firms grow, they may create some serious problems for their companies.

VENTURE MANAGEMENT AND ENTREPRENEURSHIP

The discussion to this point has focused primarily on new enterprises initiated by the entrepreneur. However, the initiative for such ventures may come from another source, either from large corporations or from independent small business investment companies. In both instances investment capital is provided by the larger organization, and an active effort is made to put this capital behind as promising new ventures as can be found. Often the new venture involves producing and marketing an invention. In any event, venture management means a new business or technology or service that did not previously exist in the sponsoring company. It is an alternative strategy to that of acquisition.

The Structure and Development of Venture Efforts

Generally, as companies move into the venture management field, they go through an evolutionary process. The initial effort utilizes a relatively informal task force. If this succeeds and the company decides to invest further, a venture management department is established with its own budget. The final stage of development is a venture management company managed separately from the sponsoring company.

All of these forms, whether task force, department, or separate company, are essentially entrepreneurial in that a new line of business is started where none existed before. Occasionally, this is true also of joint ventures, where two or more companies merge their efforts in order to combine skills or spread risks. However, more frequently the new joint venture is merely an extension of what the companies have been doing all along, and thus does not represent a *new* business. Such is the case, for instance, in the many joint ventures of the oil industry where companies pool their resources to undertake exploration and test drillings. It is also true of those combined efforts by companies headquartered in different countries, which serve to pool know-how and access to markets within a common industry [Pfeffer and Nowak, 1976].

Typically companies will staff a new venture with a team of senior managers who span the areas of needed expertise. Usually there are three or four such individuals and areas such as marketing, production, and finance are represented [Parker, 1973]. This means that more systematic, formal decision-making approaches are possible than is the case in a company started by a single entrepreneur. There is not only a greater range of expertise available within the venture but the resources of the parent company are available as well. On the other hand, this team approach does involve greater start-up costs.

The evaluation of ideas for a new venture characteristically is carried out against the twin criteria of estimated potential return and the estimated capacity of the sponsoring company to create and support the particular type of venture in terms of the resources available to it. Initial ideas for consideration may stem from within the company, the R&D department for instance, or from the outside. Companies known to be active in venture management are often approached by inventors with ideas to sell or license. Once an idea is thought to be worth considering, a senior management team is established and it is this team that prepares the business plan. If the plan is approved and implemented through the medium of a separate company with the parent firm having the major ownership position, the members of the original team may be given some equity position in the venture.

The Parent Company–Venture Firm Relationship

One thing on which there is widespread agreement is that the relationship between the sponsoring company and the new venture is a delicate one [Parker, 1973; Wilemon and Gemmill, 1973]. One reason is that if the person put in charge of the venture is a true entrepreneur and the type of individual who is most likely to make the venture a success, he is also likely to have characteristics that militate against strong control on the part of the parent company. His high level of achievement motivation means that he will be the type of person who wants to achieve success through his *own* efforts, not the efforts of the sponsoring company and its chief executive. Furthermore he is likely to have a strong distaste for bureaucratic constraints and to want to escape from authority relationships which make him uncomfortable.

The implication is clear that the nature of the venture manager is a key ingredient for success and that if one has a good manager for this purpose he should be given considerable freedom. The primary control should be in terms of the amount the parent company is willing and able to invest. Should the venture grow to sizable proportions and become firmly established, it will usually be desirable to replace the original manager simply because he is an entrepreneur and not a manager of ongoing organizations. At this point some companies sell off the new venture, thus taking a sizable profit. In other cases a new *managerial* team is installed. In either instance it is appropriate to have the venture manager start over again on yet another new business.

Although research data on venture managers are limited as compared with what is known about the more conventional type of entrepreneur, it is apparent that venture managers are not typical managers. Furthermore, as contrasted with product managers they do in fact experience much fewer bureaucratic controls [Hlavacek and Thompson, 1973]. On the other hand, as indicated in Table 16-3, some venture managers operate without the kinds of decision-making discretion that the independent entrepreneur has.

TABLE 16-3
Areas of Decision-Making Freedom for Venture Managers

AREA	PER CENT WITH CLEAR AUTHORITY
Recommending promotions	96
Rating performance	92
Assigning personnel	83
Assigning priorities	79
Terminating projects	79
Allocating funds	78
Determining salaries	71
Hiring personnel	71
Firing personnel	67
Directly promoting personnel	57
Undertaking new projects	63

SOURCE: Adapted from Wilemon and Gemmill [1973:52].

These data derive from venture managers in 24 companies [Wilemon and Gemmill, 1973]. A number of these managers are restricted in the personnel actions they can carry out and in their freedom to initiate new projects. These restraints may, of course, be entirely acceptable if the particular managers involved are not achievement motivated, enterprising men. If they are of a truly entrepreneurial bent, however, the parent company controls can only mean trouble.

Successes and Failures in Venturing

Corporate venture efforts of the type described, although originally heralded in the 1960s as the key to diversification, have in fact faired poorly [Biggadike, 1979; Dunn, 1977; Fast, 1977; Quinn, 1979]. In one sample of ten venture groups in the consumer products field, six were subsequently disbanded and the remaining four had been severely restricted by top management. All ten were considered disruptive, expensive, and unproductive; accordingly, project failures were largely due to their being "killed" by top management, rather than to a lack of performance in the marketplace. Although these failures might seem to have resulted from the difficulty of entrepreneurial entry in the consumer products area generally, similar findings have been reported for ventures in other areas including industrial goods.

One observer notes the following three problems as paramount:

1. Corporate time horizons were not long enough to play the probability game and wait for results.
2. Venture teams were staffed with professional managers balanced as to their marketing, financial, and technical skills, rather than infused with the deep-seated expertise and personal commitment a real entrepreneur needs.
3. Full costing of ventures (including all overheads) made those ventures difficult to justify in financial terms and excellent targets for cutbacks during short-term economic or organizational crunches [Quinn, 1979:23].

The data generally support these conclusions. Biggadike [1979] found that severe losses were typically experienced through the first four years of a venture, especially if a serious attempt to capture a sizable market share was made. On the average it appears to take about eight years to achieve profitability. Many companies simply do not wait that long and terminate the venture. As with entrepreneurial efforts in general, it appears to be very important to obtain sufficiently large initial commitments of capital to "go it big" both in terms of time duration and market position.

Additional findings derive from an analysis of 21 venture failures that focused on the reasons behind the lack of success [Hill and Hlavacek, 1977; Hlavacek and Thompson, 1978]. Data reported by the venture managers (entrepreneurs) and top managers (creditors) are given in Table 16-4 in a manner paralleling Table 16-2. In this case the disparity in perceptions is even more pronounced. The venture managers place the blame largely on top management decisions; top management does not. However one interprets these results, the uneasy and apparently unresolved relationship problems between the entrepreneurial and bureaucratic components of the venture process is clearly evident.

All this is not to say that successful venture efforts have not occurred; there have been many. But more often than not the results have been far below what was expected and desired. Furthermore, there is little agreement as to exactly how ventures might be structured to ensure success. A wide variety of views exist, extending all the way from close control by top management to almost total entrepreneurial freedom. A particularly popular solution at the present time is the formation of a joint venture between a large company, which supplies marketing power and capital, and a small (entrepreneurial) firm, which supplies technical know-how [Hlavacek, Dovey, and Biondo, 1977].

TABLE 16–4
Rank Ordering of Causes of Venture Failures as Indicated by
Venture Managers and Top Managers

| | RANKING OF NUMBER OF VENTURES AFFECTED | |
CAUSE OF FAILURE	BY VENTURE MANAGERS	BY TOP MANAGERS
Large overhead cost to absorb	2.5	No mention
Insufficient top management support	2.5	No mention
Inadequate distribution channels	2.5	3
Size constraints on venture	2.5	No mention
Budget too small	5	No mention
Conflicts with other divisions	7	5.5
Improper risk-reward compensation	7	No mention
Lack of sufficient authority	7	No mention
Inability to meet budget guidelines	No mention	1
Venture too small	>7	2
Wrong venture manager	No mention	4
Insurmountable technical problems	No mention	5.5
Termination of federal funding	No mention	7.5
Market too competitive	No mention	7.5

SOURCE: Adapted from Hill and Hlavacek [1977:6].

On the surface at least this approach would seem to increase the problems at the bureau-cratic-entrepreneurial boundary, but as yet there is insufficient evidence to tell.

MINORITY ENTREPRENEURSHIP

In recent years there has been a special emphasis on the development of new enterprises by minority group members. In the past this type of entrepreneurship has been quite limited, but concerns for social responsibility and the problems of the ghetto have provided a new stimulus. The federal government has been actively encouraging the development of minority enterprises, and a number of companies have become involved in venture management efforts involving minorities (America, 1980).

Although many such efforts face almost insurmountable obstacles and it is certainly too soon to evaluate the net effects of what has been done, one conclusion is emerging quite clearly already: There is a distinct need to identify and develop minority group members who are capable of playing the entrepreneurial role with skill and effectivness.

To this end, programs have been undertaken to assess and develop achievement motiva-tion among blacks who are in, or are interested in going into, business for themselves. The initial impetus for this training came from efforts undertaken in underdeveloped countries, and in particularly in India [McClelland and Winter, 1969]. From research conducted in India it became apparent that achievement motivation could be developed or aroused in certain people and that many of these people did subsequently start new businesses or markedly, expand existing ones. More recently similar results have been obtained in the United States [Miron and McClelland, 1979].

The approach appears to be a promising one, and there are a number of considerations that suggest that, in spite of its currently limited scale, minority entrepreneurship ulti-mately may become a significant economic factor in this country. As Collins and Moore [1964] point out, most entrepreneurs of the past have been to varying degrees on the fringes of the larger society. Many are foreign born (20 per cent in the Collins and Moore sample) and many more had foreign-born parents (another 35 per cent of the Collins and Moore group). They tend to come from families that are not well off finan-cially. In a very real sense they have little to lose and much to gain from undertaking the creation of a new business.

To the extent these types of considerations apply to minority group members, these groups may represent fertile ground for the nurturance of entrepreneurship. For this to happen, however, the primary rationale for the new business must be personal economic accomplishment, not the creation of new jobs for ghetto residents. Furthermore, these businesses will actively have to seek and obtain markets in direct competition with existing businesses and in many cases outside the ghetto environment where money is currently too scarce to permit sizable profits.

Studies have been conducted comparing minority and white male [Hornaday and Aboud, 1971] and minority and white female [DeCarlo and Lyons, 1979] entrepreneurs. Among the males there are few differences. The white male entrepreneurs exhibit strong achievement motivation, little need for emotional support, low conformity, considerable independence, a lack of benevolence, and good leadership skills—a pattern that fits well with the previously reported results. The minority entrepreneurs almost always show the same tendencies as the whites, but their scores on the measures used do not depart as sharply from those of the general population.

Among the white female entrepreneurs the pattern noted for the white males is also in evidence, but in addition differences from the general population appear consistently across all measures; this is also true for the minority females. It is as if one has to be very different from other females to be a female entrepreneur. Yet the white females are more achievement oriented, less conforming, more independent, and less benevolent than the minority females. Once again the personality differences tend to be somewhat muted in the minority group. Based on data available from other studies it would seem likely that minority entrepreneurs might be somewhat less likely to achieve success insofar as motivational and personality factors contribute. This too would argue for the use of approaches such as achievement motivation training.

CONCLUDING COMMENTS

The topic of entrepreneurship is a fascinating one, with origins closely allied to the early industrial development of this country. Yet there remain many unanswered questions. Studying entrepreneurship typically involves the identification of a sample of small and, as yet, not very visible firms, at an early point. It is particularly hard to study the failures because they disappear so rapidly. Thus comparisons between effective and ineffective entrepreneurial organizations are distinctly lacking. At a later point it is equally difficult to analyze the gradual process of shift from entrepreneurial to managerial, bureaucratic organization.

These and other areas related to entrepreneurship remain sadly underresearched— but understandably so, given the problem involved. Yet, for business development and growth and the economic welfare of society, there is hardly any topic of greater significance. Hopefully there will be a major expansion of knowledge in the next few years. The rate of new business failures, including the numerous venture failures at the corporate level, are testimonial to the inadequacy of current concepts.

QUESTIONS

Discussion Guides on Chapter Content
1. How is achievement motivation related to entrepreneurship?
2. "Entrepreneurs . . . cannot make a go of it in existing social structures." Explain and comment.
3. What are the different types of entrepreneurs that have been proposed? How do these types relate to types of firms and strategy formation?
4. Overall what do we know about the characteristics of entrepreneurs in general? Successful entrepreneurs?

5. What is the nature and role of a business plan? How does planning in general fit into small-business decision making?
6. What do we know about the chances for survival of new firms and the causes of failure?
7. What problems are associated with the growth of an entrepreneurial company?
8. How does venture management relate to entrepreneurship? What are the similarities and differences?
9. How has venture management worked out? What major problems has it faced?
10. What are the special problems of minority entrepreneurship? What is its future? Why?

Mind Stretching Questions
1. Do you think you are the kind of person who would enjoy being an entrepreneur and do well at it? Why do you feel as you do?
2. If you were teaching a course in business policy, would you include entrepreneurship as part of the subject matter, and, if so, what approach would you use? Explain the reasons for your decision.
3. If you were faced with the question of making a recommendation to your company regarding the possibility of entering the venture management field, what would be your approach? Explain in detail.

CHAPTER

17

Special Aspects of Policy/ Strategy in Not-for-Profit Organizations

INTRODUCTION

From time to time in preceding chapters reference was made to the policy/strategy process in nonbusiness institutions, which we shall call not-for-profit (NFP) organizations. Much of what was said in these chapters about policy/strategy in business institutions applies to NFP organizations. However, there are fundamental differences between the two sectors. In this chapter some of the principal similarities will be noted, but the emphasis will be placed upon the major differences between the two sectors.

THE NFP SECTOR

What Is The NFP Sector?

The NFP can be divided roughly into two distinct groups of organizations. The first encompasses governments and the second includes all other organizations. The differences among these organizations are probably greater than differences among companies in the private sector, as diverse as they are. The government spectrum ranges from the federal government to state and local governments. The range of organizations in the federal government is from the Congress, the Executive Branch, and the Supreme Court to special agencies of the government such as the Tennessee Valley Authority and U.S. Navy shipbuilding yards.

Other organizations in the NFP sector include savings and loan associations, trade associations, chambers of commerce, professional societies, farmers' cooperatives, trade unions, private colleges and universities, foundations, hospitals, churches, and museums. These organizations are like private institutions in that they are not a part of government. However, they perform a public service and are not operated for profit which, of course, makes them different from private firms. (Some of these institutions sometimes are operated for a profit, such as savings and loan associations, private colleges and universities, hospitals, and so on. When operated for profit they are properly included, of course, in the private sector, not the NEP.)

Some of these institutions are quite similar in structure and operation to private enterprises. Such, for example, are transportation systems of cities, toll roads, and state liquor stores. Many of these organizations have boards of directors like private companies.

Importance of the NFP Sector

We need not elaborate the point that government is the most dominant institution in society. Its policy/strategy making processes literally may mean the difference between life and death to all of our institutions and to each of us personally. Government is also growing rapidly in terms of expenditures, jobs, laws, and administrative regulations.

There has been substantial growth in our nongovernment public service institutions in recent years, especially in the areas of health. Business is still, of course, a major institution in society, but it is declining in importance relative to these other NFP institutions as measured by employment, power, control of capital, and expenditures.

On Comparing Private and NFP Organizations

Before proceeding with a detailed discussion of the major aspects of NFP policy processes that differ from those in the private sector, a few comments about comparing the two sectors provides a useful perspective.

First, our interest focuses on the formulation, implementation, and evaluation of policy/ strategy, and most of what follows will be concerned with this process. In private institutions, particularly the larger ones, these processes frequently take place in the comprehensive strategic planning process. There is no comprehensive integrated long-range national strategic planning process in the federal government, and there are grave reservations about the advisability of introducing such a system at the present time [Steiner, 1975]. The nearest approach to such a system was the introduction of a planning-programming-budgeting system (PPBS) into the federal government by President Johnson in 1965. This system was abolished by President Nixon when he assumed office. There are, however, many state and local governments, and other organizations in the NFP, using program budgeting [DeWoolfson, 1974; Novick, 1973].

Among the nongovernment institutions in the NFP there is a new thrust to develop a type of formal strategic planning quite comparable to that employed in private industry. This trend will grow because the Social Security Administration in mid-1974 made institutional planning mandatory for participation in Medicare and Medicaid. This new regulation is part of Public Law 92-603 and requires that hospitals prepare an overall plan and budget for operations and capital expenditures. The latter must cover a three-year period and be reviewed annually and updated.

The fundamental processes of formal strategic planning used in the private sector, and the lessons learned from that experience, are highly applicable to institutions in the NFP. This is especially so with respect to the many nongovernment organizations, but it is also applicable to the federal government [Steiner, 1975]. A number of writers have explained how corporate long-range planning processes apply to different types of NFP organizations. Hawkins and Tarr [1980] and Cartwright [1975] have dealt with the subject for local governments, McKay and Cutting [1974] for educational institutions, Hussey [1974a] for a church, Peters [1974] and Webber and Dula [1974] for hospitals, and Hardy [1973] for nonprofit organizations generally.

Although certain of the fundamental approaches, methods, and processes of corporate planning are applicable to planning in the public sector, there are many important differences. These will be highlighted in the following pages. The degree of similarity and/or dissimilarity varies much, depending upon the type of institution. A government-owned and operated electric utility may have a strategic plan comparable to that of its private counterpart. Strategic plans in government organizations, however, tend to be less like those in even the huge private corporations.

The policy processes in an organization take place, of course, within a larger management context. A great many of the fundamentals of operational management of private organizations apply to public organizations, and vice versa. However, there are significant dissimilarities in management between the two [Fottler, 1980; Newman and Wallender, 1978; Drucker, 1973].

FORMULATING POLICY

Politics and Pluralism in Public Sector Policy

Some years ago in a very perceptive book Appleby [1949:153] said, "Everything having to do with the government and everything the government does is political, for politics is the art and science of government." This means for this discussion that decision making in government is essentially forged on the political anvil. Here is a major difference with business decision making. Although it is quite true that decision making in business, especially in the larger corporation, is based considerably more on political and social considerations than current academic decision theorists admit, the core determinant is still economic.

Another fundamental feature of our political democracy is pluralism. A pluralistic society is one in which many individuals and groups have power that can be, and is, used to influence decision making in government. This is not only permitted but encouraged by the Constitution of the United States. No one group has overwhelming power over all others, but each may have at least an indirect impact on all the others. The basic purpose of this Constitutional right to influence government was originally designed to limit the power of the federal government. But it also has served to decentralize power, to assure a check on and balance of power, and to prevent the tyranny of a majority over a minority. Here, too, is a major difference with business decision making. Whereas business firms, especially the larger companies, must today respond to the demands of various interests focused on the enterprise, there is no legal compulsion for managers of private companies to entertain or respond to the demands of such interests. In a public institution these demands are heard, and the way in which they are weighed on the political scale decides public policy.

Drucker illustrates this dissimilarity with private firms in this way. A company with a market share of 20 per cent must pay attention to customers in this market segment. Along with stockholders, these are the two primary constituents of the company. The other 80 per cent of the market can be ignored. In a public service institution, whether a government or a voluntary hospital, management must be concerned with 100 per cent of its constituents [Drucker, 1973].

Furthermore, any group of constituents with even moderate power can, for a time at least, block action. To illustrate, President Johnson two years before he left office directed that a predominantly low-income housing development be created in the District of Columbia called the Fort Lincoln Housing Project. Despite the President's strong support, the resistance of local groups and then conflicts among government agencies blocked the program. Incoming President Nixon abandoned the project [Derthick, 1970]. Although it may be an oversimplification, it can be asserted with some truth that in the past political decision generally was based on concensus by the relatively few. That has given way to a politics today of conflict engaged in by a great many. And, as noted in Chapter 4, individual pressure groups are tending more and more to press for and accept no compromise with their own single narrow issues. This certainly complicates the decision-making processes in public service institutions. This fact of life affects all organizations in the public sector—from the federal government to "businesslike" organizations.

Determining Missions, Purposes, and Long-Range Objectives

The processes of formulating basic missions, purposes, and objectives is significantly more difficult in public service organizations than in private organizations. The Constitution of the United States, of course, sets forth a comprehensive set of missions, purposes, and objectives for this nation but no integrated, more detailed network of these aims exists. The first and only attempt to establish a set of long-range consistent national goals, for instance, was made by the Eisenhower Administration in 1960 (President's Commission on National Goals). The basic reason that this work has not been updated is not lack of interest but the extraordinary difficulty in achieving any sort of consensus of goals except at very high levels of abstraction.

The federal budget in a very real sense is a statement of national goals and priorities, but it is comparatively short-range in focus, although it naturally has significant long-range implications. It is also an extraordinarily complicated document with an endless array of explicit and implicit goals.

Even in comparatively small and "businesslike" public service institutions, such as a hospital, problems of formulating basic missions, purposes, and objectives are very complex. Such questions as these, for example, are difficult to answer. Should a hospital be the service facility for physicians? If so, which physicians? Or, should the purpose be to respond to the health needs of the community? What are they? Whose needs? Should the focus be on preventive medicine or administering to those people with current health problems? Each of these basic missions can be defended, and each would get support from major constituents of the hospital.

Coming to an agreement about which missions and purposes are of highest priority is a complex and difficult task because different constituents hold values that do not readily change. In reviewing the introduction of management by objective into British hospitals, Charnock [1975] found that among physicians, to mention but one powerful constituent group, there appeared to be no adjustment of their values to changing societal values concerning health services. Physicians were still committed, he said, to optimizing their subsystems.

Getting Problems on the Policy Agenda

There is a major difference between the way problems get to the attention of management in public as contrasted with private organizations. In business, problems come to the attention of management when something happens to alter importantly those established measures of performance used in business, such as market share, sales, profits, return on investment, cash flow, and so on. In government, the process is much different and far more complex. In a classical treatment, Truman [1951] observed that when the equilibrium of a group is seriously disturbed the group exerts pressure on government to preserve equilibrium. This is still true but, as Jones [1970] points out, there are many other ways problems attract the attention of government. Self-appointed advocates for groups (such as consumers or those interested in preserving the environment) often are successful in getting their issues on the policy agenda of government. Individual legislators, of course, can initiate legislation, and the executive branch is constantly seeking new policies to resolve existing and anticipated problems. This process of stimulating policy development is fundamentally different from that of business firms.

Disjointed Incremental Policy Making

In Chapter 12, the so-called "disjointed incremental" approach to policy making in government was discussed. With such an approach, policy makers take one little step at a time. Something is tried, then altered, then tried in a slightly different form. All the while the policy makers seek compromises with powerful interest groups until the bargaining process produces a result acceptable to all having power or until those who are dissatisfied are unable or disinterested in obstructing a decision. This is also called by Lindblom [1959] "muddling through." In an earlier paper Lindblom [1955:5] took the position that bargaining in government was akin to Smith's "jiggling of the market." A good bit of policy/strategy decision making in private enterprises can be described in this fashion, but it is not as pervasive in comparison to total decision making as in public service organizations. In public policy decision making, for instance, nonincremental alternatives are generally not within the range of choice. This is so because party politics is generally based on incremental differences in policies, not radical change. In private industry, however, no reasonable alternatives are eliminated in the policy/strategy decision-making process.

Policy and Learning

Closely associated with the idea of muddling through and the group decision-making character of policy formulation is the idea that, in the governmental sector, formulation of policy is often tentative and incremental because the state of knowledge is inadequate to be clear and precise. The democratic process is a learning process, and this fact applies to both the formulation and implementation of policy. Schattschneider expresses the idea this way:

Every statute is an experiment in learning. When Congress attempts to deal with a new problem it is likely to pass an act establishing an agency with vague powers to do something about it. The new agency makes an investigation, it issues some literature about its functions, invites comments by interested parties, assembles a library of information, tries to find some experts, tries to get people to do something about the problem, and eventually reports back to Congress, recommending some revisions of the statute. Thereafter the problem is passed back and forth between Congress, the President, the agency, interested people, the public. It is debated, criticized, reviewed, investigations are made, the statute is revised, over and over again, sometimes for years, before a policy is evolved [Schattschneider, 1969:89].

Frequently the Congress and the executive agencies of government keep the issue open deliberately precisely because the "answer" is not obvious and/or discussion is required to reach a needed concensus. Furthermore, there are very few decisions which, because of this process, are irrevocable.

Group Decision Making

In the Congress, decision making cannot be said to rest ultimately with one individual. Decisions are compromises among many. In the Executive Branch of government, however, one man is often responsible for a decision. More frequently than not, however, the decision is recommended by a group assigned the responsibility to do so. This process is pursued in the private sector but generally not as extensively as in the public sector. The result is that in the public sector there is greater dependence on group decision making with all the strengths and weaknesses of that approach. In Chapter 11 the strengths and weaknesses of group decision making were examined. It was found that grave dangers rest in group decision making for a number of cogent reasons described there. Janis [1972] and Allison [1971], as noted earlier, linked a number of major fiascos in government policy to what Janis calls "groupthink," which stresses the weaknesses in group decision making. The linkage, however, is admittedly imperfect [Janis, 1972:11]. Nevertheless, the conclusion may be tentatively set forth that the possibility of serious policy errors may be greater in public service institutions because they engage more in group decision making.

Policy Analysis

Major business policy/strategy decisions contain a good bit of judgment and reliance on unquantifiable considerations. But, generally, major decisions also rest on quantified economic analysis. In the public service area more decisions rely more heavily on judgment and nonquantifiable factors. In examining in detail the Congressional decision-making process with respect to foreign aid, for instance, Geiger and Hansen observed that in the Congress "the role of rational intellectual considerations is much less important than is commonly supposed and that it would not be greatly enhanced by changes in the volume and nature of information per se . . ." [in Bauer and Gergen. 1968:363].

Because decisions are ultimately made on "political grounds" it cannot be said that rational calculation is absent in making the decisions. Actually, relevant information and quantifiable calculations are being more and more used and are sometimes decisive in policy formation [U.S. 90th Congress Research and Programs Subcommittee, 1967; Hitch, 1966]. This technology is becoming encompassed in a new discipline called "policy science" [Brewer, 1974; Fisher, 1974]. The methods and tools of business analysis, such as return on investment, are generally inapplicable in the NFP. But comparable, although less precise, tools and processes have been developed such as cost/benefit analysis, system analysis, operations analysis, cost-effectiveness analysis, and program budgeting [Fisher, 1974].

The ultimate test of a "good" policy is conceptually the public interest. But this is an elusive test and differs much among decision makers. There are daily instances where disagreements about what is the public interest sharply distinguish positions taken by the President and Congressional leaders. Within the Congress as well as in the Supreme Court, there is not always a consensus about what the public interest is. Lindblom [1959:81] says that "The test of a 'good' policy is typically that various analysts find themselves directly agreeing on a policy (without their agreeing that it is the most appropriate means to an agreed objective)." This may serve for large overarching policies, but there are more rigorous tests that can be applied to policies of lesser magnitude, such as a program to improve highway safety, or to meet demands for new airports.

Although quantitative approaches to policy analysis are growing in usage, there are still many who caution against placing too much reliance upon them for public policy making. Strauch, for instance, is highly critical of quantitative methodology as a tool for the analysis of what he calls "soft" or "squishy" problems (that is, without any well-defined mathematical formulation that unambiguously captures the substantive problem) [Strauch, 1974]. When these limitations are neglected, he says, serious distortions in policy can result. Vickers, in his classic *The Art of Judgment* [1965], underscores the keystone role of judgment in all policy analysis. Wildavsky [1979] has skillfully shown that public policy analysis is less problem solving than problem learning.

In sum, the role of analysis in policy making in the NFP sector is different than in the private sector. Much depends, however, upon the level of policy and the organizational setting in which it is made. In both sectors, however, at high levels of policy there is no *best* solution to a policy problem. In both sectors the less significant the policy problem is, the more likely the decision makers will be to rely on pertinent information and quantitative analysis.

Policy Versus Means

The conventional view of problem solving is that means are adjusted to ends, or, policies/strategies are sought that will achieve identified objectives. As noted previously, however, strategies can bring a redefinition of objectives in business. In government, more frequently than in business, ends of public policy are governed by means. For instance, U.S. Navy shipbuilding yards were originally established to build ships. With the decline in the demand for ships, the production of ships became a means to achieve a different end, namely, that of providing employment for shipyard workers.

Also, in the public sector more than in the private sector, making a policy, any policy, is sometimes more important than the wisdom of the substance of the policy. This results from the fact, for example, that great pressures exist on politicians to meet their promises to deal with urgent demands.

Complexity of Policy Making

In the larger public service institutions, it is obvious that policy making is far more complex than in the largest private organizations. George M. Humphrey left the Hanna Company to join President Eisenhower's cabinet and to apply his no-nonsense managerial decision-making capability to straightening out the government. Later, in discussing his experiences he said:

Government is vast and diverse, like a hundred businesses all grouped under one name, but the various businesses of government are not integrated nor even directly related in fields of activity; and in government the executive management must operate under a system of divided authority . . . when a government executive decides on a course of action not already established under law, he must first check with other agencies to make certain his proposal does not conflict with or duplicate something being done by somebody else. It is common in government, much too common, for several agencies to be working on different facets of the same activity. The avoidance of overlapping or conflict calls for numerous conferences, for painstaking study of laws and directives, for working out plans in tedious detail so that what one Cabinet officer does will not bump into what another is doing—or run counter to our interests and activities abroad. . . .

Before coming to Washington, I had not understood why there were so many conferences in government, and so much delay. Now I do. Everything is more complex. . . . [Humphrey, 1954:31].

Comparable problems exist in smaller public service organizations. Figure 17-1 shows the range of influences on an administrator of a public hospital. To begin with, his board of directors is probably appointed by an elected official and will owe some allegiance to that official. Board members are influenced by individuals in various government agencies and by hospital employees. The planning committee of the hospital is composed of managers and staff working in the hospital as well as representatives of outside interests. Their role on the committee is to represent those outside interests. In sum, everyone is able to influence everyone else in the operation of the hospital. No strong influence can be ignored, and consensus on major issues is difficult to achieve. Furthermore, actions decided upon must not conflict too much with other organizations.

Although managerial skills that can be successfully applied in the private sector may also be transferrable to the public sector, the transition is not easy. One of the authors has spent a number of years in the federal service and has watched successful business managers enter into public service with visions of using "sound business methods" to improve the public service. He saw many of them in a short time become frustrated, angry, and depart because they could not adapt their managerial skills to the new demands of the public service institution they joined. On the other hand, many businessmen have made the adjustment and have used well the managerial skills they learned in business. Much or little is transferrable, depending upon the situation.

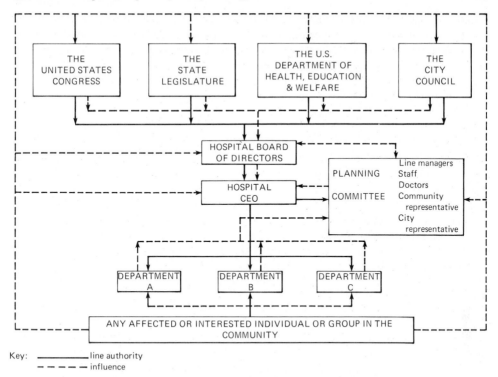

Key: ——————— line authority
— — — — influence

Figure 17-1 Influences on the planning process in a nonprofit hospital.

IMPLEMENTING POLICY/STRATEGY

Implementing policy/strategy in a private business is not easy, as discussed in earlier chapters. However difficult it may be in even the largest corporations, it is more complicated in government and other public service organizations for all the reasons given previously plus many more. President Roosevelt, a master political strategist and manipulator of government agencies, picturesquely described this state of affairs as follows:

The Treasury is so large and far-flung and ingrained in its practices that I find it is almost impossible to get the action and results I want. . . . But the Treasury is not to be compared with the State Department. You should go through the experience of trying to get any changes in the thinking, policy, and action of the career diplomats and then you'd know what a real problem was. But the Treasury and the State Department put together are nothing as compared with the Na-a-vy. . . . To change anything in the Na-a-vy is like punching a feather bed. You punch it with your right and you punch it with your left until you are finally exhausted, and then you find the damn bed just as it was before you started punching [Eccles, 1951:336].

There are many constraints on efficient implementation of policy/strategy in the NFP.

As noted before there are multiple, often conflicting, often fuzzy, and generally hard-to-measure objectives to be achieved. Policy/strategy to achieve these ends also frequently embodies the same characteristics. Try getting implemented anywhere a vague, conflicting, and unpopular policy/strategy! In the NFP, particularly the government, policy/strategy is subject to different interpretations by different people, each of whom has a power not controllable or easily controllable by someone else.

Partly because of performance measurement difficulties in the NFP, and also because of civil service regulations, rewards and penalties are not related to performance. When pay and promotions are tied tightly to seniority and external professional certification, as they are in government, the separation of rewards and performance makes it difficult for a centrally administered control system to function effectively.

Drucker [1973] observes that some differences in the measurement of performance result from the fact that in private organizations income is derived from sales to satisfied customers, whereas in NFP organizations income is received in budget allocations. Desirable objectives in such organizations, he says, associate with getting higher budgets. Efficiency and cost control are not considered virtues. Rather, spending total budget allocations is a prime objective. Such gamesmanship goes on in business, but not to the same degree. The point Drucker is making is that the public agency begins to serve its own internal needs rather than those of its constituents.

EVALUATING RESULTS

In business the evaluation of the results of policy, at least in incremental periods of time—such as months, quarters, or years—are measurable, for the most part, in quantitative terms. This is not true in government. No single or set of quantitative evaluation measures exist.

We have already noted that the extent to which the public interest is met is an ultimate measure of performance. We noted, too, how difficult it is to apply. Another final measure, much like the public interest, is what Appleby [1949:131] calls political efficiency, or that which gains the consent of the governed. Jones [1970:109] speaks of the same measure as "support for the authorities" as being applicable to all decision makers in the public service sector. He quotes Rourke with approval as follows: ". . . there are three vital centers from which political support may be drawn: the outside community, the legislature, and the executive branch itself. All these sources of political strength may be cultivated simultaneously, and usually are. . . . Basic to any agency's political standing in the American system of government is the support of public opinion" [Rourke, 1968:3].

Jones goes on to say that an evaluation of policy consequences on this standard would require answering a long list of extremely difficult-to-answer questions, such as:

1. How specific publics define the problems which policy is designed to affect.
2. The awareness of existing policy by specific publics.

3. The extent to which existing policy is associated with specific authorities.
4. Opinions toward existing policy.
5. Whether, and to what extent, opinion is divided within a public or between publics that are affected.
6. Whether, and to what extent, existing policy affecting one problem is considered significant enough for publics to grant or withhold political support [Jones, 1970:109].

To answer such questions, says Jones, would necessitate the establishment of a new government agency. Even if the evaluation process were undertaken, the results would be ambigious in recommending policy changes. This is so because of widespread differences in perception of what the basic problem is, disagreement on the effects of policy, and so on.

As a result, the evaluation process in government is not routine as in business. It varies depending upon policy and the level of activity. At lower levels of government and for most nongovernment public service organizations annual reports of activities are rather standard. The standards of measure, however, are not common to all.

MANAGERIAL CAPABILITIES AND VALUES

There is a widespread belief that business managers are generally more capable than managers in government. This is said to be due to the fact that in government there are greater political influences on managers, the civil service regulations constrain them, they have less freedom to act, and they are not invigorated by the rigors of economic competition. Miner's [1974:64] research tends to support this view, although, of course, there are many exceptions to it.

Findings of a study that compared values of managers entering or reentering the profit and nonprofit sectors suggest that in the future the quality of managers in nonprofit organizations may improve considerably [Rawls, Ullrich, and Nelson, 1975]. In this study 142 persons were evaluated and the following conclusions were reached:

1. Individuals favoring the nonprofit sector were more dominant and flexible than those favoring the profit sector.
2. Those preferring the nonprofit sector had greater capacity for status, social presence, and concern for personal relations. They expressed lower preference for obedience, responsibility, ambition, a comfortable life, cleanliness, and economic wealth.
3. Those preferring the nonprofit sector placed greater value on helpfulness, cheerfulness, and forgiveness.
4. Nonprofit sector aspirants expressed a greater need for power and a lesser need for security than those going into the profit sector.
5. Those individuals considered to be change agents were mostly destined for the nonprofit sector.

This study shows clearly that for the subjects examined there are significant differences in personality, values, and behavioral characteristics between those destined for the nonprofit as contrasted with the profit sector. Furthermore, the comparisons are, in part, just the reverse of those that stereotypes of the past have asserted. If the results of this study are correct, and persist, we may see some substantial changes in the ways in which our public service institutions are managed. We need more and continuous surveys, however, before valid conclusions can be drawn about the trend and its potential.

CONCLUDING OBSERVATIONS

An experienced manager has concluded that there are fundamental differences between administration in business and government, as follows:

It is exceedingly difficult clearly to identify the factors which make government different from every other activity in society. Yet this difference is a fact and I believe it to be so big a difference that the dissimilarity between government and all other forms of social action is greater than any dissimilarity among those other forms themselves. Without a willingness to recognize this

TABLE 17-1
Comparisons of Business and Not-For-Profit Organizations

	BUSINESS	NFP
Basic purpose	Profit	Advance the public interest
Objectives	Few	Many
	Have general concensus	No concensus
Organizational structure	Decentralized in most large companies	Generally a centralized bureaucracy
	Many large companies	Many extremely large organizations
Decision-making processes	ROI a dominant standard	Evaluating tools more blunt
	Quantitative evaluating tools widely used	Qualitative evaluating tools widely used
	Economic standard dominant	Political standards dominant
	Decisions centered in one person	Group decision making predominates
	Integrated decision making	Piecemeal decision making
	Wide policy choices considered	Policy choices narrow
Dominant constituents	Stockholders and customers	Any interest group can influence decisions
Environment	Competitive and turbulent	Monopolistic and relatively stable
Implementation of decisions	Lines of authority reasonably clear	Chain of command not clear and confused
	Common implementing mechanisms	No standard implementing systems
Source of income	Satisfied customers	Budget allocations
Measures of performance	Principally economic and quantitative, e.g., return on investment	Political and not well defined, e.g., public interest, political efficiency

fact, no one can even begin to discuss public affairs to any good profit or serious purpose [Appleby, 1945:1].

As this chapter explains there are some very significant differences in formulating, implementing and evaluating policy between private and public sector organizations. Table 17-1 summarizes in simplified form some comparisons highlighted in the chapter. Yet, as also explained, there are fundamental similarities between organizations in the two sectors in the policy process.

QUESTIONS

Discussion Guides on Chapter Content

1. What is the not-for-profit sector?
2. Set forth fundamental dissimilarities between policy/strategy formulation and implementation in the not-for-profit sector and in the profit sector.
3. What are some major similarities in policy/strategy formulation and implementation in the private and not-for-profit sector?
4. It is often said that managers in private industry are more capable than those in government. Do you agree or disagree?
5. Assume that you are the chief executive of a not-for-profit hospital. What differences would you expect to find in formulating and implementing a long-range planning program in contrast to, say, a chief executive in a manufacturing company having about the same revenues and number of employees?

Mind Stretching Questions

1. "A basic difference between decision making in the private and in the public sector is that in the former a central standard for rationality is economic theory, whereas rational action in the public sector is based upon political theory. Do you agree or disagree? Explain.
2. Is a growing pluralism likely to accentuate differences between the private and public sector in the formulation and implementation of policy/strategy?
3. "The differences in policy/strategy formulation and implementation between large and small corporations are much less than among different types of organizations in the not-for-profit sector." Do you agree or disagree with this assertion? Explain.

18

Contingency Theory of Policy/Strategy

INTRODUCTION

At various points in the preceding discussions a contingency theory approach has been advocated and various proposals of this nature have been considered. For instance in Chapter 4 certain environmental contingency variables were discussed with considerable emphasis placed on variables that have been of concern to those working in the field of organization theory. Also as noted further in Chapter 13 environmental contingencies of this kind play an important role in the design of organizations, and thus in the implementation of strategies through the medium of organizational structure.

Although applications of the contingency approach to problems of organizational planning and design appear to have the longest history, there have been relatively recent applications in other areas as well. Thus, as indicated in Chapter 8, a number of scholars have attempted to specify appropriate strategies to be used in a given set of circumstances (but not in others). Similarly Chapter 12, in considering the various decision-making approaches, provides evidence that there is no "one best way" for all circumstances; the appropriate approach will vary with the nature of the situation, and in particular with the characteristics of the firm's external environment.

This final chapter seeks to focus more directly on this contingency theory approach, to evaluate it in the context of existing research, and to derive from this analysis some conclusions regarding the future of the policy discipline. The fact that the authors choose to mold this discussion around a contingency theory theme is indicative on the one hand of their profound belief in the need to develop sound theory in this most practical of all areas and, on the other hand, of their conviction that something approximating a contingency approach is most likely to provide an effective means to this end, at least for the present.

CONTINGENCY THEORY AND LIMITED DOMAIN THEORY

The appeal of contingency theory is that it appears to provide a middle ground between the extreme situationist view that every situation is unique and that therefore theoretical generalization is well nigh impossible, and the view that organizational functioning can be fully explained in terms of broad general truths and principles, a view that is not born out by the evidence [Miner, 1978]. Furthermore, the contingency approach potentially provides a means of "getting a handle on" the almost unlimited complexity of the open system concept, which views organizations in terms of the constant dynamic interaction of internal subsystems and environmental variables [Kast and Rosenzweig, 1973]. Unfortunately, as Moberg and Koch [1975] point out this potential has not been fully realized. Yet the potential is there. Current difficulties appear to relate to efforts to achieve too much too fast, and thus to an oversimplification of the problem, and to a premature settling on key contingency variables.

These points, and at the same time the true nature of the contingency approach, may be illustrated with reference to a contingency theory of leadership developed by Fiedler [1967]. The reason for choosing this particular theory is that it has been stated in comprehensive form and has been in existence long enough to elicit a sizable body of research. (In fact this is one of the very earliest contingency theories.) A similar situation does not yet exist with regard to any of the contingency theories in the field of policy/strategy.

The essential point of Fiedler's theory is that the particular leadership styles that will lead to success and to failure are contingent upon three aspects of the leadership situation: (1) whether leader-member relations are good or poor, (2) whether the structure of the tasks to be performed is high or low, and (3) whether the leader's position power is strong or weak. With a knowledge of these three variables, according to the theory, one can specify what kind of a leader will prove effective. Taking these three variables and specifying two levels for each, the theory yields eight combinations and thus eight subtheories. Together these eight subtheories specify a comprehensive theory of leadership.

The difficulty with this approach is that when subjected to research test some of the subtheories seem to hold up and some do not [Miner, 1980a]. Furthermore, there is a question whether these three contingency variables are the right ones. In particular it appears that specific inclusion in the theory of variables drawn from the wider organizational context in which leadership occurs is essential to effective prediction.

As a theoretical and research strategy, it might be more appropriate not to attempt to develop a comprehensive theory immediately but rather to focus on a limited domain that appears particularly amenable to understanding. Thus, using the Fiedler subtheories as an example, the situation specified by good leader-member relations, high task structure, and strong leader position power might be explored in considerable detail. This could be done with a view to determining key aspects and causes of these three variable states and how they might interact with leader behavior and various indexes of success over time. To the extent one focuses on one important theoretical area in this manner, ignoring other areas and thus producing a less than fully comprehensive theory, the theory is best described as a limited domain theory. However, in the literature such theories are not always clearly differentiated from the more comprehensive contingency theories [Pinder and Moore, 1980].

The main virtue of limited domain theories is that they simplify the theoretical task to a point where it is amenable to precise conceptualization and intensive research investigation. Key variables delimiting the domain, which may later be expanded into true contingency variables, can be clearly identified. Over time as various domains are explored, the matrix of possible domains is gradually filled in, until a comprehensive contingency theory emerges. Ideally the domains explored initially will be those where the prospect of establishing valid theories is greatest *and* where the most important practical contribution can be made. One definition of the latter would be a domain in which the greatest number of organizations fall for the longest periods of time.

The obvious difficulty with the limited domain approach to developing contingency theories of policy/strategy is that many top executives and their firms will be left without precise theoretical guidance for some time to come. Yet, as will become evident in the following discussion, this is the general state of affairs for most organizations at the present time, in spite of the fact that serious attempts at theoretical generalizations are now beginning to appear. No discipline can move to complete understanding instantaneously. The task must be divided into manageable segments and subjected to intensive study over time. This is what the limited domain approach to the development of valid contingency theory attempts to accomplish [Miner, 1980c; Weir, 1979].

APPROXIMATIONS TO CONTINGENCY THEORIES OF POLICY/STRATEGY

It has been evident for some time that the strategies and policies that are appropriate for one firm under one set of circumstances are very different from those that another firm, in different circumstances, should use. It is this very fact that fostered the use of the case approach in teaching business policy. Each situation was seen as unique, and the way to have the student fully comprehend this uniqueness was to expose him or her to a variety of cases.

In its original form this approach made no attempt at the development of theoretical generalizations, but more recently various writers have proposed sets of contingency hypotheses derived from case analysis. This approach to the development of theory is very much in the tradition of the business policy field. It stands in marked contrast to a second approach to the formulation of contingency theories of policy/strategy, which is more consistent with the view that the policy field is closely intertwined with management and organization theory [Mintzberg, 1977]. This latter approach draws heavily upon the research related to organization structure and, in fact, derives its contingency variables from this source.

Theories Based on the Case Tradition

As might be expected those theories that have developed out of the case tradition tend to be quite complex. There are a number of contingency variables and many hypotheses. The objective is to retain the richness of the basic case materials in the theory to the extent possible.

A comprehensive formulation by Hofer [1975] provides a typical example. This theory attempts to develop strategies that are appropriate at different stages of the product life cycle. The variables considered are as follows:

Market and consumer behavior variables—buyer needs, purchase frequency, buyer concentration, market segmentation, market size, elasticity of demand, buyer loyalty, seasonality, cyclicality.

Industry structure variables—uniqueness of the product, rate of technological change in product design, type of product, number of equal products, barriers to entry, degree of product differentiation, transportation and distribution costs, price/cost structure, degree of technological change in process design, experience curves, degree of integration, economics of scale, marginal plant size.

Competitor variables—degree of specialization within the industry, degree of capacity utilization, degree of seller concentration, aggressiveness of competition.

Supplier variables—degree of supplier concentration, major changes in availability of raw materials.

Broader environmental variables—interest rates, money supply, GNP trend, antitrust regulations, growth of population, age distribution of population, regional shifts of population, life style changes.

Organizational characteristics and resources—quality of products, market share, marketing intensity, value added, degree of customer concentration, discretionary cash flow, gross capital investment, length of the production cycle, plant and equipment newness, relative wage rate.

Descriptive propositions are developed for each stage of the product life cycle. Thus, for example:

In the maturity stage of the life cycle, the major determinants of business strategy are the nature of buyer needs, the degree of product differentiation, the rate of technological change in process design, the degree of market segmentation, the ratio of distribution costs to manufacturing, value added, and the frequency with which the product is purchased.

Normative contingency hypotheses are then formulated using these major determinants. An example for the maturity stage is

When (1) the degree of product differentiation is *low*
      (2) the nature of buyer needs is primarily *economic*
      (3) the rate of technological change in process design is *high*
      (4) the ratio of distribution costs to manufacturing value added is *high*
      (5) the purchase frequency is *high*
      (6) the buyer concentration is *high*
      (7) the degree of capacity utilization is *low*

Then businesses should

(a) allocate most of their R&D funds to improvements in process design rather than to new product development
(b) allocate most of their plant and equipment expenditures to new equipment purchases
(c) seek to integrate forward or backward in order to increase the value they add to the product
(d) attempt to improve their production scheduling and inventory control procedures in order to increase their capacity utilization
(e) attempt to segment the market
(f) attempt to reduce their raw material unit costs by standardizing their product design and using interchangeable components throughout their product line in order to qualify for volume discounts

Other sets of strategies of a quite different nature are proposed for different combinations of states of the contingency variables. Furthermore, the relevant contingency variables themselves change at different points in the product life cycle. Obviously this is far from a parsimonious theory, but it does retain much of the richness of its case origins.

The Hofer approach to theory construction relies heavily on the inductive skills of the theorist. In contrast Miller and Friesen [1978] have used a type of statistical factor analysis of case data to achieve similar results. They defined ten different scenarios in terms of such variables as environmental stability and hostility, use of controls, environmental scanning, delegation, technocratization, availability of resources, bureaucratic constraints, strategic innovation, length of time horizons, multiplexity, extensiveness of analyses, risk taking, and so on. Again the number of contingency variables is large, but the factor analytic approach yields a grouping process such that companies may be identified with certain archetypes. Those archetypes associated with success are labelled the adaptive firm under moderate challenge, the adaptive firm in a very challenging environment, the dominant firm, the giant under fire, the entrepreneurial conglomerate, and the innovator; those associated with failure are the impulsive firm, the stagnant bureaucracy, the headless giant, and the aftermath.

Note should also be made of Summer's [1980] major theoretical effort based largely on induction from case data. Although this effort fails to achieve a full-blown contingency theory, in that specific hypotheses are not stated in a contingent form, it does present certain guidelines for strategy formation that could be elaborated further, at a lower level of abstraction, into contingent hypotheses. Among these guidelines are the following:

1. Focus the problem on the strategic concept that should receive the most weight (based on its importance to society) and the highest heuristic or sequential priority (based on the time available and limited attention span of the strategic group).
2. Search for alternatives that are value-rich, and outside the experience of the strategic group.
3. Diagnose the payoffs (outcomes) of any alternative strategy or policy in terms of (1) strategic language and (2) isolation of dominant payoffs [Summer, 1980: 323–326].

Additional examples of theory construction that is firmly embedded in case data might be cited [Steiner, 1979b]. Based on what has been done in this regard to date, however, certain potential pitfalls can be noted. One is an apparent difficulty in moving to levels of generality beyond those of the individual cases themselves. It appears difficult for the theorists to abandon the richness of the case data in the interest of generalization across multiple organizations and situations. When this bond is broken, there is a tendency to leap to very high levels of abstraction where testing of the theory becomes practically impossible. In short, writing specific, testable middle-range theory out of a case context has to date proved to be a very difficult task, primarily because of the problems inherent in identifying a limited set of salient variables around which to cast the theory. The jump from cases to such theory appears to be too great, whatever the value of cases for other purposes. It would seem to be much easier to induce theory from a body of existing research than from individual cases directly.

Theories Derived from Organization Theory

The approach to theory construction that draws upon organization theory for its key contingency variables is considerably more parsimonious than the preceding, but may suffer from limited predictive power to the extent these key variables fail to subsume important variables proposed by case-oriented theorists. An example of this approach is provided by Anderson and Paine [1975], who have developed a theory based on two environmental contingency variables. The first is the perceived uncertainty of the environment (certain or uncertain), and the second is the perceived need for strategic change (high or low). In both cases the relevant perceiver is the strategy maker (singular or plural). Different strategies are proposed for the resulting four quadrants.

Thus, under conditions of perceived environmental certainty and low need for change, strategies would stress defending the domain, expansion in "sure bet" areas only, integration to protect supplies and markets, efficient technological processes and maintenance of market share. In contrast, where uncertainty and high need for change are perceived, strategies would emphasize divestiture and selective acquisition, diversification, new ventures, and entrepreneurial risk taking. Similar guides to strategy formation as well as typical planning modes, organizational forms, and information search behaviors are presented for the other quadrants.

The results of a study conducted to test the theory in a sample of 62 organizations are given in Table 18-1 [Paine and Anderson, 1977]. Although certain environments with little need for change are much more likely to yield success than uncertain environments that require change, there still remain sizable differences between quadrants in the factors associated with success. The data do not consistently support the theoretical hypotheses, but they do support a contingency concept and the evidence is far from being devoid of relationship to the theory.

A somewhat different theory has been proposed by Cook [1975] using perceived environmental press (hostile or benign) and organizational responsiveness orientation (stable or dynamic) as the contingency variables. It is posited that benign environments elicit approach behavior and hostile ones avoidance; stable organizations elicit conventional strategies and dynamic ones creative strategies. Four basic hypotheses are thus derived:

TABLE 18-1
Factors Associated with Company Success in Different
Perceived Contexts

Environment certain and low need for change
   All firms relatively successful and characterized by
      little innovation
      little risk taking
      short planning horizons
      little proactive environmental scanning
Environment certain and high need for change
   Successful firms in contrast with unsuccessful characterized by
      optimizing of objectives
      considerable innovation
      long planning horizons
      considerable proactive environmental scanning
Environment uncertain and low need for change
   Successful firms in contrast with unsuccessful characterized by
      considerable innovation
      considerable proactive environmental scanning
Environment uncertain and high need for change
   Relatively few firms successful, but relative to the unsuccessful majority
      these few were characterized by
      less perceived environmental uncertainty
      considerable innovation

SOURCE: Adapted from Paine and Anderson [1977:156].

1. Stable organizations facing benign press tend to enact intensification (approach/conventional) strategies.
2. Dynamic organizations facing benign press tend to enact proactive (approach/creative) strategies.
3. Stable organizations facing hostile press tend to enact reactive (avoidance/conventional) strategies.
4. Dynamic organizations facing hostile press tend to enact mediative (avoidance/creative) strategies.

Cook has conducted an empirical test using 14 supermarket chains as a data base. The results do in fact provide impressive support for the hypotheses, at least in a descriptive sense. Whether strategies of the type specified yield more effective organizational performance under the indicated contingency conditions is yet to be determined.

Other examples of contingency theories of policy/strategy derived from organization theory might be cited [Litschert and Bonham, 1978; Steiner, 1979b]. In many respects this appears to be a fruitful approach. Yet it suffers from a lack of research focused directly on strategic issues, and the current disarray in macro organization theory—both theoretical and empirical—is such as to provide only a very unstable base for extrapolation [Miner, 1982].

Contingency Theories Based on Empirical Experience and Conceptualization

Steiner [1979b] notes two other categories of contingency theories in the policy/strategy field—those deriving from empirical experience and from conceptualization. The PIMS hypotheses developed out of empirical analyses of complex relationships among many variables in many organizations are an example of the former approach (see Chapters 8 and 9). In a similar mode Hatten, Schendel and Cooper [1978] analyzed data on 13 firms in the brewing industry. Groups of firms were established empirically that differed considerably from each other but had marked homogeneity within the group. Strategic models were then developed for each group, thus providing what amount to sets of contingent hypotheses based upon the posture of a firm in the industry.

Theory construction of this kind is time consuming and requires cross-validation of the findings on new samples or on the same samples at another point in time. Results may be overly dependent on circumstances at the point of study and thus fail to permit the kind of generalization a good theory should provide. However, as an initial approach to a complex field, such a contingent model-building process has much to recommend it. It should be noted also that this approach does not necessarily require the kind of multivariate computer analysis and modeling we have been considering. Hypotheses may be induced from reviews of the empirical research in the field or from the theorist's own studies. Many of the contingency formulations, especially those related to planning effectiveness and aspects of planning, considered in previous chapters are of this type.

Contingency approaches derived from conceptualization appear to be more deductive than inductive in nature, although it is often difficult to determine the exact nature of the theorist's thought processes. Ansoff's [1965] book *Corporate Strategy* provides an example.

There are in addition certain unintegrated lists of hypotheses drawn from various sources that have been proposed primarily to stimulate thinking and research. Typical of these is the list of 71 hypotheses developed by Glueck [1972]. Many of these hypotheses are stated in the general form, but a number are of a contingency nature. Contingency variables proposed are the degree of dependency of the firm; the extent to which the company is entrepreneurial; complexity of product line, technology, and environment; industry; the presence of long-linked, mediating, or intensive technology; market share; stage of the product life cycle; growth rate of the market; volatility of the market; and company size.

Some of these hypotheses refer to a specific theoretical domain rather than subsuming the full variable range as in true contingency theory. The variable terminology, lack of logical relationships among the hypotheses, and on occasion the total failure to maintain internal consistency almost automatically invalidate such a list as theory. The list is merely what the author originally presented it as—an attempt to get things started.

THE NEED FOR RESEARCH TESTS

It is clear that the policy field is moving toward conceptual maturity. In fact, it is beginning to develop an abundance of hypotheses, although not of logically consistent theories dealing with causal relationships among key variables. The problem is that the research which should serve to cull out incorrect hypotheses is only beginning. Thus, more and more hypotheses pile up with little basis for differentiating among them. This is why the authors have not set forth *a* contingency theory, or even *a* set of limited domain theories, in this chapter or the preceding ones. The state of our knowledge at the present time is simply not such that this can be done with the necessary degree of certainty. Guides for managerial strategy and policy formation that have a sufficient grounding in research to justify recommending them to practitioners are few in number. In a few years, assuming that the current progress continues, there may well be many such guides, but not at present. The data to make an accurate choice from among conflicting theoretical statements simply are not available.

Research Problems and Problems with Research

One of the major problems of the policy field is its grounding in and long-term commitment to the case approach. In terms of teaching and learning this is a real asset; in terms of theory construction and research it is not, simply because those who have learned to be good case writers and analyzers often have not at the same time learned to value research and to be good collectors and analyzers of statistical data. The two skills are not the same [Schendel, 1975; Schendel and Hatten, 1972]. "There is a need to empirically test concepts and hypotheses to evaluate their applicability to real circumstances. Models do need to be tested for their worth. It is fair to say that policy is long on models and short on empirical results" [Schendel, 1975:15].

An example of the kind of exploratory research that is currently needed is provided by a study conducted by Hofer [1973] using data derived from business case histories written up in *Fortune* from 1960–72. Although, as Hofer himself notes, the study has its drawbacks in terms of scientific precision and rests on certain assumptions that may not hold entirely, the following conclusions are supported by the data:

. . . when environmental opportunities abound and/or when resources are more than sufficient for the needs of existing product/market areas, the Firms studied typically sought to increase the scope of their present operations in some way, while, when the opposite conditions applied, they more typically curtailed increases in the present scope of operations and pursued changes in their functional policies and/or conglomerate diversification . . . the development of new products for existing markets and/or increased penetration of existing products for existing markets were almost always among the top two or three responses. . . . the attempt to increase penetration of existing products for existing markets seems to succeed more often as a response to major increases in total demand than it does as a response to major changes in technology. By the same token, the development of new products for existing markets appears to be more successful as a response to major changes in technolgy than is horizontal diversification [Hofer, 1973:51–52].

In conjunction with findings reported previously, these results provide a good beginning in gaining an understanding of the marketing strategies companies do and should develop when faced with varied environmental circumstances.

As research of this kind increases, however, there are certain pitfalls that must be avoided. One is that hypotheses should not be tested using the same case data that were used to generate them in the first place. Another is that when hypotheses are derived from analyses of a set of cases by factor analysis or some similar technique, the hypotheses cannot be assumed to be true because they derive from data; they must be tested on another independent data set. Another is that causation cannot be attributed to a particular independent variable unless other correlated variables are controlled either statistically or experimentally. And yet another is extrapolating from limited data to widespread applications. Pitfalls of this kind have marred research in the past; they are in fact inevitable in an emerging field. But to obtain valid answers to important research questions they need to be kept to a minimum.

Stages of Research

As research in a field develops it tends to appear first in the form of surveys dealing with practice, attitudes, and intentions; then in the form of correlational or correlation-type analyses relating key variables to each other; and finally in the form of experimental studies that establish *causal* relationships [Miner, 1978]. The field of policy/strategy is now moving into the second of these phases, although certain of its subareas are still in the initital, survey phase. On the other hand, some areas, such as that of behavioral decision theory (see Chapters 10, 11 and 12), are in fact well into the experimental phase.

The problem in these more advanced areas is that they have gotten to the point where causal statements can be accepted as fact through a heavy reliance on laboratory studies. The causal statements are true as far as they go, but many may need serious modification when injected into the context of an ongoing organizational setting. The ultimate need is for field experiments where key variables are manipulated and the behavior of dependent variables is observed. Such studies are very difficult to conduct with adequate controls; they should not even be attempted until the key variables have been established with high certainty by research of lesser degrees of elegance. Yet in the end, if solid guidelines for managerial practice in the policy/strategy field are to be established, such studies will be required.

In the mean time it appears likely that we will see an increasing number of correlational studies involving content analysis of case data [Jauch, Osborn, and Martin, 1980]; the use of documentary information, such as that available from the major business reporting services and federally required reports (the 10-K prescribed by the Securities and Exchange Commission for example) [Glueck and Willis, 1979]; and studies based on content analyses of company annual reports [Bowman, 1978]. This is appropriate; it is sensible to move the field as far as possible utilizing existing data sources. Then, based on what the correlational studies tell us, we can focus research involving the collection of original data to test causal hypotheses in areas where important results are most likely to be obtained.

Research Opportunities

Given the preceding, there are a number of areas in which research can have an important impact on the development of a contingency theory of strategic management:

1. Very little research has been done on the factors determining which missions, purposes, and philosophies are preferred in which environmental (internal as well as external) conditions.

2. Very little research has been done on factors influencing the design of formal strategic planning systems.

3. Not enough research has been done on preferred strategies concerning social programs pursued by an organization in light of variable environmental forces.

4. Not enough research has been done on preferred strategies to acquire environmental knowledge that is most needed in making decisions in different situations.

5. Strategic factors most significant in the success of firms in different industries . . . were found to be common to companies in the same industry, but very different among different industries [Steiner, 1969b]. Further research in this area seems warranted.

6. Much has been done . . . regarding strategies for different stages of the product life cycle [Steiner, 1979b]. This research could be pursued further.

7. More research is needed concerning results of participation under different conditions.

8. With the growth in importance of the not-for-profit area, much more needs to be done in developing contingency theories of strategic management in this area.

9. Great opportunities exist for research in the understanding of preferred relationships between headquarters and divisions and within divisions.

10. We need much replication of past research to see whether different scholars reach the same conclusions.

11. Deeper research is needed in important areas where significant research has already been done.

12. We need much more study of the manager as a variable [Steiner, 1979b:414–415].

These are merely a set of suggested foci for research, but they do point up both the significance of contingency approaches and the need for research on them.

THE EMERGENCE OF A DISCIPLINE

For many years the field of business policy has been represented by a single capstone course in the undergraduate and MBA curriculums, which relied heavily on case materials and was taught by people from diverse backgrounds and with varied areas of functional specialization. Now this situation is changing and it is changing very fast. The policy/strategy field is emerging as a full-fledged discipline in its own right. A number of considerations attest to this. Perhaps the most important of these is that some 400 pages of text can be written here describing existing knowledge, theory, and research in the field, and still only the surface has been scratched. As noted in Chapter 1, the policy/strategy discipline has developed its own body of knowledge, its own theory, and it is spawning its own research. At the same time it is reaching out and providing a scholarly home for certain subdisciplines that have previously been largely in academic limbo. The key point is that it is no longer drawing primarily on other disciplines and functional fields to create an unstable amalgam of theories, hypotheses, and data with little apparent relationship to one another. It is now a discipline that is generating its own indigenous knowledge and within which certain individuals find their primary professional identity.

Further evidence for this view derives from the fact that increasing numbers of universities are providing coursework at the doctoral level to train teachers and researchers in the field. In many cases such efforts currently are represented by one or two courses within a doctoral program in management or organizational behavior. In such cases the major thrust of the training is outside the policy field, although an individual may develop a specialization of this kind through reading, research, and in particular the choice of a dissertation topic. However, an increasing number of business schools are offering a full-scale Ph.D. program designed for those who wish to make an academic career of the policy discipline. This is a most encouraging development; it reflects a considerable degree of disciplinary maturity [Greenwood, 1977].

The core of the discipline is the organization-environment interaction as reflected in the decision-making process, the development of strategies and policies, and in planning. Policy implementation is at the interface with the management and organizational behavior areas and the development of knowledge in this regard no doubt will continue to be shared with these disciplines. At the same time certain areas of study that have not previously had a secure disciplinary home appear to be finding this home in the policy/strategy context. Among these are subject matter areas that have been variously labeled business and environment, business and government, business and society, social responsibility, management consultation, entrepreneurship, and behavioral decision theory. All of these areas have major contributions to make to our understanding of the total process surrounding policy and strategy. This is not to say, however, that these subject matter areas do not have a sufficient separate identity to warrant independent courses and even, in some cases, independent programs of study.

Increasingly, the student will have something of major practical importance to learn in this area to supplement the traditional development of analytic skills that the study of cases provides. The source of this knowledge will be the theory and research of the policy/strategy discipline. As indicated in the first chapter, the objectives of the policy/strategy course are to help students develop their analytical skills, improve their knowledge, and develop appropriate and relevant attitudes. The burgeoning theory and research make the accomplishment of all three of these objectives now increasingly feasible.

QUESTIONS

Discussion Guides on Chapter Content
1. Distinguish between contingency theory and limited domain theory.
2. In what ways do contingency theories of policy strategy derived from the case approach differ from those derived from organization theory?
3. What are the special problems in developing a sound research base that appear to be plaguing the policy field at the present time?
4. In what areas of policy/strategy study does the need for more research seem greatest? Why are these areas relatively lacking in sound research?

5. "The policy/strategy field is emerging as a full-fledged discipline in its own right." Comment.

Mind Stretching Questions

1. What do you think will be the state of the policy/strategy field in the year 2000?

2. "Theory is fine for ivory-tower academics, but it has no relevance for the practical businessman or businesswoman." Comment and document your answer.

REFERENCES

Abell, Derek F.: *Defining the Business: The Starting Point of Strategic Planning.* Englewood Cliffs, NJ, Prentice-Hall, 1980.

Abell, Derek F., and John S. Hammond: *Strategic Market Planning: Problems and Analytical Approaches.* Englewood Cliffs, NJ, Prentice-Hall, 1979.

Abernathy, William J., and Kenneth Wayne: "Limits of the Learning Curve." *Harvard Business Review,* September–October 1974.

Abramson, Robert, and Walter Halset: *Planning for Improved Enterprise Performance: A Guide for Managers and Consultants.* Geneva, Switzerland, International Labour Office, 1979.

Ackerman, Robert W.: "How Companies Respond to Social Demands." *Harvard Business Review,* July–August 1973.

Ackerman, Robert W.: *Managing Corporate Responsibility.* Boston, Harvard University Press, 1975a.

Ackerman, Robert W.: *The Social Challenge to Business.* Cambridge, MA, Harvard University Press, 1975b.

Ackoff, Russell L.: *A Concept of Corporate Planning.* New York, Wiley, 1970.

Adizes, Ichak: *How to Solve the Mismanagement Crisis.* Homewood, IL, Dow Jones-Irwin, 1979.

Adizes, Ichak, and J. Fred Weston: "Comparative Models of Social Responsibility." *Academy of Management Journal,* March 1973.

Aguilar, Francis J.: *Scanning the Business Environment.* New York, Macmillan, 1967.

Aguilar, Francis J., Robert A. Howell, and Richard F. Vancil: *Formal Planning Systems—1970.* Graduate School of Business Administration, Harvard University, 1970.

Alchian, Armen A.: "Uncertainty, Evolution, and Economic Theory." *Journal of Political Economy,* June 1950.

ALCOA Policy Guidelines for Business Conduct: March 1977.

Alexander, Larry D.: "The Effect Level in the Hierarchy and Functional Area Have on the Extent Mintzberg's Roles are Required by Managerial Jobs." *Academy of Management Proceedings,* August 1979.

Allen, M. G.: "Strategic Problems Facing Today's Corporate Planner." Speech before Thirty-sixth Annual Meeting of the Academy of Management, Kansas City, MO, August 1976.

Allio, Robert J., and Malcolm W. Pennington: *Corporate Planning: Techniques and Applications.* New York, AMACOM, 1979.

Allison, Graham T.: *Essence of Decision: Explaining the Cuban Missile Crisis.* Boston, Little, Brown, 1971.

Alutto, Joseph A., and Franklin Acito: "Decisional Participation and Sources of Job Satisfaction: A Study Manufacturing Personnel." *Academy of Management Journal,* March 1974.

America, Richard F.: "How Minority Business Can Build on Its Strength." *Harvard Business Review,* May–June 1980.

Anderson, Carl R., and Frank T. Paine: "Managerial Perceptions and Strategic Behavior." *Academy of Management Journal,* December 1975.

Anderson, Carl R., and Frank T. Paine: "PIMS: A Reexamination." *Academy of Management Review,* July 1978.

Andrews, Frederick: "Abe Briloff Tees Off on Creativity in Accounting," *Wall Street Journal,* March 13, 1973.

Andrews, Kenneth R.: *The Concept of Corporate Strategy.* Homewood, IL, Dow Jones-Irwin, 1971.

Anshen, Melvin: "Changing the Social Contract: A Role for Business." *Columbia Journal of World Business,* November–December 1970.

Anshen, Melvin (ed.): *Managing the Socially Responsible Corporation.* New York, Macmillan, 1974.

Anshen, Melvin: *Corporate Strategies for Social Performance.* New York, Macmillan, 1980.

Anshen, Melvin, and William D. Guth: "Strategies for Research in Policy Formulation." *Journal of Business,* October 1973.

Ansoff, H. Igor: *Corporate Strategy: An Analytic Approach to Business Policy for Growth and Expansion.* New York, McGraw-Hill, 1965.

Ansoff, H. Igor: "Managing Strategic Surprise Through Response to Weak Signals." *California Management Review,* Winter 1975.

Ansoff, H. Igor: "The Changing Shape of the Strategic Problem." In Dan E. Schendel and Charles W. Hofer (eds.): *Strategic Management: A New View of Business Policy and Planning.* Boston, Little, Brown, 1979a.

Ansoff, H. Igor: *Strategic Management.* New York, Wiley, 1979b.

Ansoff, H. Igor: "Strategic Issue Management." *Strategic Management Journal,* April–June 1980.

Ansoff, H. Igor, *et al.:* "Does Planning Pay? The Effect of Planning on Success of Acquisitions in American Firms." *Long Range Planning,* December 1970.

Ansoff, H. Igor, Roger P. Declerck, and Robert L. Hayes (eds.): *From Strategic Planning to Strategic Management.* New York, Wiley, 1976.

Anthony, Robert N.: "The Trouble with Profit Maximization." *Harvard Business Review,* November–December 1960.

Anthony, Robert N.: *Planning and Control Systems: A Framework for Analysis.* Boston, Graduate School of Business Administration, Harvard University, 1965.

Anyon, G. Jay: *Entrepreneurial Dimensions of Management.* Wynnewood, PA, Livingston, 1973.

Appleby, Paul H.: *Big Democracy.* New York, Alfred A. Knopf, 1945.

Appleby, Paul H.: *Policy and Administration.* University, AL, University of Alabama Press, 1949.

Argyris, Chris: *Integrating the Individual and the Organization.* New York, Wiley, 1964.

Argyris, Chris: *Intervention Theory and Method.* Reading, MA, Addison-Wesley, 1970.

Armstrong, J. Scott: *Long-Range Forecasting: From Crystal Ball to Computer.* New York, Wiley-Interscience, 1978.

Arroba, Tanya Y.: "Decision-making Style as a Function of Occupational Group, Decision Content and Perceived Importance." *Journal of Occupational Psychology,* September 1978.

Asimov, Isaac: Letter to Editor. *Time,* January 20, 1975.

Badr, Hamed, Edmund R. Gray, and B. L. Kedia: "An Empirical Examination of the Relationship between Personal Value Structures and Decision Making: A Cross-Cultural Perspective." *Southern Management Association Proceedings,* November 1980.

Bagley, Edward R.: *Beyond the Conglomerates.* New York, AMACOM, 1975.

Bailey, Earl L. (ed.): *Pricing Practices and Strategies.* New York, The Conference Board, 1978.

Bailey, Stephen K.: *Congress Makes a Law.* New York, Columbia University Press, 1950.

Bank of America: *Community and the Bank 1977*. San Francisco, Bank of America, 1977.

Barkley, Paul W., and David W. Seckler: *Economic Growth and the Environmental Decay*. New York, Harcourt, 1972.

Barmeier, Robert E.: "Public Issues Analysis in Corporate Planning." In Lee E. Preston (ed.): *Business Environment/Public Policy*. 1979 Conference Papers. St. Louis, American Assembly of Collegiate Schools of Business, 1980.

Barnard, Chester I.: *The Functions of the Executive*. Cambridge, MA, Harvard University Press, 1968.

Barron, Frank: *Creative Person and Creative Process*. New York, Holt, Rinehart and Winston, 1969.

Bartol, Kathyrn M.: "Professionalism as a Predictor of Organizational Commitment, Role Stress, and Turnover: A Multidimensional Approach." *Academy of Management Journal*, December 1979.

Bassett, Glenn A.: "The Qualifications of a Manager." *California Management Review*, Winter 1969.

Bauer, Raymond A., and Kenneth J. Gergen (eds.): *The Study of Policy Formation*. New York, Free Press, 1968.

Baumback, Clifford M., and Kenneth Lawyer: *How to Organize and Operate a Small Business*. Englewood Cliffs, NJ, Prentice-Hall, 1979.

Baumhart, Raymond: *Ethics in Business*. New York, Holt, Rinehart and Winston, 1968.

Baumol, William J.: *Business Behavior, Values and Growth*. New York, Harcourt, Brace and World, 1967.

Baumol, William J., Rensis Likert, Henry C. Wallich, and John J. McGowan: *A New Rationale for Corporate Social Policy*. New York, Committee for Economic Development, 1970.

Beach, Lee Roy, and Terence R. Mitchell: "A Contingency Model for the Selection of Decision Strategies." *Academy of Management Review*, July 1978.

Bell, Daniel: "The Corporation and Society in the 1970s." *The Public Interest*, Summer 1971.

Bell, Daniel: "The Revolution of Rising Entitlements." *Fortune*, April 1975a.

Bell, Daniel: "Too Much, Too Late: Reactions to Changing Social Values," In Neil H. Jacoby (ed.): *The Business-Government Relationship: A Reassessment*. Pacific Palisades, CA, Goodyear, 1975b.

Bell, E. C.: "Practical Long-Range Planning," *Business Horizons*, November 1968.

Biggadike, Ralph: "The Risky Business of Diversification." *Harvard Business Review*, May–June 1979.

Blake, Robert R., and Jane S. Mouton: *Consultation*. Reading, MA, Addison-Wesley, 1976.

Bleichan, Gerhard D.: "The Social Equation in Corporate Responsibility." Speech made at the Boston University Law School Centennial, 1972.

Bloom, Paul N., and Philip Kotler: "Strategies For High Market-Share Companies." *Harvard Business Review*, November–December 1975.

Boettinger, Henry M.: "The Management Challenge." In Edward C. Bursk (ed.): *Challenge to Leadership*. New York, Free Press, 1973.

Boone, Louis E., and James C. Johnson: "Profiles of the 801 Men and 1 Woman at the Top." *Business Horizons*, February, 1980.

Boston Consulting Group: *Perspectives On Experience*. Boston, The Boston Consulting Group, 1972.

Bouchard, Thomas J., Gail Drauden, and Jean Barsaloux: "A Comparison of Individual, Subgroup, and Total Group Methods of Problem Solving." *Journal of Applied Psychology*, April 1974.

Boucher, Wayne I. (ed.): *The Study of the Future: An Agenda For Research.* Washington, D.C., U.S. Government Printing Office, 1977.

Boulton, William R.: "The Evolving Board: A Look at the Board's Changing Roles and Information Needs." *Academy of Management Review,* October 1978.

Bowen, Howard R.: *Social Responsibilities of the Businessman.* New York, Harper, 1953.

Bower, Joseph L.: "Business Policy in the 1980's: Content and Method." Paper presented at the Academy of Management Meetings, Detroit, August 1980.

Bower, Marvin: *The Will to Manage.* New York, McGraw-Hill, 1966.

Bowers, David G., and Stanley E. Seashore: "Predicting Organizational Effectiveness with a Four-Factor Theory of Leadership." *Administrative Science Quarterly,* September 1966.

Bowman, Edward H.: "Strategy, Annual Reports, and Alchemy." *California Management Review,* Spring, 1978.

Bracker, Jeffrey: "The Historical Development of the Strategic Management Concept." *Academy of Management Review,* April 1980.

Brewer, Garry D.: *The Policy Sciences Emerge: To Nurture and Structure a Discipline.* Santa Monica, CA, Rand Corporation, 1974.

Bright, James R.: *Practical Technology Forecasting.* Austin, TX, Industrial Management Center, 1978.

Brightman, Harvey J., and Thomas F. Urban: "The Influence of the Dogmatic Personality upon Information Processing: A Comparison with a Bayesian Information Processor." *Organizational Behavior and Human Performance,* April 1974.

Brockhaus, Robert H.: "Risk Taking Propensity of Entrepreneurs." *Academy of Management Journal,* September 1980a.

Brockhaus, Robert H.: "Psychological and Environmental Factors Which Distinguish the Successful from the Unsuccessful Entrepreneur: A Longitudinal Study." *Academy of Management Proceedings,* August 1980b.

Brockhaus, Robert H., and Walter R. Nord: "An Exploration of Factors Affecting the Entrepreneurial Decision: Personal Characteristics vs. Environmental Conditions." *Academy of Management Proceedings,* August 1979.

Brockhaus, William L.: "How to Develop a Plan for Securing Venture Capital." *Business Horizons,* June 1976.

Broom, H. N.: *Business Policy and Strategic Action: Text, Cases and Management Game.* Englewood Cliffs, NJ, Prentice-Hall, 1969.

Brown, James K.: *This Business of Issues: Coping With the Company's Environments.* New York, The Conference Board, 1979.

Brown, James K., and Rochelle O'Connor: *Planning and the Corporate Planning Director.* New York, National Industrial Conference Board, 1974.

Brown, Julius S.: "Risk Propensity in Decision Making: A Comparison of Business and Public School Administrators." *Administrative Science Quarterly,* December 1970.

Bryan, Stanley E.: "TFX—A Case in Policy Level Decision Making." *Academy of Management Journal,* March 1964.

Buchanan, Bruce: "Building Organizational Commitment: The Socialization of Managers in Work Organizations." *Administrative Science Quarterly,* December 1974.

Buchanan, Bruce: "To Walk an Extra Mile—The Whats, Whens, and Whys of Organizational Commitment." *Organizational Dynamics,* Spring 1975.

Buchholz, Rogene A.: *Business Environment/Public Policy: Corporate Executive Viewpoints and Educational Implications.* St. Louis, Center for the Study of American Business, Washington University, 1979.

Buchholz, Rogene A.: *Business Environment/Public Policy: Corporate Executive Viewpoints and Educational Implications.* St. Louis, Center for the Study of American Business, Washington University, 1980.

Buckley, Adrian: "Competitive Strategies for Investment." *Journal of General Management,* Spring 1975.

Burns, Tom, and G. M. Stalker: *The Management of Innovation.* London, Tavistock Publications, 1961.

Burton, Gene E., Dev S. Pathak, and Ron M. Zigli: "Using Group Size to Improve the Decision-Making Ability of Nominal Groups." *Academy of Management Proceedings,* 1977.

Business Roundtable: *The Role and Composition of the Board of Directors of the Large Publicly Owned Corporation.* New York, January 1978.

Business Week: "Publisher's Memo," January 9, 1978.

Business Week: "Sears Strategic About Face." January 8, 1979.

Cammillus, J. C.: "Evaluating the Benefits of Formal Planning Systems." *Long Range Planning,* June 1975.

Campbell, Hannah: *Why Did They Name It . . . ?* New York, ACE Books, 1964.

Campbell, John P., Marvin D. Dunnette, Edward E. Lawler, and Karl E. Weick: *Managerial Behavior, Performance, and Effectiveness.* New York, McGraw-Hill, 1970.

Cannon, Warren M.: "Organization Design: Shaping Structure to Strategy." *McKinsey Quarterly,* Summer 1972.

Carroll, Archie B., and George W. Beiler: "Landmarks in the Evolution of the Social Audit." *Academy of Management Journal,* September 1975.

Carroll, John B., and Scott E. Maxwell: "Individual Differences in Cognitive Abilities." *Annual Review of Psychology,* 1979.

Carroll, Stephen J., Jr., and Henry L. Tosi, Jr.: *Management by Objectives: Applications and Research.* New York, Macmillan, 1973.

Carter, E. Eugene: "The Behavioral Theory of the Firm and Top Level Corporate Decisions." *Administrative Science Quarterly,* December 1971.

Carter, Violet Bonham: *Winston Churchill: An Intimate Portrait.* New York, Harcourt, Brace, 1965.

Cartwright, John: "Corporate Planning in Local Government—Implications for the Elected Member." *Long Range Planning,* April 1975.

Cavanagh, Gerald F.: *American Business Values in Transition.* Englewood Cliffs, NJ, Prentice-Hall, 1976.

Cecil, Earl A., Larry L. Cummings, and Jerome M. Chertkoff: "Group Composition and Choice Shift: Implications for Administration." *Academy of Management Journal,* September 1973.

Cecil, Earl A., and Earl F. Lundgren: "An Analysis of Individual Decision Making Behavior Using a Laboratory Setting." *Academy of Management Journal,* September 1975.

Chamber of Commerce of the United States: *Business and the Consumer—A Program for the Seventies.* Washington, D.C., Chamber of Commerce of the United States, 1970.

Chambers, John C., Satinder K. Mullick, and Donald D. Smith: "How to Choose the Right Forecasting Technique." *Harvard Business Review,* July–August 1971.

Chandler, Alfred D.: *Strategy and Structure: Chapters in the History of the American Industrial Enterprise.* Cambridge, MA, MIT Press, 1962.

Chandler, Alfred D.: *The Visible Hand: The Managerial Revolution in American Business.* Cambridge, MA, Harvard University Press, 1977.

Chandler, Alfred D., and Herman Daems: "Administrative Coordination, Allocation, and Monitoring: Concepts and Comparisons." In Norbert Horn and Jürgen Kocka (eds.): *Law and the*

Formation of the Big Enterprises in the 19th and Early 20th Centuries. Göttingen, Vandenhoeck and Ruprecht, 1979.

Channon, Derek F.: *The Strategy and Structure of British Enterprise.* Boston, Graduate School of Business Administration, Harvard University, 1973.

Channon, Derek F.: "Strategy Formulation as an Analytical Process." *International Studies of Management & Organization,* Summer 1977.

Channon, Derek F., and Michael Jalland: *Multinational Strategic Planning.* New York, AMACOM, 1978.

Charan, Ram: "Classroom Techniques in Teaching by the Case Methods." *Academy of Management Review,* July 1976.

Charnock, John: "Can Hospitals Be Managed by Objectives?" *Journal of General Management,* Winter 1975.

Chatov, Robert: "What Corporate Ethics Statements Say." *California Management Review,* Summer 1980.

Christensen, C. Roland, Kenneth R. Andrews, and Joseph L. Bower: *Business Policy: Text and Cases.* Homewood, IL, Irwin, 1978.

Clark, John M.: *Competition as a Dynamic Process.* Washington, D.C., The Brookings Institution, 1961.

Clark, John: *Business Today: Successes and Failures.* New York, Random House, 1979.

Clark, Russell D.: "Group-induced Shift Toward Risk: A Critical Appraisal." *Psychological Bulletin,* August 1971.

Clifford, Donald K., Jr.: "Leverage in the Product Life Cycle." *Dun's Review of Modern Industry,* May 1965.

Clifford, Donald K., Jr.: *Managing the Threshold Company.* New York, McKinsey & Company, Inc., 1973a.

Clifford, Donald K., Jr.: "Growth Pains of the Threshold Company." *Harvard Business Review,* September–October 1973b.

Clifford, Donald K., Jr.: "Thriving in A Recession." *Harvard Business Review,* July–August 1977.

Cobbs, John: "Egalitarianism: Threat to a Free Market." *Business Week,* December 1, 1975.

Cohen, Kalman J., and Richard M. Cyert: "Strategy: Formulation, Implementation, and Monitoring." *Journal of Business,* July 1973.

Cohen, Michael D., and James G. March: *Leadership and Ambiguity: The American College President.* New York, McGraw-Hill, 1974.

Cohn, Theodore, and Roy A. Lindberg: *Survival and Growth: Management Strategies for the Small Firm.* New York, AMACOM, 1974.

Collins, Orvis F., and David G. Moore: *The Enterprising Man.* East Lansing, MI, Graduate School of Business Administration, Michigan State University, 1964.

Committee for Economic Development: *Social Responsibilities of Business Corporations.* New York, Committee for Economic Development, 1971.

Connolly, Terry: "Information Processing and Decision Making in Organizations." In Barry M. Staw and Gerald R. Salancik (eds.): *New Directions in Organizational Behavior.* Chicago, St. Clair, 1977.

Cook, Curtis W.: "Corporate Strategy Change Contingencies. *Academy of Management Proceedings,* August 1975.

Cook, John, and Toby Wall: "New Work Attitude Measures of Trust, Organizational Commitment, and Personal Need Non-fulfillment." *Journal of Occupational Psychology,* March 1980.

Cooper, Arnold C.: "Strategic Management: New Ventures and Small Business." In Dan E. Schendel and Charles W. Hofer (eds.): *Strategic Management: A New View of Business Policy and Planning,* Boston, Little, Brown, 1979.

Cooper, Arnold C., and Dan Schendel: "Strategic Responses to Technological Threats." *Business Horizons,* February 1976.

Corey, E. Raymond, and Steven H. Star: *Organizational Strategy: A Marketing Approach.* Boston, Graduate School of Business Administration, Harvard University, 1971.

Corson, John J., and George A. Steiner: *Measuring Business Social Performance: The Corporate Social Audit.* New York, Committee for Economic Development, 1974.

Cummings, L. L., George P. Huber, and Eugene Arendt: "Effects of Size and Spatial Arrangements on Group Decision Making." *Academy of Management Journal,* September 1974.

Cyert, Richard M., and James G. March: *A Behavioral Theory of the Firm.* Englewood Cliffs, NJ, Prentice-Hall, 1963.

Dalton, Gene W., Louis B. Barnes, and Abraham Zaleznik: *The Distribution of Authority in Formal Organizations.* Boston, Graduate School of Business Administration, Harvard University, 1968.

Davis, James H., Patrick R. Laughlin, and Samuel S. Komorita: "The Social Psychology of Small Groups: Cooperative and Mixed-Motive Interaction." *Annual Review of Psychology,* 1976.

Davis, Keith: "Can Business Afford to Ignore Social Responsibilities?" *California Management Review,* Spring 1960.

Davis, Stanley M., and Paul R. Lawrence: *Matrix.* Reading, MA, Addison-Wesley, 1977.

Davis, Stanley M., and Paul R. Lawrence: "Problems of Matrix Organizations." *Harvard Business Review,* May–June 1978.

Day, George S.: "A Strategic Perspective on Product Planning." *Journal of Contemporary Business,* Winter 1975.

Dean, Joel: "Pricing Policies for New Products." *Harvard Business Review,* November–December, 1950.

Dearden, John: "Limits on Decentralized Profit Responsibility." *Harvard Business Review,* July–August 1962.

Dearden, John: "The Case Against ROI Control." *Harvard Business Review,* May–June 1969.

DeCarlo, James F., and Paul R. Lyons: "A Comparison of Selected Personal Characteristics of Minority and Non-Minority Female Entrepreneurs." *Academy of Management Proceedings,* August 1979.

Deets, M. King, and George C. Hoyt: "Variance Preferences and Variance Shifts in Group Investment Decisions." *Organizational Behavior and Human Performance,* July 1970.

Delbecq, André L., Andrew H. Van de Ven, and David H. Gustafson: *Group Techniques for Program Planning.* Glenview, IL, Scott, Foresman, 1975.

Derthick, Martha: "Defeat at Fort Lincoln: A Case Study of a Housing Fiasco." *Public Interest,* Summer 1970.

DeWoolfson, Bruce H.: *Pitfalls in Planning-Programming-Budgeting Systems.* Ph.D. dissertation, University of California, Irvine, CA, 1974.

Dhalla, Nariman K., and Sonia Yuspeh: "Forget the Product Life Cycle Concept." *Harvard Business Review,* January–February 1976.

Dooley, Arch R., and Wickham Skinner: "Casing Casemethod Methods." *Academy of Management Review,* April 1977.

Dror, Yehezkel: *Ventures in Policy Sciences.* New York, American Elsevier Publishing, 1971.

Drucker, Peter F.: *The Practice of Management.* New York, Harper and Row, 1954.

Drucker, Peter F.: "On Managing the Public Service Institution." *The Public Interest,* Fall 1973.

Drucker, Peter F.: *Management: Tasks, Responsibilities, Practices.* New York, Harper and Row, 1974.

Dubin, Robert: "Business Behavior Behaviorally Viewed." In George B. Strother (ed.): *Social Science Approaches to Business Behavior.* Homewood, IL, Irwin, 1962.

Dunn, Dan T.: "The Rise and Fall of Ten Venture Groups." *Business Horizons,* October 1977.

Dyas, Gareth P., and Heinz T. Thanheiser: *The Emerging European Enterprise: Strategy and Structure in French and German Industry.* Boulder, CO, Westview Press, 1976.

Eaton, William J.: "Analysts Say 20 Years of Mistakes Led to Plight." *Los Angeles Times,* August 10, 1979.

Ebert, Ronald J., and Terence R. Mitchell: *Organizational Decision Processes: Concepts and Analysis.* New York, Crane, Russak, 1975.

Eccles, M. S.: *Beckoning Frontiers: Public and Personal Reminiscences.* New York, Knopf, 1951.

Editors of *Forbes:* "Management" and "Corporate Morality, Corporate Vitality." *Forbes,* September 15, 1967.

Eells, Richard: "Business for Sale: The Case for Corporate Support of the Arts." In Ivar Berg (ed.): *The Business of America.* New York, Harcourt, 1968.

Ehrbar, A. F.: "United Technologies' Master Plan." *Fortune,* September 22, 1980.

Ehrlich, Thomas, and Anne H. Ehrlich: *The End of Affluence.* New York, Random House, 1974.

Elliott-Jones, M. F.: *Economic Forecasting and Corporate Planning.* New York, The Conference Board, 1973.

Emery, F. E., and E. L. Trist: "The Causal Texture of Organizational Environments." *Human Relations,* February 1965.

Emory, C. William, and Powell Niland: *Making Management Decisions.* Boston, Houghton Mifflin, 1968.

England, George W.: *The Manager and His Values: An International Perspective from the United States, Japan, Korea, India, and Australia.* Cambridge, MA, Ballinger, 1975.

Enis, Ben M.: "GE, PIMS, BCG, AND THE PLC." *Business,* May–June 1980.

Estes, Robert M.: "The Emerging Solution to Corporate Governance." *Harvard Business Review,* November–December 1977.

Etzioni, Amitai: "Mixed Scanning: A Third Approach to Decision Making." *Public Administration Review,* December 1967.

Ewing, David W. (ed.): *Long Range Planning for Management.* New York, Harper and Row, 1972.

Farmer, Richard N., and W. Dickerson Hogue: *Corporate Social Responsibility.* Chicago, Science Research Associates, Inc., 1973.

Fast, Norman D.: *The Rise and Fall of Corporate New Venture Divisions.* Ann Arbor, MI, University Microfilms International Research Press, 1977.

Fegley, Robert L.: "New Breed of Top Executive Takes Charge." Speech delivered to the Public Relations Society of America, New Orleans, November 1979.

Fiedler, Fred E.: *A Theory of Leadership Effectiveness.* New York, McGraw-Hill, 1967.

Field, R. H. George: "A Critique of the Vroom-Yetton Contingency Model of Leadership Behavior." *Academy of Management Review,* April 1979.

Filley, A. C., and R. J. Aldag: "Organizational Growth and Types: Lessons from Small Institutions." *Research in Organizational Behavior,* 1980.

Fisher, G. H.: *Rand Policy Analysis Course: Tools and Techniques of Analysis for Public Policy Decisions.* Santa Monica, CA, Rand Corporation, 1974.

Fisk, George: "Impact of Social Sanctions on Product Strategy." *Journal of Contemporary Business,* Winter 1975.

Folsom, Marion B.: *Executive Decision Making.* New York, McGraw-Hill, 1962.

Ford, Charles H.: "MBO: An Idea Whose Time Has Gone?" *Business Horizons,* December 1979.

Forrester, Jay W.: "Advertising: A Problem in Industrial Dynamics." *Harvard Business Review,* March–April 1959.

Forrester, Jay W.: "The Structure Underlying Management Processes." *Academy of Management Proceedings,* December 1964.

Foster, D. W.: "Developing a Product Market Strategy." *Long Range Planning,* March 1970.

Fottler, Myron D.: "Environment and Management in the Public Sector: A Comparison With the Private For-Profit Sector." Paper presented at the annual meeting of the Academy of Management, Detroit, August 1980.

Fox, Harold: "A Framework for Functional Coordination." *Atlanta Economic Review,* November–December 1973.

Franko, Lawrence G.: *The European Multinationals: A Renewed Challenge to American and British Big Business.* Stamford, CT, Greylock, 1976.

Frey, G. F., *et al.: Case Narratives.* The Phillips Awards: Value Decisions in Business Management. Greenville, NY, C.W. Post Center, School of Business, Long Island University, 1980.

Friedman, Milton: *Capitalism and Freedom.* Chicago, University of Chicago Press, 1962.

Fruhan, William E., Jr.: "Pyrrhic Victories in Fights for Market Share." *Harvard Business Review,* September–October 1972.

Fry, Fred L.: "The End of Affirmative Action." *Business Horizons,* February 1980.

Fulmer, Robert M., and Leslie W. Rue: *The Practice and Profitability of Long Range Planning.* Oxford, OH, Planning Executives Institute, 1973.

Galbraith, Jay R., and Daniel A. Nathanson: *Strategy Implementation: The Role of Structure and Process.* St. Paul, MN, West, 1978.

Gale, Bradley T.: "Cross-Sectional Analysis." *Planning Review,* March 1978.

Gershefski, George W.: *The Development and Application of a Corporate Financial Model.* Oxford, OH, Planning Executives Institute, 1968.

Gerstner, Louis V.: "Can Strategic Planning Pay Off?" *Business Horizons,* December 1972.

Ghiselli, Edwin E.: "The Validity of Aptitude Tests in Personnel Selection." *Personnel Psychology,* Winter 1973.

Gilmore, Frank F., and R. G. Brandenberg: "Anatomy of Corporate Planning." *Harvard Business Review,* November–December 1962.

Gluck, Frederick W., Stephen P. Kaufman, and A. Steven Walleck: "Strategic Management for Competitive Advantage." *Harvard Business Review,* July–August 1980.

Glueck, William F.: "Business Policy: Reality and Promise." *Academy of Management Proceedings,* August 1972.

Glueck, William F.: "Decision Making: Organization Choice." *Personnel Psychology,* Spring 1974.

Glueck, William F.: *Business Policy and Strategic Management.* New York, McGraw-Hill, 1980.

Glueck, William F., and Robert Willis: "Documentary Sources and Strategic Management Research." *Academy of Management Review,* January 1979.

Gordon, Michael E., John W. Philpot, Robert E. Burt, Cynthia A. Thompson, and William E. Spiller: "Commitment to the Union: Development of a Measure and an Examination of Its Correlates." *Journal of Applied Psychology,* August 1980.

Gordon, Robert A., and James E. Howell: *Higher Education for Business.* New York, Columbia University Press, 1959.

Gram, Harold A., and Ronald L. Crawford: "Corporate Strategies for Political Action." *Long Range Planning,* October 1979.

Green, Thad B.: "An Empirical Analysis of Nominal and Interacting Groups." *Academy of Management Journal,* March 1975.

Greenwood, William T.: "A Doctoral Field in Business Strategy-Policy." *Journal of Management,* Spring 1977.

Greiner, Larry E.: "Evolution and Revolution as Organizations Grow." *Harvard Business Review,* July–August 1972.

Greiner, Larry E., D. Paul Leitch, and Louis B. Barnes: "Putting Judgment Back Into Decisions." *Harvard Business Review,* March–April 1970.

Grieco, V. A.: *Management of Small Business.* Columbus, OH, Merrill, 1975.

Grinyer, Peter H.: "Some Dangerous Axioms of Corporate Planning." *Journal of Business Policy,* No. 1, 1973.

Grinyer, Peter H., and David Norburn: "Strategic Planning in 21 U.K. Companies." *Long Range Planning,* August 1974.

Grinyer, Peter H., Masoud Yasai-Ardekani, and Shawki Al-Bazzaz: "Strategy, Structure, the Environment, and Financial Performance in 48 United Kingdom Companies." *Academy of Management Journal,* June 1980.

Gross, Bertram M.: *The Managing of Organizations.* New York, Free Press, 1964.

Guest, Robert H.: *Organizational Change: The Effect of Successful Leadership.* Homewood, IL, Irwin-Dorsey, 1962.

Gulick, Luther, and L. Urwick (eds.): *Papers on the Science of Administration.* New York, Institute of Public Administration, 1937.

Guth, William D.: "The Growth and Profitability of the Firm: A Managerial Explanation." *Journal of Business Policy,* Spring 1972.

Guth, William D.: "Corporate Growth Strategies." *Journal of Business Strategy,* Fall 1980.

Guth, William D., and Renato Tagiuri: "Personal Values and Corporate Strategies." *Harvard Business Review,* September–October 1965.

Gutman, Peter M.: "Strategies for Growth." *California Management Review,* Summer 1964.

Haire, Mason: *Psychology in Management.* New York, McGraw-Hill, 1964.

Haire, Mason, Edwin E. Ghiselli, and Lyman W. Porter: *Managerial Thinking: An International Study.* New York, Wiley, 1966.

Hall, Jay, Vincent O'Leary, and Martha Williams: "The Decision-Making Grid: A Model of Decision-Making Styles." *California Management Review,* Winter 1964.

Hall, William K.: "Forecasting Techniques for Use in the Corporate Planning Process." *Managerial Planning,* November–December 1972.

Hall, William K.: "SBU's: Hot, New Topic in the Management of Diversification." *Business Horizons,* February 1978.

Hall, William K.: "Survival Strategies in a Hostile Environment." *Harvard Business Review,* September–October 1980.

Hammermesh, R. G., M. J. Anderson, Jr., and J. E. Harris: "Strategies for Low Market Share Businesses." *Harvard Business Review,* May–June 1978.

Hardy, James M.: *Corporate Planning for Non-Profit Organizations.* New York, Association Press, 1973.

Harrigan, Kathryn R.: *Strategies for Declining Industries.* DBA Dissertation, Harvard Graduate School of Business Administration, 1979.

Harrigan, Kathryn R.: "The Effect of Exit Barriers Upon Strategic Flexibility." *Strategic Management Journal,* April–June 1980a.

Harrigan, Kathryn R.: *Strategies for Declining Businesses.* Lexington, MA, D. C. Heath, 1980b.

Harrison, E. Frank: *The Managerial Decision-Making Process.* Boston, Houghton Mifflin, 1975, 1981.

Harrison, Roger: "Understanding Your Organization's Character." *Harvard Business Review,* May 1972.

Hatten, Kenneth J., Dan E. Schendel, and Arnold C. Cooper: "A Strategic Model of the U.S. Brewing Industry: 1952–1971." *Academy of Management Journal,* December 1978.

Hawkins, Kevin, and Robert J. Tar: "Corporate Planning in Local Government—A Case Study." *Long Range Planning,* April 1980.

Hayek, Friedrich A.: *The Road to Serfdom.* Chicago, University of Chicago Press, 1944.

Hedley, Barry: "Strategy and the 'Business Portfolio.'" *Long Range Planning,* February 1977.

Heidrick and Struggles, Inc.: *Profile of a President.* Boston, Heidrick and Struggles, Inc., 1972.

Heller, Frank A.: *Managerial Decision-Making: A Study of Leadership Styles and Power Sharing Among Senior Managers.* London, Tavistock Publications, 1971.

Henderson, Bruce D.: "The Experience Curve . . ." Boston Consulting Group, 1975.

Henderson, Bruce D.: *Henderson On Corporate Strategy.* Cambridge, MA, Abt Books, 1979.

Henderson, Bruce D.: "The Experience Curve Revisited." Boston, Boston Consulting Group, undated.

Herold, David M.: "Long Range Planning and Organizational Performance: A Cross Valuation Study." *Academy of Managerial Journal,* March 1972.

Hertz, David B.: *New Power for Management.* New York, McGraw-Hill, 1969.

Heyne, Paul T.: *Private Keepers of the Public Interest.* New York, McGraw-Hill, 1968.

Heyne, Paul T.: "The Free-Market System is the Best Guide for Corporate Decisions." *Financial Analysts Journal,* September–October 1971.

Hidy, Ralph W., and Paul E. Cawein (eds.): *Individual Enterprise and National Growth,* Boston, D. C. Heath, 1967.

Higdon, Hal: *The Business Healers.* New York, Random House, 1969.

Hill, Richard M., and James D. Hlavacek: "Learning from Failure: Ten Guides for Venture Management." *California Management Review,* Summer 1977.

Hines, George H.: "Achievement Motivation, Occupations, and Labor Turnover in New Zealand." *Journal of Applied Psychology,* December 1973.

Hitch, Charles J.: *Decision-Making for Defense.* Berkeley and Los Angeles, University of California Press, 1966.

Hlavacek, James D., Brian H. Dovey, and John J. Biondo: "Tie Small Business Technology to Marketing Power." *Harvard Business Review,* January–February 1977.

Hlavacek, James D., and Victor A. Thompson: "Bureaucracy and New Product Innovation." *Academy of Management Journal,* September 1973.

Hlavacek, James D., and Victor A. Thompson: "Bureaucracy and Venture Failures." *Academy of Management Review,* April 1978.

Hofer, Charles W.: "Some Preliminary Research on Patterns of Strategic Behavior." *Academy of Management Proceedings,* August 1973.

Hofer, Charles W.: "Toward a Contingency Theory of Business Strategy." *Academy of Management Journal,* December 1975.

Hofer, Charles W.: "Research on Strategic Planning." *Journal of Economics and Business,* Spring–Summer 1976.

Hofer, Charles W.: "Conceptual Constructs for Formulating Corporate and Business Strategy." Boston, Intercollegiate Case Clearing House, #9-378-754, 1977.

Hofer, Charles W.: "Turnaround Strategies." *Journal of Business Strategy,* Summer 1980.

Hofer, Charles W., and Dan Schendel: *Strategy Formulation: Analytical Concepts.* St. Paul, MN, West, 1978.

Holden, Paul E., Carlton A. Pederson, and Gayton E. Germane: *Top Management.* New York, McGraw-Hill, 1968.

Hornaday, John A., and John Aboud: "Characteristics of Successful Enterpreneurs." *Personnel Psychology,* Summer 1971.

Hornaday, John A., and Charles S. Bunker: "The Nature of the Entrepreneur." *Personnel Psychology,* Spring 1970.

Hosmer, La Rue T., Arnold C. Cooper, and Karl H. Vesper: *The Entrepreneurial Function.* Englewood Cliffs, NJ, Prentice-Hall, 1977.

House, Robert J., and John B. Miner: "Merging Management and Behavioral Theory: The Interaction Between Span of Control and Group Size." *Administrative-Science Quarterly,* September 1969.

Howell, Robert A.: "Managing by Objectives—A Three Stage System." *Business Horizons,* February 1970.

Hrebiniak, Lawrence G.: "Effects of Job Level and Participation on Employee Attitudes and Perceptions of Influence." *Academy of Management Journal,* December 1974.

Huber, George P.: *Managerial Decision Making.* Glenview, IL, Scott, Foresman, 1980.

Humble, John W.: "Corporate Planning and Management by Objectives." *Long Range Planning,* June 1969.

Humphrey, George M., with James C. Derieux: "It Looked Easier on the Outside." *Collier's,* April 2, 1954.

Hundal, P. S.: "A Study of Entrepreneurial Motivation: Comparison of Fast- and Slow-Progressing Small-Scale Industrial Entrepreneurs in Punjab, India." *Journal of Applied Psychology.* August 1971.

Hunsicker, J. Quincy: "The Malaise of Strategic Planning." *Management Review,* March 1980.

Hunt, Alfred: *The Management Consultant.* New York, Ronald, 1977.

Hurwood, David L., Elliott S. Grossman, and Earl L. Bailey: *Sales Forecasting.* New York, The Conference Board, 1978.

Hussey, David E.: "Corporate Planning for a Church," *Long Range Planning,* April 1974a.

Hussey, David E.: *Corporate Planning: Theory and Practice.* New York, Pergamon Press, 1974b.

Hussey, David E.: "Portfolio Analysis: Practical Experience With the Directional Policy Matrix." *Long Range Planning,* August 1978.

Hutchins, Robert: "A Center Conversation, 'Get Ready for Anything.' " *Center Report,* June 1975.

Jacoby, Neil H.: *Corporate Power and Social Responsibility: A Blueprint for the Future.* New York, Macmillan, 1973.

Jago, Arthur G., and Victor H. Vroom: "An Evaluation of Two Alternatives to the Vroom/Yetton Normative Model." *Academy of Management Journal,* June 1980.

James, Barrie G.: "The Theory of the Corporate Life Cycle." *Long Range Planning,* June 1973.

Janis, Irving L.: *Victims of Groupthink.* Boston, Houghton Mifflin, 1972.

Janis, Irving L., and Leon Mann: *Decision Making: A Psychological Analysis of Conflict, Choice, and Commitment.* New York, Free Press, 1977.

Jauch, Lawrence R., Richard N. Osborn, and Thomas N. Martin: "Structured Content Analysis of Cases: A Complementary Method for Organizational Research." *Academy of Management Review,* October 1980.

Jerome, William Travers, III: *Executive Control: The Catalyst.* New York, Wiley, 1961.

Johnson, Thomas E., and David J. Werner: "Management Education: An Interdisciplinary Problem Solving Approach." *Academy of Management Journal,* June 1975.

Johnston, Russ: "Review of *Organizations and Their Members: A Contingency Approach.*" *Administrative Science Quarterly,* March 1975.

Jones, Charles O.: *An Introduction to the Study of Public Policy.* Belmont, CA, Wadsworth, 1970.

Karger, Delmar, and F. A. Malik: "Long Range Planning and Organizational Performance." *Long Range Planning,* December 1975.

Karmel, Barbara: "Group Decision-Making: Effects of Attitude, Sample and Leader Variables." *Academy of Management Proceedings,* August 1972.

Kast, Fremont E., and James E. Rosenzweig: *Contingency Views of Organization and Management.* Chicago, Science Research Associates, 1973.

Kastens, Merritt L.: "Who Does the Planning?" *Managerial Planning,* January–February 1972.

Katz, Daniel, and Robert L. Kahn: *The Social Psychology of Organizations.* New York, Wiley, 1978.

Kelley, Lane, and Clayton Reeser: "The Persistance of Culture as a Determinant of Differentiated Attitudes on the Part of American Managers of Japanese Ancestry." *Academy of Management Journal,* March 1973.

Kerr, Steven: "On the Folly of Rewarding A, While Hoping for B." *Academy of Management Journal,* December 1975.

Khandwalla, Pradip: "Effect of Competition on the Structure of Top Management Control." *Academy of Management Journal,* June 1973.

Kilman, Ralph H.: *Social Systems Design: Normative Theory and the MAPS Design Technology.* New York, North-Holland, 1977.

Kinnunen, Raymond M.: "Hypotheses Related to Strategy Formulation in Large Divisionalized Companies." *Academy of Management Review,* October 1976.

Kipnis, David, Arnold Silverman, and Charles Copeland: "Effects of Emotional Arousal on the Use of Supervised Coercion with Black and Union Employees." *Journal of Applied Psychology,* February 1973.

Kirchoff, Bruce A.: "Empirical Assessment of the Strategy/Tactics Dilemma." *Academy of Management Proceedings,* August 1980.

Klein, Harold, and William Newman: "How to Use SPIRE: A Systematic Procedure for Identifying Relevant Environments For Strategic Planning." *Journal of Business Strategy,* Summer 1980.

Klimoski, Richard J., and Barbara L. Karol: "The Impact of Trust on Creative Problem Solving Groups." *Journal of Applied Psychology,* October 1976.

Knight, Kenneth: *Matrix Management: A Crossfunctional Approach to Organization.* Westmead, England, Gower Press, 1977.

Kono, Toyohiro: "An Analysis of Corporate Growth in Japan." *Management Japan,* No. 4, 1970.

Koontz, Harold, and Robert W. Bradspies: "Managing Through Feedforward Control: A Future-Directed View." *Business Horizons,* June 1972.

Kotler, Philip: "Harvesting Strategies For Weak Products." *Business Horizons,* August 1978.

Kraut, Allen I.: "The Entrance of Black Employees Into Traditionally White Jobs." *Academy of Management Journal,* September 1975.

Kubr, M.: *Management Consulting: A Guide to the Profession.* Geneva, Switzerland, International Labour Office, 1976.

Kudla, Ronald J.: "The Effects of Strategic Planning on Common Stock Returns." *Academy of Management Journal,* March 1980.

Lang, James R., John E. Dittrich, and Sam E. White: "Managerial Problem Solving Models: A Review and Proposal." *Academy of Management Review,* October 1978.

Lawler, Edward E., and John G. Rhode: *Information and Control in Organizations.* Pacific Palisades, CA, Goodyear, 1976.

Lawrence, Paul R., and Jay W. Lorsch: *Organization and Environment: Managing Differentiation and Integration.* Boston, Graduate School of Business, Harvard University, 1967.

Lear Siegler, Inc.: *Corporate Planning Guide 1980.* Santa Monica, CA, Lear Siegler, Inc., 1979.

Leavitt, Harold J.: "It's a Valuable Management Tool, But . . . Motivation is Not Enough." *Stanford Graduate School of Business Bulletin,* Autumn 1966.

LeBell, Don, and O. J. Krasner: "Selecting Environmental Forecasting Techniques from Business Planning Requirements." *Academy of Management Review,* July 1977.

Lee, James A.: "Leader Power for Managing Change." *Academy of Management Review,* January 1977.

Lenz, R. T.: "Strategic Capability: A Concept and Framework for Analysis." *Academy of Management Review,* April 1980.

Leontiades, Milton: "Unrelated Diversification: Theory and Practice." *Business Horizons,* October 1979.

Leontiades, Milton: *Strategies for Diversification and Change.* Boston, Little, Brown, 1980.

Leontiades, Milton, and A. Tezel: "Planning Perceptions and Planning Results." *Strategic Management Journal,* January–March 1980.

Levitt, Theodore: "Exploit the Product Life Cycle." *Harvard Business Review,* November–December 1965.

Levitt, Theodore: "The Dangers of Social Responsibility." *Harvard Business Review,* September–October 1968.

Life Office Management Association: "Creating a Corporate Plan for a Life Insurance Company: A Case Study." *Financial Planning and Control Report No. 17.* New York, Life Office Management Association, 1970.

Likert, Rensis: *New Patterns of Management.* New York, McGraw-Hill, 1961.

Likert, Rensis, and Jane G. Likert: *New Ways of Managing Conflict.* New York, McGraw-Hill, 1976.

Lindblom, Charles E.: *Bargaining: The Hidden Hand in Government.* Santa Monica, CA, Rand Corporation, 1955.

Lindblom, Charles E.: "The Science of 'Muddling Through.' " *Public Administration Review,* Spring 1959.

Lindblom, Charles E.: *The Intelligence of Democracy: Decision Making Through Mutual Adjustment.* New York, Free Press, 1965.

Linneman, Robert E.: *Shirt-Sleeve Approach to Long-Range Planning.* Englewood Cliffs, NJ, Prentice-Hall, 1980.

Lippitt, Gordon, and Ronald Lippitt: *The Consulting Process in Action.* La Jolla, CA, University Associates, 1978.

Lipset, Seymour Martin, and William Schneider: "How's Business? What the Public Thinks." *Public Opinion,* July/August 1978.

Litschert, Robert J., and T. W. Bonham: "A Conceptual Model of Strategy Formation." *Academy of Management Review,* April 1978.

Livingston, J. Sterling: "Myth of the Well-Educated Manager." *Harvard Business Review,* January–February 1971.

Locke, Edwin A., and David M. Schweiger: "Participation in Decision-Making: One More Look." *Research in Organizaitonal Behavior,* 1979.

Lodge, George Cabot: "Business and the Changing Society." *Harvard Business Review,* March–April 1974.

Lodge, George Cabot: *The New American Ideology.* New York, Alfred A. Knopf, 1975.

Lorange, Peter: *Corporate Planning: An Executive Viewpoint.* Englewood Cliffs, NJ, Prentice-Hall, 1980.

Lorange, Peter, and Richard F. Vancil: *Strategic Planning Systems.* Englewood Cliffs, NJ, Prentice-Hall, 1977.

Lorsch, Jay W., and Stephen A. Allen, III: *Managing Diversity and Interdependence: An Organizational Study of Multidivisional Firms.* Boston, Graduate School of Business Administration, Harvard University, 1973.

Lorsch, Jay W., and John J. Morse: *Organizations and Their Members: A Contingency Approach.* New York, Harper and Row, 1974.

Luck, David J., and O. C. Ferrell: *Marketing Strategy and Plans.* Englewood Cliffs, NJ, Prentice-Hall, 1979.

Luck, David J., and Arthur E. Prell: *Market Strategy.* New York, Appleton-Century-Crofts, 1968.

Lundberg, Olof, and Max D. Richards: "A Relationship Between Cognitive Style and Complex Decision Making: Implications for Business Policy." *Academy of Management Proceedings,* August 1972.

Lundstedt, Sven: "A Note on Asking Questions." *Journal of General Psychology,* 1968.

Lusk, Edward J., and Bruce L. Oliver: "American Managers' Personal Value Systems—Revisited." *Academy of Management Journal,* September 1974.

McAdam, Terry: "How to Put Corporate Responsibility Into Practice." *Business and Society Review/Innovation,* Summer 1973.

McAllister, Daniel W., Terence R. Mitchell, and Lee Roy Beach: "The Contingency Model for the Selection of Decision Strategies: An Empirical Test of the Effects of Significance, Accountability, and Reversibility." *Organizational Behavior and Human Performance,* October 1979.

McCarthy, E. Jerome: *Basic Marketing: A Managerial Approach,* rev. ed. Homewood, IL, Richard D. Irwin, Inc., 1964.

McCaskey, Michael B.: "The Management of Ambiguity." *Organizational Dynamics,* Spring 1979.

McClelland, David C., and David G. Winter: *Motivating Economic Achievement.* New York, Free Press, 1969.

McConkey, Dale D.: "MBO—Twenty Years Later, Where Do We Stand?" *Business Horizons,* August 1973.

McConkey, Dale D.: *MBO For Nonprofit Organizations.* New York, AMACOM, 1975.

McDonald, Alonzo: "Conflict at the Summit: A Deadly Game." *Harvard Business Review,* March 1972.

McFarland, Dalton E.: *Management: Principles and Practices.* New York, Macmillan, 1967.

McGrath, Phyllis S.: *Corporate Directorship Practices: The Public Policy Committee.* New York, The Conference Board, 1980.

McGregor, Douglas: *The Human Side of Enterprise.* New York, McGraw-Hill, 1960.

McKay, Charles W., and Guy D. Cutting: "A Model for Long Range Planning in Higher Education." *Long Range Planning,* October 1974.

McKenney, James L., and Peter G. W. Keen: "How Managers' Minds Work." *Harvard Business Review,* May–June 1974.

MacMillan, Ian C.: *Strategy Formulation: Political Concepts.* St. Paul, MN, West, 1978.

McNair, Malcolm P.: *The Case Method at the Harvard Business School.* New York, McGraw-Hill, 1954.

Macchiaverna, Paul.: *Internal Auditing.* New York, The Conference Board, 1978.

Mahoney, Thomas A., Thomas H. Jerdee, and Stephen J. Carroll: *Development of Managerial Performance . . . A Research Approach.* Cincinnati, OH, South-Western, 1963.

Mahoney, Thomas A., Thomas H. Jerdee, and Stephen J. Carroll. "The Job(s) of Management." *Industrial Relations,* February 1965.

Maier, Norman R. F.: *Problem Solving and Creativity in Individuals and Groups.* Belmont, CA, Brooks/Cole, 1970.

Mann, Roland (ed.): *The Arts of Top Management.* New York, McGraw-Hill, 1971.

Manne, Henry G.: "Shareholder Social Proposals Viewed by an Opponent." *Stanford Law Review,* February 1972.

March, James G., and Johan P. Olsen: *Ambiguity and Choice in Organizations.* Bergen, Norway, Universitetsforlaget, 1976.

March, James G., and Herbert A. Simon: *Organizations.* New York, Wiley, 1958.

Marino, Kenneth E.: "A Preliminary Investigation into the Behavioral Dimensions of Affirmative Action Compliance." *Journal of Applied Psychology,* June 1980.

Marrow, Alfred J., and John R. P. French: "Changing a Stereotype in Industry." *Journal of Social Issues,* May 1945.

Mason, Edward S.: "The Apologetics of 'Managerialism.'" *Journal of Business,* January 1958.

Mason, Richard O., and Ian I. Mitroff: "Assumptions of Majestic Metals: Strategy through Dialectics." *California Management Review,* Winter 1979.

Meadows, Dennis, *et al.: The Limits to Growth.* New York, Universe Books, 1972.

Michael, Donald N.: *On Learning to Plan—and Planning to Learn.* San Francisco, Jossey-Bass, 1973.

Michael, George.: "Product Petrification: A New Stage in the Life Cycle." *California Management Review,* Fall 1971.

Mihalasky, John: "Questions: What Do Some Executives Have More Of? Answer: Intuition. Maybe." *Think,* November–December 1969.

Miles, Raymond E., and Charles C. Snow: *Organizational Strategy, Structure, and Process.* New York, McGraw-Hill, 1978.

Miller, Arjay: "New Roles for the Campus and the Corporation." *Michigan Business Review,* November 1966.

Miller, Danny: "Common Syndromes of Business Failure." *Business Horizons,* December 1977.

Miller, Danny, and Peter H. Friesen: "Archetypes of Strategy Formulation." *Management Science,* May 1978.

Miner, Frederick C.: "A Comparative Analysis of Three Diverse Group Decision Making Approaches." *Academy of Management Journal,* March 1979.

Miner, John B.: *Studies in Management Education.* Atlanta, Organizational Measurement Systems Press, 1965.

Miner, John B.: *The School Administrator and Organizational Character.* Eugene, OR, University of Oregon Press, 1967.

Miner, John B.: "Bridging the Gulf in Organizational Performance." *Harvard Business Review,* July 1968.

Miner, John B.: *Management Theory.* New York, Macmillan, 1971.

Miner, John B.: *Intelligence in the United States.* Westport, CT, Greenwood, 1973.

Miner, John B.: *The Human Constraint: The Coming Shortage of Managerial Talent.* Washington, D.C., BNA Books, 1974.

Miner, John B.: *The Challenge of Managing.* Philadelphia, Saunders, 1975.

Miner, John B.: *Motivation to Manage: A Ten-Year Update on the "Studies in Management Education" Research.* Atlanta, Organizational Measurement Systems Press, 1977.

Miner, John B.: *The Management Process: Theory, Research, and Practice.* New York: Macmillan, 1978.

Miner, John B.: "The Role of Organizational Structure and Process in Strategy Implementation: Commentary." In Dan E. Schendel and Charles W. Hofer (eds.): *Strategic Management: A New View of Business Policy and Planning.* Boston, Little, Brown, 1979.

Miner, John B.: *Theories of Organizational Behavior.* Hinsdale, IL, Dryden, 1980a.

Miner, John B.: "The Role of Managerial and Professional Motivation in the Career Success of Management Professors." *Academy of Management Journal,* September 1980b.

Miner, John B.: "Limited Domain Theories of Organizational Energy" and "A Rationale for the Limited Domain Approach to the Study of Motivation." In Craig C. Pinder and Larry F. Moore (eds.): *Middle Range Theory and the Study of Organizations.* Boston, Martinus Nijhoff, 1980c.

Miner, John B.: *Theories of Organizational Structure and Process.* Hinsdale, IL, Dryden, 1982.

Miner, Mary G., and John B. Miner: *Employee Selection Within the Law.* Washington, D.C., BNA Books, 1978.

Mintzberg, Henry: *The Nature of Managerial Work.* New York, Harper and Row, 1973.

Mintzberg, Henry: "The Manager's Job: Folklore and Fact." *Harvard Business Review,* July–August 1975.

Mintzberg, Henry: "Planning on the Left Side and Managing on the Right." *Harvard Business Review,* July–August 1976.

Mintzberg, Henry: "Policy As a Field of Management Theory." *Academy of Management Review,* January 1977.

Mintzberg, Henry: *The Structuring of Organizations: A Synthesis of the Research.* Englewood Cliffs, NJ, Prentice-Hall, 1979.

Mintzberg, Henry, Duru Raisinghani, and André Théorêt: "The Structure of 'Unstructured' Decision Processes." *Administrative Science Quarterly,* June 1976.

Miron, David, and David C. McClelland: "The Impact of Achievement Motivation Training on Small Businesses." *California Management Review,* Summer 1979.

Mishan, Ezra J.: "On Making the Future Safe for Mankind." *The Public Interest,* Summer 1971.

Mitroff, Ian I., and James R. Emshoff: "On Strategic Assumption-Making: A Dialectical Approach to Policy and Planning." *Academy of Management Review,* January 1979.

Moberg, Dennis J., and James L. Koch: "A Critical Appraisal of Integrated Treatments of Contingency Findings." *Academy of Management Journal,* March 1975.

Mohrman, Susan Albers: "A New Look at Participation in Decision Making: The Concept of Political Access." *Academy of Management Proceedings,* 1979.

Monieson, D. D.: "An Overview of Marketing Planning." *Executive Bulletin,* The Conference Board in Canada, 1978.

Moose, Sandra O., and Alan J. Zakon: "Divestment—Cleaning Up Your Corporate Portfolio." *European Business,* Autumn 1971.

Moose, Sandra O., and Alan J. Zakon: "Frontier Curve Analysis: As a Resource Allocation Guide." *Journal of Business Policy,* Spring 1972.

Morris, James H., and Richard M. Steers: "Structural Influences on Organizational Commitment." *Journal of Vocational Behavior,* August 1980.

Morse, John J., and Francis R. Wagner: "Measuring the Process of Managerial Effectiveness." *Academy of Management Journal,* March 1978.

Moskowitz, Herbert: "Managers as Partners in Business Decision Research." *Academy of Management Journal,* September 1971.

Mulder, Mauk: "Power Equalization through Participation?" *Administrative Science Quarterly,* March 1971.

Mulder, Mauk, and Henk Wilke: "Participation and Power Equalization." *Organizational Behavior and Human Performance,* September 1970.

Muldrow, Tressie W., and James A. Bayton: "Men and Women Executives and Processes Related to Decision Accuracy." *Journal of Applied Psychology,* April 1979.

Murray, Edwin A.: "The Social Response Process in Commercial Banks: An Empirical Investigation." *Academy of Management Review,* July 1976.

Murray, Edwin A.: "Strategic Choice as a Negotiated Outcome," *Management Science,* May 1978.

Nanus, Burt: "QUEST—Quick Environmental Scanning Technique." Center for Futures Research, University of Southern California, 1979.

Nanus, Burt: *Eighth Annual Report, Center For Futures Research.* Los Angeles, CA, Graduate School of Business Administration, University of Southern California, 1980.

Naylor, Thomas H.: "PIMS: Through A Different Looking Glass." *Planning Review,* March 1978.

Naylor, Thomas H.: *Corporate Planning Models.* Reading, MA, Addison-Wesley, 1979.

Neal, Alfred C.: "Immolation of Business Capital." *Harvard Business Review,* March–April 1978.

Neuschel, Robert P.: "Presidential Style: Updated Versions." *Business Horizons,* June 1969.

Newgren, Kenneth E., and Archie B. Carroll: "Social Forecasting in U.S. Corporations—A Survey." *Long Range Planning,* August 1979.

Newman, William H.: "Shaping the Master Strategy of Your Firm." *California Management Review,* Spring 1967.

Newman, William H.: "Strategy and Management Structure." *Academy of Management Proceedings,* August 1971.

Newman, William H.: *Constructive Control: Design and Use of Control Systems.* Englewood Cliffs, NJ, Prentice-Hall, 1975.

Newman, William H., and Harvey W. Wallender, III: "Managing Not-for-Profit Enterprises." *Academy of Management Review,* January 1978.

Norman, Richard A.: "Business Decision Making: A Phenomenological Approach." *California Management Review,* Winter 1967.

Novick, David (ed.): *Current Practice in Program Budgeting: Analysis and Case Studies Covering Government and Business.* New York, Crane, Russak, 1973.

O'Connell, Jeremiah J.: *Managing Organizational Innovation.* Homewood, IL, Irwin, 1968.

O'Connell, Jeremiah J., and John W. Zimmerman: "Scanning the International Environment." *California Management Review,* Winter 1979.

O'Connor, Rochelle: *Corporate Guides To Long-Range Planning.* New York, The Conference Board, 1976.

Odiorne, George S.: "MBO: A Backward Glance." *Business Horizons,* October 1978.

Odiorne, George S.: *MBO II: A System of Managerial Leadership for the 80s.* Belmont, CA, Fearon Pitman, 1979.

Organ, Dennis W.: "Linking Pins Between Organizations and Environment." *Business Horizons,* December 1971.

Paine, Frank T., and Carl R. Anderson: "Contingencies Affecting Strategy Formulation and Effectiveness: An Empirical Study." *Journal of Management Studies,* May 1977.

Paine, Frank T., and William Naumes: *Organizational Strategy and Policy.* Philadelphia, Saunders, 1978.

Palesy, Steven R.: "Motivating Line Management Using the Planning Process." *Planning Review,* March 1980.

Palmer, Michael: "The Application of Psychological Testing to Entrepreneurial Potential." *California Management Review,* Spring 1971.

Pandey, Janek, and N. B. Tewary: "Locus of Control and Achievement Values of Entrepreneurs." *Journal of Occupational Psychology,* June 1979.

Parker, Treadway C.: *The Formation and Management of New Business Ventures.* New York, The Presidents Association of the American Management Association, 1973.

Patchen, Martin: "The Locus and Basis of Influence on Organizational Decisions." *Organizational Behavior and Human Performance,* April 1974.

Patton, Arch: "Top Management's Stake in the Product Life Cycle." *Management Review,* June 1959.

Patz, Alan L.: "Notes: Business Policy and the Scientific Method." *California Management Review,* Spring 1975.

Pavan, Robert J.: "Strategy and Structure: The Italian Experience." *Journal of Economics and Business,* Spring–Summer, 1976.

Pelz, Donald C., and Frank M. Andrews: *Scientists in Organizations: Productive Climates for Research and Development.* New York, Wiley, 1966.

Pennington, Malcolm W.: "Why Has Planning Failed?" *Long Range Planning,* March 1972.

Perrow, Charles: "A Framework for the Comparative Analysis of Organizations." *American Sociological Review,* April 1967.

Peters, Joseph P.: *Concept Commitment Action.* New York, United Hospital Fund of New York and the Health and Hospital Planning Council of Southern New York, Inc., 1974.

Peterson, Richard B.: "A Cross-Cultural Perspective of Supervisory Values." *Academy of Management Journal,* March 1972.

Pfeffer, Jeffrey: *Organizational Design.* Arlington Heights, IL, AHM Publishing, 1978.

Pfeffer, Jeffrey, and Phillip Nowak: "Joint Ventures and Interorganizational Interdependence." *Administrative Science Quarterly,* September 1976.

Pfeffer, Jeffrey, and Gerald R. Salancik: *The External Control of Organizations: A Resource Dependence Perspective.* New York, Harper and Row, 1978.

Pierson, Frank C., *et al.: The Education of American Businessmen.* New York, McGraw-Hill, 1959.

Pinches, George E., Arthur A. Eubank, and Kent A. Mingo: "The Hierarchical Classification of Financial Ratios," *Journal of Business Research,* October 1975.

Pinder, Craig C., and Larry F. Moore: *Middle Range Theory and the Study of Organizations.* Boston, Martinus Nijhoff, 1980.

Pitts, Robert A.: "Strategies and Structures For Diversification." *Academy of Management Journal,* June 1977.

Polli, Rolando, and Victor Cook: "Validity of the Product Life Cycle." *Journal of Business.* October 1969.

Popp, Gary E., and Herbert G. Hicks: "Teaching Business Policy and Entrepreneurship: An Experiential Approach Revisited." *Academy of Management Proceedings,* August 1973.

Porter, Lyman W., William J. Crampon, and Frank J. Smith: "Organizational Commitment and Managerial Turnover: A Longitudinal Study." *Organizational Behavior and Human Performance,* February 1976.

Porter, Michael E.: *Competitive Strategy: Techniques For Analyzing Industries and Competitors.* New York, The Free Press, 1980.

Preble, John F.: "Corporate Use of Environmental Scanning." *Michigan Business Review,* September 1978.

President's Commission on National Goals: *Report of the President's Commission on National Goals.* Washington, D.C., U.S. Government Printing Office, 1960.

Preston, Lee E. (ed.): *Research in Corporate Social Performance and Policy.* Volume 1. Greenwich, CT, JAI Press, 1978.

Preston, Lee E. (ed.): *Business Environment/Public Policy,* 1979 Conference Papers. St. Louis, MO, American Assembly of Collegiate Schools of Business, 1980.

Price, James L.: *Organizational Effectiveness: An Inventory of Propositions.* Homewood, IL, Irwin, 1968.

Purcell, Theodore V.: "How GE Measures Managers in Fair Employment." *Harvard Business Review,* November 1974.

Quinn, James Brian: "Strategic Goals: Process and Politics." *Sloan Management Review,* Fall 1977.

Quinn, James Brian: "Technological Innovation, Entreneurship, and Strategy." *Sloan Management Review,* Spring 1979.

Quinn, James Brian: *Strategies for Change: Logical Incrementalism.* Homewood, IL, Irwin, 1980.

Radford, K. J.: *Strategic Planning: An Analytical Approach.* Reston, VA, Reston, 1980.

Rapoport, Leo A., and William P. Drews: "Mathematical Approach to Long-Range Planning." *Harvard Business Review,* May–June 1962.

Rawls, James R., Robert A. Ullrich, and Oscar Tivis Nelson, Jr.: "A Comparison of Managers Entering or Reentering the Profit and Nonprofit Sectors." *Academy of Management Journal,* September 1975.

Reimann, Bernard C.: "The Public Philosophy of Organizations." *Academy of Management Journal,* September 1974.

Rhenman, Eric: *Organization Theory for Long Range Planning.* New York, Wiley, 1973.

Richards, Max D.: "An Exploratory Study of Strategic Failure." *Academy of Management Proceedings,* August 1973.

Richards, Max D.: *Organizational Goal Structures.* St. Paul, MN, West, 1978.

Richman, Barry M.: "The Corporation and the Quality of Life: Part I: Typologies." *Management International,* 1973.

Ringbakk, K. A.: "Why Planning Fails." *European Business,* Spring 1971.

Ringbakk, K. A.: "The Corporate Planning Life Cycle—An International Point of View." *Long Range Planning,* September 1972.

Roberts, John C., and Carl H. Castore: "The Effects of Conformity, Information, and Confidence Upon Subjects' Willingness to Take Risk Following a Group Discussion." *Organizational Behavior and Human Performance,* December 1972.

Robinson, Richard: *An Empirical Investigation of the Impact of SBDC-Strategic Planning Consultation Upon the Short-Term Effectiveness of Small Business in Georgia.* Unpublished doctoral dissertation, University of Georgia, 1980.

Robinson, Richard, and William F. Glueck: "The Role of 'Outsiders' In Small Firm Strategic Planning: An Empirical Study." Unpublished paper, University of Georgia, 1980.

Rockefeller, John D., III: *The Second American Revolution.* New York, Harper and Row, 1973.

Rohrbaugh, John: "Improving the Quality of Group Judgment: Social Judgment Analysis and the Delphi Technique." *Organizational Behavior and Human Performance,* August 1979.

Rokeach, Milton: *The Nature of Human Values.* New York, Free Press, 1973.

Rosen, Benson, and Thomas H. Jerdee: "Influence of Subordinate Characteristics on Trust and

Use of Participative Decision Strategies in a Management Simulation." *Journal of Applied Psychology,* October 1977.

Rosen, Benson, and Thomas H. Jerdee: "Coping with Affirmative Action Backlash." *Business Horizons,* August 1979.

Ross, Joel E., and Michael J. Kami: *Corporate Management in Crisis: Why the Mighty Fall.* Englewood Cliffs, NJ, Prentice-Hall, 1973.

Rothschild, William E.: *Putting It All Together: A Guide to Strategic Thinking.* New York, AMACOM, 1976.

Rothschild, William E.: *Strategic Alternatives: Selection, Development and Implementation.* New York, AMACOM, 1979.

Rourke, Francis E.: *Bureaucracy, Politics and Public Policy.* Boston, Little, Brown, 1968.

Rubin, Jeffrey Z., and Bert R. Brown: *The Social Psychology of Bargaining and Negotiation.* New York, Academic Press, 1975.

Rue, Leslie W., and Robert M. Fulmer: "Is Long Range Planning Profitable?" *Academy of Management Proceedings,* August 1973.

Rumelt, Richard P.: *Strategy, Structure, and Economic Performance.* Boston, Graduate School of Business Administration, Harvard University, 1974.

Said, Kamal, and Robert E. Seiler: *Implementation of Long-Range Plans Through Current Operating Budgets.* Oxford, OH, Planning Executives Institute, 1978.

Salancik, Gerald R.: "Commitment and the Control of Organizational Behavior and Belief." In Barry M. Staw and Gerald R. Salancik (eds.): *New Directions in Organizational Behavior.* Chicago, St. Clair, 1977.

Salveson, Melvin E.: "The Management of Strategy." *Long Range Planning,* February 1974.

Saunders, C. B., and J. C. Thompson: "A Survey of the Current State of Business Policy Research." *Strategic Management Journal,* April–June 1980.

Sawyer, George C.: *Business and Society: Managing Corporate Social Impact.* Boston, Houghton Mifflin, 1979.

Sayles, Leonard R.: *Managerial Behavior.* New York, McGraw-Hill, 1964.

Schaeffer, Ruth Gilbert, and Edith F. Lynton: *Corporate Experiences in Improving Women's Job Opportunities.* New York, The Conference Board, 1979.

Schattschneider, E. E.: *Two Hundred Million Americans in Search of Government.* New York, Holt, Rinehart, and Winston, 1979.

Schendel, Dan E.: "Needs and Developments in Policy Curricula at the Ph.D. Level." Unpublished paper, Krannert Graduate School of Industrial Administration, Purdue University, 1975.

Schendel, Dan E., and Kenneth J. Hatten: "Business Policy or Strategic Management: A Broader View for an Emerging Discipline." *Academy of Management Proceedings,* August 1972.

Schendel, Dan E., and Charles W. Hofer: *Strategic Management: A New View of Business Policy and Planning.* Boston, Little, Brown, 1979.

Schendel, Dan E., G. R. Patton, and James Riggs: "Corporate Turnaround Strategies: A Study of Profit Decline and Recovery." *Journal of General Management,* July 1976.

Schmidt, Richard: "The Board of Directors and Financial Interests." *Academy of Management Journal,* December 1977.

Schoeffler, Sidney: *Key Impacts on Profitability.* Cambridge, MA, Strategic Planning Institute, 1975.

Schoeffler, Sidney, Robert D. Buzzell, and Donald F. Heany: "Impact of Strategic Planning on Profit Performance." *Harvard Business Riview,* March–April 1974.

Schoner, Bertram, Gerald L. Rose, and G. C. Hoyt: "Quality of Decisions: Individual Versus Real and Synthetic Groups." *Journal of Applied Psychology,* August 1974.

Schroder, Harold M., Michael J. Driver, and Siegfried Streufert: *Human Information Processing.* New York, Holt, Rinehart, and Winston, 1967.

Schumacher, E. F.: *Small is Beautiful.* New York, Harper & Row, 1973.

Scott, Bruce R.: "The Industrial State: Old Myths and New Realities." *Harvard Business Review,* March–April 1973.

Sethi, J. Prakash: *Up Against the Corporate Wall.* Englewood Cliffs, NJ, Prentice-Hall, 1974.

Sethi, J. Prakash: "Who, Me? (Jail as an Occupational Hazard)." *Wharton Magazine,* Summer 1978.

Shapira, Zur, and Roger L. M. Dunbar: "Testing Mintzberg's Managerial Roles Classification Using an In-Basket Simulation." *Journal of Applied Psychology,* February 1980.

Sheehan, Gary. *Long-Range Strategic Planning and Its Relationship to Firm Size, Firm Growth, and Firm Variability."* Unpublished doctoral dissertation, University of Western Ontario, 1975.

Shetty, Y. K.: "New Look at Corporate Goals." *California Management Review,* Winter, 1979.

Shin, Bong-Gon P., and Jerry L. Wall: "An Investigation of Product Life Cycle Curvatures: Their Frequency and Their Occurrence by Industry." College of Business, Western Illinois University. Working paper, 1979.

Shull, Fremont A., André L. Delbecq, and L. L. Cummings: *Organizational Decision Making.* New York, McGraw-Hill, 1970.

Simon, Herbert A.: *Administrative Behavior: A Study of Decision-Making Processes in Administrative Organization.* New York, Free Press, 1976.

Simon, Herbert A.: *The New Science of Management Decision.* Englewood Cliffs, NJ, Prentice-Hall, 1977.

Simon, Herbert A.: "Information Processing Models of Cognition." *Annual Review of Psychology,* 1979.

Sims, Henry P., and W. Harvey Hegarty: "Policies, Objectives, and Ethical Decision Behavior: An Experiment." *Academy of Management Proceedings,* 1977.

Sloan, Alfred P., Jr.: *Adventures of the White Collar Man.* New York, Doran, 1941.

Sloan, Alfred P., Jr.: *My Years with General Motors.* New York, Doubleday and Company, 1964.

Smith, Norman R.: *The Entrepreneur and His Firm: The Relationship Between Type of Man and Type of Company.* East Lansing, MI, Graduate School of Business Administration, Michigan State University, 1967.

Snow, Charles C., and Lawrence G. Hrebiniak: "Strategy, Distinctive Competence, and Organizational Performance." *Administrative Science Quarterly,* June 1980.

Snyder, Neil, and William F. Glueck: "How Managers Plan—The Analysis of Managers' Activities." *Long Range Planning,* February 1980.

Soden, John V.: "Planning for the Computer Services Spin-Out." *Harvard Business Review,* September–October 1972.

Soelberg, Peer: "Unprogrammed Decision Making." *Academy of Management Proceedings,* December 1966.

Solomons, David: *Divisional Performance: Measurement and Control.* New York, Financial Executives Research Foundation, 1965.

Stagner, Ross: "Corporate Decision Making: An Empirical Study." *Journal of Applied Psychology,* February 1969.

Steele, John E., and Lewis B. Ward: "MBAs: Mobile, Well Situated, Well Paid." *Harvard Business Review,* January–February 1974.

Steers, Richard M.: "Antecedents and Outcomes of Organizational Commitment." *Administrative Science Quarterly,* March 1977.

Steiner, George A.: "Approaches to Long Range Planning for Small Business." *California Management Review,* Fall 1967.

Steiner, George A.: *Strategic Factors in Business Success.* New York, Financial Executives Research Foundation, 1969a.

Steiner, George A.: *Top Management Planning.* New York, Macmillan, 1969b.

Steiner, George A.: *Comprehensive Managerial Planning.* Oxford, OH, Planning Executives Institute, 1971.

Steiner, George A.: "The Redefinition of Capitalism and Its Impact on Management Practice and Theory." *Academy of Management Proceedings,* August 1972a.

Steiner, George A.: *Pitfalls in Comprehensive Long Range Planning.* Oxford, OH, Planning Executives Institute, 1972b.

Steiner, George A.: "National Policy Assessment and Action Program." *Planning Review,* 1975.

Steiner, George A. (ed.): *The Changing Role of Business in Society.* Los Angeles, CA, UCLA Graduate School of Management, 1976.

Steiner, George A.: *Strategic Planning: What Every Manager Must Know.* New York, Free Press, 1979a.

Steiner, George A.: "Contingency Theories of Strategy and Strategic Managment." In Dan E. Schendel and Charles W. Hofer (eds.): *Strategic Management: A New View of Business Policy and Planning.* Boston, Little, Brown, 1979b.

Steiner, George A.: "Can Business Survive Its Environment." *Business,* January–February 1980.

Steiner, George A.: "The New Class of Chief Executive Officer," *Long-Range Planning,* August 1981a.

Steiner, George A.: *The New Chief Executive Officer.* New York, Macmillan, 1981b.

Steiner, George A., and William G. Ryan: *Industrial Project Management.* New York, Macmillan, 1968.

Steiner, George A., and John F. Steiner: *Business, Government, and Society.* New York, Random House, 1980.

Steinmetz, Lawrence L., and Charles D. Greenidge: "Realities that Shape Managerial Style." *Business Horizons,* October 1970.

Stevenson, Howard H.: "Defining Corporate Strengths and Weaknesses." *Sloan Management Review,* Spring 1976.

Stewart, Robert F.: *A Framework for Business Planning.* Report No. 162, Long Range Planning Service. Menlo Park, CA, Stanford Research Institute, February 1963.

Stieglitz, Harold: *The Chief Executive—And His Job.* Personnel Policy Study No. 214. New York, National Industrial Conference Board, 1969.

Stonich, Paul J.: "How to Use Strategic Funds Programming." *Journal of Business Strategy,* Fall 1980.

Stonich, Paul J., and Carlos E. Zaragoza: "Strategic Funds Programming: The Missing Link in Corporate Planning." *Managerial Planning,* September–October 1980.

Stopford, John M., and Louis T. Wells: *Managing the Multinational Enterprise: Organization of the Firm and Ownership of the Subsidiaries.* New York, Basic Books, 1972.

Strauch, Ralph E.: *A Critical Assessment of Quantitative Methodology as a Policy Analysis Tool.* Santa Monica, CA, Rand Corporation, 1974.

Strauss, George: "Adolescence in Organization Growth: Problems, Pains, Possibilities." *Organizational Dynamics,* Spring 1974.

Streufert, Siegfried, and Susan C. Streufert: "Effects of Increasing Failure and Success on Military and Economic Risk Taking." *Journal of Applied Psychology,* October 1970.

Stumpf, Stephen A., Richard D. Freedman, and Dale E. Zand: "Judgmental Decisions: A Study of Interactions Among Group Membership, Group Functioning, and the Decision Situation." *Academy of Management Journal,* December 1979.

Suler, John R.: "Primary Process Thinking and Creativity." *Psychological Bulletin,* July 1980.

Summer, Charles E.: *Strategic Behavior in Business and Government.* Boston, Little, Brown, 1980.

Summer, Charles E., and Jeremiah J. O'Connell: *The Managerial Mind.* Homewood, IL, Irwin, 1964.

Summers, Irvin, and David E. White: "Creativity Techniques: Toward Improvement of the Decision Process." *Academy of Management Review,* April 1976.

Tannenbaum, Arnold S., Bogdon Kavcic, Menachem Rosner, Mino Vianello, and Georg Wieser: *Hierarchy in Organizations: An International Comparison.* San Francisco, Jossey-Bass, 1974.

Tannenbaum, Robert, and Warren H. Schmidt: "How to Choose a Leadership Pattern." *Harvard Business Review,* March 1958.

Taylor, Alexander: "Detroit's Uphill Battle." *Business Week,* September 8, 1980.

Taylor, Calvin W.: *Climate for Creativity.* Elmsford, NY, Pergamon Press, 1972.

Taylor, Ronald N.: "Age and Experience as Determinants of Managerial Information-Processing and Decision-Making Performance." *Academy of Management Journal,* March 1975.

Taylor, Ronald N., and Marvin D. Dunnette: "Influence of Dogmatism, Risk-taking Propensity, and Intelligence on Decision-Making Strategies for a Sample of Industrial Managers." *Journal of Applied Psychology,* August 1974.

Tersine, Richard J., and Walter E. Riggs: "The Delphi Technique: A Long-Range Planning Tool." *Business Horizons,* April 1976.

TFX Contract Investigation. Hearings Before the Permanent Subcommittee on Investigations of the Committee on Government Operations, U.S. Senate, 88th Congress. Washington, D.C., U.S. Government Printing Office, 1963.

Thain, Donald H.: "Stages of Corporate Development." *Business Quarterly,* Winter 1969.

Thomas, Philip S.: "Environmental Scanning—The State of the Art." *Long Range Planning,* February 1980.

Thompson, James D.: *Organizations in Action.* New York, McGraw-Hill, 1967.

Thompson, Stewart: *Management Creeds and Philosophies.* New York, American Management Association, 1958.

Thorelli, Hans B.: *Strategy + Structure = Performance: The Strategic Planning Imperative.* Bloomington, IN, Indiana University Press, 1977.

Thune, Stanley S., and Robert J. House: "Where Long Range Planning Pays Off." *Business Horizons,* August 1970.

Tilles, Seymour: "How to Evaluate Corporate Strategy." *Harvard Business Review,* July–August 1963.

Tilles, Seymour: "Strategies for Allocating Funds." *Harvard Business Review,* January–February 1966.

Toffler, Alvin: *Future Shock.* New York, Random House, 1970.

Truman, David B.: *The Governmental Process.* New York, Alfred Knopf, 1951.

Tuason, Roman V.: "Corporate Life Cycle and the Evolution of Corporate Strategy." *Academy of Management Proceedings,* August 1973.

Tyler, Leona E.: *Individuality: Human Possibilities and Personal Choice in the Psychological Development of Men and Women.* San Francisco, Jossey-Bass, 1978.

U.S. News & World Report: "Complaints About Lawyers." July 21, 1978.

U.S. 90th Congress, 1st Session, House of Representatives, Research and Technical Programs Subcommittee of the Committee on Government Operations: *The Use of Social Research in Federal Domestic Programs, Part I,* 1967.

U.S. v. Park: 421 US 658 (1974).

Vance, Stanley C.: *Managers in the Conglomerate Era.* New York, Wiley-Interscience, 1971.

Vancil, Richard F., and Peter Lorange: "Strategic Planning in Diversified Companies." *Harvard Business Review,* January–February 1975.

Van de Ven, Andrew H., and André L. Delbecq: "The Effectiveness of Nominal, Delphi, and Interacting Group Decision Making Processes." *Academy of Management Journal,* December 1974.

Van Voorhis, Kenneth R.: *Entrepreneurship and Small Business Management.* Boston, Allyn and Bacon, 1980.

Vesper, Karl H.: *New Venture Strategies.* Englewood Cliffs, NJ, Prentice-Hall, 1980.

Vickers, Geoffrey: *The Art of Judgment: A Study of Policy Making.* New York, Basic Books, 1965.

Vogel, David: *Lobbying the Corporation: Citizen Challenges to Business Authority.* New York, Basic Books, 1978.

Vroom, Victor H., and Arthur J. Jago: "Decision Making as a Social Process: Normative and Descriptive Models of Leader Behavior." *Decision Sciences,* December 1974.

Vroom, Victor H., and Philip W. Yetton: *Leadership and Decision-Making.* Pittsburgh, PA, University of Pittsburgh Press, 1973.

Wainer, Herbert A., and Irwin M. Rubin: "Motivation of Research and Development Entrepreneurs: Determinants of Company Success." *Journal of Applied Psychology,* June 1969.

Walton, Clarence C.: *Corporate Social Responsibilities.* Belmont, CA, Wadsworth, 1967.

Warren, E. Kirby: *Long Range Planning: The Executive Viewpoint.* Englewood Cliffs, NJ, Prentice-Hall, 1966.

Warren, E. Kirby: "Perspective on Planning Trends and Changes." *Resource,* July–August 1980.

Wasson, Chester: *Product Management: Product Life Cycles and Competitive Marketing Strategy.* St. Charles, IL, Challenge Books, 1971.

Webber, James B., and Martha A. Dula: "Effective Planning Committees for Hospitals." *Harvard Business Review,* May–June 1974.

Weber, John A.: "Market Structure Profile Analysis and Strategic Growth Opportunities." *California Management Review,* Fall 1977.

Webster, Frederick A.: "Entrepreneurs and Ventures: An Attempt at Classification and Clarification." *Academy of Management Review,* January 1977.

Weiner, Edith: "TAP: How One Group Identifies Trends That Affect Its Members." *Manager's Forum,* February 1977.

Weir, James E.: "Toward the Theoretical Foundations of a Contingency Theory of Policy Making Behavior." *Academy of Management Proceedings,* August 1979.

Weiss, Howard M., and Patrick A. Knight: "The Utility of Humility: Self-Esteem, Information Search, and Problem-Solving Efficiency." *Organizational Behavior and Human Performance,* April 1980.

Weston, J. Fred: "ROI Planning and Control." *Business Horizons,* August 1972.

Weston, J. Fred, and Eugene F. Brigham: *Essentials of Managerial Finance.* New York, Holt, Rinehart and Winston, 1981.

Wheelwright, Steven C., and Spyros Makridakis: *Forecasting Methods for Management.* New York, Wiley, 1980.

Whitely, William, and George W. England: "Variability in Common Dimensions of Managerial Values Due to Value Orientation and Country Differences." *Personnel Psychology,* Spring 1980.

Whybark, D. Clay: "Comparing an Adaptive Decision Model and Human Decisions." *Academy of Management Journal,* December 1973.

Wiener, Yoash, and Yoav Vardi: "Relationships between Job, Organization, and Career Commitments and Work Outcomes—An Integrative Approach." *Organizational Behavior and Human Performance,* August 1980.

Wildavsky, Aaron: *Speaking Truth to Power: The Art and Craft of Policy Analysis.* Boston, Little, Brown, 1979.

Wilemon, David L., and Gary R. Gemmill: "The Venture Manager as a Corporate Innovator." *California Management Review,* Fall 1973.

Williams, Harold M.: "The Mood of America." Speech at World-Wide Management Meeting of the Bank of America, San Francisco, January 23, 1975.

Wilson, Ian H.: "Socio-Political Forecasting: A New Dimension to Strategic Planning." *Michigan Business Review,* July 1974.

Wilson, Ian H.: "Environmental Scanning and Strategic Planning. In Lee E. Preston (ed.): *Business Environment/Public Policy.* 1979 Conference Papers. St. Louis, American Assembly of Collegiate Schools of Business, 1980.

Woo, Carolyn Y., and Arnold C. Cooper: "Strategies of Effective Low Market Share Business." *Academy of Management Proceedings,* August 1980.

Woodward, Joan: *Industrial Organization: Theory and Practice.* London, Oxford University Press, 1965.

Wrigley, Leonard: *Divisional Autonomy and Diversification.* Unpublished Doctoral Dissertation, Harvard Business School, 1970.

Zand, Dale E.: "Trust and Managerial Problem Solving." *Administrative Science Quarterly,* June 1972.

Zander, Alvin: "The Psychology of Group Processes." *Annual Review of Psychology,* 1979.

Author Index

A

Abell, Derek F., 93, 132, 146, 153, 317
Abernathy, William J., 162, 317
Aboud, John, 272, 275, 285, 328
Abramson, Robert, 201, 317
Acito, Franklin, 259, 317
Ackerman, Robert W., 66, 223, 317
Ackoff, Russell L., 93, 95, 208, 317
Adizes, Ichak, 58, 88, 317
Aguilar, Francis J., 120, 232, 317
Al-Bazzaz, Shawki, 231, 326
Alchian, Armen A., 157, 317
Aldag, R. J., 276, 324
Alexander, Larry D., 73, 317
Allen, M. G., 136f, 317
Allen, Stephen A., 226, 232, 234, 240, 331
Allio, Robert J., 93, 317
Allison, Graham T., 151, 157, 223, 294, 317
Aluminum Company of America (ALCOA), 66, 67, 317
Alutto, Joseph A., 259, 317
America, Richard F., 285, 317
Anderson, Carl R., 129, 160, 308, 309t, 318, 334
Anderson, M. J., 160, 326
Andrews, Frank M., 180, 335
Andrews, Frederick, 159, 318
Andrews, Kenneth R., 8, 17, 32, 58, 61, 318, 322
Anshen, Melvin, 13, 58, 61, 68, 318
Ansoff, H. Igor, 31, 32, 115, 129, 208, 209, 310, 318
Anthony, Robert N., 96, 157, 318
Anyon, G. Jay, 271, 318
Appleby, Paul H., 24, 291, 298, 301, 318
Arendt, Eugene, 197, 323
Argyris, Chris, 256, 261, 318
Armstrong, J. Scott, 126, 318
Arroba, Tanya Y., 172, 318
Asimov, Isaac, 116, 318

B

Badr, Hamed, 175, 318
Bagley, Edward R., 82, 318

Bailey, Earl L., 126, 146, 318, 328
Bailey, Stephen K., 151, 318
Bank of America, 67, 319
Barkley, Paul W., 59, 319
Barmeier, Robert E., 68, 128, 319
Barnard, Chester I., 156, 261, 319
Barnes, Louis B., 153, 261, 323, 326
Barron, Frank, 181, 319
Barsaloux, Jean, 188, 319
Bartol, Kathryn M., 259, 319
Bassett, Glenn A., 78f, 319
Bauer, Raymond A., 169, 294, 319
Baumback, Clifford M., 279t, 280, 319
Baumhart, Raymond, 59, 319
Baumol, William J., 61, 157, 319
Bayton, James A., 179, 334
Beach, Lee Roy, 170, 215, 319, 331
Beiler, George W., 68, 321
Bell, Daniel, 47, 49, 59, 319
Bell, E. C., 256, 319
Berg, Ivar, 324
Biggadike, Ralph, 283, 319
Biondo, John J., 284, 327
Blake, Robert R., 201, 319
Bleichan, Gerhard D., 60, 319
Bloom, Paul N., 146, 319
Boettinger, Henry M., 7, 319
Bonham, T. W., 309, 330
Boone, Louis E., 172, 319
Boston Consulting Group, 142, 319
Bouchard, Thomas J., 188, 319
Boucher, Wayne I., 127, 320
Boulton, William R., 197, 320
Bowen, Howard R., 58, 320
Bower, Joseph L., 8, 13, 32, 320, 322
Bower, Marvin, 30, 78, 320
Bowers, David G., 75, 320
Bowman, Edward H., 312, 320
Bracker, Jeffrey, 31, 320
Bradspies, Robert W., 250, 329
Brandenburg, R. G., 96, 325
Brewer, Garry D., 295, 320
Brigham, Eugene F., 146, 341
Bright, James R., 127, 320

Brightman, Harvey J., 179, 320
Brockhaus, Robert H., 277, 320
Brockhaus, William L., 278, 320
Broom, H. N., 8, 320
Brown, Bert R., 190, 337
Brown, James K., 68, 125*t*, 320
Brown, Julius S., 179, 320
Bryan, Stanley E., 151, 320
Buchanan, Bruce, 258, 260*t*, 320
Buchholz, Rogene A., 52, 68, 320, 321
Buckley, Adrian, 135, 321
Bunker, Charles S., 272, 328
Burns, Tom, 226, 321
Bursk, Edward C., 319
Burt, Robert E., 258, 325
Burton, Gene E., 188, 321
Business Roundtable, 198, 199, 321
Business Week, 32, 34, 321
Buzzell, Robert D., 141, 337

C

Cammillus, J. C., 115, 321
Campbell, Hannah, 143, 321
Campbell, John P., 173, 321
Cannon, Warren M., 225, 321
Carroll, Archie B., 68, 129, 321, 334
Carroll, John B., 175, 321
Carroll, Stephen J., 72, 205, 252, 321, 332
Carter, Eugene, 212, 321
Carter, Violet B., 162, 321
Cartwright, John, 291, 321
Castore, Carl H., 192, 336
Cavanagh, Gerald F., 178, 321
Cawein, Paul E., 33, 327
Cecil, Earl A., 192, 211, 321
Chamber of Commerce of the United States, 62, 321
Chambers, John C., 126, 129, 321
Chandler, Alfred D., 28, 52, 84, 87, 211, 227–230, 234, 321
Channon, Derek F., 31, 93, 229, 322
Charan, Ram, 12, 322
Charnock, John, 293, 322
Chatov, Robert, 24, 322
Chertkoff, Jerome M., 192, 321
Christensen, C. Roland, 8, 32, 322
Clark, John M., 37, 38, 157, 322
Clark, Russell D., 191, 322
Clifford, Donald K., 19, 86, 135, 139, 145, 226, 322
Cobbs, John, 47, 322
Cohen, Kalman J., 96, 322
Cohen, Michael D., 213, 322

Cohn, Theodore, 124*t*, 144, 322
Collins, Orvis F., 274, 275, 280, 285, 322
Committee for Economic Development, 59, 60, 63, 322
Connolly, Terry, 170, 322
Cook, Curtis W., 308, 322
Cook, John, 258, 322
Cook, Victor, 139, 335
Cooper, Arnold C., 145, 146, 276, 279, 310, 323, 327, 328, 342
Copeland, Charles, 4, 263, 329
Corey, Raymond E., 233, 323
Corson, John J., 63, 68, 323
Crampon, William J., 258, 335
Crawford, Ronald L., 145, 325
Cummings, Larry L., 169, 186, 192, 197, 321, 323, 338
Cutting, Guy D., 291, 331
Cyert, Richard M., 96, 157, 227, 322, 323

D

Daems, Herman, 228, 321
Dalton, Gene W., 261, 323
Davis, James H., 191, 323
Davis, Keith, 58, 63, 323
Davis, Stanley M., 234, 323
Day, George S., 135, 323
Dean, Joel, 139, 323
Dearden, John, 159, 232, 323
DeCarlo, James F., 285, 323
Declerck, Roger P., 31, 318
Deets, M. King, 192, 323
Delbecq, André L., 169, 186, 187, 188*t*, 323, 338, 341
Derieux, James C., 328
Derthick, Martha, 292, 323
DeWoolfson, Bruce H., 290, 323
Dhalla, Nariman K., 160, 323
Dittrich, John E., 154, 330
Dooley, Arch R., 12, 323
Dovey, Brian H., 284, 327
Drauden, Gail, 188, 319
Drews, William P., 142, 336
Driver, Michael J., 174, 338
Dror, Yehezkel, 149, 323
Drucker, Peter F., 27, 28, 100, 153, 246, 251, 291, 292, 298, 323
Dubin, Robert, 205, 324
Dula, Martha A., 291, 341
Dunbar, Roger L. M., 73, 338
Dunn, Dan T., 283, 324

Dunnette, Marvin D., 173, 179, 321, 340
Dyas, Gareth P., 229, 324

E

Eaton, William J., 37, 324
Ebert, Ronald J., 179, 191, 194, 324
Eccles, M. S., 297, 324
Eells, Richard, 59, 324
Ehrbar, A. F., 38, 324
Ehrlich, Anne H., 50, 324
Ehrlich, Thomas, 50, 324
Elliot-Jones, M. F., 126, 324
Emery, F. E., 45, 324
Emory, William C., 324
Emshoff, James R., 195, 196*f*, 333
England, George W., 176, 324, 341
Enis, Ben M., 139, 324
Estes, Robert M., 198, 324
Etzioni, Amitai, 210, 324
Eubank, Arthur A., 159, 335
Ewing, David W., 246, 324

F

Farmer, Richard N., 59, 324
Fast, Norman D., 283, 324
Fegley, Robert L., 52, 324
Ferrell, O. C., 132, 331
Fiedler, Fred E., 304, 324
Field, R. H. George, 217, 324
Filley, A. C., 276, 324
Fisher, G. H., 295, 324
Fisk, George, 146, 324
Folsom, Marion B., 151, 325
Forbes, 88, 324
Ford, Charles H., 252, 325
Forrester, Jay W., 5, 139, 325
Foster, D. W., 134, 325
Fottler, Myron D., 291, 325
Fox, Harold, 141, 325
Franko, Lawrence G., 229, 325
Freedman, Richard D., 215, 339
French, John R. P., 264, 332
Frey, G. F., 68, 325
Friedman, Milton, 59, 60, 325
Friesen, Peter H., 307, 332
Fruhan, William E., 160, 325
Fry, Fred L., 262, 325
Fulmer, Robert M., 115, 325, 337

G

Galbraith, Jay R., 87, 234, 235*f*, 325
Gale, Bradley T., 142, 160, 325
Geiger, Theodore, 294
Gemmill, Gary R., 282, 283*t*, 342
Gergen, Kenneth J., 294, 319
Germane, Gayton E., 205, 328
Gershefski, George W., 142, 325
Gerstner, Louis V., 115, 150, 325
Ghiselli, Edwin E., 173, 261, 325, 326
Gilmore, Frank F., 96, 325
Gluck, Frederick W., 31, 325
Glueck, William F., 8, 32, 115, 211, 211*t*, 310, 312,
    325, 336, 338
Gordon, Michael E., 258, 325
Gordon, Robert A., 3, 4, 325
Gram, Harold A., 145, 325
Grant, John H., 146
Gray, Edmund R., 175, 318
Green, Thad B., 189, 326
Greenidge, Charles D., 82, 339
Greenwood, William T., 314, 326
Greiner, Larry E., 86, 153, 232, 326
Grieco, V. A., 278, 326
Grinyer, Peter H., 116, 152, 231, 326
Gross, Bertram M., 17, 24, 326
Grossman, Elliott S., 126, 328
Guest, Robert H., 261, 326
Gulick, Luther, 226, 326
Gustafson, David H., 186, 323
Guth, William D., 13, 19, 20, 144, 175, 318, 326
Gutman, Peter M., 19, 133, 326

H

Haire, Mason, 261, 262, 326
Hall, Jay, 75, 326
Hall, William K., 38, 111, 126, 326
Halset, Walter, 201, 317
Hammermash, R. G., 160, 326
Hammond, John S., 93, 132, 146, 317
Hansen, Roger D., 294
Hardy, James M., 291, 326
Harrigan, Kathryn R., 145, 326
Harris, J. E., 160, 326
Harrison, E. Frank, 149, 152*f*, 327
Harrison, Roger, 79, 80*t*, 327
Hatten, Kenneth J., 310, 311, 327, 337
Hawkins, Kevin, 291, 327
Hayek, Friedrich A., 60, 327
Hayes, Robert L., 32, 318

Heany, Donald F., 141, 337
Hedley, Barry, 135, 139, 326
Hegarty, W. Harvey, 178, 338
Heidrick and Struggles, Inc., 205, 327
Heller, Frank A., 76, 215–218, 216*t*, 256, 326
Henderson, Bruce D., 135, 142, 144, 327
Herold, David M., 115, 327
Hertz, David B., 158, 327
Heyne, Paul T., 60, 327
Hicks, Herbert G., 272, 335
Hidy, Ralph W., 33, 327
Higdon, Hal, 200, 327
Hill, Richard M., 284, 284*t*, 327
Hines, George H., 272, 273*t*, 327
Hitch, Charles J., 151, 295, 327
Hlavacek, James D., 282, 284, 284*t*, 327
Hofer, Charles W., 18, 31, 32, 89, 115, 128, 129, 133,
     134, 139, 141, 142, 145, 146, 155, 160, 306, 311,
     312, 318, 323, 327, 328, 333, 337, 339
Hogue, W. Dickerson, 59, 324
Holden, Paul E., 205, 328
Horn, Norbert, 322
Hornaday, John A., 272, 275, 285, 328
Hosmer, La Rue T., 279, 328
House, Robert J., 115, 197, 328, 340
Howell, James E., 3, 4, 325
Howell, Robert A., 232, 252, 317, 328
Hoyt, George C., 189, 192, 323, 337
Hrebiniak, Lawrence G., 83, 258, 328, 338
Huber, George P., 194, 197, 323, 328
Humble, John W., 96, 328
Humphrey, George M., 296, 328
Hundal, P. S., 273, 328
Hunsicker, J. Quincy, 116, 328
Hunt, Alfred, 200, 328
Hurwood, David L., 126, 328
Hussey, David E., 93, 96, 139, 291, 328
Hutchins, Robert, 10, 328

J

Jacoby, Neil H., 58, 319, 328
Jago, Arthur G., 76, 215, 216, 328, 341
Jalland, Michael, 93, 322
James, Barrie G., 87, 328
Janis, Irving L., 192, 193, 294, 328
Jauch, Lawrence R., 312, 328
Jerdee, Thomas H., 72, 205, 256, 266, 332, 336, 337
Jerome, William T., 248, 328
Johnson, James C., 172, 319
Johnson, Thomas E., 174, 329

Johnston, Russ, 234, 327
Jones, Charles O., 293, 298, 299, 329

K

Kahn, Robert L., 88, 329
Kami, Michael J., 36, 144, 145, 241, 337
Karger, Delmar, 115, 329
Karmel, Barbara, 196, 329
Karol, Barbara L., 188, 329
Kast, Fremont E., 304, 329
Kastens, Merritt L., 116, 329
Katz, Daniel, 88, 329
Kaufman, Stephen P., 31, 325
Kavcic, Bogdon, 257, 340
Kedia, B. L., 175, 318
Keen, Peter G. W., 174, 331
Kelley, Lane, 177, 329
Kerr, Steven, 262, 263*t*, 329
Khandwalla, Pradip, 76, 329
Kilman, Ralph H., 195, 329
King, William R., 146
Kinnunen, Raymond M., 155, 329
Kipnis, David, 263, 329
Kirchoff, Bruce A., 154, 329
Klein, Harold, 129, 329
Klimoski, Richard J., 188, 329
Knight, Kenneth, 234, 329
Knight, Patrick A., 180, 341
Koch, James L., 304, 333
Kocka, Jürgen, 322
Komorita, Samuel S., 191, 323
Kona, Toyohira, 133, 329
Koontz, Harold, 250, 329
Kotler, Philip, 145, 146, 319, 329
Krasner, O. J., 126, 129, 161*f*, 330
Kraut, Allen I., 264, 329
Kubr, M., 200, 329
Kudla, Ronald J., 115, 329

L

Lang, James R., 154, 330
Laughlin, Patrick R., 191, 323
Lawler, Edward E., 173, 262, 321, 330
Lawrence, Paul R., 226, 234, 323, 330
Lawyer, Kenneth, 279*t*, 280, 319
Lear Siegler, Inc., 125, 330
Leavitt, Harold J., 201, 330
LeBell, Don, 126, 129, 161*f*, 330
Lee, James A., 261, 330

Leitch, D. Paul, 153, 326
Lenz, R. T., 225, 330
Leontiades, Milton, 84, 87, 115, 330
Levitt, Theodore, 60, 139, 141, 330
Life Office Management Association, 142, 330
Likert, Jane G., 256, 330
Likert, Rensis, 61, 226, 256, 257, 319, 330
Lindberg, Roy A., 124*t*, 144, 322
Lindblom, Charles E., 207, 293, 295, 330
Linneman, Robert E., 93, 330
Lippitt, Gordon, 201, 330
Lippitt, Ronald, 201, 330
Lipset, Seymour M., 48, 330
Litschert, Robert J., 309, 330
Livingston, J. Sterling, 171, 330
Locke, Edwin A., 257, 330
Lodge, George C., 48, 331
Lorange, Peter, 93, 96, 155, 232, 242, 331, 341
Lorsch, Jay W., 226, 232, 234, 240, 330, 331
Los Angeles Times, 151
Luck, David J., 19, 132, 134, 134*t,* 140*t,* 331
Lundberg, Olof, 174, 331
Lundgren, Earl F., 211, 321
Lundstedt, Sven, 146, 331
Lusk, Edward J., 176, 331
Lynton, Edith F., 68, 337
Lyons, Paul R., 285, 323

M

McAdam, Terry, 59, 331
McAllister, Daniel W., 215, 331
McCarthy, E. Jerome, 242, 331
McCaskey, Michael B., 212, 331
Macchiaverna, Paul, 67, 331
McClelland, David C., 273, 285, 331, 333
McConkey, Dale D., 251, 252, 331
McDonald, Alonzo, 82, 331
McFarland, Dalton E., 19, 331
McGowan, John J., 61, 319
McGrath, Phyllis S., 68, 331
McGregor, Douglas, 226, 256, 331
McKay, Charles W., 291, 331
McKenney, James L., 174, 331
MacMillan, Ian C., 190, 331
McNair, Malcolm P., 4, 331
Mahoney, Thomas A., 72, 205, 332
Maier, Norman R. F., 256, 332
Makridakis, Spyros, 126, 332
Malik, F. A., 115, 329
Mann, Leon, 193, 328
Mann, Roland, 133, 332

Manne, Henry G., 60, 332
March, James G., 156, 157, 212, 213, 227, 322, 323, 332
Marino, Kenneth E., 264, 265*t,* 332
Marrow, Alfred J., 264, 332
Martin, Thomas N., 312, 328
Mason, Edward S., 157, 332
Mason, Richard O., 195, 332
Maxwell, Scott E., 175, 321
Meadows, Dennis, 50, 321
Michael, Donald N., 210, 332
Michael, George, 141, 332
Mihalasky, John, 143, 332
Miles, Raymond E., 82, 83*t,* 84*t,* 86, 87, 332
Miller, Arjay, 60, 332
Miller, Danny, 88, 307, 332
Miner, Frederick C., 189, 332
Miner, John B., 23, 72, 75, 77, 81, 87, 173, 190, 197, 198, 205, 213, 217, 224, 226, 229, 234, 235, 252, 255, 257, 259, 261, 262, 264, 266, 299, 304, 305, 310, 312, 328, 332, 333
Miner, Mary G., 262, 264, 333
Mingo, Kent A., 159, 335
Mintzberg, Henry, 7, 73, 74*t,* 115, 151, 154, 174, 205, 207, 213, 271, 305, 333
Miron, David, 285, 333
Mishan, Ezra J., 50, 333
Mitchell, Terence R., 170, 179, 191, 194, 215, 319, 324, 331
Mitroff, Ian I., 195, 196*f,* 332, 333
Moberg, Dennis J., 304, 333
Mohrman, Susan, 259, 333
Monieson, D. D., 137*t,* 333
Moore, David G., 274, 275, 280, 285, 322
Moore, Larry F., 305, 333, 335
Moose, Sandra O., 135, 333
Morris, James H., 258, 259, 333
Morrison, J. Roger, 133
Morse, John J., 73, 234, 331, 333
Moskowitz, Herbert, 172, 333
Mouton, Jane S., 201, 319
Mulder, Mauk, 217, 334
Muldrow, Tressie W., 179, 334
Mullick, Satinder K., 126, 129, 321
Murray, Edwin A., 66, 334

N

Nanus, Burt, 128, 129, 334
Nathanson, Daniel A., 87, 234, 235*f,* 325
Naumes, William, 201, 202, 334
Naylor, Thomas H., 93, 142, 158, 160, 334

Neal, Alfred C., 45, 334
Nelson, Oscar T., 299, 336
Neuschel, Robert P., 77*t*, 336
Newgren, Kenneth E., 129, 334
Newman, William H., 45, 129, 132, 249, 291, 329, 334
Niland, Powell, 324
Norburn, David, 152, 326
Nord, Walter R., 277, 320
Norman, Richard A., 209, 334
Novick, David, 290, 334
Nowak, Phillip, 281, 335

O

O'Connell, Jeremiah J., 9, 127, 261, 334, 340
O'Connor, Rochelle, 101, 121, 121*t*, 125*t*, 320, 334
Odiorne, George S., 252, 334
O'Leary, Vincent, 75, 326
Oliver, Bruce L., 176, 331
Olsen, Johan P., 212, 332
Organ, Dennis W., 6, 334
Osborn, Richard N., 312, 328

P

Paine, Frank T., 129, 160, 201, 202, 308, 309*t*, 318, 334
Palesy, Steven R., 139, 160, 335
Palmer, Michael, 271, 335
Pandey, Janek, 273, 277, 335
Parker, Treadway C., 281, 282, 335
Patchen, Martin, 218, 325
Pathak, Dev S., 188, 321
Patton, Arch, 139, 335
Patton, G. R., 89, 146, 337
Patz, Alan L., 10, 335
Pavan, Robert J., 229, 335
Pederson, Carlton A., 205, 328
Pelz, Donald C., 180, 335
Pennington, Malcolm W., 93, 116, 317, 335
Perrow, Charles, 226, 335
Peters, Joseph P., 291, 335
Peterson, Richard B., 177, 177*t*, 335
Pfeffer, Jeffrey, 199, 214, 215, 226, 281, 335
Philpot, John W., 258, 325
Pierson, Frank C., 4, 335
Pinches, George E., 159, 335
Pinder, Craig C., 305, 333, 335
Pitts, Robert A., 146, 335
Polli, Rolando, 139, 335
Popp, Gary E., 272, 325

Porter, Lyman W., 258, 261, 326, 335
Porter, Michael E., 131, 132*t*, 139, 146, 335
Preble, John F., 127, 336
Prell, Arthur E., 19, 134, 134*t*, 140*t*, 331
President's Commission on National Goals, 292, 336
Preston, Lee E., 68, 128, 319, 336, 342
Price, James L., 173, 336
Purcell, Theodore V., 264, 336

Q

Quinn, James B., 154, 205, 283, 336

R

Radford, K. J., 93, 336
Raisinghani, Duru, 151, 154, 213, 333
Rapoport, Leo A., 142, 336
Rawls, James R., 299, 336
Reeser, Clayton, 177, 329
Reimann, Bernard C., 81, 336
Rhenman, Eric, 45, 336
Rhode, John G., 262, 330
Richards, Max D., 88, 174, 252, 331, 336
Richman, Barry M., 58, 336
Riggs, James, 89, 146, 337
Riggs, Walter E., 188, 340
Ringbakk, K. A., 89, 96, 116, 336
Roberts, John C., 192, 336
Robinson, Richard, 115, 336
Rockefeller, John D., 47, 62, 70, 336
Rohrbaugh, John, 189, 336
Rokeach, Milton, 176, 336
Rose, Gerald L., 189, 337
Rosen, Benson, 256, 266, 336, 337
Rosenzweig, James E., 304, 329
Rosner, Menachem, 257, 340
Ross, Joel E., 36, 144, 145, 241, 337
Rothschild, William E., 93, 132, 145, 337
Rourke, Francis E., 298, 337
Rubin, Irwin M., 273, 341
Rubin, Jeffrey Z., 190, 337
Rue, Leslie W., 115, 325, 337
Rumelt, Richard P., 134, 230, 231, 337
Ryan, William G., 233, 339

S

Said, Kamal, 242, 337
Salancik, Gerald R., 199, 214, 215, 259, 322, 335, 337

Salveson, Melvin E., 111, 150, 337
Saunders, C. B., 13, 337
Sawyer, George C., 68, 337
Sayles, Leonard R., 205, 337
Schaeffer, Ruth G., 68, 337
Schattschneider, E. E., 294, 337
Schendel, Dan E., 18, 31, 32, 89, 115, 128, 129, 139, 145, 146, 155, 310, 311, 318, 323, 327, 328, 333, 337, 339
Schmidt, Richard, 198t, 337
Schmidt, Warren H., 75, 76, 340
Schneider, William, 48, 330
Schoeffler, Sidney, 141, 142, 337
Schoner, Bertram, 189, 337
Schroder, Harold M., 174, 338
Schumacher, E. F., 50, 338
Schweiger, David M., 257, 330
Scott, Bruce R., 85, 85t, 338
Seashore, Stanley E., 75, 320
Seckler, David W., 59, 319
Seiler, Robert E., 242, 337
Sethi, J. Prakash, 45, 50, 338
Shapira, Zur, 73, 338
Sheehan, Gary, 115, 338
Shetty, Y. K., 100, 338
Shin, Bong-Gon P., 160, 338
Shull, Fremont A., 169, 186, 338
Silverman, Arnold, 263, 329
Simon, Herbert A., 156, 157, 172, 207, 210, 227, 261, 332, 338
Sims, Henry P., 178, 338
Skinner, Wickham, 12, 323
Sloan, Alfred P., 35, 143, 166, 232, 338
Smith, Donald D., 126, 129, 321
Smith, Frank J., 258, 335
Smith, Norman R., 219, 275, 276, 276t, 338
Snow, Charles C., 82, 83, 83t, 84t, 86, 87, 332, 338
Snyder, Neil, 115, 338
Soden, John V., 232, 338
Soelberg, Peer, 211, 338
Solomons, David, 232, 338
Spiller, William E., 258, 325
Stagner, Ross, 212, 212t, 338
Stalker, G. M., 226, 321
Star, Steven H., 233, 323
Staw, Barry M., 322, 337
Steele, John E., 171, 338
Steers, Richard M., 258, 259, 333, 338
Steiner, George A., 24, 31, 35, 45, 51–53, 54t, 63, 65, 66, 68, 93, 94, 98, 107t, 116, 127, 144, 157, 174, 206, 233, 239, 279, 290, 308–310, 313, 323, 339
Steiner, John F., 45, 51, 65, 66, 339

Steinmetz, Lawrence L., 82, 339
Stevenson, Howard H., 129, 339
Stewart, Robert F., 96, 339
Stieglitz, Harold, 52, 105, 339
Stonich, Paul J., 242, 339
Stopford, John M., 229, 339
Strauch, Ralph E., 295, 339
Strauss, George, 112t, 339
Streufert, Siegfried, 174, 191, 338, 339
Streufert, Susan C., 191, 339
Strother, George B., 324
Stumpf, Stephen A., 215, 339
Suler, John R., 181, 340
Summer, Charles E., 9, 307, 308, 340
Summers, Irvin, 181, 340

T

Tagiuri, Renato, 20, 175, 326
Tannenbaum, Arnold S., 257, 340
Tannenbaum, Robert, 75, 76, 340
Tarr, Robert J., 291, 327
Taylor, Alexander, 37, 340
Taylor, Calvin W., 181, 340
Taylor, Ronald N., 173, 175, 179, 340
Tersine, Richard J., 188, 340
Tewary, N. B., 273, 277, 335
Tezel, A., 115, 330
TFX Contract Investigation, 153, 340
Thain, Donald H., 85, 86, 340
Thanheiser, Heinz T., 229, 324
Théorêt, André, 151, 154, 213, 333
Thomas, Philip S., 128, 340
Thompson, Cynthia A., 258, 325
Thompson, James E., 227, 240, 340
Thompson, J. C., 13, 337
Thompson, Stewart, 24, 340
Thompson, Victor A., 282, 284, 327
Thorelli, Hans B., 226, 340
Thune, Stanley S., 115, 340
Tilles, Seymour, 135, 162, 340
Toffler, Alvin, 50, 340
Tosi, Henry L., 252, 321
Trist, E. L., 45, 324
Truman, David B., 293, 340
Tuason, Roman V., 85, 85t, 340
Tyler, Leona E., 182, 340

U

Ullrich, Robert A., 299, 336
U.S. Congress, 295, 340

U.S. News and World Report, 49, 50, 339, 340
U.S. v. Park, 50, 341
Urban, Thomas F., 179, 320
Urwick, L., 226, 326
Utterback, James M., 128

V

Vance, Stanley C., 88, 169, 274, 275, 341
Vancil, Richard F., 93, 155, 232, 242, 317, 331, 341
Van de Ven, Andrew H., 186, 187, 188*t,* 323, 341
Van Voorhis, Kenneth R., 279, 341
Vardi, Yoav, 259, 342
Vesper, Karl H., 276, 279, 328, 341
Vianello, Mino, 257, 341
Vickers, Geoffrey, 295, 341
Vogel, David, 48, 341
Vroom, Victor H., 76, 215–218, 328, 341

W

Wagner, Francis R., 73, 333
Wainer, Herbert A., 273, 341
Wall, Jerry L., 160, 338
Wall, Toby, 258, 322
Walleck, A. Steven, 31, 325
Wallender, Harvey W., 291, 334
Wallich, Henry C., 61, 319
Walton, Clarence C., 64, 341
Ward, Lewis B., 171, 338
Warren, E. Kirby, 116, 341
Wasson, Chester, 141, 341
Wayne, Kenneth, 162, 317
Webber, James B., 291, 341
Weber, John A., 132, 341
Webster, Frederick A., 276, 341
Weick, Karl E., 173, 321
Weiner, Edith, 128, 341
Weir, James E., 249, 341

Weiss, Howard M., 180, 341
Wells, Louis T., 229, 339
Werner, David J., 174, 329
Weston, J. Fred, 58, 146, 159, 232, 317, 341
Wheelwright, Steven C., 126, 341
White, David E., 181, 214, 340
White, Sam E., 154, 330
Whitely, William, 176, 341
Whybark, D. Clay, 172, 341
Wiener, Yoash, 259, 342
Wieser, Georg, 257, 340
Wildavsky, Aaron, 149, 295, 342
Wilemon, David L., 282, 283*t,* 342
Wilke, Henk, 217, 334
Williams, Harold M., 49, 342
Williams, Martha, 75, 326
Willis, Robert, 312, 325
Wilson, Ian H., 68, 127, 342
Winter, David G., 273, 285, 331
Woo, Carolyn Y., 145, 342
Woodward, Joan, 226, 342
Wrigley, Leonard, 230, 342

Y

Yasai-Ardekani, Masoud, 231, 326
Yetton, Philip W., 76, 216, 218, 341
Yuspeh, Sonia, 160, 323

Z

Zakon, Alan J., 135, 333
Zaleznik, Abraham, 261, 323
Zand, Dale E., 199, 215, 339, 342
Zander, Alvin, 197, 342
Zarogoza, Carlos E., 242, 339
Zigli, Ron M., 188, 321
Zimmerman, John W., 127, 334

Subject Index

A

Academic backgrounds of top executives, studies of, 171
Accounting system of a company, 159
Achievement-motivated entrepreneur, 280
Achievement motivation, 272–274, 273t, 276
Acme Markets, Inc., 50
Adaptive approach, to decision making, 172, 208, 209, 219, 279
Adaptive firms, 275
Administrative coordination, 228
Administrative man, 210
Aerospace industry, 233
Affirmative action policies, an example, 262–266
Age, and decision making, 175
Ajax Corporation, 22
Aluminum Company of America (ALCOA), 66, 67
America, 34. *See also* United States
American Assembly of Collegiate Schools of Business, 4
American business, 36, 126, 161
American Council of Life Insurance, 128
American industrial enterprise, 227
American Motors Corporation, 223
American Revolution, 47
American Telephone and Telegraph Company (A.T. & T.), 100, 128
Americans, 48
Antitrust Division of the Department of Justice, 163
Apollo program, 47
The Art of Judgment, 295
Attitudes
  managerial, 233
  worker, 163
Australia, 177
Authoritarian leadership, 77
Authority, 48, 261–264, 266
Automobile companies, 37, 126, 127, 163

B

Baldwin Locomotive Works, 38, 126
Battelle Memorial Institute, 143

Bay of Pigs invasion, 192
Behavioral decision theory, 312
A Behavioral Theory of the Firm, 157
Bich, Baron Marcel, 131
Blacks, 263
Bloomingdale's, 34
Boards of directors, 53, 197–200, 198t. *See also* Chief executive officers (CEOs)
Boston Consulting Group, 135, 136, 139, 142
Bottom-up approach, to planning, 105
"Bounded rationality," 157
Brain research, 174
Brewing industry, 310
British corporations, study of, 152
British firms, studies of, 229
Budgets, 243–248, 247f
Bureaucratic (hierarchic) systems, 235
Burnham, James, 275
Burroughs Corporation, 160
Business
  criticism of, 48
  environment, 31, 52–54
  failures, 279, 279t, 280, 286
  initiating a new, 277–281
  managers, study of values, 175. *See also* Managers; Values
  policies, types and classifications of, 24
  policy courses, 3, 4, 8–11, 272, 313
  schools, 314
  studies, 172
  success, 28, 144–146
  units, 233. *See also* Strategic business units (SBUs)
Business Week, 32, 47

C

Cambria Steel, 88
Carlson, Chester, 143
Carnegie Corporation of New York, 3, 4
Carter, President James, 36
Case method, 7, 305–308, 311
Casey, William, 159

351

Causal relationships, 312
Central Leather Co., 88
Centralized company, 105, 120
Chief executive officers (CEOs), 4, 5, 31, 52, 53, 71, 73, 76, 77, 86, 105, 110, 111, 154, 155, 171, 177, 257, 279. *See also* Boards of directors
Chrysler Corporation, 36, 37
Churchill, Winston, 162
Civil Aeronautics Board (CAB), 127
Civil War, 227
Climate, organizational, 71
Coalitions, 202
Coca-Cola Co., 18, 20, 128
Cognitive
    complexity, 174, 234
    styles, of decision making, 174, 175, 183
College textbook industry, 83
Committee for Economic Development (CED), 59
Communications network, 227
Competitive
    conditions, 76, 84, 126
    strategy, 131, 132
Competitive Strategy: Techniques for Analyzing Industries and Competitors, 131
"Comprehensive rationality," 156, 157
Computer models, 142, 158
COMSAT, 47
Conceptual models of decision making, operational versus, 154
Conference Board, 52
Conflict, 5, 82, 94, 194, 198, 199, 217, 224
Congress, United States, 289, 294, 295
Connelly, John F., 32
Consolidated Edison of New York, 156
Constituencies, in boards of directors, 199
Constitution of the United States, 291, 292
Consultants, 200–203, 201*t*
Consulting firms, 195, 200, 201, 203
Contingency theory
    of organizations, 226, 227
    of policy/strategy, 303–315
Control process, management, 248–251
Cooptation, 199, 214
Coordination, 240, 241
Corporate life cycle, 85*t,* 87, 271
Corporate Strategy, 310
Craftsman entrepreneur, 275
Creativity, in decision making, 180–183, 186–189, 194, 196, 217
Crown Cork and Seal Company, Inc., 32, 33, 160
Cuba, 192

D

Data bases, 98, 99, 121, 124
Decentralized companies, 105, 120, 231, 234, 240
Decision making
    alternative approaches to, 205–220
    within boards of directors, 197–200
    characteristics of process, 150–155, 152*f*
    cognitive factors in, 170–175
    defined, 169, 170
Decisional roles, 73, 74*t*
Decisions
    acceptance of, 256
    -based variability, studies of, 215–218
    and environments, 179
    shared, 76, 216–218, 257
    theory, 149
Decline, in organizational life cycles, 88, 89
Delphi technique, 187, 197, 262
Democratic leadership, 77
Department of Defense, United States, 153
Descriptive theory, 149, 210
Dialectical approach, to decision making, 195, 196, 196*f*
Discussion group technique, 187, 188
Diversification strategies, 229
Divisionalized companies, 124, 242
Dixie Cups Co., 143
Dogmatism, in decision making, 179, 180, 183
Douglas Aircraft Co., 132
DuPont, 49, 128, 143, 228
Durant, Will, 143

E

Eastman Kodak Co., 45
Economic
    forecasts, 121, 122*t,* 126
    man, 149, 210
    theory, 156, 157
Ehrlich, Thomas, 49
Eisenhower Administration, 292
Eisenhower, President Dwight D., 296
Engagement teams, 195, 200, 201. *See also* Consulting firms
The Enterprising Man, 274
Entrepreneurial-opportunistic approach, to decision making, 207, 209, 218, 219, 278
Entrepreneurs, study of, 277
Entrepreneurship, 271–287
Environment(s), 71, 81, 120, 162, 163, 199, 218, 279
    changing, 28–31, 43–55, 97, 98, 122

Environment(s)—*Continued*
  competitive, 76
  economic, 45, 46, 52
  external, 77, 128, 182, 202
  future, 51, 52, 124
  governmental, 46, 47
  hostile, 309
  impact of business policy/strategy on, 51
  influence of in decision making, 213–215
  internal, 49, 77, 202
  legal, 49, 50
  uncertain, 129, 234, 308
Environmental
  analysis, 128, 129
  contingencies, 303, 308
  impacts on organizations, 6
  problems, 280
  scanning, 127–129
Ethics, 7, 8, 59, 178
Europe, 29, 229
European Economic Community, 229
European market, 126
Evaluation
  of plans, 103
  of policies and strategies, 149–167
Evolutionary management, 84
Executive Branch of the U.S. government, 289, 294
Expertise, in decision making, 217, 218, 257

F

Feasibility testing, 104
Federal Drug Administration (FDA), 127
Federal Trade Commission (FTC), 127, 163
Female entrepreneurs, 285, 286
Field research, 7, 312
Firm(s)
  dealing with others, in decision making, 214, 215
  strategies, 82
Food processor company, 127
Ford Foundation, 3
Ford, Henry, 275
Ford Motor Co., 34–37, 128
Forecasts, 99, 127, 162, 208
  environmental, 121, 126
  of market, 159
  techniques, 161*f*, 162
Formal
  planning, 28, 29, 252
  systems, 239–253
Formal-structured approach, to decision making, 206, 207, 209, 212, 218, 219, 279

Fort Lincoln Housing Project, 292
Fortune, 311
Fortune 1000 companies, 52
Fortune 500, studies of firms, 38, 230, 231
France, 36
The Franklin Mint, 131
French firms, studies of, 229
"Future Shock," 50

G

Gap analysis, 130, 170
Garbage can model, of decision making, 213
General Electric Co., 68, 111, 127, 128, 136, 137, 139, 141, 264
General Foods Co., 160
General Motors Corporation, 34–36, 67, 68, 128, 147, 163, 232
Generalists, 73, 277
Gerber Products Company, 130
German firms, studies of, 229
Germany, 22, 36
Gillette Company, 131
Goals, 79, 80*t*, 100, 157, 170, 200, 232, 256, 263–264, 292
Government, 36, 86, 127, 192, 251, 264, 271, 285, 289–291, 295–297, 299
  dealing with in decision making, 213, 214
  enforcement agencies, 280
  organizations, 219
W. T. Grant Company, 37
Gray, Harry, 38
Great Britain, 36, 231
Gross national product (GNP), 46, 126, 127
Group(s)
  cohesion, 192, 193
  decision making, 185–204, 293, 294
  homogeneous, 195, 196, 257, 310
  inhibition, 187–189
  norms, 193
  size, 197, 203
  structures, 236
"Groupthink," 192, 193, 203, 294
Growth, 133
  problems of, 280, 281
  strategy, 82, 228, 231

H

Hanna Company, 296
Harvard Business School, 4

Hefner, Hugh, 132
Hewlett-Packard Company, 160
Hierarchic control, 261
Hospitals, 83, 290, 293, 296
Humphrey, George M., 296

I

Identification of policies and strategies, 119–147
Implementation, of plans, 103, 241, 242
Incremental approach, to decision making, 207–209,
    213, 219, 279, 293
India, 177, 285
Individuals, 49, 202, 203
    as decision makers, 169–184, 187, 188
Inducement-contribution, 261–262
Information systems, computerized, 172
Informational roles, 73
Insurance industry, 142
Integration
    role of, 231–234
    of systems, 239–243
Intelligence, 173–175, 173t, 183
Interdependence, 239, 240
Internal Revenue Service, 50
International Business Machines (IBM), 35, 36, 143
International markets, 229
Interstate Commerce Commission (ICC), 127
Interventions, 202
Intuition, 143, 159
Intuitive-anticipatory
    approach to decision making, 206, 207, 209, 218,
        278
    planning, 28, 29, 93, 94
Intuitive thinkers, 174
Invention, 143
Inventor-entrepreneur, 276
Israel, 257
Italian firms, study of, 229

J

Japan, 29, 176, 177
Japanese companies, 133
Job choice decision, 211, 211t
John Hancock Mutual Life Insurance Company,
    60
Johnson, President Lyndon B., 290, 292
Joint ventures, 215
The Journal of Business Strategy, 32

K

K-Mart Corporation, 34
Kennedy, President John F., 223
Knowledge, 120, 150, 170–174, 183, 207, 277, 286,
    293, 314
Korea, 177
Korean War, 192

L

Labor unions, 81, 199, 258
Laboratory studies, 312
Laissez-faire approach to decision making, 78
Leadership, 75–77, 189, 215, 216, 304
"Leading edge" consulting, 203. *See also* Consultants;
    Consulting firms
Lear Siegler, Inc., 124
Lear Siegler Market/Business Audit, 124
Learning curve, 142, 160, 162
Limited domain theory, 304, 305
Linkage, among plans, 242, 243
Linking pin concept, 257
Lockheed Aircraft Corporation, 38, 132
Long-range objectives, in public service organizations,
    292, 293
Long-range planning, 29, 30, 93, 94, 100, 103, 104,
    108, 114, 115, 206, 233, 242, 243, 279, 291
Long Range Planning, 96

M

McDonald's Corporation, 37
McKinsey and Company, 136
McNamara, R., former Secretary of Defense, 153
Male entrepreneurs, 285, 286
Management
    process, 72, 73
    teams, 193–197
Management by objectives (MBO), 239, 251, 252, 293
Managerial
    environment, 205
    jobs, 71–75
    philosophies, 57, 58
    planning, defined, 94, 95
    styles, 71–90, 110. *See also* Leadership
    values, in different countries, 176–178, 177t
    work roles, 73–75, 74t
Managerial Planning, 96
Managerial Revolution, 275

Managers
  backgrounds of, 171, 172
  creative, 181–183
  study of, 215, 216*t*, 218
  successful, 176
  tasks of, 27, 28
  venture, 282–284, 284*t. See also* Venture
    management
Manufacturing firm, 262
Marcor Company, 33, 34
Market
  environments, 233
  niches of, 131, 132, 165
Marshall Field and Company, 34
Matrix structures, 233, 234
Maximizing concept, 210, 211, 211*t*
MBA curriculums, 313
MBA students, 171, 178
Medicaid, 290
Medicare, 290
Medium range planning, 241, 243, 279
Medium range programming, 15, 17, 101–103, 241*f,*
  242
Mexico, 98
Michigan State University, 274
Midvale Steel Company, 88
Minnesota, Mining, and Manufacturing (3M), 143
Minorities, 263
Minority entrepreneurship, 285, 286
Mission statements, 100
Missions, in public service organizations, 292, 293
Money, as an inducement, 262
Monsanto Chemical Company, 240, 241
Moran, Joseph T., 34
Morgan, J. P., 275
"Mother-daughter" firms, 229
Moyers, W., former White House Press Secretary,
  151
"Muddling through," 208, 210, 293
Multidivisional structures, 229
Multinational markets, 87
Multinationals, study of European, 229
My Years with General Motors, 166

N

National Aeronautics and Space Administration, 47
Negotiated decision making, 186, 190, 191, 212
The New Class of Chief Executive Officer, 53
New Zealand, 272
Nixon, President Richard, 192, 290, 292
Nominal group technique, 187, 188, 197

Nonbusiness organizations, 7
Normative theory, 149, 203, 210
Not-for-profit (NFP) organizations, 117, 251, 271,
  289–301

O

Occupational Safety and Health Administration, 50
Open system concept, 304
Operating plans, 243–248
Operational
  management, 5, 6
  models of decision making, conceptual versus, 154
  strategies, 31
  theory, 13
Opportunistic entrepreneur, 275, 276
Organization(al)
  change, history of, 227, 228
  commitment, 257–261, 260*t,* 264
  development (OD), 201, 202, 224
  environment interactions, 5–10
  fit, concept of, 234–236, 235*f*
  life cycles, 84–89, 234, 276
  policy and strategy, research on, 7
  structures and processes, 223–237
  styles, 71–90
  theory, 13, 157, 308–310
Organizations, 157
Organized anarchies, 212, 213

P

Park, John R., 50
Participation, 76, 255–257, 264, 266
Participative management, 202
Partners, business, 280
Pearl Harbor, 192
J. C. Penney, 34
Pentagon, 127, 142
People, role of in implementation, 255–267
Performance
  of firms, 230, 231
  measurement of, 249–251, 298
Person orientation, 79, 80*t*
Personality, in decision making, 178–180
Planning
  models, 96
  objectives, 100, 101
  systematic (formal), 93–118
  systems, types of, 111–114
Planning-Programming-Budgeting System (PPBS),
  290

Planning Review, 96
Playboy, 132
Pluralism, 48, 52, 291, 292, 294
Policy
    analysis, 294, 295
    master, 24, 28, 30, 99–101
    nature of, 22–25
Portfolio matrix, 159, 160
Power
    in decision making, 217, 218
    motivation, 81
    orientation, 79, 80*t*
    sharing, 215, 216
President's Commission on National Goals, 292
Procedures, 23, 94
Product life cycles, 139–141, 139*f,* 140*t,* 160, 165,
    306, 307
Product/market matrix, 133–135, 133*f*
Product portfolio approach, to identifying strategies,
    135–139
Professional commitment, 260
Professional structures, 235, 236
Profile, policy/strategy, 130
Profit Impact of Market Strategies (PIMS), 141, 142,
    158, 160, 310
Profit maximization, 157, 212
Program
    policies/strategies, 16*f,* 18, 29, 30, 101, 130
    structures, 233
Program Evaluation and Review Technique (PERT),
    158
Programmable decisions, 186, 189, 194, 202, 203
Programmed approach, to decision making, 78
Project
    management, 234
    managers, 233
    teams, 194
Protestant Ethic, 48
Public(s), 50, 81
    school administrators, 179
    sector, 24, 25, 291, 292, 294, 296
    service organizations, 292, 293, 297
Public Law 92–603, 290

Q

Quick Environmental Scanning Technique (Quest),
    128

R

Ratio analysis, 159
Rationality, 116, 117, 155, 158, 212, 219, 274

RCA Company, 35, 36
Remington Rand Company, 143
Report on Progress in Areas of Public Concern, 68
Research, in the policy field, 311–313
Return-on-investment (ROI), 141, 153, 159, 160
Rigid firms, 275
Risk-taking propensity, 164, 165, 179, 183, 262, 277
Risky shift, 191–193, 203
Rockefeller, John D., 275
Rohr Industries, Inc., 38
Role
    ambiguity, 234
    conflict, 234
    orientation, 79, 80*t*
    prescriptions, 255
    theory, policy and, 23
Rolls Royce Company, 38, 166, 241
Romney, George, 223
Roosevelt, President Franklin D., 297
Rootes Motors Ltd., 36
Rules, 23

S

Sanctions, 266
Satisficing, 210, 211, 211*t*
Scientific Data Systems, Inc., 38
Scientific method, 10
Sears, Richard Warren, 33, 34
Sears, Roebuck and Company, 28, 33, 34, 68, 128
The Second American Revolution, 70
Securities and Exchange Commission, 50, 159, 182,
    312
Self-esteem, in decision making, 180, 183, 190
Shapiro, Irving, 49
Shell Oil Company, 128
Short-range planning, 15, 17, 103, 241–243
Simca Company, 36
Simulation models, 142, 158
Situation audit, 97–99, 119–130, 122*t,* 123*t*–124*t*
Sloan, Alfred, 231
Smith Brothers Company, 143
Social
    audit, 68, 69
    demands, corporate response to, 62–68
    environment, 68, 212
    forecasts, 127, 129
    programs, corporate, 59, 62, 63
    responsibilities, 7, 57–70
    skills, in decision making, 196, 197
Social Security Administration, 290
Societé Bic, 131

Sociological open systems, 227
Sociopolitical environment, 47–49, 121
Spans of control, 216
Specialist, 5
Standard operating plans, 23
Standards, in the control process, 249, 250
Stanford University, 49
Steady state management, 84
Steering controls, 247, 248
Stone Corporation, 138
Strategic
  business units (SBUs), 111, 112, 113*f*, 120, 137
  funds programming, 242
  management, 4–7, 30–32, 93–118
  planning, 6, 7, 15–22, 16*f*, 27–31, 241
  thinking, 14, 125*t*
Strategic Management Journal, 32
Strategic Planning Institute, 141
Strategies
  and policies, questions to test, 162–166
  successful, 20, 27
  types of, 18–20
Strategy
  definition of, 17, 18
  master, 16*f*, 18, 24, 30, 99–101, 130
Strategy and Structure, 52, 84
Student dormitory counselors, study of, 187, 188, 188*t*
Sullivan, Reverend Leon H., 67
Sun Oil Company, 142
Supermarket chains, 312
Supreme Court, United States, 50, 289, 295
Swiss watchmakers, 126
Synergy, 143, 144
Systematic procedure for identifying relevant
    environments (SPIRE), 129
Systematic thinkers, 174

T

Tactical planning, 16*f*
Tactics, strategy versus, 20–23
Task(s), 137, 234, 235*f*
  orientation, 79, 80*t*
  structures, 236
Team approach, to planning, 105, 108
Technological
  environment, 50, 51
  forecasting, 126, 127
Technological Forecasting, 127
Tennessee Valley Authority, 289
"Threshold" companies, 135
Time, in decision making, 205, 206, 217

Timex Company, 20
Tire and rubber producers, 121, 121*t*
Top-down approach, to planning, 105
Top management strategic activities, 31
Trend Analysis Program (TAP), 128
Trust, 199, 200, 203
Turbulent environments, 127
Turkey, 223

U

Union Camp Corporation, 160
United Aircraft Company, 38
United States, 3, 29, 32, 37, 46, 109, 126, 173, 175–
    178, 199, 208, 223, 229–231, 243, 285
United States Navy, 289, 295
United States, President of, 24, 25
United Technology, Inc., 38
Universities, 127, 203, 212, 213, 314
University of Southern California, 129
Utility company, 214

V

Value(s), 19, 20, 79, 80*t*, 183
  changes, 47, 48
  culture-based, 177
  in decision making, 175–178
  definition of, 176
  of managers, 121, 176, 178, 299, 300
  systems, 98
Venture management, 271, 281–285
Vertically integrated companies, 227
Vietnam War, 192
Voluntarism, concept of, 62

W

Watergate, 50, 193
Women, 262, 263
World War I, 34
World War II, 34, 35, 126, 228, 230
WOTS-Up Analysis, 99, 129
Wright Patterson Air Force Base, 142
Wright, T. P., 142

X

Xerox Corporation, 38, 143

Y

Yugoslavia, 257